DANCE IN ELEMENTARY EDUCATION

Harper's School and Public Health Education,
Physical Education and Recreation Series
Under the Editorship of Delbert Oberteuffer

DANCE IN ELEMENTARY EDUCATION

A Program for Boys and Girls

Third Edition

Ruth Lovell Murray

Wayne State University
Professor Emeritus

Harper & Row, Publishers
New York   Evanston   San Francisco   London

PHOTO CREDITS: Parts I, II, III, IV, Desmond L. Kelly; Part V, Detroit Public Schools; Part VI, Thomas Halsted; Part VII, O. R. Peterson III

Sponsoring Editor: Joe Ingram
Project Editor: Holly Detgen
Designer: Andrea Clark
Production Supervisor: Stefania J. Taflinska

Dance in Elementary Education: A Program for Boys and Girls,
THIRD EDITION

Library of Congress Cataloging in Publication Data

Murray, Ruth Lovell.
    Dance in elementary education.
    (Harper's school and public health education,
physical education and recreation series)
    Bibliography: p.
    1. Dancing—Children's dances. I. Title.
GV1799.M85   1974   372.8'7   74-11386
ISBN 0-06-044681-1

To my mother and father,
Clara Southwick Murray
and Neil William Murray,
and to their two-year old great-granddaughter,
Claire Catherine, who does her own dancing
without benefit of teacher, model, or book.

Contents

Foreword

As the current Divisional Director of Health, Physical Education and Safety for the Detroit Public Schools, I feel privileged to follow such eminent predecessors as Vaughn S. Blanchard and Delia P. Hussey in writing an introduction to the third edition of the Ruth Lovell Murray book, *Dance in Elementary Education*.

Since its initial publication in 1953, this book has become a classic in the literature of physical education and dance education in this country and elsewhere and, undoubtedly, has significantly influenced the thinking and educational methodology of many teachers and many school systems. As a result, several generations of school children, boys and girls, have experienced the joy and satisfaction of movement exploration and dance-making as a vital part of a well-balanced physical education program.

The schools and the staff of the Detroit Public Schools are particularly fortunate in having enjoyed the educational influence of Ruth Murray in a long-enduring relationship which by now has encompassed more than five decades. Many of the ideas and methods contained in this book were developed by her use of the classrooms and gymnasiums of our city as her laboratory.

Ruth Murray has demonstrated an ability during her long career for functioning as an inspiring teacher in the university, while at the same time retaining her keen insight and understanding of the practical problems of the public schools. Not only has she been a teacher of physical education and of dance, but she was a dance performer herself and studied with some of our American modern dance pioneers—Martha Graham, Doris Humphrey, Charles Weidman, and José Limón—as well as at the Bennington College School of Dance during the 1930s. From 1928 to 1954 she directed the Wayne State University Dance Workshop and choreographed a number of dances for this performing group and also for the University Theater.

It was precisely this unique combination of talent, interest, and broad philosophy that prompted Blanchard in his introduction to the first edition of *Dance in Elementary Education* to note that:

> The author of this book although considered a specialist in the area of dance has always recognized its place in education and has striven to have its contribution recognized. This has meant, then, an ability to see the whole program of physical education and the relationship of its component parts to general education. Dance is one of these component parts and a very important one. Miss Murray's broad perspective, a very necessary attribute for the Chairman of a women's department in a large university and a person who has been engaged in teacher education for many years, gives even more meaning to this book than to one penned by an individual with a narrower point of view.

Ruth Murray has received a number of awards in her illustrious career that should be noted in this introduction. In 1955 she received an honor award from the American Association for Health, Physical Education and Recreation. She received a similar award in 1959 from the Michigan Association for Health, Physical Education and Recreation and was elected to membership in the American Academy of Physical Education.

She has been Chairman, Member-at-Large, and Advisory Member of the Dance Division of the American Association for Health, Physical Education and Recreation; and in April 1969, the division, now the National Dance Association, chose her as the recipient of its highest honor, the Heritage Award. In the spring of 1973 she was given both the Annual Medal Award of the Michigan Academy of Sciences, Arts, and Letters and the Annual Award of the American Dance Guild.

In this third edition of her book, one can be certain that perfectionist Ruth Murray has painstakingly reshaped, brought up to date, and expanded the materials that she had originally compiled. The revised edition takes into account new ideas and methods that have been developed in recent years, including the contribution of schools of thought in the area of movement education. Selections on "Experiences in Dance Movement" and "Learning Dances" have been partially reorganized; and new, nonpartner dances have been added to the latter. Additional games and problems have been described, many new records added, and lists of films for both teachers' and children's viewing are included.

Up-to-date photographs of children are dispersed throughout the book to assist the understanding of readers and to add to their perception and enjoyment of the skills portrayed.

This edition adds to the reputation of the book as an invaluable dance guide and should serve to inspire both experienced and inexperienced teachers, men and women, and specialists and classroom teachers to initiate creative new programs or to add new dimensions to old programs. The precision of writing in this text and the many approaches and integrative themes suggested will be of great assistance in this endeavor.

Robert R. Luby
Divisional Director
Health, Physical Education and Safety
Detroit Public Schools

Preface and Acknowledgments

Dance in Elementary Education has had a long history of preparation before the first edition was published more than twenty years ago. Many of the children who danced in the pages of its two editions have their own children now, some of whom, hopefully, are dancing, too. Many of the book's materials, in the early days used primarily in the Detroit schools, now enjoy a much wider reputation. To judge from questionnaires received prior to the preparation of the book's third edition, it has been found helpful for teachers of teachers as well as teachers of children, and not only in this country but as far afield as Israel, Kenya, and New Zealand.

Instructors of modern dance in secondary schools and colleges have also found much in its pages pertinent to the development of movement and rhythmic skills and dance-making. Many students come to classes in these institutions with little background in dance skill or creative improvisation. While they may move ahead more quickly than do children, their initial experiences must be beginning ones.

More to the point, the book is beginning to be a major reference in classes for classroom teachers. In most localities, at least in the primary grades, it is they who are responsible for helping children learn how to use their bodies in functional and expressive movement. Because the medium of dance is such an intimate one, its opportunities and successes are closely related to a child's positive acceptance of himself. Because dance movement provides for the physical needs of the child, his biological development is thus sustained. Because dance is an art that adapts itself so easily to creativity and sentient expression, it becomes truly significant as an aesthetic area of the child's education.

For these reasons, it is fervently hoped that classroom teachers will accept this responsibility and that many parts of this book will provide for their guidance and inspiration.

So many persons in the past and present have encouraged and criticized and contributed that it is difficult to know where to begin to offer acknowledgments. I shall start with my two dear friends, Laurentine Collins and Delia Hussey, both now deceased. On this third edition their assistance has been gravely missed—Laurentine for her considerable flair for correct and telling English usage and Delia for her inspired teaching and understanding of children's creative dance.

From the past are two more influential names: Martha Hill Davies, now of the Juilliard School, whose movement analysis and terminology I have used as a basis for teaching since the early thirties; and Elizabeth Hunt Gottesleben, the superb accompanist-musician during the twenty-five years of my direction of Wayne University's Dance Workshop.

For assistance with the present volume my deep gratitude goes to these former colleagues at Wayne State University (former only in the sense that I am now retired).

To Ann Zirulnik for her generous assistance in many areas, especially in teaching for the photographs taken at two of the Detroit schools, for her superior abilities as a dance teacher at all levels, and for her critical review of some of the book's first chapters.

To Jane Fink for her considerable help on movement education and for the loan of many useful books from her library.

To Lillian Cassie of the Department of Music Education for bringing me up to date on school songbooks and making her music book collection available to me.

To Charles Rybacki, former accompanist-musician at Wayne and now a teacher of public school music on Long Island, for his very special help in suggesting music of appeal to older elementary school youngsters.

To Georgia Reid for her critical review of Part IV, Learning Dances.

To Alex Cushnier, folk and ethnic dance expert, for advice and counsel.

The pictures in the book come from sources both close to home and far from it, all of those cooperating being former students. The Detroit Public Schools are most generously represented; and Dr. Robert Luby, Division Director of Health, Physical Education and Safety, is responsible for making that possible. The elementary schools and their teachers are: Bow, Beatrice Baskin; Couzens, Lillian Buckner; Chrysler, Marie Dean; Fitzgerald, Sharon Kirkland; McColl, Mildred Wobrock.

Harriet Berg, Director of Dance at the Detroit Jewish Community Center and always encouraging and solicitous, offered pictures taken by her husband and helpmate, Irving Berg.

Jacqueline Davis of the State University College of New York at Brock-port sent pictures of children at the University School where she has been teaching.

Annette Golding of Wellington Teachers College in New Zealand, a former Fulbright scholar at Wayne, sent pictures of some of the children with whom she demonstrates.

Patricia Brooks Welling of the Dance Department at Ohio University taught children at the Stone School in Belpre, Ohio, and contributed special pictures which show a classroom environment.

My deepest obligation for the completion of this project is to Kathryn Ellis, a former student, friend, and teacher of secondary school dance. The responsibility of typing the manuscript, both the first rough drafts and the final copy, was hers. Many of our long sessions of discussion, interpretation, and review were indeed beyond the call of duty, and to her I extend heartfelt thanks.

Users of the second edition will recognize some reorganization of con-tent, new materials in several chapters, and the general appearance of the seventies in the pictures. May this third edition continue to serve teachers well.

RUTH MURRAY

Part I | OVERVIEW

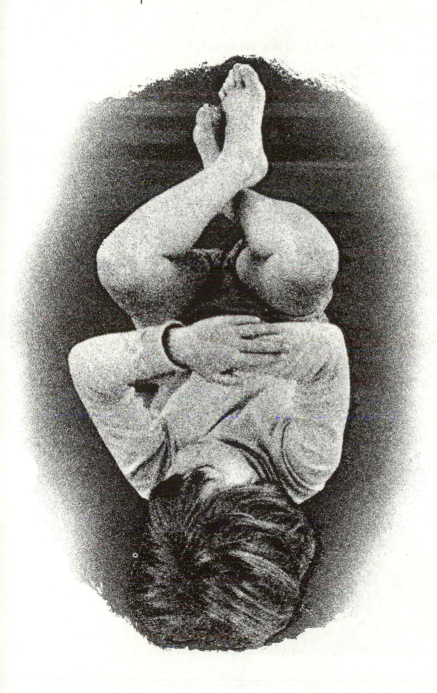

Chapter Preview

"I'm Dancing"

DETROIT PUBLIC SCHOOLS

1   *Basic Orientation*

*. . . A work of art is an expressive form created for our
perception through sense or imagination, and what is expressed
is human feeling.*[1]

*The pivotal role of dance among the arts is due to the fact
that the kinesthetic element, which gives sensuous reality to
aesthetic perception in all of the arts, is deliberately and
systematically cultivated in the art of dance.*[2]

*The little Gardiners, attracted by the sight of a chaise, were
standing on the steps of the house . . . ; and, when the carriage
drove up to the door, the joyful surprise that lighted up their
faces, and displayed itself over their whole bodies, in a
variety of capers and frisks, was the first pleasing earnest
of their welcome.*[3]

This is a book for teachers of boys and girls. It is not intended exclusively for
those who teach dance but for the use of all teachers everywhere who wish to
know more about dance in the education of children. It proposes to look at
the elements which make up a comprehensive dance experience.

    Some schools where the children are privileged to come to the teachers
in small groups, with all the advantages in attention and equipment which
that implies, may have programs of dance education equal to or surpassing
the content set forth here. Studios specializing in a particular dance area may

[1] Susanne Langer, *Problems of Art*, New York, Scribner, 1957, p. 15.

[2] Philip H. Phenix, "Relationships of Dance to Other Art Forms," *Dance—An Art in
Academe*, Martin Haberman and Tobie Meisel, eds., New York, Teachers College, 1970, p. 12.

[3] Jane Austen, *Pride and Prejudice*, New York, Macmillan, 1962, p. 272.

not find such an extensive program practical. But this book is written for that tremendous group of children and young people who attend our public schools, so they may be helped to know all the joys and satisfactions that dance can offer them. It is intended to be of use for the teachers in these schools, to contain material as well as references, to present methods as well as theories.

Part I tries to answer some questions having to do with dance—how this author chooses to define it, why it is an essential educational experience for children, and what should be its scope in elementary education. Teaching methods and the teacher's attributes are discussed in Chapter 2.

Part II is concerned with children's exploratory and creative experiences in dance movement, their occasions of discovery of its expressive qualities, and the conceptual learnings which should accompany such experiences.

Parts III and IV discuss in some detail the basic skills of locomotor and nonlocomotor movement, and the skills of rhythmic performance, especially as it is involved in the relationship of movement to an accompaniment.

Parts V and VI are devoted to the acts of making and learning dances, since children should have the experience of doing both.

Part VII offers certain supplementary aids to dance teaching such as references for films and accompaniment, suggestions for solving some problems related to dance teaching, and minimum standards for performance of certain dance skills at different levels of experience.

Some chapters, notably 5, 6, 8, 9, 10, 13, 14, and all of those in Part V (Making Dances) offer, as part of the chapter content, concentrated and quite advanced materials which could well be used by dancers at any level, even in college classes or with adults. In many other places (Chapters 5, 6, 8, 17, 18, and 19) activities may be found which preschool and kindergarten teachers can adapt for their children's play.

Today, more and more men are becoming interested in teaching in elementary schools. Because the English language provides no pronoun which includes both sexes, it is necessary to choose one or the other when referring to a teacher of children. Traditional literary practice uses masculine word symbols whenever there is any doubt about the specificity of the sex. In this book this tradition will be observed in all references to children. For references to the teacher, however, it seems artificial and inaccurate, considering the present multiplicity of women over men teachers of children. Continual use of the neutral plural (*teachers, they,* etc.) diminishes the personal effect of the point being made. Consequently, where it seems necessary to be concise and distinct, the teacher will be a "she" rather than a "he." Young men need only make the substitution of *he* for *she* to actuate a more personal meaning for them.

It is hoped that this book will provide new impetus for teaching dance to children, that it will help the teacher and also the administrator to understand the areas which should make up a comprehensive elementary school dance program and how each contributes to the others and to other aspects of the school curriculum. Special emphasis is given to the creative and expressive elements of the dance experience. Too many adults, and therefore children as well, find anything other than the use of movement for functional or practical purposes somewhat disconcerting. Yet dance, being an art, is essentially expressive, a holistic act of movement for an aesthetic purpose. Its use as a medium for creativity is far-reaching. In the pages ahead there are ideas, principles, materials, and guidelines that may help to make the dance experience both an exhilarating and a significant educational venture.

Dance, Past and Present

The human race has danced for pleasure and purpose from time immemorial. Until quite recently, however, very little study was made of dance—its range of form and content, its reason for being, and its contribution to physical, emotional, and social existence. Anthropologists, it is true, have studied the dance of primitive tribes in an effort to understand the behavior of those cultures. Ballet masters evolved a system of transcribing their dance movements into notations so that teaching and composing in that style were made simpler. Industrious collectors of ethnic dances have reproduced dances of many cultures in publications designed for American school children. A few historians have described the chronological development of dance, and a very few philosophers have accorded it an impressive place in human activities. But for the most part, dance has remained an art of the people, unrecorded and unexplored. Moralists in certain ages, who have held to the ascetic theory that the body is necessarily evil, have tended to condemn it. Conversely, it has been a source of communal strength, a manly test of skill and agility, a festive and cheery act in an otherwise arduous existence. Through all such periods of love and hate, dance has endured, has appeared in new patterns, has bestowed new meanings.

The twentieth century has made considerable progress in according to dance its deserved place as a major area of artistic expression. The contemporary dance artist has affirmed its importance as an intensification of human experience and a significant language of communication. Whereas in the past no comprehensive system of recording dance movement was available to teachers and choreographers, today several systems of dance notation have been developed. Of these systems, that most widely used for the notation of recent choreographic masterpieces and beginning to be part of the education of dance specialists is Labanotation, created by the great movement analyst, the late Rudolph Laban. The literature of dance has expanded, and its unique and historic contribution to man's aesthetic nature is being examined in scholarly volumes. It has achieved prominence on the concert stage, in the theater, in films, on television, as well as in the many places where people get together for fun and relaxation.

Thus the dance room in the school, whether it be one designed for dance activity, a gymnasium, a multipurpose room, or merely a classroom with the chairs pushed back, is becoming more and more significant. It is here that the activities described in this book will find their most appropriate setting. There can be no doubt that dance under wise and competent leadership is part of the total educative process. It holds all the satisfactions of both play and art. Its opportunities for group as well as individual expression are manifold. It can fulfill many of the needs which psychologists tell us have such a profound effect on developing personalities. And most important for the child, its purpose is inherent in its performance. For him it is doing, it is being, it is acting, it is fun!

Dance, a Dance, and Dancing Defined

For a long time the layman has confused the words *dance, a dance,* and *dancing,* substituting *dancing,* used as a noun, for each of the others.

Most people today in the arts and many in education understand that the word *dance* (like that of the word *music*) describes the whole body of the art. Until recently, however, we have had this and that kind of *dancing, dances* which one performed or attended or viewed, times and places where one *danced,* but nothing that was called purely and simply *dance.* In many cases, dictionaries have not caught up to this definition of the word *dance* and continue to apply outdated meanings to it. And some persons, still uncomfortable with the usage, find the word more acceptable if it is preceded by *the,* as in "the dance"!

Educators as well as scholars and the general public have been at fault in not giving to dance its rightful name. Several years ago the term *rhythms* came into favor to describe some of the dance activities of young children. To teachers at that time, the word *dance* meant learning dances and therefore did not cover the movement in dancelike form which was beginning to find its way into school acivities. Creative activity in dance was rarely attempted beyond the third grade, but where it did occur, usually only among girls, it was referred to as *creative dancing.*

Another factor delaying the general use of *dance* in place of *rhythms* was the attitude that dance was suitable only for girls and offered little that was physically challenging to boys in comparison with the more acceptable participation in sports. Antagonistic attitudes toward dance were and still are found in many communities because of religious scruples or because of a negative reaction to anything in the educational program which might be classified as "fads and frills."

Thus confusion in terminology extended even to professional educators. *Rhythms* is a nonword deriving from only one aspect of the dance experience. Whether used as a camouflage or for convenience, it misleads and denies to dance those experiences which are essential to it.

If *dance* is to be all-inclusive, then what is *a dance?* A dance is movement put into rhythmic and spatial form, a succession of movements which starts, proceeds, and finishes. How complex this progression must be, or how simple it can be and still be called *a dance* may be a point of disagreement among terminologists. This author maintains that the simplest combination of movement phrases, say only two, which a child puts together and performs may be legitimately called *a dance*. Who can say when random experimenting with an art medium ends and expression of an idea begins? When the first attempts with paint and paper are more than merely absorbing activity and become "my painting" or "my picture"? When the beginning of a form is recognizable, at least to the child?

Is a child who moves in a flying action about the room doing a dance? To make the definition more precise, let us call this *dancing* and not *a dance*. A dance implies the arrangement of parts into a sequential form, and form demands contrast, even if it is only that of one part to another. Hence the child makes a dance only if he progresses far enough in his project to have his flight come to a point of rest on the floor and then resumes the sequence of flight and stillness. Whether such action personifies airplane or bird is immaterial. Some children's imaginations will immediately objectify the movement; others will enjoy the sensation of the moving sequence for its own sake.

Again, a child skipping forward is dancing, for a skip is a dance step. When a skipping turn is added to the forward skip and this succession of movements is repeated, the beginning of a dance has been made. These movements may be further structured *in time* if it is decided to take a certain number of skips for each part, say six skips forward and four turning; *in space* if a high skip forward and a low skip turning are used. Such a sequence of movements contains the beginning of formal movement structure; and on the child's level it is, indeed, a dance.

So we come to the participle *dancing,* perhaps the most familiar and most commonly used term, yet the most difficult to define. Dancing is moving in a "dancelike" way. This could include many activities not considered dancing at all, however—the gyrations of a drum major, or even the act of marching in a parade or procession, inasmuch as this often includes movement formations and group patterns. The word in an even more general reference may refer to the use of movement in any way which investigates, extends, or strengthens its potentialities for dance expression—for example, engaging in the techniques of ballet or modern dance. The goal of a program of *movement education,* now becoming an important part of many elementary physical education programs, is the mastery of body movement in all its infinite variety. The exploration of movement in such programs, however, will usually lead to the functional uses of movement discoveries, such as those characteristic of work, play, and sport, because teaching content and method are oriented in that direction. In this book, the experiences of exploration and discovery are described only in their "dance-like" connotations—which is to say those of organically aesthetic intent.

It is not enough, therefore, to say that dancing is movement for its own sake, for that takes us over the thin line separating gymnastics, stunts, and acrobatics from movement specifically related to dance. Perhaps the best interpretation is one that emphasizes not only body mastery and discipline in movement but even more the use of movement for expressive, imaginative, and sentient purposes. Dance may borrow from and lend to other kinds of

Some Shapes of Dancers

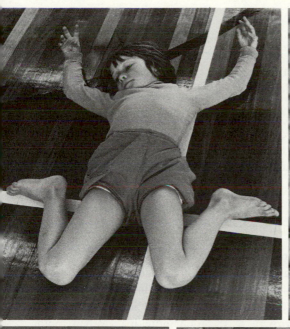

movement activities. It is when the ultimate concern is with the meaning of movement, rather than its practical function, that the terms *dance, a dance,* and *dancing* are accurately applied.

> We are here concerned with movement as an art. This implies an attitude towards movement which is quite different from our approach to swimming or gymnastics, for example, because we shall be concerned not with movement as a means of performing some feat, but with its expressive quality. . . .[4]

Why Boys and Girls Need to Dance

Probably the first reason children need to dance is that they have a hunger for movement which must be satisfied if their proper biological development is to be achieved. ". . . The child's movement fulfills a biological law, often stated as 'structure demands function.' "[5] Further, "The growth of the musculature is crucial to the growth of the total individual. When motor activities play no part in life, the individual develops little socially, becomes sluggish nutritionally and is subject to many of the somatic problems that derive from muscular atrophy."[6]

Psychomotor skills aid in successful school achievement:

> The primary process is *motor development.* This is the basis upon which is built the child's ability to control his body. . . . In addition to being the result of an order from the brain each movement made by a developing child is, in itself, an experience which contributes to the basic store of information held by the brain. In other words movements are not only *output,* they are *input* as well.[7]

Finally, control and mastery of the body's movement relate to emotional as well as physical and mental development. "Control of one's own body can mean the beginning of self control in general. Having controlled this most obvious part of his environment, control of temper and other emotions are, for most people, easier."[8]

[4] English Ministry of Education and the Central Office of Information, *Moving and Growing, Physical Education in the Primary School,* Part I, London, 1959, p. 59.

[5] Elizabeth Halsey and Lorena Porter, *Physical Education for Children,* New York, Holt, Rinehart & Winston, 1963, p. 5.

[6] Delbert Oberteuffer and Celeste Ulrich, *Physical Education,* 4th ed., New York, Harper & Row, 1970, p. 23.

[7] D. H. Radler and Newell C. Kephart, *Success Through Play,* New York, Harper & Row, 1960, pp. 23–24.

[8] Marian E. Breckenridge and E. Lee Vincent, *Child Development,* 5th ed., Philadelphia, Saunders, 1965, p. 229.

Boys and girls, then, need to move vigorously and often if their proper development is to be achieved. Physical play and games, and aquatics provide some of such movement. But just as important is dance.

All of the arts provide ways in which man can bring shape and order to his fragmented and rapidly changing world. But dance provides a primary medium for expression involving the total self, not just a part, like the voice, or totally separated from the physical self, like painting or sculpture. Dance and the movement that produces it is "me," and as such, is the most intimate of expressive media. A child's identity, self-concept, and self-esteem are improved in relation to such use of the body's movement.[9]

Many adults whose movements have been restrained by convention and circumvented by push buttons, steering wheels, and other machine-age accouterments find no joy in rhythmic action. They are content to be spectators, to sit on the side lines, to watch the game, the race, the ubiquitous TV. For a child, however, movement is both an organic need and a constant delight. Witness the light in his eyes when he demonstrates how he can skip, his joyous abandonment when he jumps, spins, falls, and challenges his space in a myriad of ways. Dancing to him is good for its own sake; but should meaning or purpose be required, it is easily supplied by the rich imaginative resources of childhood.

Again, the intellectual, social, and mechanical occupations of the average adult make the release of energy much less of a biological necessity. With such channels not yet a part of the life pattern of children because of their stage of physiological growth, expressive movement is one of their greatest resources for energy release, for proper organic and coordinated growth, and for exploration, discovery, and communication.

Movement is as clearly related to emotional as to physical and intellectual development. Jumping for joy, shaking with fear or excitement and standing in awe literally happen to young children. They express such feelings fully and freely, whereas in the adult the action may be minimized, reduced or controlled.[10]

. . . However movement is viewed it remains a visible expression of the wholeness of life since movement is indivisible from life. This not only applies to the utilitarian aspect of living but because of the fact that every

[9] Ruth L. Murray, "A Statement of Belief," *Children's Dance*, Gladys Andrews Fleming, ed., Washington, D.C., AAHPER Publications, 1973, p. 5.

[10] Molly Brearley, ed., *The Teaching of Young Children—Some Applications of Piaget's Learning Theory*, New York, Schocken Books, 1970, p. 88.

movement of man is expressive of himself, his aims, struggles and achievements, it reflects the inner activity of the person. For these reasons alone we should satisfy the movement appetite of the young children in our schools.[11]

A child who is forced to resist these natural outlets will often explode or retreat in less desirable directions. Certainly his physical welfare will be impaired. It should be recognized that movement which helps to free the body of awkwardness and inhibitions, makes it more rhythmic, enables it figuratively to say, "Let us join hands and dance together," is worthy of a large place in the life of a child.

The Scope of Dance in Elementary Education

While the word *dance* does refer to a totality of the art, what is set down in this book as being suitable in the dance education of children represents only certain aspects of the whole. The classical system of dance traditionally called ballet is not included, nor is tap dance, or modern jazz dance, or modern ballroom dance, or so-called fad dance.

In the opinion of Bruce King, a professional dancer who has had extensive experience in teaching dance to children,

> The stylized forms of dance (ballet, specific modern dance styles, jazz, etc.) are unnecessary to children. Introducing these adult-style forms to children too soon can inhibit their imaginations and strain their bodies. The child should find himself in movement and the teacher should help him develop that self.[12]

Allegra Fuller Snyder says,

> There is a difference between children's dance and much of the dance which is taught to children. The first recognizes the particular qualities of learning and doing of the child and builds an approach based upon these. The second focuses on a body of knowledge which, in fact, can be taught interchangeably to either a child or adult.[13]

[11] Ibid., pp. 85–86.

[12] Bruce King, *Creative Dance, Experience for Learning*, New York, Bruce King Studio, 1968, p. 6.

[13] Allegra Fuller Snyder, "Films That Show How Children Learn by Dancing," *Film News*, Vol. 26, No. 2, April 1969.

While folk dance might be included in the latter body of knowledge, those folk dances considered desirable for elementary school children are natural and informal in their movements rather than complex and precise.

Ballet has been omitted for the above reasons and because it takes highly trained teachers and much practice and drill to achieve a satisfying dance experience, with little opportunity for creativity. However, a teacher who becomes aware that a nine- or ten-year-old displays special talent as a dancer should inform the parents so that if possible extra out-of-school instruction in a modern dance or ballet class may be provided. Every effort should be made to give the child talented in dance the special instruction needed to develop that talent, just as is done in art or music.

Tap dance is theatrical and unchildlike and employs highly refined and complicated foot movements. It does contain an exciting rhythmic quality, has the advantage of being considered more masculine than certain other kinds of dance expression, and appears frequently on television programs. However, it is limited in expressive scope, sophisticated in movement style, and demands too much mechanical drill for children.

Social dance, including ballroom dance and "fad" dancing, while an important social skill for boys and girls to learn during their adolescent years, is not included because it is fundamentally an adolescent and adult dance activity. Although certain dances referred to in Part VI use the social dance position, they do not require the close embrace necessary if an effective lead is to be provided. Folk dances using the social dance position merely repeat the same step, such as the polka or two-step. They do not demand the improvisational use of steps characteristic of good ballroom dance.

It is questionable whether children in elementary school should be encouraged to try out certain of the isolated hip, shoulder, foot, and head movements characteristic of the "fad" dances of today, and performed to the heavy beat of rock music. To impose adult dance patterns upon children during the latency period, especially those of frankly erotic implications, is to force many of them beyond their maturation level. Preserving the innocence and spontaneity of childhood in the face of the many assaults on it is a worthy but sometimes futile task.

Teachers who specialize in dance instruction in studios or schools of dance employ specific exercises and techniques for the development of strength, flexibility, balance, and precision. These conditioners of body coordination and control relate very definitely to expertness in dance performance. As developmental essentials of body movement, they should be desirable outcomes of a progressive and comprehensive program of movement education. Therefore, they do not belong exclusively to the area of dance.

Older children, however, interested in improving their dance performance, may well discover, invent, and practice body movements which increase flexibility, strength, and balance control. Long discarded in progressive programs of physical education is the practice of lining up children and directing them through a series of imposed exercises designed to "train" the body. This has been superseded by problem-centered movement experiences—to be preferred in all aspects of children's movement education. Since the nurturing of creativity is of great importance in dance, much more desirable educational results are obtained through exploration, improvisation, and invention than through prescribed exercises or activities, unless the latter are intended for therapeutic or remedial effect or to prepare the body for a specific use.

This book presents more fundamental dance experiences than such specialized areas provide. The child should learn through experimentation how he can move, how he can manipulate movement to discover its potential for use and for communication, and how he can build it into simple forms, thereby making symbols for expression. He should understand how to respond to the time structure of an accompaniment and should be able to adjust his own movement to it in various ways. He should learn patterns of movement which have been made by others, some over hundreds of years. Thus, he begins to develop a vocabulary of dance movement and an understanding of the many uses to which it can be put.

Understanding the Elementary Dance Curriculum

A new body of knowledge about movement and movement practices has been developing among elementary physical education practitioners during the past fifteen years. This has as its source a program of movement education adopted by British educators after World War II.[14] Based upon theories of the nature of movement postulated by Rudolph Laban, *movement education,* or *basic movement education,* or, inaccurately, *movement exploration* (which describes method, not content) is becoming a significant part of the elementary physical education curriculum in this country.

The relationship of movement education to dance education is sometimes misunderstood by elementary school teachers who are beginning to

[14] Elizabeth Ludwig, "Toward an Understanding of Basic Movement Education in the Elementary Schools," *Journal of Health, Physical Education, and Recreation,* Washington, D.C., American Association for Health, Physical Education, and Recreation, March 1968. (The *Journal* is hereafter referred to as *JOHPER.*)

investigate these new materials and their effectiveness. It should be noted that the problem-solving method is used in both dance and movement education. There are differences in terminology, especially when the movement educator uses the language of Laban exclusively, although the essential elements of movements are the same.[15] Since the early thirties, American modern dance theorists have used the elements of time, space, and force to analyze and describe movement, and, as Marion Broer suggests, "efficient movement [of any kind] results only when these three elements are employed in proper relationship."[16]

True basic movement education should encompass all purposes for which movement is used, those that are functional and those that are expressive and communicative. But the latter purposes are related to the art of dance and hence are close to the affective as well as the psychomotor domain. Not all teachers are sensitive to manifestations of emotional and aesthetic expression in movement performance. Nor is their preparation for teaching sufficiently enriched by knowledge and participation in dance and the other arts. Dance education, therefore, should be considered a separate aspect of movement education—related closely to it, growing out of it in many ways, but having its own special approaches and content. For dance as a performing art has deeper aesthetic values than any functional movement, however skillful, or any gymnastic feat, however spectacular. Its substance is the structuring of movement for an expressive purpose, the stripping of the facade of the everyday to the inner self, rather than the doing of a task, the winning of a race, the manipulation of an implement, the overcoming of an obstacle.

There are two large areas which the teacher of dance must be equipped to present: the movement and rhythmic components of dance and the dances themselves, whether composed by the children or learned by them. These two bodies of material must be interrelated, one leading into the other and then back again. To make a dance or perform a dance may be the ultimate goal, but much satisfying activity can come from the exploration and manipulation of movement, putting familiar movements into new forms, testing one's rhythmic response, and improvising ways of moving in response to imagery and to sensory and rhythmic experiences. With younger children particularly, such dance activity may conceivably constitute the bulk of the dance program; children of an early school age need to find themselves in movement before they can relate well to others, in either the making or the learning of group dances.

[15] See Chapter 3 for a listing of movement concepts.
[16] Marion R. Broer, "Movement Education: Wherein the Disagreement?" *Quest*, Monograph II, April 1964, pp. 19–25.

A child should be helped to become aware of the wonderful potentialities of his body for movement of all kinds: to carry him through space, or around, or up and down, or out and in; to allow it to burst into great speed or to control it into slow motion; to exert immense energy into violence or to restrain it into lightness and gentleness; to stretch tall and wide with tension or to relax into the floor with loose and effortless abandon; to move a part or all of himself from one point to another in space on a straight, zig-zag or roundabout path; to crawl close to the floor or leap high to avoid it; to use his knees, his back, his shoulders, his hands as well as his feet as a base of support. The way these things feel when he makes them happen with his body will soon become a part of his general kinesthetic awareness when he moves in any way or for any reason.[17]

For a clearer understanding of the essentials of a complete dance program, the large areas of exploring movement, acquiring specific dance skills, and making and learning dances have been kept separate in this book. It is the responsibility of the teacher to fit these various aspects of dance learning together, so that experiences are comprehensive and each supports or supplements the other. It would be less of a task if all these experiences could be provided in the form of lesson sheets, with what should be taught today, tomorrow, and the next day planned and ready to be handed to the children and even the words of the teacher included as the lesson is taught. Fortunately, or unfortunately, this cannot be done, because communities of children differ as much from group to group in abilities and interests as individual children differ from one another. The denial of such differences, as well as of group dynamics, is implied in "lessons" of this sort.

Thinking about children in terms of layer upon layer, age level upon age level, each with its particular ceiling, has blinded us to the development of, and has weakened our confidence in, our own perceptions. The generalizations, unfortunately, became substitutes for thinking for ourselves. Can we really say there are kindergarten rhythms, third-grade rhythms, fifth-grade rhythms? There is movement—all children are interested in it, all explore it, if we allow them. The nursery-school child, as he propels himself across the floor, rolling, swimming, crawling, is using not only his arms and legs, but, more especially, his torso. The difference between his use of these floor movements and that of the older child and of the trained dancer is one of purpose and skill.[18]

[17] Ruth Lovell Murray, "Observations on the Teaching of Dance to Children," *Impulse, Annual of Contemporary Dance,* 1957, p. 2.

[18] Emma Sheehy, *Children Discover Music and Dance,* New York, Teachers College, 1968, p. 123.

Teachers, too, have their own styles of teaching practice which may make adherence to a prescribed program of class direction unnatural and artificial. Also, in these days of open schools and open classrooms, children's inclinations toward particular activities may make a series of planned lessons impractical. It is best, then, for a teacher to have a variety of *approaches* at her fingertips, so to speak, so that lessons are open-ended and subject to change, tangents may be pursued, and children's reactions to the presentation may be taken into account and its successive steps altered, if necessary.

The dance activities presented here are not categorized by grade levels or specific age levels. In the sections on movement exploration (Part II) and movement skills (Part III), much of the material except certain kinds of imagery could be used with beginners in dance at any age—children, adolescents, or adults. Activities for the development of rhythmic skill (Part IV) are classified as introductory and advanced. Upper-grade children, however, whose movement and musical backgrounds are meager will need to start with the simplest activities in this area. In differentiating activities in other sections, reference is made to younger (five or six through eight years or younger) and older (nine through eleven years or older) children. Materials listed for older children in the sections on making dances and learning dances will also be useful in secondary schools and even in colleges. The teacher and students planning together, exploring together, appraising together, will always be the most authentic guide to the proper selection of dance activities.

It is possible to suggest what children at particular levels of development under normal circumstances and with competent direction should be able to accomplish in dance skills. Outlines which describe such skills in terms of minimum standards for performance are presented in Chapter 27. How the teacher weaves into these suggested standards of accomplishment the creative acts of exploring, discovering, and inventing movement, of structuring it into dance forms, and how she decides which dances her children shall learn depends largely upon her own sensitive discrimination. Content areas should lead into each other naturally and inevitably and move ahead together to augmented and richer dance experiences. There is much to choose from in this book. There is much more within the children themselves, ready to be expressed in the right situation and under knowledgeable and sympathetic guidance.

Chapter Preview

2   *The Teaching of Dance*

> *. . . A school is not a place where you do something to children, but a place which makes something possible. That "something" is the most efficient possible growth toward self-realization. This makes of the teacher not a director or coercer, but a situation provider. . . .*[1]

The Environment and Costume for Dance

Dance is a generous, not a meager, activity. In good dance something of the self must be given out; otherwise the spark that makes it exhilarating, dynamic, and vital is extinguished. If presented or engaged in where the atmosphere is one of fear, suppression, or imposition, dancing emerges as a series of wooden imitations. But in a friendly, cooperative milieu it can become creative and enlivening.

The Emotional Environment

The environment created by the teacher for dance learning must be one in which the principles of democratic living are constantly practiced. The act of dancing implies voluntary participation by the dancer. A person can be forced to march, dig, lift, carry on complicated movement under sufficient pressure, but to dance, no! One's heart must be in it if the dance experience is to be genuine for both dancer and observer. Unless teacher and children are *en rapport*, and conflicts of interests and purposes are absent, it would be better for everyone, including the teacher, if dance were left unexplored as a

[1] Association for Supervision and Curriculum Development Yearbook, *Perceiving, Behaving, Becoming*, Washington, D.C., NEA, 1962, p. 90.

Talking It Over

curricular activity until another time, when a more effective leader can introduce it, or a more positive atmosphere prevails.

While certain types of dance activity necessitate more teacher direction than others, there need be no conflict here. Children are willing, even eager, to take direction, to practice incessantly, if they wish to learn, if they as well as the teacher are totally involved, if their emotional response toward the learning situation is favorable.

The Physical Environment

A school built without a room where children can stretch their legs, move about freely, play, and dance has failed to consider this most vital need of children. Such an activity area should be spacious, light, and free of encumbrances which might be unsafe for a child engaged in vigorous movement, sometimes "airborne," sometimes "earthbound." Immediately adjacent should be sufficient storage space for a record player, a tape recorder, records and cassettes, a piano, props, percussion instruments, a box or shelving for masks and simple costume pieces, and apparatus (poles, boxes, blocks, mats, stools, etc.) which occasionally may change the environment where movement will be explored and improvised. The walls should have bulletin boards for visual aids and a screen for film projection. The floor should be of wood, of resilient construction, and should be kept immaculately clean.

Such an ideal facility is what children deserve and need for a comprehensive program of movement and dance education. It will, unfortunately, not be available in a great many places. Instead, some schools will be equipped with a gymnasium designed primarily for basketball games, and often so large that young children become disoriented; others may have a multipurpose room with so many purposes that daily movement or dance sessions, especially for the younger children who need it the most, are out of the question. If convinced teachers, however, continue to emphasize and validate the need for movement and dance programs, eventually their efforts should be rewarded. Meantime, compromise is necessary and possible.

In some old schools, seats can be taken out of an unused classroom and a dance-play room results. Even a large hall may serve. As far as noise goes, it is no longer believed that the best learning goes on in a hushed atmosphere, that the sounds of conversation, or activity, are taboo. On the contrary, today the ever-quiet class, like the very quiet child, is looked upon with suspicion.

Lacking any of the above facilities, one can (and must) conduct the dance experience in the classroom. There are some advantages, in spite of the lack of space. For one thing, children are surrounded (or should be!) with evidence of their work in other aspects of the curriculum, such as mathematics, science, and social studies, and particularly their creative efforts in art and literature. The relationship of dance movement to these learnings is more easily recognized than in a room entirely devoid of such exhibits.

Obviously, the whole class often cannot be active at one time. The half of the class that watches (and five minutes is the outside limit for such physical inactivity) must be actively involved as an audience, observing with a critical but sympathetic and appreciative eye the solutions to problems their classmates present. It is the teacher's responsibility to deepen the perception of the observers so that their reactions are more than merely cursory ones; to minimize the self-consciousness of the performers; to reward inventiveness or special progress with suitable comment.

Performing for their peers by half the class at one time (and the random division should include both boys and girls) is good procedure regardless of the physical setting. It may serve as the first introduction to children's perception of dance movement as a performing art, audience-centered as well as movement-centered.

Preparing the room, encumbered as it is with chairs, tables, desks, bookshelves, and other objects, should be the children's responsibility, supervised by the teacher. There are times in the school day when, for the sake of efficiency and time-saving, imposed tasks should be performed capably and with dispatch by children. Pushing tables back and storing chairs beneath them should allow sufficient space for all the children to engage in activities in a personal space or self-space, and half of them at a time in those which involve traveling through space.

Shoes and socks should be removed and the floor used for sitting, lying, kneeling, as well as standing. If a desirable teacher-pupil relationship has been established, this preparation for activity, which represents a break in routine classroom procedures, will be engaged in willingly by boys and girls.

If the seats in her room are fastened to the floor (and there are still such rooms in our schools), the teacher's ingenuity is taxed to the utmost. The front of the room may be used, of course, and seats may serve as obstacles to mount, to climb through or over, or as a base for other movement explorations. Many activities can be adapted so that the children may experience creative movement even in such a static environment.

The Costume

Movement performance is freest and most effective when unhampered by tight clothes and heavy or slippery footgear. Long pants, especially if they are tight over the knees, and, in some cases, long skirts for girls, inhibit movement in obvious ways. However, if constructed of material that stretches, long pants are useful. Most desirable are shorts and a sleeveless or short-sleeved shirt or blouse. Except for fads which come and go, children these days usually wear comfortable, durable clothes to school. At least they can generally be persuaded to do so on dance days if there is no place in school to change into pants or shorts.

The worst offenders to effective movement are shoes; they make the feet heavy to lift and difficult to move in quick and complex patterns, and they prevent one from feeling the floor's surface or gripping it for strength and balance. Thus the development of consciousness of the sentient qualities of the feet is curtailed. ". . . We probably do a great deal of sensory 'masking' by keeping children in sneakers for all activity sessions. Children should do more of their activities barefooted. The tactile receptors on the soles of the feet and toes are extremely important for signaling shifts of weight and changes in surface textures."[2]

[2] Hope M. Smith, "Implications for Movement Education Experiences Drawn from Perceptual-Motor Research," *JOHPER*, April 1970, p. 33.

"Concern with the desensitizing effects of our present culture has led to much emphasis on body awareness, affective learning, nonverbal communication, and self-realization. The feet *can* sense, feel and know if not always encased in armor."[3]

The feet are the base of the body's support for most locomotor and nonlocomotor movement, and it is vitally important that they be as strong and flexible as possible. Barefooted activity, of course, must take place on a clean, smooth floor. Mothers may then be assured that there is a minimum of danger from stepping on small objects or from such infections as athlete's foot, which thrives only when considerable moisture is present. Of course, a clean floor is necessary in any case if movement is to be explored on any level or in any way except in a vertical stand.

The feeling of both freedom and security that moving in bare feet affords rapidly overcomes objections. Not too long ago having children sit on the floor of playrooms, gymnasiums, art rooms, or elementary classrooms was a shocking innovation. Now in modern schools it is standard procedure. Should there be reluctance to remove shoes, a teacher might say casually, "Anyone who would like to try moving without shoes and socks should certainly do so. It's much the best way to support your movement and to make your feet strong." It should be understood, however, that both shoes *and* socks are to be removed, that the feet are indeed to be bare. Socks or stockings are slippery and hence dangerous foot-covering for movement on bare floors.

The best costumes, then, for movement exploration and creative dance are shorts, playsuits, or stretch pants of any kind and bare feet. If for one reason or another having bare feet is not feasible, clean, lightweight tennis shoes or flexible leather sandals are possible substitutes.

Other Elements Affecting Dance Learning

The Importance of Purpose

There are many elements that control, direct, and affect a successful learning experience, and psychologists are continually discovering more about this complex process. It is well established, however, that a most important element is the learner's purpose, his motivation, his will to persevere through momentary failure, inconveniences, and obstacles. The purpose may come from within the child himself or arise out of the innumerable forces which impinge upon his developing personality. The indispensable

[3] Harriet Forkey Stone, "The Case Against Sneakers," *JOPHER*, May 1971, p. 26.

aspect of his purpose as a powerful implement in the learning process is that he accept it completely as his, whatever its source. It is then that his drive toward the goal begins.

There are probably few areas of education in which the child's purposes and the teacher's are more successfully coordinated than in dance. Exploring movement arouses physical and mental challenges and leads to an awareness of its expressiveness and powers of communication. Imaginative movement in which one assumes another identity or communicates an idea is a natural product of curiosity about one's world, more natural indeed than verbal description could be. Rhythmic movement for its own sake is organically congenial and satisfying. Moving with others helps give a sense of belonging, of both security and purposeful relationship in the group.

There is no basis for the assumption that girls like these things any better than boys. Men have always liked to dance and have been more enthusiastic in their participation than women. In the past the great dancing teachers were men, not women. For illogical reasons, dance in America in the past century became associated in the minds of boys with effeminacy. The dances selected for teaching and the way they were taught were in part responsible for this feeling, which, fortunately, is not nearly so strong as it was. The skillful teacher, by selecting dance experiences for boys and girls which are in accord with their interests and goals, by avoiding highly stylized and meaningless dance patterns, by dealing with the movement potential of the body in varied, daring, and challenging ways, can easily make dance a joyous and sought-after activity for all children.

Problem-Solving in Dance

Learning takes place through problem-solving. When a situation demands action from the learner to fulfill a purpose, to alleviate tension, to move toward a goal, he will act as a total organism, bringing to bear all of his physical, mental, social, and emotional equipment to do something about it. This exercise of powers improves efficiency in attacking new problems, with the result that an ever-broadening cycle of learning takes place.

The [dance] teacher's first task is to identify or structure the problem. What follows, through exploration and discovery, . . . is a variety of acceptable solutions. The selected solution may be one which feels good to do, or is the most innovative or daring, or is judged best for other reasons, sometimes perceived only by the child himself. Then should follow the refinement, through practice, of the chosen solution so that it is performed with greater control, better logical flow, more authority, and greater expressive awareness or is developed into a more complex sequence. The learning principles of discovery, perception, and actualization are thus applied to the child's increasingly discerning use and mastery of his own body's movement.[4]

Dance education offers vast learning opportunities if these principles are accepted and implemented. In quite obvious fashion children are solving problems when, through exploration, they discover the body's capabilities in releasing and controlling energy; in traveling through space; in forming the innumerable moving and static shapes its joints allow; in learning how various patterns of movement can be constructed, when working alone and with others. In self-testing and gamelike activities for developing rhythmic acuity, they must discover how best they can synchronize many different kinds of movement with the time structure of an accompaniment.

Children are working intensely as problem-solvers when they are involved in making a dance study with its process of experimenting with movement ideas, of choosing what fits best into the project and eliminating what is superfluous or unsuitable. In partner or group dance-making, even when a solution is accepted which is different from theirs, they have been involved in experimentation, deliberation, and selection. They may even have learned the virtues of compromise in achieving an aesthetically satisfying resolution.

Learning a dance, too, where the process of problem-solving is less feasible, presents challenging situations. For example, absorbing, understanding, and remembering a series of movement patterns, orienting oneself with the movement, or with a partner or with the group, is assurance that the dance proceeds smoothly and satisfaction accrues to all.

The Element of Success

In a school environment standards of right and wrong are often rigid. If experimental opportunities are provided, the child's sincere effort to arrive at a solution to a problem, to perform a task, to explore or improvise is an indicator of success merely because it has been attended to, is his alone, and is therefore satisfying. A continual diet of failure distorts development in a variety of ways, particularly if it is publicized by parents, teachers, and peers.

It is important in all dealings with children to see that no adult approach occurs which would cause feelings of inferiority or self-consciousness to

[4] Ruth L. Murray, "A Statement of Belief," *Children's Dance*, Gladys Andrews Fleming, ed., Washington, D.C., AAHPER Publications, 1973, p. 7.

"tie-up" motor skills. Ridicule, sarcasm, scolding or laughing at children's clumsiness in the early learning stages . . . may cause an emotional blocking that may result in tense movement and awkwardness through the child's life.[5]

Nor should a child feel the constant need to seek adult approval for his choices and actions. Independence is gained when, having applied himself to the problem and arrived at a solution, he is pleased with the result and feels a sense of achievement without adult reassurance.

If a child sees himself as fairly competent and successful, lovable and loving, he is usually happy and well-adjusted. If this feeling is not established in childhood, if what he identifies himself with, expresses himself by, is continually found wanting or unworthy by teachers or parents . . ., his confidence in himself is shaken and he either rebels or becomes overly-dependent upon others for guidance.

The development of self-regard is continually set back or interrupted by the accumulation of experiences of failure. To miss, to make mistakes, to be left out, to "spoil," to fail "to be as good as," or "to do as well as" do not increase self-confidence, even in adults. For children they can be dangerous. Nevertheless in traditional dance teaching, occasions for such set-backs are manifold and sometimes become so easily a part of the teaching procedure that their use by teachers is almost automatic and their long-range ill effects generally disregarded.[6]

Very young children and inexperienced older ones will undoubtedly imitate others in creative and exploratory movement. While imitation certainly should not be encouraged except where movement experiences are being shared with others, it does offer a sort of security to timid children who hesitate at first to strike out on their own. Care should be taken with young children that the teacher is not the pattern for imitation. Rhoda Kellogg observes:

Adult gestures are distracting always and often appear to the child as entertainment provided for him, or as instructions to be followed rigidly. In the first case, he observes only; in the second, he gives up or goes through motions that may or may not be natural and easy for him. In either case, the effect is undesirable; whereas imitation of other children is more likely to lead to activity that is genuine and not self-conscious.[7]

[5] Marian E. Breckenridge and E. Lee Vincent, *Child Development,* 5th ed., Philadelphia, Saunders, 1965, p. 238.

[6] Ruth L. Murray, "Observations on the Teaching of Dance to Children," *Impulse, Annual of Contemporary Dance,* 1957, p. 1.

[7] Rhoda Kellogg, "Dance in the Nursery School," *Impulse, Annual of Contemporary Dance,* 1957, p. 9.

And from Gray and Percival:

> Children must be given time to learn *how* to move. . . . Their rate of development may be slow, but once they have evolved their own individual style of movement it will remain with them whether they are playing games, dancing, or miming. . . . Adult movements imposed on a child may appear to get quicker results but will look as artificial as powder and lipstick on a five-year-old.[8]

Most children are sensitive to an atmosphere of encouraging acceptance of each person's effort and will begin to share the teacher's interest and satisfaction in the progress of less-gifted classmates. When the objective is to lead children away from imitation and to find satisfaction and success in their own efforts, a teacher's natural reaction to the most creative children must often be suppressed. Singling them out repeatedly for special commendation should be avoided; rather, all children should be praised for the degree of advance made over previous efforts.

The Element of Creativity

" 'Creativity' . . . refers to people's behavior when they do such things as (1) invent a new pattern, form, or idea; (2) rearrange already established objects, patterns, or ideas; and (3) integrate a new or borrowed factor into an already established organization."[9] This is one way creativity is defined by an art teacher, and it applies to dance as well as to art. But are these processes present in school experiences? Are they cultivated, nurtured, encouraged? Are children aided in developing their creative potential?

> To a child the arts are not play, they are meaningful work. They are ways of saying how he feels and who he is. And if the curiosity and eagerness the arts stir in him are turned off . . . by boredom, lack of involvement, or insensitive adults . . . the fragile structure of ego built upon confidence in his capacity to make judgments, to risk failure, to try and try again until he is satisfied . . . will shrink, hide, and sometimes collapse. It needs support in the form of gentle guidance and respect.[10]

While the creative use of movement is not at all the exclusive province of the dance program, it is here that the horizons are broadest, that self-

[8] Vera Gray and Rachel Percival, *Music, Movement and Mime for Children*, London, Oxford University Press, 1962, p. 71.

[9] June King McFee, *Preparation for Art*, 2nd ed., Belmont, Calif., Wadsworth, 1970, p. 158.

[10] Lydia Joel, "The Impact of IMPACT: Dance Artists as Catalysts for Change in Education," *Dance Scope*, Spring/Summer 1972, p. 14.

expression flourishes, and that possibilities for individual and group creative effort are endless. Perhaps because of this very fact, teachers are sometimes frightened of it, preferring the narrow boundaries of the circle singing game or the line folk dance, where a modicum of expressiveness may be present but no creativity whatever.

Art educators have progressed much farther than either music or dance educators, not only in fostering children's creativity in their several media but in studying its relationship to the development of personality. For one thing, music and dance are performing arts, and it is erroneously considered that the degree of technical skill must be reasonably high before they can be engaged in as part of a creative enterprise. Creativity is therefore disregarded in favor of direct instruction and drill to enable the child to perform in a way acceptable to the expectations of a preconceived "model."

This author questions whether young children should *perform* dance in the conventional interpretation of the idea of performing before an older audience that expects to be amused or entertained. Spontaneity, as well as creativity, becomes suspect and even dies when children begin to develop a self-conscious awareness of the response of such a group, untutored in and insensitive to a child's world of expressive movement.

> Inhibition may begin with the unexpected reaction of an observer who makes the child self-conscious. The laughter of peers, parents or teachers, whether in amusement or delight, can bring sudden and painful embarrassment. The child becomes aware that when he is spontaneously, freely responsive, he may be exposing himself to ridicule from others. . . . [He] then tends to become guarded, distorting his original movements as if to indicate that he too agrees that they are laughable.[11]

Many uninformed and insensitive adults still regard dance, including children's dance performance, as light entertainment preferably with a slight seasoning of sex. Unfortunately, they then find it difficult to take it seriously, to identify with and understand the child's dance expression. With children's choral and instrumental groups and child musical soloists they are usually respectful and do not look for "cuteness." But then music is a serious art in our culture, and dance has yet to fully attain that status.

Creative dance is resisted by teachers for many reasons, but the fact that creativity is an important attribute to be developed in children is strongly established by educators everywhere. It is a false assumption that children of limited backgrounds respond less successfully to opportunities for expression than those more broadly privileged. Mr. A. L. Stone describes his engrossing

[11] Miriam B. Stecher, "Concept Learning Through Movement Improvisation," *Young Children*, January 1970, p. 147.

experiences in a creative arts program in a school of which he was head-master:

> These few words give you a glimpse of the stark ugliness of the surroundings in which these children lived, . . . but the amazing thing was that when they were allowed to express themselves freely in certain media of expression, they created something which was beautiful. . . . The obvious fact was that the children in this school . . . had within them, as their birthright, an ability to create true beauty within all the media of the arts.[12]

It seems obvious that movement should be among the easiest means with which teachers can cultivate this significant potential in children. One can start wherever the children are and grow with them in knowledge, skill, and understanding. This emphatically does not mean that the children take over and the teacher becomes merely a member of the group. A teacher is always a leader, whether she wills it so or not, and whether her leadership is effective or weak. Where control and authority are lacking or inconsistent, creativity flounders. But control need not be dogmatic or authority repressive. Freedom combined with controls and responsibilities, spontaneity with trust and respect, an expectancy that children will respond wholeheartedly to assigned tasks rather than a suspicion that they will not—in this kind of wholesome environment children's creative efforts flower.

The Child as Audience

Just as an important part of the musical education of children is listening to good music with awareness and appreciation, so their dance education should include opportunities to view dance programs of quality on film or in live performance. A wide variety of dance styles should be shown, ethnic and folk as well as contemporary concert dance and classic ballet. Tap dance and modern jazz routines can be omitted because their visibility on television is high. The primary intention is that children should see dance which has artistic merit.

Teachers should use discretion and judgment in choosing such programs, but they should not underestimate children's ability to understand and enjoy those which are not planned exclusively for them. While a film or demonstration or concert should not be too long, considering the attention span of children, dance movement engages their attention in a vital and exciting way. The kinesthetic response to movement necessary for dance appreciation obviates the need for previous verbal description. Nevertheless, some preparation regarding the kind of dance that will be viewed and who

[12] A. L. Stone, *Story of a School,* Pamphlet No. 14, London, English Ministry of Education, pp. 7–8.

the performers are is indicated. A detailed explanation should be avoided, so that the children may react to the performance spontaneously, and not with ideas as to what they are supposed to see already supplied by the teacher.

Time should be provided for discussion after the performance, and children's comments and reactions, although naive, should be accepted as honest perceptions. Verbalizing about dance is not easy and teachers should not try to force a child to describe a reaction when none is forthcoming.

There is a kind of film which is a valid and essential adjunct to children's viewing experience—the kind that motivates or inspires movement, illuminates kinesthetic and aesthetic concepts, or relates to dance and to other art disciplines in possibly indirect but very telling ways. A listing of such films is found in Chapter 29.

Actually the children's experience as audience commences when they observe with interest and involvement the dancing of their classmates. Perceptions of another's problem-solving are sensitized, and sharing such movement experiences broadens one's own movement vocabulary.

If films, dance demonstrations, and concerts for children are impossible to come by, visual aids such as dance photographs, sketches, and sculpture—some perhaps created by the children themselves—can be used to great advantage. This kind of visual aid should always be a part of the environment of a room used for dancing.

What of the Teacher?

There are many more women than men teachers of children in our elementary schools at the present time. This will not always be the case, nor should it be. Men to whom young children have a special appeal, and who themselves possess attributes which induce happiness and security as well as achievement in the classroom, should definitely be recruited so that they may be properly prepared in our teacher education institutions. In the meantime, it seems more appropriate to use the feminine gender in referring to a teacher of children.

All the characteristics of a good teacher should be possessed by the teacher of dance. She needs to be sympathetic, patient, stimulating, and, above all, imbued with friendliness and respect toward all persons, with a special affinity for children. She should be playful, fun-loving, able to understand and appreciate children's humor, and able to ease tense situations with a light touch. She should create, certainly for all dance lessons and as much as possible otherwise, a noncompetitive environment, where each child's contribution is noted and respected for its own sake, and never in comparison with others. She must try to keep her own house in order so that she can

Appraising Others

be sensitively aware of the children under her guidance and successfully discharge her responsibility to them. As a professional person she must bring to her teaching—and constantly renew through study and inquiry—certain knowledge of boys and girls, their needs and interests, their ways of learning and growing, and how they can best be helped to become happy and contributing persons.

The following qualifications for a teacher of dance may seem formidable. The new generation of young teachers, however, is likely to be more flexible and adventurous than their predecessors. It should be possible to find more than one in a school willing and able to take on the dance program. No child should be denied a dance experience because "the teacher doesn't know how to teach it."

Enjoyment of Movement

Does she find physical movement exhilarating? Does she feel free to perform simple expressive movements without fear or embarrassment? Does she enjoy watching movement?

The dance teacher should not only find movement pleasurable but be able to help others to move with freedom, ease, and enjoyment. The disciplined body of a dancer is not needed, nor is the ability to move in the ways the children can. Trying out movements herself, however, will strengthen her perception and understanding of their responses. Chiefly, there must be a deep sense of children's need to move, to move well, and to move creatively in their own ways.

. . . Expertise can sometimes narrow the view of a classroom teacher so that she finds it difficult to be open to fresh innovations of young children.

Children need the supportive encouragement to pursue their own style. This allows each child to hold on to the integrity of his own personal response. It recognizes that there can be no specific right or wrong.[13]

The teacher of younger children need not move with or for them if she so prefers. Demonstrations by the teacher tend to confuse children for the various stated reasons, and also because their bodily structure and skills are so dissimilar from those of adults. However, if simple dance performances are engaged in, as in singing games and action songs, they should be done wholeheartedly and with gusto. Self-consciousness is quickly communicated to children, and the activity may be interpreted as being trivial.

Older children have higher skill demands. A qualified teacher should possess sufficient skill to perform basic locomotor and nonlocomotor movements and the common dance steps. A kinesthetic comprehension of the whole skill to be learned is desirable in order to understand how its parts relate to one another and what learning procedure can be used most satisfactorily. If it is to be "discovered" by them, knowledge of what problems to set is necessary so that discovery is assured. Mostly, she should recognize natural, free, efficient, and expressive movement when she sees it, take delight in it, sharing the sense of discovery with the child, and have at her command a variety of ways to help all of the children to achieve it.

Rhythmic Skill

Can she chant a rhyme? Can she sing a simple song with rhythmic, though not necessarily tonal, accuracy? Can she hear the beat and reproduce it with hand movements or on an instrument?

[13] Stecher, op. cit., p. 152.

If two particulars were to be cited as required of all dance teachers, they would be a love of movement and a sense of rhythm, the term used to describe an accurate response to aspects of musical rhythm.[14] Music teachers should possess rhythmic skill as a matter of course, although some trained in older methods may have rhythm in their voices and fingers but not much beyond that. Children cannot learn to move rhythmically if their teacher cannot perceive the difference between moving on the beat and off the beat, with the accent and out of accent, or doesn't recognize the beginning and ending of a musical phrase. A person who cannot keep time and who fails to recognize faults of rhythmic performance in others is greatly handicapped in dance teaching. While she could perhaps work successfully with movement alone, she would be unable to guide children in any part of the dance program involving rhythmic response to an accompaniment.

The case is not hopeless. Most young adults can develop sufficiently accurate response to become adequate teachers. In fact, tests of rhythmic response, with provision for remedial work if necessary, should be part of the preparation of all elementary school teachers. Teacher-education curriculums which do not provide such training not only preclude the experiences dance can offer to children but deny the student the personal satisfaction of good rhythmic performance.

Abilities Related to Accompaniment

Does her musical background extend beyond pop tunes? Can she play pulse beats or rhythmic patterns on a drum or other simple instruments? Are note symbols more than an unfamiliar foreign language?

While it is not necessary for dance teachers to know how to play pieces of music on the piano, a knowledge of how to use the piano and/or percussion instruments for improvising accompaniment is an aid to good dance teaching. Sticks (claves) are the easiest instruments with which to start, with the drum a close second. Rich improvisation is possible on the piano and can be rewarding for adventurous souls with little musical knowledge. A discriminating ear and inventiveness in the use of sounds of all sorts are more important than musical ability.

It follows, though, that a dance teacher should be familiar with note symbols and their relative time values, how they can be arranged into simple patterns, where accents fall in a series of beats, what constitutes a musical

[14] For a poetic account of rhythm for children, see Langston Hughes, *The First Book of Rhythms,* New York, F. Watts, 1954.

phrase. So many good records are available today for accompaniment that one's ability to accompany dance is less important than one's understanding of its relation to movement and how the two are integrated.[15]

The teacher's repertoire of chants, rhymes, songs, poems, pieces of music, and recordings which may be used for dance accompaniment need not be extensive but should have appeal for children. While the market for children's records is booming, the products often are educationally worthless. Great care should be taken, therefore, that recorded songs are not trite, vulgar, or overly sentimental. Some popular songs and music are acceptable for dance use, but they should be selected with good taste and with children's understandings and interests in mind.

Because of the extensive use today of recordings and tapes as accompaniment, a teacher should know how to operate the instruments which reproduce them. It is important, too, that the library of records be varied. Always peforming a particular movement to the same selection is a limiting and unsound dance experience. Tape machines, if available, have countless uses for dance lessons. A short section of a record can be taped, or a suitable television song, or children singing a song in the music room, or a collage of instruments and voices made for an invented movement sequence or dance study.

The teacher should be familiar with simple ways to make percussion instruments, so that children can be helped to construct their own. Often the art teacher is of assistance here. Such instruments are useful to dance with if they can be manipulated in the hands, and can be catalysts for movements suggested by their sound. Directions for making instruments are available in many references.[16] It should be remembered, however, that metallic instruments such as bells, triangles, gongs, and chimes can rarely be made at home or school, yet children should not be denied the experience of these sounds and the kind of movement they may induce. Triangles and gongs may be purchased at most instrumental music stores; tin whistles, kazoos, and other metallic sound-makers in dime stores and variety stores.

Personal Attributes

Is her voice a versatile instrument? Are her posture and general demeanor alert, alive, accepting? Can she use her body, and especially her hands, to describe and motivate movement?

---

[15] A good reference is Ruth White, *The Fundamentals of Music for Dancers* (see References for Recordings, Chapter 29).

[16] See footnote 5 in Chapter 16.

Certain characteristics of the teacher as leader affect children's responses either favorably or unfavorably. Hand gestures, for example, may be overdone. However, since children's visual perceptions are often stronger than those received through other senses, effective use of the hands can point up comments or directions which may otherwise be vague and obscure.

Probably the most cogent personal trait is the voice. An expressive and dramatic as opposed to a monotonous or an affected voice quality—one that can convey natural (never false) enthusiasm, that can calm excited youngsters, that can be forceful when the occasion demands—is a potent teaching aid. A harsh or nasal quality causes tension in children; a simpering, artificial voice "turns them off." A course in the speech or drama department which emphasized the use of a good natural voice in teaching, and which would include, besides routine procedures, the reading of poetry, storytelling, and vocal improvisation for movement accompaniment, would improve immeasurably the fledgling teacher's chances of success in initial encounters with young children.

Posture and manner and the ability to move about easily, without self-consciousness, relate positively to success in dance teaching. A leader who appears tired or slovenly can expect that kind of response from the class. One who is cold and unapproachable will find it extremely difficult to establish a "danceable" environment or to free the creative propensities of children. A presence which is friendly but not familiar, vital but not dominating, enthusiastic but not noisy or theatrical, which can evoke fun and excitement but also serenity, is the ideal all teachers should seek.

Creative Imagination

Lastly, does she have some creative imagination? This is indispensable for all teachers, but particularly if they are to help children develop artistic expression. A successful teacher must understand and nurture children's imaginations, know how to direct them into productive channels and to use them to enrich personalities and powers of communication. This is an impossible task if her own imagination is sluggish, yet it is hard to tell exactly how one sharpens it. Certainly active participation in some artistic enterprise of her own will help—even the reading of good literature and poetry or "Sunday painting." Success also derives from understanding each child as a unique person and from an affectionate and enjoyable relationship with him. Perhaps most of all it comes from identifying with the insights of childhood and realizing that all of life should be a continuum of fresh learnings, deepening appreciations, widening horizons.

The Teacher's Objectives for Children's Dance

Following is a list of objectives for dance teaching which has been excerpted from the booklet *Children's Dance*.

Through movement-centered dance activities to assist children to:

Realize their biological urge to experience primal patterns of movement.

Develop an adequate degree of satisfaction in and mastery of their body movements for their pleasure, confidence, and self-esteem.

Expand their movement resources by affording many opportunities to explore, discover, invent, and develop different ways of moving and to structure sequences using them.

Increase their aesthetic sensitivity by emphasizing the expressive and imaginative potential of movement, as well as its physical and athletic aspects.

Develop their appreciation of dance as art, by relating it to appropriate experiences in music, literature, painting, and sculpture.

Relate their movement effectively to accompanying sounds and to music.

Participate with others in recreational folk and ethnic dances by helping them to learn traditional dance steps and to understand the different ways they have been used through centuries of people dancing together.

Make dances alone and with others and, when ready for the experience, to perform them for peer audiences.

Through audience-centered dance activities to assist children to:

Understand the ancient and honorable tradition of dance as art and ritual.

Develop sensitivity to the essence of movement as communication as they observe performances of their peers.

Appreciate the many forms of dance which have evolved in different cultures, all based on common movement resources from which man has drawn for expressive purposes.

Understand, as they grow older, something of the demanding discipline and training of the body which are necessary in order to qualify as a professional dancer.

Enjoy viewing concert and theatre dance and develop a discriminating awareness of movement as an artistic medium.[17]

[17]Murray, "A Statement of Belief," pp. 6, 7.

Part II | *EXPERIENCES IN DANCE MOVEMENT*

Chapter Preview

"I Make My Own Path"

3 Experiences in Dance Movement: Orientation

Movement does not need mind for its existence, but it does for its clarification.[1]

Conceptual Understandings

Until recently creative dance has been mostly neglected in our schools. Many books for children have been written about the use of other art media, but those about dance movement are only recently beginning to appear. Even books, pamphlets, and articles which profess to advance the cause of creativity for children in all the arts approach dance movement timidly and with an apparent lack of knowledge of its possibilities, except as they relate to the other performing arts.[2]

One reason for the lack of attention to the significance of dance as a creative province of children's activity may be ignorance on the part of educators of the "stuff" of movement, its properties, possible classifications, qualities, and uses. This chapter will supply definitions and descriptions of terms, and analyses and classifications of movement used throughout the book. These definitions and analyses will provide concepts about movement which should be part of children's understanding as they use them for creative and expressive purposes. For the teacher they offer points of departure, activators, for those dance lessons in which the primary focus is the creative use of movement.

---

[1] Margaret H'Doubler (to whom the edition was dedicated), quoted in "Extensions of Dance," *Impulse, Annual of Contemporary Dance,* 1969–1970, p. 5.

[2] A favorable augury is a recent series for teachers and children: *Self-Expression and Conduct—The Humanities,* New York, Harcourt Brace Jovanovich, 1974.

In connection with such dance lessons, an elementary principle of motor learning now recognized by psychologists is especially relevant. Many kinds of free exploratory and experimental movements should be experienced before more complex, specialized movement patterns are required to be learned. A great variety of such experiences provide rich resources for later athletic and dance endeavors.

What are children like during this early age period, roughly from three to eight years—in the context of this book, "younger children"? We know that there is rapid physical growth, so rapid that muscular development is uneven; that there is a drive to be active, but that until late in the period the attention span is short; that movement is exuberant, experimental, dramatic, with a tendency to accept that which pleases and to reject that which does not; that interest in a multiplicity of activities makes continuous practice of any one of them unappealing, and often ineffective; that complex movements and rules confuse and irritate.

Only toward the end of this period do we get an increasing desire to learn how, to practice, to become more proficient in activities that earlier were performed merely for the sake of doing them. During the years roughly from eight to eleven, the small muscles are developing, the coordination is improving; but even so, many children "tighten up" and withdraw if driven too hard by adults.

At the early age then, more than at any other, it is imperative that children have freedom to explore movement, to experiment, manipulate, improvise in a spontaneous and creative fashion; to experience many ways of moving rather than only certain specific ways. The child should become aware of the demands each way of moving makes upon his body, how it feels, and finally how movement can be used expressively, dramatically, as well as for the delight and release of just dancing in his own way.

It follows that excursions into movement of all sorts should constitute dance experiences in the elementary school, certainly during the first four years there. Much of the material in Part II is based on this theory.

Children are continually asked to solve intellectual and creative problems with words and numbers during the school day. They should have opportunities to do the same with musical sound, with paint and other art materials, and particularly with movement. They therefore need some knowledge of the components of human movement, comprehension of its special features and the ability to give a verbal description of them as well as an active demonstration. "If a child who has no knowledge of movement is asked to dance, he will probably run and skip and swing his arms about. He is creating *movement things*. When he is taught the alphabet of movement and how it can be used, he will be able to create *movement words*. If he is never taught the words of dance, he may still be dancing 'things' when he goes to college."[3]

Concepts about human movement should be understood not only by children as they test its medium for functional and expressive purposes but by teachers, administrators, and laymen. The public is knowledgeable about the dance of spectacle, of entertainment, of "show biz." Relatively few parents (and even educators) recognize its study as having profound educational and aesthetic values for children. This chapter, therefore, provides a list of body parts used in dance, a description of what, where, and how human motion is achieved; its essential elements and the factors attributed to each; a simple but useful movement classification; a list of movement qualities effected by varying uses of force; and a glossary of some of the action terms used in dance teaching.

Body Parts Used in Dance Movement

Head	Shoulders	Upper and lower arms	Upper and lower legs
Face	Chest	Elbows	Knees
Neck	Trunk	Wrists	Ankles
	Hips	Hands	Feet
	Back	Fingers	Heels
			Toes

Most children know the names of these body parts before they enter kindergarten. For those who seem confused and who cannot touch the part when it is named there are games and action songs which will help. (See Chapter 18.)

Children should be able to identify parts before they are asked to isolate that part in movement. For example, "While sitting on the floor, can you put one of your elbows on one of your knees?" "Can you tap the drumbeat on the floor with fingers, with both feet, with one heel?" "Can you put the top of your head on the floor and see upside down?"

---

[3] Gertrude Blanchard, "Dance in the Modern Elementary School," unpublished article used by permission.

A Descriptive Outline of the Properties of Movement[4]

Human movement has:

    A. Body Actions—*What* the body can do
        1. Move through general space with locomotor movements—walk, run, hop, jump, and all combinations
        2. Move within a personal space with nonlocomotor movements—stretch, bend, twist, and all combinations
        3. Transfer weight
        4. Receive weight
        5. Support weight
        6. Become elevated or airborne
        7. Initiate and terminate movement actions
    B. Space Aspects—*Where* the body moves (alone or with others)
        1. In personal space or self-space
        2. In general space
        3. In differing directions
        4. In differing paths
        5. On differing levels
        6. In differing dimensions
        7. In relation to others' movement
    C. Intrinsic Components—*How* the body moves
        1. In time—both freely, and in an organized or structured sequence
        2. With force—on an energy scale from little to much
        3. In a sequential flow—a logical joining of one movement to the next

An Analysis of Movement

Before explaining the movement analysis used in this book, we should make certain points regarding movement sequences and the contrast between motion and stillness.

All movement is sequential. It is made up of a succession of body actions or action sequences, some involuntary, others voluntary. This characteristic is observed in the many small body changes which constitute, for example, the stamp of a foot, the blink of an eyelid, the pointing of a finger. It is apparent

---

[4] This outline with agreed-upon minor changes appeared in "Movement Education and Creative Dance Experience," by Ann Zirulnik, in the *Journal of the Michigan Association for Health, Physical Education and Recreation*, Vol. 1, No. 10, January 1971, p. 4.

in the repetition of a single movement, as in walking, and when one movement is followed by a different one and then joined logically to a third, in what might be called the extension of an initial movement into a *movement phrase*. This sequential nature of movement and its differentiated actions has been called "flow" by one authority, with "free flow" characterized by a continuous sequence of body action impelled by the force of the initial impulse, and its opposite, "bound flow," by interruption of the sequence with controlled stops and starts as it proceeds.[5]

In this book it is taken for granted that all movement is ensuing, successive, and consecutive, and differentiation is made between that succession of movement events represented by several different movement qualities. Six of these recognizable qualities of movement are described later in this chapter.

When movement is stopped, even momentarily, the result is a *position* in space, an arrested body shape. Such a position may be the point from which movement is initiated, i.e., the starting position; the pause or point of stillness from which it continues to another position in space; or the place where it is brought to a conclusion.

Movement takes place in *space* and in *time* and requires some degree of *force* to perform. Further, movement has a certain *shape* which can be described and can now be notated. Any natural movement has certain definite characteristics because it uses these movement elements in particular ways.

Let us take the basic *walk* as an example. Its body *direction* is forward, it transfers weight from one foot to another with steps of moderate *size* (there are, of course, individual differences), it maintains a standing *level* with the body erect, its *path* is straight, and the eyes *focus* in the direction in which the walk is moving. These characteristics are related to *space* and may be said to be the spatial factors of a natural walk.

In *time,* the basic walk moves at a moderate *rate of speed*, and because the intervals between the steps are usually equal it has a regular *pulse*, like the beat of the heart.

The *way* one walks usually refers to the way one expends and controls *force* or *energy*. An efficient walk is light and springy with a nice balance between tension and relaxation, falling about in the middle between strong and weak on a scale of dynamics. (When a person says of another, "I can tell she's coming when I hear her walk," the telltale factors are usually timing and quality.)

The *shape* of the walk has changed very little since our remote ancestors began to travel on two feet instead of four. It has become more erect, but it

[5] See Rudolph Laban, *Modern Educational Dance*, London, MacDonald & Evans, 1948, p. 24.

still moves the body through space by transferring weight from one foot to the other. Its shape characteristics are described in detail in Chapter 8.

Following is án analysis of the force, shape, space, and time elements of movement and the factors pertaining to each.

THE ELEMENT OF Force (ENERGY, EFFORT, WEIGHT, DYNAMICS)[6] AND FACTORS THAT RELATE TO IT

Force is released and controlled by the body's joint and muscular action. The quantity of such energy affects the *quality* of the resulting movement, which may be described as tense, heavy, strong, hard; or, on the opposite side of the scale, relaxed, light, weak, soft.

Changes in force: May be gradual or sudden (crescendo or diminuendo in musical terms).

THE ELEMENT OF Shape (BODY ACTION, USE OF BODY) AND FACTORS THAT RELATE TO IT

Position or movement of the head, trunk, arms, legs, hands, feet, alone or in combination with other body parts; vertical, horizontal, or intermediary body posture.

THE ELEMENT OF Space AND FACTORS THAT RELATE TO IT

Direction of movement: Forward, backward, sideward, diagonal, turning, in, out, up, down. (See also Glossary of Dance Terms.)

Dimension (size, range, amplitude) *of movement:* Large, big, tall, high, wide; or small, little, short, low, narrow.

Level (plane) *of movement:* Low, middle, high, airborne; or, of body posture, prone, sitting, squatting, kneeling, standing, elevated.

Path of movement: Straight (direct) or curved, twisted, crooked (indirect, flexible), zigzag, serpentine, random.

Focus of gaze in movement: Constant toward any direction, wandering, near, far, dual, outward, inward. Focus may also relate to the focal point of a movement, which may be in any direction and may oppose or concur with eye action.

THE ELEMENT OF Time AND FACTORS THAT RELATE TO IT

Rate of speed (tempo, pace) of movement: Slow, moderate, fast.

Changes in speed: May be gradual or sudden (acceleration or retardation in musical terms).

---

[6] The words in parentheses have been used in others' writing on movement and dance and have similar meanings.

"When You're Down, I'm Up"

An Airborne Skip

Even timing: When intervals defined or measured by pulse beats (metric or underlying beats), or divisions *within* these intervals are *equal.*

Uneven timing: When divisions *within* the intervals between pulse beats are *unequal.*

Unstructured timing: When the timing sequence, rather than being metrically structured, is dictated by the nature of the movement itself, as in breath rhythms, the movements of young children, the ebb and flow of energy.

Increased understanding of the elements of movement and their factors is afforded by a list of contrasting actions and descriptive words which appears in a recent publication of the Dance Division of AAHPER.[7]

The contrasting words were chosen for their simplicity and descriptive qualities. Children may well find others that are just as accurate and more appealing to them. For the most part, the first contrasts of each factor are the simplest and easiest to use for exploration and experimentation. Some of the later ones should be reserved for older children. Some contrasts, such as degree of force, speed, size, and level of movement, range from least to most. The intermediate points on the scale may be "middle," "moderate," "medium," "neutral," or similar words.

Element	Factor	Contrast
Force	Control of	Moving–stopping
	Degree of	Much–little
		Heavy–light
		Strong–soft
		Tight–loose
	Quality of	Explosive–smooth
Space	Level	High–low
	Size	Big–little
	Direction	Toward–away
		Up–down
		Out–in
		Forward–backward
		Right–left (one side–other side)
		Around right–around left
	Path	Straight or curved, twisted, angular
	Focus of gaze	Constant–changing
Time	Rate of speed	Fast–slow
	Progress of speed	Increasing–decreasing
	Duration	Short–long
	Interval	Equal–unequal (even–uneven)

[7] Gladys Andrews Fleming, ed., *Children's Dance,* Washington, D.C., AAHPER Publications, 1973, p. 10.

Shape	Design	Large–small
		Wide–narrow
		Straight–crooked or curved
		Round–pointed
		Smooth–sharp
		Fat–thin
		Symmetrical–asymmetrical

A Movement Classification

Movement may be classified according to differences in its characteristics or in its use. Alice Gates lists several classifications, of which the following are quoted for a better understanding of movement in general.

1. Movements may be *voluntary* (or) *Involuntary* (movements of organic body functioning and expressive gesturing)
   (those consciously selected, controlled, and directed)
2. *Functional* actions (or) *Expressive* (gestures and stylized movements)
3. *Natural* body movements (or) *Contrived* movements (as in ethnic forms, classical ballet, etc.)
4. *Movements of the whole body* (or) *Peripheral movements* (of arms, legs, head, or those limited to particular parts of the body)
5. *Locomotor movements* (which propel the body through space) (or) *Axial or nonlocomotor movements* (contained spatially in relation to the body axis)[8]

The final classification has been part of this author's dance teaching over the years. It is explained here in detail. Simple to understand, it is related to "general space" and "personal space," based on the kind of movement that goes from "here to there" or that "stays here."

Locomotor movement: Movement that carries the body from one place to another through space
  1. Using the feet as a base for moving
     a. The simplest, primary, or basic locomotor movements—the walk, run, jump, and hop
     b. Variations and combinations of these movements, resulting in all the different kinds of dance steps, as well as all locomotor movement used in work and play—for example, the leap, skip, slide, gallop, polka, waltz, schottische, etc.

[8] Alice A. Gates, *A New Look at Movement, A Dancer's View*. Minneapolis, Burgess, 1968, p. 116.

    2. Using another part of the body as a base for moving
       a. Crawling, rolling, somersaulting, cartwheeling, walking on hands, moving on knees, buttocks, etc.

Nonlocomotor movement: Movement performed over a more or less stationary base, within the space in one place

    1. The simplest, primary or basic nonlocomotor movements—the bend, stretch, twist, and swing[9]
    2. Variations and combinations of these movements resulting in many movements that may involve the whole body and are called by descriptive action words: pull, push, strike, dodge, spin, shake, sit, collapse, rise, lift, etc.
    3. Other such movements, some of which have no specific names and some of which use only the arms or legs or head—such as clapping, striking, pressing, or slapping the hands together, or striking another part of the body with the hands or arms, nodding or shaking the head, stamping, brushing, slapping, or tapping the feet, etc.

These two large categories of movement (locomotor and nonlocomotor) are usually combined in everyday movement activity. We swing our arms when we walk, twist our bodies and necks to watch our opponents when we are running in a game, bend or stretch our arms to carry things from place to place. Endless combinations of movements are possible not only from these two categories, but within them as well. They form the materials of which dance experiences are born and dances are made.

Movement Qualities

Forces within the body and outside it which are induced, expended, or reacted with or against in various ways result in distinctive qualities of movement. They attain their special characteristics through the particular way body energy is used, as in the extreme tension accompanying vibratory movement, or body reaction to the force of gravity, as in the release into gravity of the swing. Those qualities in the movement of children, especially older ones who are physically ready for this kind of experience, are explained below.

    Sustained movement is characterized by a constant, even flow of energy, resulting in movement that is ongoing, smooth, and equal in force expenditure. The latter may be little or much, so that the movement may be very

---

[9] These should be considered basic not necessarily in a kinesiological sense but as described in Chapter 9.

soft or very strong, and in timing it may be fast or slow. The lack of perceptible accents and sharp beginnings or endings is typical of sustained movement.

Percussive (sometimes known as propulsive or ballistic) movement is the opposite of sustained movement. It begins with a strong impetus, expends energy in spurts and small or large explosions, stops suddenly at any point, and then may start again. While energy expenditure may be small, resulting in light movement, it is more often intense, with sharply defined accents or points of additional stress.

Swinging movement, described in detail in Chapter 9, is characterized by a reaction to the force of gravity, inasmuch as the swinging body part is relaxed and allowed to drop. Because of its attachment to a fixed joint, the path in space is curved and the momentum of the drop carries it up on the other side of the curve, where it hangs suspended for an instant before dropping back. Many sustained and percussive movements follow a curved or circular path, and an adapted swing is often used as a partial preparation for such movements as throwing and striking. Without the relaxed release into gravity and the suspension at the top of the curve, however, the movement cannot be called a true swing.

Vibratory movement results when the extreme of tension is applied to the vibrating part, which responds with a series of fluttering, quivering movements. Force is generally released after a short time and then may be initiated again, so that the vibrations recur. The easiest parts of the body to bring to a state of vibration are the hands and arms, then the head, and lastly the total body. The movement of "shaking," if tension is considerably increased and continued, will result in vibratory movement.

Collapsing movement, like swinging, is characterized by a relaxed release into gravity, usually in the trunk or knees, resulting in a folding, curling, or telescoping of the body or body part downward. It may continue its downward path to the floor or stop at any point, when the force resisting the pull of gravity is renewed.

Suspended movement results when the initial force is expended for an instant and a momentary stillness in space is achieved although the sense of movement continues. It can be compared to breath-holding after a deep inhalation, and this simile is helpful in attaining it. Suspension is the exciting quality present when an expert leap hangs in the air; when a swing attains the top of its arc before dropping back; when balance hangs for a moment between loss and recovery. Whether it occurs on springboard or trampoline, in the aerialists' upper reaches of the circus tent or in the dance room or studio or stage, suspended movement arouses interest and excitement. This is because, for a minute period in time, it does not acknowledge gravity.

A Short Glossary of Dance Terms

Action words typical of creative dance teaching are often used so indiscriminately that distinctions between them are lost. While certain words do have somewhat similar meanings, it is best to use a precise activity term when planning, directing, or discussing what is to be done. Teachers use certain words to signal or direct action. Such words, as they are used in this book, are also included in this glossary.

Compose: To make a dance study by joining together parts into a logical sequence. This term will be used in children's dance, rather than *choreograph,* which implies a more advanced and complex act of creating dance forms.

Dance study: A "little" dance or a "mini-dance." This term describes the dance compositions of children, especially those growing out of the manipulation of movements and their combination into simple sequences.

Demonstrate: To perform a dance movement or part of a dance sequence for the purposes of clarification, imitation, motivation, showing the quality of response or the variety of possible responses.

Direction (body): That movement in which the front, back, or either side of the body or body part leads into the movement, so that *forward, backward,* or *sideward* may be applied to it.

Direction (spatial): That movement which proceeds toward the front, back, sides, or corners of the space or place where the movement occurs. The body direction may remain constant or may also change.

Discover: To come upon a movement, a way of moving, or a combination of movements that bestows a new awareness of their nature and possible use.

Duration: The length of time employed for the performance of a single movement, a movement phrase, or a dance study.

Evaluate: To establish criteria for assessing a movement experience in terms of movement concepts, skill, artistic principles, and aesthetic impact.

Explore: To search for, to investigate, to try out, in order to find solutions to problems.

Finish (bring to a conclusion, come to a stillness, make an ending): All of these directions indicate that movement should cease—not suddenly, but as soon as the individual or group perceives an opportunity to conclude it in a shape that relates to what has gone before.

Freeze (hold, stop): To cease all movement at once and to remain immobile in the shape the body presented when the signal word was given. *Stop* may also suggest merely ceasing to move without freezing the final shape.

General space (outer space): In contrast to self-space, this term refers to all the space beyond it available for movement purposes. As others will also be occupying the general space, the child must be aware of them in order to avoid collision as he travels through it.

Identify (with): To establish as being a particular person, action, or thing; to move in a similar way as something assumed.

Imitate: To reproduce in movement and manner; to duplicate or copy as closely as possible.

Improvise: To move without previous planning, but with identified purpose; to perform on the spur of the moment.

Invent: To devise, originate, or create a new or at least unfamiliar dance movement, a part of a dance study, or a dance sequence of unique organization.

Neutral: In a movement this term may refer to that place which is midway between fast and slow, small and big, moderate in its use of force and with a path beginning at any place in space.

Opposition: A contrasting movement phrase performed simultaneously with another person or persons. The phrases are usually of the same duration, and they may precede or follow each other in a sequential order.

Perform: To execute or participate in dance movements or a dance study, usually before some kind of audience and often as a culminating experience.

Place-shape (position, still-shape, body design): This hyphenated expression means the shape of the body when it is not visibly moving—when, in other words, it is holding a position. This is in contrast to a moving shape, or sequential shapes.

Practice: To perform repeatedly a dance movement or dance so as to gain in clarity, skill, and proficiency.

Self-space (personal space): This hyphenated expression means the space occupied by a single child. It is the space appropriated when all body parts are extended to the fullest in all directions, in a lying, sitting, kneeling, or standing place-shape.

Shape: The design of a body in a spatial area in which it is held still or immobile or in which it is continually changing.

Succession: Immediate and identical reproduction of a movement or movement phrase performed by another person (or persons) after he has completed it and is still, or has moved on to the next phrase.

Unison: Performance of a movement or movements identically and simultaneously with another or others.

Chapter Preview

Movement Experiences Through Teacher Direction

Movement Experiences Through Guided Exploration
  and Problem-Solving

Movement Experiences Through Free Exploration,
  Improvisation, Invention

Permutations

Properties as Aids in Exploration and Improvisation

Altering the Physical Environment

The Uses of Accompaniment in Movement Exploration
  For Movement-Centered Problems
  For Rhythm-Centered Problems

Evaluating Themselves and Others

4 *Presenting Movement Experiences*

Children learn whenever the environment allows them the opportunity to become involved . . . in activity, investigation, choice, participation, interaction.

Exploring one's movement potential, experiencing rhythm, discovering music through organizing sounds, these are essentials in relating to one's world.[1]

The teacher's role in providing experiences in dance movement to children may vary widely, from one in which she continuously calls the turn, so to speak, to one in which such direction is given over almost completely to the child after the general purpose of the experience has been made clear to him. In any creative use of movement, however, the child makes movement choices, even though the range of such choices may be limited. Where there is no single or standard solution to the problem, where more than one way of moving is possible, any movement is right if it is his selection and a solution. When kinds of movement and ways of moving are being investigated and manipulated, children must rely on their own judgments and problem-solving abilities. This is an initial aspect of creativity.

To structure problems so that there is a variety of activity and both progression and continuity in the mastery of body movement requires sensitive observation of children's responses and careful planning from one lesson to the next. It is far easier to tell the class what to do, to show by demonstration or other illustrative means, and then to cue responses so that they approximate as nearly as possible the movement pattern desired by the

[1] Nik Krevitsky, Project Director, *A Gift of Heaven,* A Report on Project Creates, Tucson, Arizona, Public Schools, 1968.

teacher. In the beginning it also takes less time to learn movement skills in this fashion if one's purpose is only skill attainment.

The creative method of the teaching of dance, however, has other goals. Growth in self-direction, in understanding one's own movement potential, in the ability to judge how and why certain movements provide certain results is a concomitant that must not be denied the child if the experience is to be one of education and not merely training. The teacher who is both adventurous and patient in her use of this method will soon observe and appreciate the integrated learnings that evolve from it. Eventually even skill attainment itself progresses at a much more rapid rate, for the child teaches himself as much as he is taught.

Imagery or descriptive action words may or may not be used, depending on (1) the age of the children; (2) the sort of experiencing or exploring or improvising sought; (3) whether the movement experience is self-contained as a solution of a kinetic problem or related to literature, drama, art, or music; and (4) the teacher's skill in using images to stimulate better, more individual movement response.

The judicious use of cue words having imaginative color and dramatic flavor effects more effort in any lesson in movement—baseball, golf, folk dance, or merely jumping or stretching or collapsing. "Can you be as tiny as a bug; as big as a house; float in the air; scrunch yourself up; investigate the ceiling; hug the floor?" Such imagery adds emphasis to the kinesthetic feeling for the movement and a subtle expressiveness to the performance that brings it closer to the dance experience.

Movement Experiences Through Teacher Direction

Complete teacher direction is a time-honored and perfectly legitimate way of getting children to move well in both familiar and unfamiliar ways. The teacher's approach may be autocratic or gentle, but the movement result is the same. The children are put through their paces by her commands— usually with their full cooperation, for it is fun to move, even though someone else starts one off and makes all the decisions. This method should not be belittled, but it should not be called something it is not. The teacher may be exploring the children's movement abilities for any number of purposes, but the children themselves are not doing any exploring. Experiencing, yes, and often with great satisfaction; making choices, investigating, manipulating, inventing, improvising—no. These words imply self-directed activity, and one cannot be self-directed when he is being told what to do and how to do it, even though the "how" is couched in interesting imagery.

Many teachers believe they are conducting a lesson in movement exploration or creative movement when all they have done is modify a formal command into a signal or a question or a challenge in an informal setting with less insistence on exact and immediate response. There is one standard way of following the direction, rather than several acceptable ways. Children may run, jump, bend, twist, swing, but the movement is ordered and controlled by the teacher. It goes something like this:

Direction: Everyone bend over and, keeping knees straight, touch the floor with your fingers.

Challenge: Try to bend over and touch the floor . . . (etc.).

Request: Let me see you . . . (etc.).

Question: Can you . . . ? (etc.).

Direction plus imagery: Show me how you can make a bridge by bending over to touch the floor.

These movement signals, or any combination of them, will almost always produce the same results, there being few variables possible in the movement. The teacher's expectations are clear when phrases like "I want you," "Show me," "Let me see you" are sprinkled throughout the dance lessons. The children usually comply, for most children are tractable and are used to having the demands of authority couched in the language of inquiry or challenge, or at the very least in courteous phrases, especially in school.

"What a nice, big, strong bridge Jimmy has made! See if you can make your legs long and straight, too" still does not offer the child any choice but that of emulating Jimmy's bridge. It may, however, improve his performance of the movement, which was what it was intended to do.

Complete teacher structuring of movement experiences in dance should be seen, then, for what it is. It may have many worthy purposes. Children may increase their movement vocabularies considerably, may achieve better control and flexibility, strength and balance, may learn to move with greater ease and freedom and security. And they will have fun doing so if the atmosphere is informal and playful and imaginative and if they gain the satisfaction of meeting the challenges offered them and noting their own improvement. But this must not be called exploratory or creative or a problem-solving use of movement, for it is not that.

Creativity implies choices, even if the choice is between only two things. Exploration implies discovering for oneself that straight knees make a tall bridge and bent knees a smaller one and that there are lots of other ways of bending, twisting, supporting, and balancing to make body bridges.

Nevertheless, when all children are responding in the same way, they can be helped to perform basic movements in the most efficient, natural, and correct fashion. Posture, carriage, correct use of feet, legs, arms, suspension, spring and buoyancy, control in landing, relaxation, precision—these can be readily checked by the teacher and guidance offered for improved execution. Children need to be able to move well in basic natural ways if their movements are to be used as points of departure for exploration.

For very young or shy children, sitting on the floor around the teacher, playing action-song games or following simple directions affords reassurance. Since the majority of these children have not yet established a firm and secure identity (something the teacher should be sensitive to), they should not be asked to individualize their activity.

A simple procedure reinforcing the "motion and stillness" action which is the kernel of any movement activity might be this: By verbal signal and hand gesture the teacher has the children move away from her; on another signal such as a word or clap, they stop; on a third verbal and hand signal, they return. This simple "away, stop, and toward" pattern can be elaborated, with giant walks, jumps, tiptoe walking, crawling, galloping, or any other locomotor movement within the children's repertoire. Nonlocomotor movement—high and low, out and in, turning and stopping—may also be attempted. After several different tries, children can make choices, perhaps between only two or three movements at first. Thus they begin to approach their own decision-making.

Dance lessons often have some teacher-directed movement in them, if only as a warm-up and review at the beginning. The purpose at all times is to help the child to become master of his body's movement, and many kinds of experiences will work toward that goal.[2]

Movement Experiences Through Guided Exploration and Problem-Solving

In this large middle area between teacher-directed and child-directed experiences, a choice is given, an area of exploration is stated, a problem is set, and the child makes decisions, discovers another way, or solves the problem to the best of his ability. Giving a child the whole world to choose from will confuse and often bewilder him. Channeling his efforts toward a satisfying solution, limiting the choices, setting boundaries to his investigation will allow him to apply himself productively.

In a lesson in movement exploration children must first of all be enjoined to move. To this end the teacher must provide a *purpose* for the

2 For a detailed list of mostly teacher-directed activities for very young children see Vera Gray and Rachel Percival, *Music, Movement and Mime for Children,* London, Oxford University Press, 1962, Appendix A.

A Nose Lead

An Elbow Lead

movement which makes sense to the children. Merely to be told to "move in any way you wish" or "move the way the music makes you feel" will embarrass and inhibit some children, make others try to discover how the teacher wants them to move, and be a signal to others to engage in disruptive actions not at all pertinent to the activity.

Purposive catalysts can take many forms of direction, inquiry, illustration, or suggestion. Most of the following examples have many possibilities for development into a single lesson or a series of lessons. While two or more might be used together, they are not meant to represent a series of movement experiences to be presented one after another. Rather they are single points of departure into movement which may then be developed and clarified.

With children standing, sitting, or lying in self-spaces, a movement to start with may be achieved in many ways.[3]

SOME MIGHT BE

Try to make yourself very, very small; now move into a big shape (and vice versa).

Stretch very high; now down very low (and vice versa).

Reach to a wide shape; now make yourself very narrow (and vice versa).

Try to be very round; now very flat.

Twist (bend) your arm (leg, body) and then straighten it.

Put an elbow on the floor and then take it as far away as you can (and vice versa).

Stretch a leg far away from you and bring it back without touching the floor.

Make a big, straight movement; a little one.

Make a big, curving movement; a little one.

Turn yourself around in different ways, fast and then slowly.

Move very quickly and freeze suddenly into stillness.

Move slowly and come gradually to stillness.

Bounce one part of yourself; another part; your whole self.

Float one part of yourself; another part; your whole self.

Push with one part of yourself; another part; your whole self.

Collapse one part of yourself; another part; your whole self.

Walk (run, jump, hop) from "here to there" and back.

Gallop or skip from "here to there" and back.

Spin in place and stop suddenly without falling; spin and gradually slow down and stop; start slowly, spin fast, and stop suddenly or slowly.

---

[3] Sometimes movement is freer and more inventive if children are first asked to close their eyes before exploring or improvising.

Move as though you were very tall (tiny, wide, round, crooked, stiff, floppy, star-gazing, earth-gazing, etc.).

THEN EACH MIGHT BE FOLLOWED WITH QUESTIONS LIKE ONE OF THESE–(*not all will apply to all of the above movements*)

Can you change . . . (the direction of your movement? its level? its speed? its path? its force or intensity?)

What would happen if . . . (you make it curved or crooked or straighter or spiraled?)

Can you make your body into a different shape? . . . another? . . . another?

Can you do it if you are . . . (crouching low, sitting down, lying down, standing very tall?)

How many different things can you do with your feet (knees, arms) when you walk (run, jump)?

How many different ways can you move your feet (legs, arms, hands) when you are lying on your back?

OR SUGGESTIONS LIKE ONE OF THESE

Try to make the movement bigger and then smaller (faster and then slower, higher and then lower, stronger and then softer).

See if you can do the same movement with another part of yourself.

Try to change the way your fingers and hands are moving so that they are stronger (lighter, slower, faster, closed, open, higher, lower, and then several ways in succession).

When you come up from the floor (or go down into it) try to let your head (one hand, your nose, an elbow) be the leading part that starts the movement, with the rest following.

Try to move around the room letting one part of you lead your movement and change to another part after a while.

OR DIRECTIONS LIKE ONE OF THESE

Go across the room using three different movement speeds.

Move one part of yourself fast and another slowly (or big and small).

Lift something that is heavy (light, big, small) and carry it to a definite place, putting it down.

Change quickly from high to low, slowly from low to high, and then change the timing as you wish.

In your own space draw any form you see in the room (triangle, square, arc, circle, rectangle) as big as you can with one hand (vertically); in the space overhead with both hands (horizontally); in front of you with your leg or chin or head or trunk; now on the floor with one foot. Now to make it even bigger, move around on the floor using any locomotor movement you wish.

OR ILLUSTRATIONS LIKE ONE OF THESE

The rope is slithering into the floor in a tangle. Can you move like that?

Jim bends and extends his arm when he raises his hand. What other ways can you raise one hand or both?

Could you twist yourself like a dishrag and then shake yourself out again?

How many different masks can your face make?

Many people are running with legs lifted high in front. Could they be lifted high in another way?

Show whether you are walking on ice, hot sand or pavement, in a hurry, around things that are in your way.

In all of the above, children must make decisions about their activity. There may be only one, as: "Shall I make a big or small shape?" or several, as: "Shall I make it low or high, on how many bases of support, twisted or straight?"

It is important that children learn the names of movements, at least basic ones (walk, run, jump, hop, stretch, bend, twist), and simple combinations (gallop, skip, slide, push, pull, lift, fall) as soon as they have been experienced. Factors of time, space, and force that affect their movement performance should also be part of their vocabulary. They should recognize their application to movement and perceive that often they provide a contrast from one way of performing a movement to the opposite way. The list of contrasting factors in Chapter 3 will be of assistance here. Gradually, fewer directions and explanations from the teacher will be necessary. Children themselves can experiment with the ways a particular movement may be done, and the teacher need be concerned only with improvement in skill, control, freedom, and creativity.

At the same time there should come an increasing kinesthetic awareness of the body in movement—for example, the knowledge that stillness in dance as opposed to moving "is *not* not doing. It is mental and emotional preparation for the ensuing activity . . . a stillness in which there is still tension, latent action. . . ."[4] The feel of a twist, bend, stretch, of a strong takeoff and a light landing, a drop with complete relaxation, the placing of body parts in various spatial relationships to each other—awareness of these and many

[4] Peter Lofthouse, *Dance,* London, Heinemann, 1970, p. 12.

other kinesthetic elements of body movement will be developed through such methodology.

Movement Experiences Through Free Exploration, Improvisation, Invention

Even when a child is given freedom to move as he wishes, there must be a reason, a purpose, a catalyst, possibly assigned but better self-selected, to evoke movement. It may be a movement problem of balance or design or energy contrasts which is to be investigated. It may be a piece of music of a certain quality to which movement is to be improvised. It may be a scarf, a piece of plastic film, and a newspaper whose similarities and differences need examining as the child moves them and moves with them. It may be any one of hundreds of images he has chosen to interpret in movement.

The choices at this end of the creative scale are much greater. Children may proceed at their own pace, and anything within the problem which seems right to them is legitimate and useful. However, the activity loses its value as an educational experience if the movements are merely at random, performed with no concentration or absorption in the project, and constitute only a sort of laissez-faire release of energy. The children should therefore be encouraged to consider their purposes and be able to explain them, if explanation is necessary.

When, through the practice of many decision-making activities, children are ready for self-directed exploration, they should also be ready to set their own problems. Discovery of possible solutions or potential developments should follow, some being eliminated, others, perhaps only one, retained. The ensuing creative product is the movement sequence or study or mini-dance showing the development or solution of the problem. As children become more mature these movement phrases acquire dancelike qualities; they are imbued with inner feeling; they evidence rhythmic flow, design, texture, balance, and other principles of artistic form that should characterize good dance composition.

Children working creatively with movement materials should be encouraged to think of them in terms of a sequential form which from a definite position or place-shape starts on an action impulse, proceeds, and then arrives at a point of completion. In other words, it has a beginning, a middle, and an end. The results of free invention or improvisation should exhibit a sequence of this kind. Other limitations and restrictions to self-directed enterprises which should be heeded follow.

Control of Space. When many children are moving at once, certain regulations must be made by the teacher or class[5] so that each child has an equal chance to move as he wishes. These might consist of:

1. Assigning to him only the space which he can reach by stretching in all directions (self-space).
2. Allowing him to move only in that half or quarter of the room in which he starts.
3. Allowing free movement about the room if it can be done without collision. It helps to have each child "carry his self-space" with him.

Children should learn early how to weave about among others, making their own paths without interfering with their classmates' progress.

Control of Speed. If the music, song, image, or technical problem demands explosions of locomotor speed, space allowance must be made for it unless it can be simulated with movement in place or with nonlocomotor movement. The noncollision rule applies here as well. Children should be encouraged when moving about the room to watch for open spaces and to take quick spurts into them, being ready to stop short or change direction quickly if necessary. Quick stops and starts are skills which are extremely useful in sport and "daily" movements as well as in dance.

Control of Force. When a problem is given or chosen, a piece of music is decided upon, images are selected, environment is altered, or properties are distributed, some agreement should be reached as to the quality of movement suitable to the proposed interpretations, improvisations, or inventions. A teacher must not be surprised when music which seems calm and peaceful to her sounds uncommonly sprightly to a child's ears, or when an image that seems merely ponderous and slow has sinister or ominous overtones. Assigning space according to the vigor of the invented movement after this has been determined may be a partial solution. If the dance space is too crowded and children are unable to experiment as they wish, taking turns is the only answer. It is not a bad one if the watchers are encouraged to be a serious audience and their critical or encouraging comments are requested.

Options. When a lesson or part of a lesson is devoted to free movement experimentation on the part of children who are not new to such an experience, it is sometimes desirable to offer certain options to them as they work on a movement problem. Inspiration may come from stopping for a bit to

---

[5] Sometimes a class is asked to make so many organizational decisions that the activity itself has to be postponed. To accept and abide by them, children should understand what the rules are and why they need to be made. It is not necessary that they themselves make them.

think through what has been done, from watching others work, or from copying some of their movements, as well as from continuing the improvisational process.

A former colleague of mine who has taught both children and adults specifies the following options when a class is improvising. Children may use one or all of them in the course of a problem-solving session.

1. Movement may be continuously improvised in search of a satisfying solution of the problem.
2. Movement may be frozen in a specific shape as mental reconstruction of the satisfying (or unsatisfying) sequence up to that point takes place. Also reaction to the movement occurring around them may trigger new ideas.
3. Anyone may quietly leave the floor or working space at any time, watch for a while, and then return.
4. Anyone may copy part of another's movement if he so wishes (it is desirable to give credit) and thinks it will help him to construct a more satisfying sequence.

Permutations

The author is indebted to Shirley Ririe, master teacher, concert dancer, and Associate Professor of Dance at the University of Utah, for the following table of movement elements. It should appeal not only to teachers but to children, who, starting with any "neutral" movement, may choose from one, two, three, or four of the columns to change their movement according to the listed qualities.

By reading across the columns, it will be seen that an assigned or chosen movement may be altered in several ways:

Using any single column, there are *two* possible permutations. For example, using only column one, the movement may change from slow to fast.

Using any two columns, there are *four* possible permutations. For example, using columns one and two, movements that are slow may change from curved to straight, and fast movements similarly.

With each additional column, possible permutations are multiplied by two, so that the use of all four columns makes possible sixteen different movements.

Time	Shape	Space	Force
slow	curved	big	much
slow	curved	big	little
slow	curved	small	much
slow	curved	small	little
slow	straight	big	much
slow	straight	big	little

slow	straight	small	much
slow	straight	small	little
fast	curved	big	much
fast	curved	big	little
fast	curved	small	much
fast	curved	small	little
fast	straight	big	much
fast	straight	big	little
fast	straight	small	much
fast	straight	small	little

Properties as Aids in Exploration and Improvisation

The process of encouraging children to move freely without embarrassment and in a variety of ways is greatly aided by the use of simple *props*. Here interest is centered not so much on one's own movement as on making something else move in every possible and interesting way. The prop may also be an object that does not move or is not touched or handled, in which case the action may consist of a constant or intermittent focus with resultant reactions.

There are many precedents for dancing with something in the hands. The mask, the fan, the flower of court dance, the swords and sticks of folk dance ritual all were used for specific movement purposes, usually definitely prescribed. One not so prescribed but more related to the free use we are discussing here is a large handkerchief held in the hand when performing folk dance. Sometimes held only by the man (the women have skirts to hold, flick, and swing) but often by dancers of both sexes, they provide a light, gay touch and help dancers overcome the stilted use of the upper body so often seen in elementary and secondary school folk dance.

Very light silk scarves of all shapes, or their more available substitute, lengths of colored plastic film, can be flicked, waved, swung, tossed with one or both hands or by one or more persons, depending upon their size. The movement after the scarf is tossed in the air and floats downward to the floor can be observed and imitated. The scarf can be tossed high and allowed to cover the body, standing, sitting, or lying, as it drifts down; it can be swung or sailed or flicked; it can be made to be gentle or angry. It is one of the best "dance things" there is, for its movement can be both brisk and dreamy, as in the flames of a fire or in the smoke that curls up from them.

Some of the same feats can be performed with pages of newspaper or paper toweling. In each case—with silk, plastic, newsprint, or toweling—their different as well as similar movement properties, how they are affected by air currents, their clinging or slipping qualities, their translucence or opacity are interesting subjects for investigation.

Long strips of crepe paper or other sturdier material make curves, snails, and serpentines in the air or may be placed on the floor for tight rope walking or jumping or leaping over. Or several shorter pieces can be doubled over, fastened at the bend with a string handle, and made into a kind of fluttery mop. Bandannas or short pieces of soft rope are useful to pull against in different hand and arm relationships while movement is made from one position to another. Grasped at either end and held taut, they keep the hands and arms in varying positions of tension against which the body may make nonlocomotor movements on different levels and in differing designs.

Ropes provide another movement aid if they are not too heavy, and hence dangerous to swing and toss when others are near. They are particularly good to twirl around the body, or in circles, serpentines, and figure eights near the floor in imitation of cowboy rope tricks. They can be used to make visible forms on the floor when the problem assigned is to describe a circle, triangle, or part of a square in a position or in movement. Elastic or stretch ropes are now available for purchase at many stores.[6] Children love to explore with them, making shapes and experiencing the tautness of a stretch and the limpness of relaxation by manipulating them on their own bodies.

Light wooden hoops, or as a second choice plastic ones, which are not too large have many possibilities. The hula hoop craze of years ago ended so quickly that other movement uses of the hoop went unexplored. Besides being twirled, a hoop can be swung, turned, climbed or crawled through, lifted high in large arcs or circles, rolled from one part of the body to another, or held aloft to run with. It may be placed on the floor as a focus for many kinds of dramatic movement, or several hoops may be used together in lines or circles for leaping from one to the next.

Any small percussion instrument that can be made at home or in the art room can be a prop for movement if it is light and easily manipulated. Rattles and shakers are probably best, although tambourines, rhythm sticks (claves), small cymbals, clappers, and light hand drums are also useful. Children at first may have to be encouraged to be active while using such sound-makers. The movement produced with them is likely to be much more strongly pulsed than that with the other props described and hence is excellent for rhythmic skill training. Any object held in the hands, of course, can be pressed into service to beat time, wave, or swing in response to the pulse beats, accents, or phrases of a musical accompaniment.

Beanbags, feathers, baskets or boxes, pipe cleaners, pie tins, lengths of contrasting fabrics, yarn balls or any balls, cardboard tubes, wands, hats, gloves, belts, shoes, flowers, paper cups—the list is endless. Children may be

---

[6] They may be ordered from The Dancer's Shop, Children's Music Center, 5373 W. Pico Blvd., Los Angeles, Calif. 90019.

encouraged to bring a "found object" to class. Each one will provide certain limitations to its manipulation because of its special characteristics. Inventing movement that takes cognizance of those characteristics often results in interplay which is fresh and humorous.

Two other props could also be regarded as partial costumes. One is a length of tubular jersey or other stretchy synthetic material, within which the child moves. The other is the mask constructed according to each child's design in the art room or at home, or purchased in a novelty store. Movement inside the tube of material produces amazing sculptural effects, which after a few trials can be partially controlled. Three yards is sufficient for one person's inward manipulation; eight yards if two or three persons are to be involved. The mask can be made either to symbolize movement of a certain type or to suggest it. A child quickly becomes whatever the mask depicts (or he thinks he does), and the fact that it is a disguise offers the same kind of anonymity that closed eyes do. Hence inhibitions are decreased.

With the prop as a catalyst, then, movements exploring its possibilities may fall into the following categories:

Dancing with a Scarf

Dancing with a Newspaper

1. With continuous, intermittent, or no contact.
2. With movement around, toward, away, above, below, inside, under.
3. With constant or recurrent focus.
4. With or without manipulation.
5. With involvement of another person or persons.

Props are a quick means of helping children to explore many ways of moving. The next step would be to reproduce the invented movements with only imaginary props. It must be remembered, too, that many professional dancers use props for dramatic or absurd effect. Too much use, however, can become boring, and the substitution of novelty for thematic material and/or technical facility is undesirable.

Altering the Physical Environment

The best environment in which to conduct a dance lesson is undoubtedly a spacious, well-lighted room free of encumbrances. Occasionally, however, certain large objects set up in the dance room, possibly only one for a small class, offer a challenge to children. They must show awareness of these intruders into their dance place and change their movement or movement sequences in order to relate to them.

Changing the dance environment by presenting obstacles to free locomotion, or perhaps unusual objects of which the dancers must take notice, is another aid to movement discovery. It is a way of impelling children to find methods to move around an obstacle, to move on it or over it or in it, above or below it, to use it as an object of attraction or rejection, to examine it or ignore it.

Such objects may be chairs or tables or stools, one or several of them; wooden boxes that can support weight; the supporting standards for volleyball nets; a heap of the nets themselves. They may be hoops on the floor, balance beams if they are available, blown-up balloons, large balls, plastic swimming tubes, or elastic tape draped about to move over, under, or to tunnel through.

It perhaps should be decided beforehand whether the objects can be moved during the course of the experimentation with them or should remain in place. Another ground rule might be one that prevents monopoly of a particular object. Transitional movements from one object to another should be part of a sequential form using the altered environment.

There are other ways of changing the dance environment. The space can be made smaller so that more nonlocomotor movement must be used, and young dancers become more aware of their classmates' self-spaces. The room can be darkened, or at least be made darker; almost at once the quality of the movement will change. Or dancing can take place in a different setting entirely—outside on the grass, in a park with trees, or in a school court or patio. It is valuable, occasionally to find or create a new setting for children's dancing, for motivation and challenge.

The Uses of Accompaniment in Movement Exploration

"Movement arises from and returns to points of stillness. Sound arises from and returns to silence. Children should experience states of stillness and silence and feel the contrast between moving silently and moving to their own accompaniment in sound."[7]

For Movement-Centered Problems

When a child is absorbed in trying out a movement in different ways (How fast can it be? how slow, high, low, big, little, heavy, light?), an accompaniment is usually distracting unless it is specifically related to the problem being solved. When many children are finding their unique solutions to a problem, a general accompaniment restricts invention. Music tends to structure movement, and if beats which must be followed are imposed too soon, the breadth of discovery may be limited.

This is not to say that sound is taboo during such problem-solving. The child's own vocalization may add impetus and insight to the nature and flavor of the movement with which he is experimenting. High, thin sounds for elevated movements; glissando sounds for rises or descents; deep, growly ones for low movements—there are innumerable ways to match human sound to movement. Like all ingredients used for flavor, vocalization should not be overdone and it should never interfere with another's endeavor. Used sparingly, however, the sound the child makes can reinforce the quality of his movement and enrich it. Although the use of onomatopoetic words is legitimate, here we are considering vocalization, not verbalization. The use of words with movement will be discussed in later chapters.

Teachers and children who have become oriented to the teaching of dance to a musical or percussion accompaniment may find movement without the control it exerts strange and regard it as an invitation to disorder. The following quotation illustrates this point.

> Since the practice of having children dance to music is so deeply established in our teaching, we have come to depend on it. We feel insecure without music. It affords a beginning and an end. By building up certain associations with certain sounds from the piano the group responds, and what might seem to be the spark of an "out-of-hand" idea or a really creative impulse is brought under control. Teaching cannot go on without group control by the teacher but there are different ways of achieving and exercising [it]. Gradually breaching the gap between our dependence on music as a control and working with movement in and of itself will help us hold on to our security.[8]

[7] Department of Education and Science, *Movement—Physical Education in the Primary Years,* London, Her Majesty's Stationery Office, 1972, p. 58.

[8] Emma Sheehy, *Children Discover Music and Dance,* New York, Teachers College, 1968, p. 126.

For the solving of movement problems, then, no accompaniment is necessary unless it arises from the movement itself, or unless the problem originates in or relates to some sort of musical or rhythmic response. For example, the sudden or gradual change in a movement from fast to slow is aided by an accompaniment which does the same, *after* such changes in timing have been tried without it. If the *quality* of the movements being investigated is the same for all (even though the movements themselves are quite different), appropriate background sound effects may be provided by the teacher. Suitable percussion instruments or improvised piano sounds can make what a musician friend calls a "sound landscape" to stimulate improvisation.

Accompaniment may be introduced by having each child provide his own with a small instrument he can play while moving. If children are working in small groups, they may provide accompaniment for each other. If the final solution of a problem is worthy of a subsequent performance, a "score" of the accompaniment may be made and played by assisting children or the teacher. If a collage of sounds is used (children's voices, snatches of song or other music, periods of stillness) a tape recorder is indispensable.

For Rhythm-Centered Problems

The improvisation of movement to fit a series of pulse beats, accents, rhythmic patterns, or musical phrases is part of the development of rhythmic skills. It also has a place in the total program of dance movement experiences, particularly for older children. Problems of movement invention which stem from aspects of rhythm are commonplace in the dance program, and many kinds of accompaniment will be helpful in solving them. Body sounds, rhymes, chants of actions, names, places, colors, slogans, and similar rhythmic sequences are suggested in Part IV and are not repeated here.

Very often appropriate music or other auditory accompaniment initiates movement improvisation. A response in movement should follow a recognition of the quality, timing, and rhythmic structure of the music. Most younger children, however, will do little more than observe its timing and quality in their improvised dancings, and even that perception may be of short duration. It must be remembered that when children move to music they have to do three things simultaneously: move, observing spatial rules; listen carefully; and translate the quality, timing, and rhythmic structure of the music into their movement. This is a lot to expect from a five- or six-year-old. "Music is also a possible starting point—but one which should be used sparingly with young children when they are busy establishing their own personal rhythms and find it difficult to conform to such highly structured sound not of their own making."[9]

Music selected for young children's dancing, then, should be short, and have a specific descriptive quality (lilting, ponderous, eerie, etc.) a specific speed (fast, moderate, slow) or a strong rhythmic structure (as in a march, skip, or swing). Even at an early age, its rhythm will have a subconscious effect on their movement which may not be noticeable until later.

Evaluating Themselves and Others

Important as it is for each child to receive recognition for his efforts, it is equally important, especially for the older child, that he learn why a particular movement phrase is better coordinated, more inventive, a more accurate solution to the problem set by the teacher or the child's own purpose. Such learning comes through observation, through discussion and evaluation, and through the sharing of movement experiences. While it has been suggested that children should not spend too much time verbalizing about their movement experiences, pertinent observation of and discussion about the successful solution of movement problems may certainly take place in a lesson. Such evaluation not only helps to reassure children who are on the right track and to clarify their intent but stimulates the others to greater effort.

Occasionally particular children may be called upon to demonstrate if their movement is especially commendable. It is desirable, in this case, to choose more than one child, although they may be asked to perform individually. Under most circumstances a more acceptable method is to have half of the class, or a smaller fraction, demonstrate for the others. In this way, each child's accomplishment is brought to attention and recognition of prowess noted in the evaluation discussion which should follow the demonstrations. It is every teacher's prerogative to remark on good work as long as favors are distributed impartially: for a burst of inventiveness from an otherwise unresponsive class member; to a child who has "turned a corner" in his exploration; to someone who worked out a successful solution and performed it with authority. A teacher's choices, and the reasons for them, should be explained to the rest of the class, and eventually the children will make their choices in the same way.

[9] Molly Brearley, ed., *The Teaching of Young Children,* New York, Schocken Books, 1970, p. 80.

Chapter Preview

5 Exploration Through Movement Manipulation

. . . It is a waste of time to tell a child things that the child cannot experience through his senses. The child must be able to try things out to see what happens, manipulate objects and symbols, pose questions and seek their answers, reconcile what he finds at one time with what he finds at another, and test his findings against the perceptions of others his age.[1]

The body can move in an almost infinite variety of ways. Contemporary concert dancers have pushed the horizons of possible body movements far beyond their former confines to make the art of dance a much richer and more compelling area of human expression. One can learn the techniques of performing some of these movements, but in true creative dance they serve only to prepare the body as an instrument for its own expressive idiom. A dancer who makes his own forms must go on from there, just as a writer must manipulate the words, phrases, and sentences he knows into his own combinations and sequences. In like manner a child, if he is to have broad and rich creative movement experiences, must learn to make new movements from familiar ones, to change, to combine, to invent on the basis of what he already knows.

The technical investigation of movement is the process by which movements are manipulated and/or combined to achieve other and new ways of moving. It is best described as the solution of kinetic problems and hence does not depend on the use of images, dramatic references, or other similes and metaphors for motivation of movement activity.

This is not to say that imagery's use in children's movement exploration

[1] Beatrice and Ronald Gross, "A Little Bit of Chaos," *Saturday Review,* May 1970, p. 84.

is not substantial, if the type adapts to their age and level of interests. Its overuse in the past, however, has caused younger children (and their teachers) to think of dance movement only in terms of animals, toys, and the like, and older children to reject its pretense as being beneath their dignity.

Overtones of meaning beyond that of the action itself may be evoked by a change in the movement or in the contrast between one movement and another. Imagery and dramatic meaning are inherent in some of the movement sequences and contrasts described in this chapter. They will often be obvious to the children, and comment about them should not be discouraged. But the response should be made in terms of what can be done with the movement and not in terms of what can be expressed, identified with, or interpreted by performing it in a particular way. Such experimentation is obviously more abstract and scientific than one which depends on imagery for its motivation, and is useful for all ages of children. It has particular appeal for older ones, who are interested in maneuvering their bodies to accomplish desirable purposes in all kinds of movement activities.

Traveling Low

O. R. PETERSON III

Changing Basic Movements

The basic locomotor and nonlocomotor movements listed in Chapter 3 lend themselves to innumerable variations and combinations, and a logical way to guide exploration of movement is to use the elements and their factors that influence changes in movement performance. These, too, are to be found in Chapter 3 and in specific detail in Part III. Many of the activities in the current chapter are based on those concepts.

By starting with any single movement like the walk or a simple combination of movements, and applying any of the factors of the elements of movement, one can change the original action and something new evolves. Thus the child's repertoire of movements is continually enlarged, and he has many more sources to draw upon for his dance-making proclivities.

The activities listed below are highly concentrated and represent materials which might well be used in several lessons, on any age level. They range from relatively simple to quite difficult. Most of the last steps in the series should be reserved for older children.

Some Procedures for Exploring Movement

USING BASIC MOVEMENTS IN PLACE AND THROUGH SPACE

Moving first in place and later through space, using a walk, run, jump, hop, or bend/stretch, as points of departure (not all factors will result in satisfying or even feasible movement):

1. Move and stop suddenly on a signal, freezing the movement in the arrested shape.[2]
2. Change the speed to faster or slower, gradually or suddenly.
3. Change the force to heavier or lighter, gradually or suddenly.
4. Change the level to higher or lower.
5. Change the direction by turning right or left.
6. Change the natural shape by changing the position or movement of the feet, legs, arms, head, or trunk.
7. Make combinations of any two or more of these factors.

---

[2] Young children should not be asked to hold a shape for more than three seconds; older children may hold for longer periods.

USING LOCOMOTOR MOVEMENTS TO EXPLORE BODY AND
SPATIAL DIRECTIONS (*see Glossary in Chapter 3 for
description of terms*)

With a walk, run, or simple dance step:

1. Move forward to an assigned or chosen point, turn, and come back.
2. Move forward to two or three assigned or chosen places and back to self-space, making own sequence of places and turning around on impulse.
3. Move forward to an assigned or chosen place, and move backward or sideward to own place, without colliding.
4. Move forward, half turn, and move backward in the same spatial direction.
5. Move in circles, triangles, squares, zigzags, or curving paths, at first always going forward and later changing body direction to sideward and backward.
6. Move in paths of own choice, avoiding others and consciously using a variety of body and spatial directions.

USING NONLOCOMOTOR MOVEMENT, STANDING, KNEELING,
SITTING, LYING

1. Starting with hands and feet, explore all movement potential of different parts of the body.
2. Extend in different directions body parts which permit such movement.
3. Twist, bend, and swing body parts which permit such movement.
4. Rise to a high standing shape and then sink to a low shape (or the reverse), adding turns and exploring different shapes on the repetitions.
5. Reach out from any level to a very wide shape and then move into as curled and narrow a shape as possible. Explore different wide and narrow shapes on the repetitions.
6. Explore the transitional movement in going from one shape to another by stressing
   a. Speed, by doing it faster and slower.
   b. Force, by doing it lightly and easily, and then strongly, against resistance with much tension.
   c. Path, by taking the movement in a straight or curving or twisted line.
   d. Level, by doing it high and low (only procedure 5 adapts itself to this factor).

(This next series of exploratory activities should be used with older children.)
7. Having consciously moved into different "up and down" or "out and in" shapes, choose three place-shapes that are a reasonable distance from each other—for example, one that is high, one that is low, and one that is wide. Assign a sequence to the three, as starting shape, second shape, third shape.

a. Move slowly from the first to the second to the third and then return to the first, pausing for a moment when each place-shape is attained before going on to the next.

b. Move without pause from one to the next and continue, always moving into and out of the three shapes.

c. Move at times slower and then faster than a moderate speed from one shape to the next.

d. Move at times strongly and against resistance, and then easily and lightly from one shape to another.

e. Move at times with a smooth, sustained quality, and then with strong accents or pulsations from one shape to another.

f. Interpolate a short phrase of locomotor movement that seems to "grow out of" each of the three shapes. This might be a few steps or jumps from a high shape, a turn from a wide shape, and a roll or somersault from a low shape.

g. Make a sequence or dance phrase using any of the material under procedure 7 which shows variety and sequential interest.

Suggested Procedures for Specific Movements

In the following sequential procedures a beginning is made from a few specific locomotor and nonlocomotor movements directed by the teacher. Then children are called upon to move more and more on their own, making decisions as to direction, speed, stops, etc. Two things should be noted in the use of these procedures:

1. In no sense do they represent a series of steps to be covered in a single lesson; rather, they are for use in a series of lessons over a period of time. Single steps should, of course, be repeated several times, and altered or expanded as the teacher sees fit. The order may be reorganized or reversed. Some procedures may be omitted, as later ones are intended for older rather than younger children. Individual teachers are the best judges of their children's ability to solve problems of movement exploration.

2. The responsibility for allowing children to explore, investigate, and invent movement does not negate the responsibility to help children improve the execution of movement. Inadequate solution of problems and poor performance of movement assignments should be discussed and measures taken for improvement. It may be that the movements attempted are too complex or demanding and a return to simpler problems may be indicated.

Locomotor Movement—*Running Among Others*

This involves running in place, forward, and on straight and curved paths; turning; making one's own path; changing spatial directions; and finally speed and body directions—all without colliding with other persons. (A brisk walk may be used to initiate this series.)

1. Perform an easy, basic run in place.
2. Turn around in place in either direction on impulse, using a running turn.
3. Use the run forward on a straight line (as from one side or end of the room to the other).
4. Turn when convenient, and without pause run forward again to the starting place. Make three or four trips in this manner.
5. Run on a curved line counterclockwise around the room.
6. With half of the class stopped and standing still, others continue a counterclockwise run, avoiding those standing by weaving in and out.
7. With all running again counterclockwise, each turns on his own impulse and runs clockwise for a while, then returns to the original direction (successive turns should be alternated with a forward run at least half-way around the room). On signal, stop suddenly and freeze the movement. Hold shape until signal to resume run.
8. From one end or side of the room run on a serpentine path to the other side.
9. From one end or side of the room run on a zigzag path, making quick, sharp-angled changes in spatial direction.
10. Run anywhere in the room, weaving in and out among others, using all the open spaces, never following another person, never colliding, running sometimes in place if necessary, freezing the movement on impulse for not more than five seconds, changing spatial direction often. (This activity can be made more difficult by decreasing the amount of space used by the class in running.)
11. Change speed of movement, slowing to a walk at times and then changing to quick spurts or leaps for short distances when open spaces are seen, and making sudden stops to avoid colliding.
12. Change body direction of run, from forward to backward. At first, run forward on a straight line and then backward to the starting point. Then change from a forward to a backward run, going in the same spatial direction. Progress to changes in body direction on curved lines, serpentines, zigzags. Use sideward runs in the same way.
13. Using the run with turns, stops, and body direction and speed changes, invent a floor pattern (figure eight, square, diamond, triangle, double serpentine) which has a consistent form and can be repeated.

A Light Stroke

"My Mirror"

Nonlocomotor Movement—*Out From and Into the Body Center Using Breath Rhythms*

This sequence primarily involves changes in shape from small to large and consists of stretches outward in all directions and bends or curls inward around the body center. The directions a child first learns are "toward myself" and "away from myself." Their similarity to the inhaling and exhaling of breath is obvious. Taking a deep breath extends size, and can involve arms, legs, and head as well as trunk. The slow exhalation then diminishes the stretched shape into a small bent-in one. Alternation of "out and in" of body movement and "in and out" of breath may be tried in any of the following ways.

1. Make a large shape by inhaling deeply and letting the body expand as far as possible. Make a small shape by exhaling slowly and curling inward close to the body center.
2. Move out to the large shape and in to the small shape fast by breathing in and out quickly.
3. Move out to the large shape and in to the small shape very slowly, by breathing in and out deeply and slowly.
4. Move out to the large shape fast, in slowly, and then the reverse.
5. Move out and in against resistance, exerting strong force, and then with little force.
6. Move out and in with a series of three or four sharp accents or pulsations, breathing in and out with sudden sniffs.
7. Move out with a series of pulsations, in with one smooth sustained movement, and the reverse, breathing similarly.
8. Using a series of different shapes resulting from outward and inward movements, make a dance phrase using perceptible changes in some of the factors of time, force, and space combined with breath rhythms.

Nonlocomotor Movement—*Use of the Hands*

Movement involving the hands might seem too small in scale to be included in movement exploration for dance purposes. It is true that because hand movements require control and coordination they should be used with older children rather than younger ones. Nevertheless, hands are very expressive and revealing instruments, used to stroke and to slap, to point and to press, to punch and to bless. They perform in a myriad of functional ways.

Because children remain in self-spaces for most of this series, it is interesting to experiment with the eyes closed to see whether a different feeling occurs. Although the movement dimension may be small at times, hands are attached to arms which move as well, and they to the trunk. Thus it can lead into total body movement in many instances.

1. Stretch the hands and fingers out as wide as possible, then bend them into a tight fist, as though gripping hard.
2. Move them out and in very fast and then very slowly.
3. Try procedure 2 at the same time extending the arms outward and inward in any direction.
4. Move the hands in opposite directions across the body as far as possible, closing them in or opening out at the same time; move them back to their own sides, opening them out or closing in at the same time.
5. Try procedure 4, moving them downward toward the feet and up again.
6. Try procedures 4 and 5 in own timing; sometimes very fast and very slow.
7. Lift open or closed hands above head and then down, gripping with increasing force. Change on impulse to limp hands and arms as they are raised and lowered.
8. Bring the hands together hard with much force, as though to clap them, but do not allow them to touch. Try in different levels and directions. Then use little force, making the movements soft, curving, and light.
9. Press hands together hard in front and then release them quickly to a wide sideward reach. Bring them back slowly and then touch them softly, separating with a light, relaxed movement into the sideward reach. Experiment with the use of a hard press and quick rebound and a soft touch and easy lift using hands on different surfaces of the body (the thighs, trunk, head) and on the floor.
10. Using the hand open, bend only the first and second joints, making it clawlike and tense. Move up and down, in and out, together and alternately, with level, focus, and direction changes and sudden changes in speed.
11. Using the hands open and flat as in pushing or pressing movements with palms up or down, move them together and alternately, out and in, up and down, with size, level, focus, path, and direction changes. Try sudden changes in force and speed.
12. Clasp hands together and stretch and bend elbows, making as many direction, level, focus, force, and speed changes as possible.
13. Place palms of hands and fingers together, and make similar changes as in procedure 12.
14. Make a "hand study" using one and/or both hands in any of the ways suggested by this series.

Nonlocomotor Movement—*The Swing*[3]

The swing helps to release tensions and to develop the feeling of suspension and collapse, of yielding to the pull of gravity, of moving vigorously without the necessity for strict precision. When its characteristic timing of a release or drop into gravity is changed, or if the movement is performed with tension, it loses its swinging identity. It may then be used as a point of departure into movement on different kinds of curving paths, such as arcs and circles. The following procedure is for the arms only. Trunk and head swings are more difficult to control.

1. Stand and let one arm and then the other hang freely, loosely, and heavily from the shoulder.
2. As the arm hangs, *let* it swing back and forth from the shoulder in a small arc, retaining the feeling of "giving in" to gravity.
3. Try with both arms, moving them in a parallel fashion back and forth.
4. Bend slightly forward, letting arms hang down in front, and try the same thing with the arms moving from side to side like a pendulum.
5. Try both forward and back or side-to-side swings with parallel arms and with an increase in dimension to a large arc.
6. Using one arm and then both, increase the arc of the pendular swing until it suspends overhead and drops to the opposite side to make a large circle. Try to describe an arc-circle path in space, and repeat it starting to one side and then to the other.
7. Try to do the last two swinging activities with the arms moving in opposite directions rather than parallel to each other.
8. Try to combine a parallel sideward circular swing with a sideward slide. (Both the arms and the leading foot start off in the same direction.)
9. Try to combine a backward and forward circular swing with a forward gallop. (The arms start backward as the leading foot steps forward.)
10. Try doing any of the movements in the arcs and circles resulting from the swings at a much slower or faster rate of speed. (The swinging quality is lost in both instances as a release into gravity requires its own special speed. However, the path of the movement remains.)
11. Try doing any of the arcs or circles with greater force applied and a slight hold at the top of the arc so that the arms are controlled with some tension throughout.
12. Use the curving paths to describe many different movements in space, exploring them with one or both arms moving in the same or different directions. Alternate such spatial paths with true swings in a sequence.

[3] See Chapter 9.

Nonlocomotor Movement—*Shaking*

Shaking has many variations and can be performed by several parts as well as the total body. It is usually a combination of quick twisting, bending, and extending and is characterized by both tension and extreme relaxation. Being a movement that is in constant functional use, it is familiar to children and can be performed on signal without hesitation.

When its characteristic factors of speed and force are changed, it loses its identity as a shaking movement. It therefore makes an easy point of departure into related but quite different movement experiences.

The following exploratory sequence uses shaking and movements evolving from it. Other nonlocomotor movements such as turn, push, and strike as well as the basic movements of bend, stretch, and twist can be substituted for shaking in certain of these sequential steps.

1. Standing or sitting, shake one hand, the other, both together, then arms, shoulders, head, feet, legs; in front, at either side, up high, down low.
2. Stand and shake the whole body (this will result in quick knee bends, bounces, jiggling and dangling arms, twisting and shrugging shoulders, turning head, swinging hips, and intermittent hand shaking at a more or less rapid rate of speed).
3. Either standing or lying, try small shakes of the hands, arms, or head exerting great and continuous tension so that vibratory movement results. Release tension and shake loosely after a short period.
4. Sit and shake the hand, observing its direction (up and down will be most common).
5. Shake one or both hands another way (forward and back, side to side, or in small circles). Make them go in opposite directions.
6. Slow down the movement so that it becomes "slow motion." Make the path much bigger, as far as possible either up and down, forward and back, side to side, or in circles. The extension of the arm movement may change the body position from a sit to a kneel or a stand and the opposite, from vertical to horizontal. (In slowing down and extending the size it is important that the flexible wrist and elbow of the loose shaking movement be retained.)
7. Keep the arm movement big, but make it suddenly fast again, and then suddenly slow. Then accelerate and retard so that the speed change is gradual.
8. Keep the movement big and slow, but add tension so that it is done against resistance (like pulling taffy or strong elastic). Keep the same dimension and force, but increase and decrease speed.
9. Move in the large, strong, and slow pattern of movement in all of the

three directional contrasts (up, down, forward, backward, side to side) and alternate with small quick, light, relaxed shakes. Add travel through space and turns to these movements.

Variations on Movement Phrases of Work, Sport, or Gesture

The beginning of this process of exploration designed for older children is made from a familiar or "known" movement phrase. Each child may choose his own phrase, the choice may be a group one, or the teacher may suggest several from which a selection is made. The phrase should be one that uses the total body and involves some locomotor movement in its execution. Obvious examples in sports are: delivering a bowling ball, dribbling and shooting a basketball, a tennis serve, fielding a fly ball; in work areas: sweeping the floor, washing a wall, chopping or digging, lifting and placing heavy objects; in gesture: greeting or farewell, searching and finding, "come here" or "leave here".

The movement phrase is first performed in its natural shape. Awareness of exactly how the body moves in respect to space, force, and time should be demonstrated by repeating it several times. The phrase should be long enough so that its beginning, middle, and end are observable. Transitional movements may need to be added so that the phrase can be repeated continuously.

The following variations may then be tried.

1. Perform the phrase in very slow motion continuously, keeping all parts of the movement in the same timing.
2. When moving very slowly, freeze on impulse in a place-shape. Then resume movement.
3. Perform the movement phrase continuously, but at a very fast speed.
4. Perform the movement phrase in its natural timing, but make it bigger than life size; that is, increase the dimension of the movements so that they cover a much greater space area.
5. Start the bigger-than-life-size movement phrase very slowly and, as it is repeated, gradually increase the speed until it is very fast. Then reverse the timing from fast to slow.
6. Add great tension to the performance of the movement phrase and then repeat it in a greatly relaxed fashion.
7. Try the total movement backward, starting at the end of the phrase, finishing at the beginning, and repeat.

8. Separate the phrase into three or four parts and repeat one part several times in slow, moderate, or fast timing before going on to the next. Try repeating another part the next time through.
9. Change the sequence of the parts so that the middle becomes the first or last and the others are used accordingly. Conclude the phrase in one of the place-shapes.

As the "known" movement is explored for its "unknown" possibilities, the series of variations will be found to change it so considerably that an entirely new series of movements results.

Gamelike Activities and Projects That Help to Explore Movement

There are many ways of "playing" with movement which promote spontaneity, improvisation, and enrichment of movement resources. Certain of these gamelike activities are described here. For most of them a long duration of participation should be avoided, a few "rounds" of a relatively simple game being sufficient. Thus, it can be used again in future lessons.

Individual Activities

Signal Lights. Traffic signal lights may be used in a simple game by having a visual or an auditory signal of red mean *stop*, of amber or orange mean *walk in place*, and of green mean *skip forward*. Sometimes red and green signals can follow each other so that practice in quick stops and starts is given. This is a good activity for quite young children as it offers them the security of moving by themselves in a group and increases their awareness of what is involved in moving and stopping on a signal.

Bridges and Tunnels. Children may vie with each other individually or in couples to make bridges and tunnels by changing their body shapes. The body makes a bridge when one part of it or the total length curves into an arc from points of support on the floor. A tunnel is a more or less rounded space completely surrounded by parts of the body. The activity may be made more vigorous by having a second or third child make his way through the bridges or tunnels without interfering with their structure.

Alphabet and Number Shapes. Children make letter or number shapes with their bodies on the floor as they are signaled by the teacher. Later, children can perform the leadership role, or each child may make his own letter or number sequence, such as his initials or nickname or address. Several letters of the alphabet lend themselves well to this activity (I, C, L, V, T, U, J, X, Y, A, O, S, Z); others are more difficult, but children like to try them anyway. The teacher or "watchers" take turns acting as judges of the success of the imitation. Some of these symbols, of course, can be formed in standing shapes and a few (I, X, T, J) can be made while jumping in the air. Cursive letters can also be traced on the floor by means of various kinds and directions of locomotor movements, a jump indicating the end of the two- or three-letter sequence.

What Shape Are You In? In this contest place-shapes, assumed after a quick stop, are judged for their originality and immobility. The teacher chooses two or three "watchers" and then gives a descriptive word like *crooked, round, tall, small, wide, thin, flat,* or *pointed;* or later two combined words like *tall-crooked, wide-round, flat-pointed,* or *low-straight.* On the

A "Holdup" for Three

DETROIT PUBLIC SCHOOLS

signal Go! the players run as fast as they can. On the signal Stop! each assumes his version of the indicated shape and holds it. The watchers quickly choose those judged best, tap them, and change places with them. Then the next shape-descriptive words are given by the teacher and the game proceeds. If the teacher wishes another variation on the same shape the next time around, she can say "Try again" before she gives the starting signal. As this is a vigorous game, it should be played only for a short period of time.

Space-Writing and Sky-Writing. Children of any age, standing or sitting by themselves, write letters (their initials) or numbers (three or four numbers of their address or zip code) or short names or words they may choose, or paint a pretend picture in the space before them. One hand or both hands may be used at first, but later an elbow, the nose, or the top of the head can also serve. The movement can be very small, as on a black-board, then evolve to moderately large, as on a traffic sign, and then to very large, as on a billboard. The latter may involve sideward locomotion, jumping reaches, and stooping close to the floor. The writing can be hard and strong, as though chiseling stone, or very light and delicate, as though on a misted picture window, and as fast as a scribble or as slow as signing a birthday card. Contrasts from one movement factor to another can be sig-naled by the teacher or initiated by the children themselves, the objective being to have as many different kinds of movement experiences as possible. The game can be played in partners by having one "mirror" the other's movement as they face each other, and then change roles.

Sky-writing is done lying on the back and using one or both feet high in the air to make the arcs, circles, angles, lines, or loops involved. More movement is possible if the back is lifted off the floor and supported by the hands, with the bulk of the weight taken on the shoulders. Obviously much less movement differentiation is possible in this variation of the game.

Think of a Number. The number can be anyone's age, coins in a pocket, or the date of the month. Even for older children it should not be over 25 or the individual turns can take too long. This is a mathematical guessing game with only one person active at a time. Each child divides his number into three or four parts which, when added together, equal it. He then makes a locomotor floor pattern, not only changing spatial direction sharply at the beginning of each part but using three different basic loco-motor movements. The walk, jump, and hop (as they have the same relative timing) are the easiest to use. For example, five hops, four jumps, six walks, two jumps equal the number 17. Children should be allowed time to practice their number pattern before performing it for the others, who then try to discover the number in each part and to add them to arrive at the total.

The Movement Word Game. This activity has several ramifications. Movements emanating from improvisation to the signal words can be used as phrases for many other creative activities. They can be joined to other movement phrases to make a dance sequence. Because of the spur-of-the-moment necessity to do something, movements are attempted which would not necessarily evolve if more time were available for planning. Thus imaginations are stretched and movement vocabularies extended.

At a word signal from the teacher or leader, children must perform *continuous* movement that is in some way appropriate to the word given. Different interpretations should be tried rather than repetitions of only one. Action changes when another word is signaled. Unless children are being especially inventive, words should follow each other in fairly quick succession, and it is more fun if the new word is somewhat of a surprise, and not merely a contrast to the one being performed. Sometimes an unusual word is given that evokes little response, or one that demands strenuous activity. It should be followed by a word with the opposite characteristics. At a "stop" word (freeze, still, hold, halt, stay, cease, pause) movement is interrupted and held in whatever shape it occurs until the next word is given. "Sound" words may also be used (whisper, laugh, speak, hiccough, sneeze, cough, giggle, shout, sing) but must be reproduced in suitable silent movement.

Words used at first may be those of movement factors with which children are familiar and which they have already explored (low, high, fast, slow, small, big, heavy, light, tight, loose, bumpy, smooth, straight, curving, twisted, fat, thin) although not given in that kind of contrasting sequence. Basic locomotor and nonlocomotor movements and their simple combinations (push, pull, lift, sit, turn, skip, schottische) may also be interspersed with the factoral words above. Children who are more experienced in improvisation can handle words suggesting differing movement qualities (stiff, sticky, soft, prickly, floppy, soaring), words having a dramatic connotation or describing a feeling (stare, listen, grin, scowl, lost, excited, scared, cold), design words (angular, zigzag, serpentine, symmetrical, on- and off-balance), and partner or group words (join, connect, unite, combine, meet, together, mingle), and, for a real surprise, a nonsense word or phrase that will bring "crazy" responses. See Chapter 21 for other movement word suggestions.

At first the teacher should be the leader. Later children who are inventive in their response and have adequate vocabularies of movement words may act as leaders. After several trials with the class as a whole, the game may be played in groups, each one with a child leader. Children who have made unusual or sometimes humorous responses to a movement word may demonstrate for the others.

Activities with a Partner or Group[4]

Mirrored Movement. This may be played using partners, but at first it works better if the teacher or a competent leader faces the group and initiates its movement. The leader moves in any way he wishes. The others, who face him, imitate everything he does but on the same side, as a mirror reflection would. Although movement should for the most part be nonlocomotor, traveling short distances forward, backward, and sideward is possible if there is room. At first the movement should be rather slow and sustained, but later short, quick movements may be alternated with slow ones provided they are clear in shape, short in duration, and easily followed. The leader may freeze his movement for a few seconds at intervals to check on the success of its reproduction. He should remember that he must always be able to see his reflection if his reflection is to see him.

When this activity is done using partners, one person assumes the active role and the other focuses on him in order to present a mirrored imitation of his movement. After a short time, the active partner and his reflection change roles.

Mirrored Movement may also be played like Copy Cat in Chapter 15, the active partner performing a short phrase and freezing the final shape, after which the other reproduces it as faithfully as possible. This version is more difficult than simultaneous imitation but develops movement memory, an important skill. Variety and complexity can be added by having the copyist perform the imitated movement faster or slower or more strongly or lightly than the original. The factor changing it may be assigned to him by his partner, or he may make the choice himself.

Palm Touch. In this game one child starts and his partner follows him as fast as he can. With partners facing and standing about a foot apart, the first person moves his arms into any position he wishes with the palms of his hands flat and toward the partner. The partner responds by quickly placing his palms against the other's palms, so that they lightly touch, and holding them there. As soon as the touch is made (but not before), the first person changes his position and the game proceeds. It is more fun and more challenging if the arm and hand positions taken are not symmetrical but different (one high, other one to the side, etc.). After a short time partners reverse roles. The game may be varied by having the changes from one position to the next slow and sustained rather than quick; the palms of the two partners maintain a continuous light contact as the leader initiates

---

[4] Most of these are designed for older children with good backgrounds in movement improvisation and invention.

continuous movement. In this version Palm Touch resembles the next game, Touch and Move.

Touch and Move.   The teacher suggests a contact to be made—opposite hands, right feet, tops of heads, left knees, one shoulder or hip, etc. Partners attach the assigned parts and move in as many ways as possible with this handicap. The touch contact may not be released until the hold or freeze signal is given. Partners exchange often and may devise their own points of attachment, which may differ for each person—as right hand and left ankle, or top of head and right elbow, etc. This activity can become very strenuous and should be continued for a relatively short time.

A Holdup.   Partners who are fairly well matched in size and strength experiment with different ways of receiving and "holding up" each other's weight. An easy way to begin is to sit back to back, one person leaning on his partner's back as far as possible as the other carries the weight by bending forward. The lean is then reversed. The next step is to stand back to back and link elbows. The active partner (the one receiving and holding the weight) then crouches forward, lifting his partner a short distance off the floor as he takes his weight on his back. This movement is then alternated as the other child assumes the active role.

Again, the partners can stand one behind the other, facing in the same direction. The inactive partner then rests his total length on the back of his partner, who, standing slightly crouched with feet strongly planted, grasps the upper arms or elbows of his "holdup" as they are extended over his shoulders and lifts him a short distance off the floor. The maneuver should be done slowly and carefully, and when balance is achieved, a slow walk forward may be tried.

Variations are the stunt of lifting the inactive person (who lies supine on the floor with his body straight and stiff) up to a stand as the straight position is maintained; weight may also be taken by the active partner as he lies on his back and supports his inactive partner with hands and knees, or soles of feet. Boys particularly will enjoy experimenting with these and other "holdups" in partners or in groups of three or four.

A Contest with Time.   It is sometimes interesting to discover three things about one's ability to move within a specific time limit. For example,

1. How many *different* movements can be made during the time span of 10 seconds?
2. Can one prolong a *single* movement (like raising or lowering an arm, or making a single turn) for 10 seconds?
3. Can one perform *exactly* 25 *different* movements in 10 seconds?

Some exact method of timing must be available such as a stopwatch or a sweep-second hand, and warning signals are given two or three seconds before the time is up: Children can do their own counting and must use both locomotor and nonlocomotor movement procedures in 1 and 3.

In 1, each movement counted must be different from the preceding one (a series of runs or hand claps will not count).

In 2, the movement must be continuous, with no pause to take up time.

In 3, each movement must be different from the one before, as in 1, and timing may be slow or fast as long as the twenty-fifth movement comes at the tenth second.

Group Design. Eight to twelve children join hands lightly in a circle or a curved or straight line with feet firmly planted in a forward-backward stride position. Any possible movement is attempted, care being taken not to move the feet, not to lose hand contact with the persons on either side, and, most important, not to throw these persons off balance. Hands must maintain contact but can turn within the other's grasp. The purpose is for each child to move in as great a range and in as many different ways as possible with these restrictions. The persons on either side will undoubtedly influence the movement of the one between, but he can respond to this influence in any way he wishes or finds possible.

The next step is to free one foot while keeping the other in place. The last step is to free both feet but keep hands joined in the original formation. The group shape may now change considerably, becoming much smaller or elongated or entirely different, depending on the impulse of its members. The teacher should call a halt when experimentation has gone on for a brief time, and the resulting group design is then observed for interest and originality. Two or three groups may perform at a time for the rest of the class.

Moving Echo. This activity may be done with partners, with a leader and group, or even in two groups with group members improvising individually. The objective is to have the short, strongly dynamic movement phrase of one partner, the leader, or one group *echoed* by the opposite partner or group. The echoing movement is performed after a brief pause very lightly, softly, and a bit slower than the original movement. Sometimes just the strongest part of the movement or the last part is echoed. Individuals or groups should reverse roles after two or three trials.

Active and Passive Partners. Two persons successively improvise movement phrases. They maintain contact with loosely joined right or left hands and decide who will start first. The first person, using primarily slow sustained nonlocomotor movement, begins a movement phrase and carries it through to completion. The partner cooperates by moving as he is affected by the movement of the first person, reacting only passively through the hand contact. The movement phrase should come to a definite conclusion in a "frozen" shape so that the partner can tell when it is his turn to begin. Starting in whatever shape he finds himself, the latter performs his movement phrase, with the first person following where the movement leads him.

Symmetry and Its Opposite. In art classes children become acquainted with the principles of symmetrical and asymmetrical form as seen in architecture and sculpture. To contrive a symmetrical place-shape is not difficult; to make one that moves is harder. Because the body skeleton is symmetrical, a movement done on one side and repeated on the other demonstrates a symmetrical process.

Asymmetry can make use of a great number of variations on the "ordered whole" of symmetry, and children should be encouraged to find and use them: one arm lifted instead of both, or, if both, one not a parallel copy of the other; the juxtaposition of bent and straight, curved and angular, forward and backward; the use of one side but not the other.

One half of a divided class can be assigned asymmetrical place-shapes; the other, symmetrical ones. They may be constructed individually or in twos or small groups. Evaluation of the others' product can then take place. Another assignment might be moving shapes. Each group should have a chance to construct all four kinds of shapes, moving and still, symmetrical and asymmetrical, although such a problem should extend beyond a single lesson.

Kaleidoscopes. Many older children are familiar with kaleidoscopes. Sudden and complex new designs result from each movement of the tube, and each design is always symmetrical. After experimentation with symmetrical and asymmetrical forms, making a group kaleidoscope can be an interesting activity. From three to six children construct a symmetrical starting shape in which all are involved. Sequential symmetrical changes in the group shape are then planned which may include all group members or only one or two at a time. Changes occur smoothly and suddenly, and each is held immobile for two or three seconds before going to the next. At least four symmetrical designs can be made, which may then be repeated. Each group should have a chance to perform its kaleidoscope for the others.

Positive and Negative Space. These are academic terms for what is, in effect, *occupied* and *unoccupied space*. Positive space is that which is occupied by a body shape (or more than one). Negative space is that which is unoccupied—for example, a hole completely enclosed by an arm and leg, or partially enclosed by a curved trunk. In other words, negative space is any space not occupied by the body parts of a place-shape.

One of two partners assumes a shape or is placed in a shape by the other. At first, this may be easier if it is a horizontal one. Later, it may be on any level. The second child then invents movement which relates to the negative spaces, either by moving through them with a part or all of his body (if that is possible), moving in and out of them, or with head, hands, feet, or focus, using them otherwise. Invention ends with a place-shape involving both persons. Roles are then changed on the next trial.

In a variation, movement may be continuous when the second child constructs a new place-shape using the unoccupied spaces of his partner. The latter then removes himself from the design of two related bodies and improvises a new shape in the negative spaces of the second place-shape.

Three children or more may participate, taking turns, each contributing to a trio or group shape by relating in some way to the unoccupied spaces left by the others when they "freeze" their place-shapes.

Mobiles and Stabiles. Before deciding on the construction of a movement mobile or stabile as a group project children should first see examples of the two kinds of art forms and consider their similarities and differences. Since mobiles are suspended, some travel through space is possible; stabiles are supported on the floor or ground, and movement is more firmly rooted. Movement in both is caused by air currents or by the reverberating movement resulting from tangential contacts with other moving parts. Consequently, it is usually slow, spasmodic, and irregular, and should display the sort of unsubstantial quality of an object made to move by outer rather than inner forces. The group must decide whether all the shapes making up the art object shall be alike, some alike and some different, or all different, as in a free-form series. Movement can occur on different levels, in different turning directions, and in changing relationships to other shapes. Mobiles and stabiles, in which the individual sequences are partly planned and partly improvised, are rather difficult but interesting group projects in creative dance.

Chapter Preview

Using Imagery

Examples of Movement Imagery
Some Images Classified
Be, Do, Feel
"Moving Like" Similes

Sensory Sources for Movement Invention
Visual
Auditory
Tactile

"Character" Movement

States of Feeling and Imaginary Situations

The Word Is "Fizzy"

DETROIT PUBLIC SCHOOLS

6 Exploration Through Imagery

Imagery is the catalyst that makes possible the bridging of movement-as-function and movement-as-expression so that the child is not merely moving or merely imagining but feeling, *experiencing, if even for a moment, that exhilaration of being at one and the same time both the creator and the creation, the shaper and the shaped.*[1]

In young children movement is often related to dramatic meaning if only because it is most often used for a functional or dramatic purpose. Movement performed in a particular way can arouse images in both performer and viewer, even though the movement problem is technical and abstract, and even though there may be no intent to do so and no need or even willingness to manifest the imagery in words.

Using Imagery

It is, of course, advisable that children try out various kinds of movements before assigning them imaginary or dramatic qualities. An important part of early movement education is helping children to become aware of the body's potential, how it feels to move in certain ways, how movements can be described and demonstrated and changed.

The use of direct imagery, however, supplements and enhances the "bare bones" of movement elements and their factors, and emphasizes their subjec-

[1] Jack Wiener and John Lidstone, *Creative Movement for Children,* New York, Van Nostrand Reinhold, 1969, p. 97.

tive, expressive powers. As Gray and Percival say, "The heaviness of an elephant contrasted with the lightness of a sparrow will give a new experience in movement and mime to a child."[2] Imagery also nurtures and quickens the child's imagination if it is presented in a playful, pretend kind of way.[3]

Some writers on children's dance argue that children should not "be" or "become" something other than themselves, implying that to do so is somehow harmful. To distinguish between the real and the imaginary is not easy for young children, and they move readily from one to the other. To say that they cannot "be" anything whose movement qualities appeal to them is to force an adult response to reality and imagination on the child's world. What differences in movement will be observed if the motivation is "I am walking on a balance beam" rather than "I am a tightrope walker?" Probably very few. The same body tensions, aids to balance, focus downward, slow cautious steps will be present. What will be missing in the first, however, is the exciting aura of the circus performer, a sense of his dangerous profession, perhaps, and the acclaim it brings. Such use of the imagination is lost if a child is not allowed "to personify," "to pretend," "to imagine," "to be" if that is his wish.

Imagery, then, may either grow out of or elicit movement. "The movement you are doing is heavy and slow. Does it remind you of anything?" or "I'm thinking of something that is floppy and loose. Can you think of something, too, and let us guess what you are by the way you move?" or "Can you move like something scary? Is it huge and strong, soft and slinky, twisted, jerky, stiff, crawly?"

Images may be real or fanciful, and may have dramatic implications to a greater or lesser degree. Their use to initiate or enrich a movement response will heighten the communicative aspects of the movement. Just as drama initially grew out of dance, the line between creative dance and creative drama with children is a thin one. "Although there is a close relationship between dramatic imagery and dance, in that both involve an identification with people, things, or activities, in dance, children imagine themselves in these states of being by abstracting only those qualities which they can best express in movement terms."[4] Thus dance, with its medium of expressive

[2] Vera Gray and Rachel Percival, *Music, Movement and Mime for Children,* London, Oxford University Press, 1963, p. 41.

[3] All teachers of young children should be familiar with Ruth Shaw Radlauer's *Of Course, You're a Horse,* New York, Abelard-Schuman, 1959, and Helen Borten's *Do You Move as I Do?,* New York, Abelard-Schuman, 1963.

[4] Geraldine Dimondstein, *Children Dance in the Classroom,* New York, Macmillan, 1971, p. 217.

movement used for its own sake, must sustain its differentiation from drama and pantomime, with their storytelling actions.

Numerous words[5] offer the image of a special kind of movement: verbs (jump, bounce, grab, push, flop, fly), adverbs and adjectives (softly, high, angrily, swiftly, crooked), nouns (snake, bird, miser, clown, queen). There are similes and metaphors which emphasize the quality or shape of movement: flat as a pancake, tall as a pole, smooth as glass, little as a peanut, straight as an arrow; shoot up, melt down, soften your steps, soar through the air, twinkling fingers, pounding feet.

The good teacher's creative imagination is in evidence here. If the images used are hackneyed, repetitive, or stereotyped, her muscles of imagination need exercise! Reading children's stories or poetry helps, as does watching children's television programs of good quality. One of the best ways is to ask the children to provide descriptive words or similes. "What is this movement like?" "How does it make you feel when you do it?" will often bring responses of amazingly apt movement imagery.

Examples of Movement Imagery

Young children, as noted above, often identify with things and activities in their environment. The child becomes the thing to the extent of abstracting its movement characteristics to fit the range of his human movement. Each child's interpretation may be different, but usually a constant factor is present: the movement quality (a snowflake will move softly and lightly, a marionette will be jerky, a bear heavy and relaxed); the direction of the movement as in "up" movements (growing things, airplanes); or the dimension (as in giants).

When imagery is used with older children, identification may differ in terms of *being* and *doing*. To illustrate, younger children will take delight in *being* the kite flying in the air; older children prefer reenacting the process of flying a kite, thus retaining their own identity—*doing* rather than *being*.

Feeling is more difficult for children to communicate in movement except as it relates to their direct sensory experiences. Images evoking kinesthetic sensing of the desired movement quality can be derived from the sharpness, vibration, and tension of certain machine movements, the whirling and spinning aspects of whirlpools, the swinging feel of a pendulum or an elephant's trunk, the suspension and collapse of large waves breaking

[5] See Chapter 19.

against the shore, the sustained glide of the ice skater. Specific and easily identifiable movements connected with feeling cold, hot, wet, tired, energetic, windblown can be drawn upon. Children learn very early, however, to guard against outward and active manifestations of emotional feelings, and these are best depicted through a story character with whom they may identify or movement interpretation of music that sounds angry, sad, or scary. A teacher must know her children well and be sensitive to individual personality differences before asking them to "move the way you feel."

The following categories of suggested images might be used to illuminate certain ways of moving, either locomotor or nonlocomotor. They can serve two purposes for the teacher: add color and motivation to a particular type of movement she wishes the children to experience and make her aware of the variety of ideas which the performance of such movement may evoke from the children. Because they are mostly things to *be,* they will appeal especially to younger children.

Some Images Classified

Fast: an arrow, a little clock, a fire engine, an express train, jugglers, leaves in a storm, a jet plane, reindeer, a speedboat, a squirrel, a top, the wind, a wink.

Slow: a big clock, a farm horse, flowers growing, a freight train, ice or ice cream melting, an inchworm, a snowman, a tugboat, a turtle, big trees, the sun, walking in snowshoes.

High: airplanes, climbing a ladder, kites, prancing horses, sailboats, stilt walkers, white clouds.

Low: caterpillars, ducks, Indians hunting in the woods, seals, tired horses, turtles, white mice, worms, snakes.

Up and/or down: airplanes, a seesaw, bats, birds, bouncing balls, candles, clowns, elevators, falling stars, firemen, growing things, Humpty Dumpty, jack-in-the-box, kites, rockets, sliding down the slide, snowflakes, the sun, umbrellas.

Across or back and forth: a beam, bells, cowboys roping, elephants, lightning, lions in cages, paddling a canoe, raking leaves, riding a bicycle, rocking dolly, rocking horses, rowing a boat, swings, trees.

Turning or spinning: bicycling, clock hands, curling smoke, gears, helicopters, hoops, leaves, merry-go-round, paper in the wind, pinwheels, propellers, records, revolving doors, skaters, snowflakes, spools of thread, tape recorders, telephone dials, tops, tumbleweed, weather vanes, wheels, windmills.

Strong and heavy: fishermen with their nets, a woodchopper, bears, bulldozers, elephants, farmers, ferryboats, giants, moving men, plow horses, prehistoric monsters, tanks, seals, storm clouds, stormy waves, trains, well diggers.

Soft and light: balloons, birds flying, butterflies, candles flickering, cobwebs, dandelion puffs, echoes, fairies and elves, floating feathers, flowers nodding, ghosts, kites sailing, kittens, leaves falling, moonbeams, reindeer, sailboats, smoke, snowflakes, soap bubbles, the Sandman.

Silent and quiet: floating clouds, flying saucers, ice melting, mice, shadows, smoke, spooks, thistledown.

Stiff: board, icicle, poker, tin soldier, uncooked spaghetti.

Sharp or pulsed: bacon sizzling, bees, cuckoo clocks, crickets, frogs, grasshoppers, hummingbirds, Jack Frost, a jumping jack, jugglers, machines, mechanical dolls, monkeys, a pounded nail, popcorn, puppets, scarecrows, sparklers, stilt walkers, trains, turkeys and roosters, woodpeckers.

Floppy and loose: broken or scrambled eggs, clothes on the line, cooked spaghetti, mops, puppets, rag dolls.

Smooth and sustained: airplanes, birds and butterflies, caterpillars, cats, fish swimming, things growing, ice melting, kites, molasses pouring, rocket ships, skaters, swings, a top, the moon, the sun, a rainbow.

Spiraling: cones, circular stairs, corkscrews, shells, snails.

Twisted and crooked: the Crooked Man, gnarled driftwood, knots, an octopus, pretzels, snarled rope, screws, sorcerers, taffy, witches.

Curving and round: curling smoke, bridges, mushrooms, rainbows, seashells, umbrellas, whirlpools, "whirlybirds."

Sudden, explosive: bucking broncos, dynamite blast, fireworks, lightning, spurts of a fountain or geyser.

Be, Do, Feel

Images may be grouped around a central theme and relate to it (many examples are given in Chapter 17 in the section Making Dances). In the following list each image merely suggests a kind of movement related to *being, doing,* or *feeling,* and can be used for various kinds of exploration and invention.

WATER

Be: bubbles, dripdrops, meandering or rushing brooks, rain, ripples, splashing fountains, sprinklers, waves, waterfalls, whirlpools, whitecaps.

Do: blow and play with bubbles, carry water in pails, hose the lawn and the side of the house, pump water, splash, swim on top of and under water, wade, water-ski.

Feel: the resistance of swimming under water, the rising and sinking of fountains, the shock of walking out into cold water, the weightlessness of floating, the whirling of whirlpools, the undulation of waves.

WINTER

Be: an icicle, Jack Frost, sleet and hail, a snowflake, a snowman being built, the wind.

Do: drive a snowplow or snowmobile, make angels in the snow, make snowballs and snowmen, move with and against the wind or in deep snow, push cars, shovel snow, skate, ski, sled, walk on snowshoes.

Feel: cold, shivery, strong wind blowing you, warmth of fire or a bed.

CHRISTMAS

Be: bells, candles, lights twinkling on and off, reindeer, Santa Claus, stars, toys of all kinds, trees glittering.

Do: carry presents, chop tree and drag it home, pick out tree and carry to car, put up lights, trim the tree.

Feel: excited, glad, reverent.

MAGIC

Be: an elf, a fairy, gnome, goblin, leprechaun, magician, sorcerer, spirit, witch, wizard, in a magic place, spot, woods.

Do: appear, cause miraculous happenings by mysterious movement patterns, change into a fabulous animal, toy, or creature, make magic potions, weave a magic spell, use a magic wand or cloak.

Feel: courageous, frightened, powerful, strange.

NATURE

Be: clouds, lightning, a plant or tree growing and blossoming, rain, a rainbow, seashells, stars, something crawling or hopping or jumping or flying, thunder rumbling and crashing.

Do: cross a stream on stones, dance with moonbeams or flickering shadows, explore a cave, the moon, lift and carry heavy stones to make a fire circle, make a tree house, meet a creature from outer space, reach for a cloud, play with it, float on it, sleep on it, spin a cobweb, split logs and cut wood, stand on a hilltop in the wind.

Feel: cool, floating, quiet and still, relaxed, strong, weightless.

FIRE

Be: a bonfire blazing, a candle flickering, a forest fire raging, a match being lit, smoke puffing and curling.

Do: build a fire, hose a burning house, smother a bonfire.

Feel: dreamy, hot, smoke-blinded.

"Moving Like" Similes

Verbs of action can suggest different kinds of "being" or "doing" imagery. Groups of children, having been assigned or having chosen a verb, think of several images illustrating the possible actions (i.e., rises like a mist, a jacked-up car, a sail, dough). They then have the option of *being* one of the illustrations or *doing* it—in other words, becoming what is acted upon or causing the action. The group may divide into segments according to choice, and a child may work alone, or a group working together may construct movement illustrating one of the chosen similes. Because the latter choice is theirs, and the two options in working it out are given, this activity may be used successfully with older children.

Following are some similes produced by a class after the action words were assigned. Some of them were then used for "being" or "doing."

Closes like: a book, curtains, a bridge, a blink.

Collapses like: a pile of blocks, a sand castle, a balloon.

Covers like: a plastic bag, a tent, fallen leaves.

Expands like: an accordion, elastic, yeast dough.

Floats like: feathers, a parachute, a kite.

Gathers like: a rake, a steam shovel, a fishing net.

Glides like: a surfboard, a sailboat, a Frisbee.

Melts like: a candle, a snowman, ice cream.

Opens like: a door, a can, blinds.

Revolves like: a sprinkler, an electric beater, a reel.

Springs like: a yo-yo, a pogo stick, a takeoff board.

Stretches like: taffy, animals, elastic rope.

Surrounds like: an octopus, a tunnel, a bedroll.

Swings like: a rope swing, young trees in a storm, an elephant's trunk.

Works like: a propeller, a washing machine, a spider.

Sensory Sources for Movement Invention

"Movement may be considered the primary source of dancelike activity, but things that can be touched, heard and seen are also excellent and readily obtainable starting points for dance."[6]

[6] Molly Brearley, ed., *The Teaching of Young Children: Some Applications of Piaget's Learning Theory,* New York, Schocken Books, 1970, p. 80.

". . . It is commonly assumed that the word image refers only to a visual picture in one's mind, but psychologists point out that auditory, tactile, gustatory, kinesthetic and haptic images are also formed."[7]

Sensory experiences have great potential for reproduction into movement, provided one's imagination is free and unfettered. Here movement is invented that relates to the thing seen, heard, or felt. For some children the relationship may be quite obvious and quite literal; for others, imaginative and even farfetched. In most cases, a particular aspect of the experience will be seized upon for translation into movement. If it is a sincere attempt to arrive at a solution to the problem, it is always acceptable.

Visual

Most common are the visual experiences which are immediately available wherever one happens to be. Using memory of visual cues, a dance class can make movements associated with the following things:

In the house: broom, can opener, clock, dryer, dust mop, fireplace, popcorn popper, rocking chair, steam iron, telephone, toaster, vacuum cleaner, washing machine.

In the garage or workroom: drill, garbage crusher, hammer, lawn mower, pliers, propeller, rake, saw, shovel.

In the school: books, clock, designs (circles, triangles, rectangles, squares) on the board, doors, pencils being sharpened, pointers, wastebaskets, windows.

In the street: cars, bicycles, flags, policemen, steam shovels, traffic lights.

In the office building: drinking fountains, elevators, escalators, fire escape, office machines, typewriters.

In the park: cotton candy, Ferris wheel, fireworks (rockets, Roman candles, sparklers), ice-cream cones, merry-go-round, seesaw, climbing ladders, slides, sprinklers, swings.

In the river: buoys, drifting boats, freighters, lighthouse, speedboats, submarines, suspension bridge, tugboats.

Paintings (both objective and nonobjective), designs, kaleidoscopes, free-form sculpture, driftwood, mobiles, and masks have all been used with older children and adults. With younger children simpler materials such as feathers, scarves or newspaper floating, kites of various shapes, toys that move, hand puppets, and marionettes all evoke an approximation of their movements.

Colors[8] provide unusual visual cues. The concepts they suggest and the

---

[7] Ibid., pp. 162–163.

[8] A poetic account of color images is Mary O'Neill's *Hailstones and Halibut Bones,* Garden City, N.Y., Doubleday, 1961.

feeling reactions to them should be discussed. The response to red might be excitement, gaiety, anger, danger; on the other hand, as one student said, "it might suggest red barns in the country," a quiet, peaceful symbol.

Auditory

Auditory catalysts are especially good. Sounds made by percussion and musical instruments are obvious ones to suggest movement response. Less commonly used are sounds made by the children themselves. Some may imitate city machines or alarms, or the sounds of nature (wind shushing or howling, bees humming or buzzing, animals growling or purring). Others may produce quite abstract clickings, whistlings, blowings, wailings, hissings, hummings, "oh-ings and ah-ings." What kind of movement does a shout suggest, or a whisper?

Nonsense words and phrases can be made up or borrowed from counting-out rhymes, nursery rhymes, or limericks. Single words (no, yes, well, there, here, me) can be repeated with changes in pitch, dynamics, inflection, and timing for hilarious but often highly dramatic movement response. Records[9] are available with environmental urban sounds of bells, alarms, sirens, steam engines, and other sound effects used in television and radio stations.

Perhaps the easiest and in one sense the most ridiculous sounds to translate into movement are those we inadvertently make when we cough, sneeze, yawn, hiccup, snore, giggle, or indulge in a "belly" laugh. The characteristic movements attending these sounds can be exaggerated, expanded, transferred from one part to another or to the total body. A sneeze usually has several small tensions leading up to an explosive climax. A yawn accents the first action which is a deep inhalation, and then usually ends in a slow collapsing exhalation. Hiccups produce a series of sharp paroxysms at unexpected intervals. A snore might be a long grating expansion followed by a series of quick snorting releases. It may be difficult for younger children to make such translations into movement without resorting to the sound itself. Older children solve this problem quickly and enjoy the visible but silent movement manifestations of human sound effects, as in silent movies.

Music traditionally has been used to start people dancing, and it is undoubtedly the richest of auditory sources. It has the advantage also of leading children from simple movement experimentation with the rhythm and quality of its sound to a study of its structure. Music for young children should be chosen because it has a definite quality—lilting, tranquil, or explosive—or because it is strongly rhythmic. Older children should move in

[9] See Chapter 29.

accordance with the formal structure of the music, and the process of dance-making to music thus begins.

Tactile

Textures that are delicate, smooth, rough, prickly or spiny, spongy or soft, shapes that are round or curving or jagged or angular may suggest movement counterparts. It is sometimes desirable for children, without seeing them, to feel objects such as a smooth glass paperweight, a large seashell, a scrubbing brush, a piece of light thin silk, a large sponge, a piece of sandpaper, or any other object of distinctive tactile properties. Closing their eyes, a few children at a time may touch one of the objects. They then proceed to improvise movement consistent with its tactile qualities.

A good way to share movement perceptions and at the same time to guess the object felt, or at least its properties, is the leader-and-group method. The leader touches an object which is invisible to him. He then leads the group in movement approximating his tactile sensations. The other children judge the appropriateness of the movement when the object is shown to them. Leaders and objects should change as the activity is repeated.

Most children know the sensation of walking barefoot on a hot or cold or prickly or pebbly surface and can reproduce their reactions in movement. Slippery ice, thick gooey mud, heavy slush, a bouncy surface like a trampoline, grasping the thorny stem of a plant or bush, stroking the soft fur of a kitten all can be expressed in characteristic ways. Even the pressure of a strong wind against one's back or front, the sensation of extreme heat or cold, the feeling of being rain-soaked or mud-spattered or sticky all over may evoke movement reactions of many kinds.

The senses of taste and smell present more limited possibilities. Nevertheless, sweet, sour, spicy, peppery may suggest movement reactions of face and body. Pleasant odors (the fragrance of flowers or perfumes, the invigorating smell of saltwater, woodsmoke, pine woods, or just good fresh air) also offer material for movement interpretation. Unpleasant ones such as burning food, dead fish, exhaust fumes, and the proverbial skunk should evoke comic dramatic movement.

"Character" Movement

Mention has been made of the dislike by many older children and adults of emotional display. However, the use of a character to show emotional or

"As If" Frightened   "As If" Embarrassed

personality traits removes them from the self and is in no sense taboo. Even young children, when they put on their "trick or treat" Halloween masks, try to assume traits to fit their disguise. Older children will identify in movement with favorite characters or character types encountered in their reading and in their observation of other persons. In this way, an understanding of the communicative potential of posture, gesture, and especially movement becomes a part of their direct experience.

In the following list of classic characters some will appeal in their interpretation to girls, some to boys, and some to both. The characters chosen are not complex personalities, but represent a consistent dramatic type.

HEROES AND HEROINES

Possible movement qualities: brave, strong, proud, confident, poised, outgoing, competent, kind, humane.

Possible characters: Aladdin, Beauty ("Beauty and the Beast"), Bellerophon ("The Winged Horse"), Buffalo Bill, Daniel Boone, Galahad, Lancelot, Nathan Hale, Pecos Bill, Robin Hood, the Sleeping Beauty Prince and Princess, Snow White, William Tell, such biblical characters as Daniel, David, Moses.

KINGS AND QUEENS

Possible movement qualities: dignified, regal, grand, somewhat condescending, perhaps haughty.

Possible characters: Alexander the Great, Julius Caesar, King Arthur, King Midas, Queen Elizabeth I.

VILLAINS

Possible movement qualities: arrogant, blustering, swaggering, insolent, vain, crafty, sly, skulking, furtive, fawning, sinister.

Possible characters: Captain Hook (*Peter Pan*), the Ogre ("Jack and the Beanstalk"), the Red Queen and the Duchess (*Alice in Wonderland*), Rumpelstiltskin, Scrooge (Dickens's *Christmas Carol*), the Sheriff of Nottingham (*Robin Hood*), Snow White's and Cinderella's stepmothers, the tailors (*The Emperor's New Clothes*), Uriah Heep (*David Copperfield*), all bad witches in fable and fiction.

CLOWNS, PRANKSTERS, SIMPLETONS

Possible movement qualities: silly, giddy, bemused, detached, mischievous, happy-go-lucky.

Possible characters: the Gingerbread Man, Joey the Clown, Pinocchio, Simple Simon, most of the "Jacks" in fairy tales and legends.

EXTROVERTS

Possible movement qualities: hearty, jolly, friendly, expansive.

Possible characters: Mr. Apple ("Mr. Apple's Family"), Mr. Micawber (*David Copperfield*), Old King Cole, Santa Claus.

ECCENTRICS (PLEASANT)

Possible movement qualities: preoccupied, slow, detached, strange, uncanny.

Possible characters: the Ghost of Marley (Dickens's *Christmas Carol*), Merlin the Magician, the Pied Piper, the White Queen and the White Knight (*Alice in*

Wonderland), Big Bird and His Imaginary Friend, Mr. Snuffle-Upagus ("Sesame Street").

ECCENTRICS (UNPLEASANT)

Possible movement qualities: sullen, sulky, petulant, quarrelsome, naughty, dirty.

Possible characters: Lazy Mary, the Little Girl with a Curl, Slovenly Peter, many of Gelett Burgess's *Goops*.

GROTESQUES

Possible movement qualities: distorted, crooked, twisted, bulging, stiff or floppy, slithery or jerky, sometimes scary.

Possible characters: the Beast ("Beauty and the Beast"), My Father's Dragon, Moon or Mars Men, the Scarecrow and the Tin Woodman (*The Wizard of Oz*), the borogoves, jub-jub birds, mome raths and slithy toves of Jabberwocky (*Alice in Wonderland*), the Cooky Monster ("Sesame Street").

LEGENDARY GIANTS

Possible movements: big, bold, strong, heavy, fierce.

Possible characters: Cyclops (the story of Odysseus), Goliath, John Henry, Mike Fink, Paul Bunyan, Samson.

MINIATURE PEOPLE

Possible movements: dainty, light, small, quick.

Possible characters: Hope (Pandora), Hop O' My Thumb, Tinkerbell (*Peter Pan*), Thumbalina, Wee Willie Winkie.

States of Feeling and Imaginary Situations

As they grow older, boys and girls no longer find it necessary to be Santa Claus or a witch to reproduce movement which is jolly or mysterious. Exploration of abstracted feelings or behaviors helps broaden movement vocabularies and improve expressiveness in movement. It may also help a child externalize inhibitions and frustrations. The imitation in movement of a blustering, dominating person, for instance, may have a salutary effect on small aggressions that manifest themselves in other ways.

Several examples of imagined emotional states or experiences which produce differing kinds of movement are given in the following list.

Walking as if: gay, tired, big and strong, afraid, fat and jolly, angry, sad, sly and secretive, shy and embarrassed, showing off, lame, blindfolded, proper and prim, very curious, sleepwalking, in a dream, in a frenzy, boasting and blustering, anxious and worried, with soap in the eyes, carrying a lighted candle, with a basket on the head, with a pack on the back, on a narrow plank over a ditch, in shoes filled with sand, on air, on ice, in thick mud, on hot sand, in a jungle, crossing a crowded playground, on the moon.

Running as if: pursued, avoiding being seen, catching a bus, overtaking a friend, dodging missiles, on a busy street, warning of danger.

Jumping as if: at a loud noise, shooting a basket, with joy, in a tantrum.

Turning as if: in a revolving door, on a turntable, twirling a rope, pushing a waterwheel.

Reaching and stretching as if: straightening a picture, walking out into cold water, picking fruit from a tree, putting things on a high shelf, yawning, putting on tight clothes, waking up, swatting flies.

Lifting, carrying, and placing as if: the object were something small and fragile, very heavy, very bulky, very wide, very hot or cold, filled with liquid, as if there were too many small objects.

Striking as if: angry, against a locked or stuck door, boxing in a ring, in a volley-ball game.

Sitting as if: careful of new clothes, in a jeep or bus, trying to keep awake.

Falling as if: dizzy, exhausted, shot, dodging, in a dream, from a stumble.

Focusing gaze as if: searching for something small, in a dark room, looking out of a bus window, gazing at a flying saucer, being hypnotized, watching a parade, a race, an airplane, a tennis game.

Moving as if: threatening, teasing, coaxing, calming, bewitched, having a nightmare, caught in something very sticky, catching something very big and heavy or very small and fragile, inhibited by a heavy load, a ball and chain, a severe wound, bound hands and feet, a massive headdress, a tight girdle, a large neck ruff, a hoop skirt, tremendous sleeves, too large or too small shoes, in darkness or when blindfolded in a large or small room or in a place with many or no objects, inside a cocoon, a beach ball, a large balloon, a small cave, a small or large box, a long narrow cylinder (hollow pole, hollow log, tunnel), under a lowering and/or lifting ceiling, without gravitational pull (as on the moon), taking a cold shower, being pulled by a huge magnet, through heavy fog or smog, unsnarling a ball of wool, in a limitless space, tasting something sour or hot, putting on tight clothes, being tickled with a feather, something were crawling on one's back and swatting, scratching, or overt movement is impossible (as in church or driving a car).

These imaginary states suggesting different kinds of movement reactions offer rich sources for dance-making and are best used with older children.

Part III THE SKILLS OF DANCE MOVEMENT

Chapter Preview

**Analyses of Locomotor Movements, Nonlocomotor
Movements, and Traditional Dance Steps
Exploring Variations and Combinations
Discovering Dance Steps**

Up and Down and In-between

7 The Skills of Dance Movement: Orientation

Man sometimes thinks like a tree . . . but he was built to move. All anywhere about man, within and without is eternally, ceaselessly motion, whether he senses it or not.[1]

A teacher can teach a movement skill in all of its several ramifications by constant dictation and direction. She can also *let* the child learn it, under competent guidance, by experimenting, exploring different ways of doing it, discovering why some are not satisfactory whereas others work well. It is true that learning a dance step set in a specific pattern to definite timing may need special attention. The important thing is to follow a logical procedure, building upon what the child already knows and can do, until the new combination is achieved.

The teacher must be prepared both to give help herself and to direct children to help each other. In teacher-directed method a particular skill is usually grasped by approximately half the group if a clear explanation and a good demonstration are given. Correction of the most common error observed brings another quarter of the group up to performance standards. To help the rest, and to assist other children in helping them, the teacher must be able to diagnose the difficulties and how to overcome them. To do this, she must have analyzed the movement skill and know exactly how part follows part, how one part is related to another, and how all are built into the total.

[1] *Buckminster Fuller to Children of Earth,* compiled and photographed by Cam Smith, Garden City, N.Y., Doubleday, 1972.

Analyses of Locomotor Movements, Nonlocomotor Movements, and Traditional Dance Steps

Three kinds of material are presented in outline form in Part III. The basic movements of locomotion (the walk, run, jump, hop, and leap—a variation of the run—and certain adapted movements) are analyzed and suggestions made for exploring, combining, varying, and discovering certain concepts about their use. Basic nonlocomotor movements (the bend, stretch, twist, and swing) are described and some familiar combinations, ways of exploring them and imagery examples suggested. Locomotor movements are combined into dance steps, and eleven common dance steps are analyzed and suggestions made for variations, teaching procedures, and ways in which they may be used in dancing with others.

The systematic order of presentation of the materials used here need not be followed in dance classes. It is meant to enable the teacher to understand them better and to establish goals for performance. Basic locomotor movements are analyzed in their natural form—that is, the form most functional for their use; dance steps in their most commonly used form; and nonlocomotor movements in accordance with the name of the movement.

Exploring Variations and Combinations

The natural or most functional form of a basic movement or dance step serves as a point of departure for the exploration and discovery of *variations* of the movement. For example, a natural walk is performed at a standing level; but in exploring other levels it is found that one can walk with knees half bent and also in a full squatting position. Such activity should not be forced to follow the laws of logic. The exploration done by younger children rarely conforms to a mechanical and scientific procedure unless the teacher so plans it.

Older children, on the other hand, are more interested in the problems presented by the movement itself. A logical order for movement exploration may enlarge their repertoire of movements in a more systematic way and make available to them materials for making their own dances. After a new movement or a combination of movements has evolved through the process of investigation, the question "How might this be used in a dance?" is often sufficient to lead older children directly from exploration of dance movement to dance-making.

Not all items in the outline offer possibilities of variation for every movement. For example, to change the level of a hop to any great extent is not only difficult but unsatisfactory as a movement experience. A swing loses its swinging character if tension is applied. Many dance steps do not lend themselves to variation because they are set in specific time and space patterns which, if changed, would change the nature of the step entirely. Therefore certain attempted variations will prove unsatisfactory. Further, some variations are much more difficult than others. Children exploring a walk for the first time are not expected to discover how to do a grapevine walk successfully. Older children experimenting with a sideward walk will probably discover it rather quickly and be able to perform it with little difficulty.

Discovering Dance Steps

Many who have taught folk dance over the years will have their own methods for teaching the traditional dance steps which are the substance of Chapter 10. For others, suggested teaching procedures, mostly teacher directed, may be found there after the analysis and variations of the steps.

At the end of that chapter a method involving greater participation by the children is presented for those who wish to make this part of the dance program more of a problem-solving experience. It will allow one to make children more aware of the special skills called for by the step, such as floor pattern, equal or unequal timing, weight change, direction in space. For older children, working out the step themselves following written or verbal directions has some of the same interest as finding the solution to a puzzle. It also encourages children to help each other master the step, and may be used not only for individual problem solving, but in partners and groups.

With this method, especially in small groups working together, the use of the step in an invented dance sequence is a logical progression.

Chapter Preview

Basic Locomotor Movements—walk, run, (leap), jump, hop

Analysis
Exploring Variations
Combining Variations
Discovering Movement Concepts

Adapted Locomotor Movements—crawl, roll

Description
Exploring Variations

Using Other Body Parts for Traveling

Getting There with a Run

MAX ROBERTSON

8 *Locomotor Movements: Basic and Adapted*

A walk, a run, a jump, and a hop are four ways of moving the body through space from a standing base. In the first two, the weight is transferred from one foot to the other. In the second two, the weight is maintained on one or both feet as the body is lifted in the air. These locomotor movements are considered basic for the following reasons:

1. All movement which projects the body in space in any direction and in which the feet are used as a base, regardless of the purpose of the movement, is made up of one of these four elements or a variation or combination of them.
2. A single unit of movement of the leg or legs transfers weight or lifts the body into the air. It is repeated when continuous progress through space is desired.
3. When starting from a standing level on one or both feet in any given place, a single unit makes only one contact with the area on which the movement is made.

Walking, running, jumping, and hopping—and a variation of the run, leaping—are described in outline form in this chapter. The analyses in I are for the teacher's understanding. Children may be assigned the problems of exploring, combining, and discovering in II, III, and IV.

Basic Locomotor Movements

Walk

I. Analysis of a Basic Walk

A. *Shape:* A walk carries the body through space by transferring weight from one foot to the other with a push from the ball and toes of the foot to the heel of the other. Continual contact with the floor is kept as the transfer is made, there being a brief period of support by both feet. The leg swings freely from the hip and knee and lifts the foot clear of the floor on each step. The position of the body is erect and easy. There is flexion and extension of the ankle, the toes point forward, and the arms swing in opposition to the leg swing.

B. *Space Design:* Direction, forward; level, standing; dimension of step, varying with each individual;[1] path, straight; focus of gaze, forward.

C. *Timing:* Tempo, moderate; intervals, equal. In a continuing series of walks the heel strike which begins the transfer of weight represents the climax of the movement or the beat from which time intervals are measured.

D. *Force:* Movement quality, swinging, springy; contact with floor, moderately light.

II. Exploring the Walk for Variations

A. *Changes in Shape*—Feet and Legs: On tiptoe or with balls of feet touching the floor first;[2] with knees bent up high in front or sideward; with knees stiff; with toes turned in or out; with legs kicking up high in front, in back, or sideward; with legs crossing on each step; with legs apart or together.

Hands and Arms: With arms held at the sides; with arms held overhead or folded in front or in back; with hands on knees or clasped behind the back; with fists clenched and arms thrusting forward or sideward together or alternately; with one or both hands flicking in any position; with hands clapping in front or back or overhead or slapping chest or thighs; with arms swinging together from side to side or forward and backward or out and in; with only one arm swinging in any direction; with arms held still in any position; with arms moving in counteropposition.

Trunk: With body bent forward, backward, or sideward.

B. *Changes in Space Design*—Direction: In place, backward; sideward; turning around; in a step-together or a step-cross floor pattern sideward.

Level: On tiptoe; with knees half bent; with knees fully bent.

---

[1] Younger children have shorter legs, in comparison with the rest of their bodies, than do older children. Therefore their walking steps are shorter and faster.

[2] This is the walk most often used in ballroom, folk, and square dance.

Dimension of Steps: With longer or shorter steps.

Path: On a curving or crooked path.

Focus: Gazing sideward, backward, upward or downward, or at a fixed or moving spot.

C. *Changes in Timing*—Tempo: With slower or faster steps.

Intervals: In a pattern of unequally divided intervals (such as short-long).

D. *Changes in Force:* With heavier or lighter steps; with smoothly flowing steps; with sharply staccato steps.

III. Combining Variations

Many other variations may be discovered or invented by experimenting with the walk as well as with the other three basic movements. Combinations may be made from variations that have been found. The only principle to be followed is that the combination be physically congenial in performance. For example, walking fast on tiptoe is a satisfying combination, but walking fast with knees fully bent is not. Following are some simple combinations:

Footprints (Walk Variations)

Walk forward, clapping hands in front on one step and behind on the next; walk, lifting legs high and clapping hands under one leg and then the other; walk on tiptoe with feet apart, rocking from side to side and clapping hands above head.

Walk forward, kicking legs up in front with knee straight (as in the goose step) and arms held stiffly at sides.

Walk very slowly and then gradually increase speed from natural timing to fast timing. Reverse sequence to a very slow timing.

Walk forward and then change to a backward and/or a sideward walk while continuing in the same spatial direction.

Walk, bending backward with knees lifted high in front and hands clasped behind back.

Walk, bending knees upward to touch hands extended in front; bending knees sideward to touch hands extended at side.

Walk very fast with small steps, head forward, elbows in, and hands folded in front.

Walk forward in a series of diagonal lines to make a zigzag; in three straight lines to make a triangle; in four straight lines to make a square; in a curved line to make a circle; in two circles to make a figure eight; in a weaving line to make a serpentine; in a continuously smaller curved line to make a snail.

Walk, turning once around in place with four steps; with three steps; with two steps; with one big step.

Walk with long steps, hand on knees and keeping gaze always focused on same spot on floor; with slow dragging steps, hands clasped behind back, gaze focused downward; with quick steps, gaze focused upward at a moving spot.

IV. Discovering Movement Concepts

When walking slower or faster, one tends to take longer or shorter steps respectively, although the process may be reversed.

When walking backward, one tends to incline the body slightly forward.

When one walks sideward, the following foot can be brought up to the leading foot (step-together), it can cross always in front or always in back (side-cross step), or it can cross alternately in front and in back (grapevine step).[3] When walking sideward and crossing feet, one must turn the knees and toes out.

When pivoting all the way around with one step, it is easier to use the foot toward the direction of the turn.

When one walks with heavy steps, the whole foot may be placed on the floor at once, as in tramping, or the heel strike may be especially accented. When one walks with light steps, the heel strikes gently or not at all.

When one walks with smooth steps, the ball of the foot takes the weight first;

[3] The side-cross step and the grapevine step are used extensively in eastern European line dances.

with sharply staccato steps, the heel strike is emphasized, and the hip and knee action is decreased.

Run

I. Analysis of a Basic Run

A. *Shape:* A run carries the body through space by transferring its weight from the ball and toes of one foot to the ball and toes of the other. There is a short period of nonsupport while the body is lifted completely off the floor during this transfer of weight; a slight suspension in the air occurs, and then the body drops to a landing on the other foot. The toes point forward and the body is inclined slightly forward. There is free swinging action of the hip, knee, and ankle as the free leg is lifted in the air. The arms, slightly bent at the elbows, swing in opposition to the leg movement.

B. *Space Design:* Direction, upward, forward; level, standing to elevated; dimension of step, somewhat longer than a natural walk; path, straight; focus of gaze, forward.

C. *Timing:* Tempo, faster than that of a basic walk; intervals, equal. (In a continuing series of runs the landing on one foot and takeoff into the air are identical for timing purposes and represent the climax of the movement or the beat from which time intervals are measured.)

D. *Force:* Movement quality, percussive, buoyant, resilient; contact with floor, moderately heavy.

II. Exploring the Run for Variations

A. *Changes in Shape*—Feet and Legs: With knees bent up high in front or at the side; with legs kicking up high in front, at the side, or in back; with toes and knees turned in or out; with legs crossing on each step.

Hand and Arms: With arms held still at sides; with hands on knees; with hands flicking forward, sideward, or overhead, together or alternately; with hands pressed over ears; with arms folded behind back or in front; with arms extended in any direction; with arms swinging together from side to side; with one or both arms held still in any position.

Trunk: With body bent backward or sharply forward.

B. *Changes in Space Design*—Direction: In place; backward; sideward; turning around; in a combination of directions to make different floor patterns.

Level: Springing high into the air; crouching low toward the floor.

Dimension of steps: With longer or shorter steps.

Path: On a curving or crooked path.

Focus: Gazing sideward, backward, upward, or downward or at a fixed or moving spot.

C. *Changes in Time*—Tempo: With slower or faster steps.

Intervals: In a pattern of divided and undivided intervals (a longer run in combination with one or more shorter runs becomes a leap).

D. *Changes in Force*—Contact with Floor: With heavier or lighter steps.

III. Combining Variations

Run very fast and then gradually decrease speed through natural timing to slow timing. Reverse sequence.

Getting There with a Leap

DETROIT PUBLIC SCHOOLS

Run forward and then change to a run backward without changing the spatial direction of the run.

Run forward, changing the spatial direction two times to make a triangle; three times to make a square; several times to make a zigzag.

Run forward in a curved line to make a circle; a figure eight; a serpentine; a snail.

Run a definite number of steps forward, sideward, backward, and again sideward to make a square, facing continuously forward.

Run forward with arms extended forward, then in place with elbows bent.

Run forward with arms extended forward, keeping gaze focused backward over one shoulder.

Run a definite number of steps with knees bent high in front and then with feet lifted high in back; with legs kicking forward and then backward.

IV. Discovering Movement Concepts

When one runs slowly, the body is held in the air longer; similarly, when one springs higher into the air or covers a greater distance, the tempo of the run is slower. The result in both cases is a *leap*.

When running fast to cover distance, one increases knee action; when running fast to take many small steps in a short time, one decreases knee action.

When landing from a high spring into the air, one increases flexion of the knee and ankle.

When exaggerating either the forward or backward movement of the legs, one inclines the body in the opposite direction to maintain balance.

When one uses the run in dancing, balance is easier to maintain if the size of the step is short to moderate.

Leap

I. Analysis of a Leap (A Variation of the Run)

A. *Shape:* A leap is a run in which the upward and/or forward dimension is increased and the timing is decreased. Much of the analysis of a basic run applies to a leap. In comparison with the run, the knee and ankle action is increased. The knee leads forward after the takeoff into the air and then is extended as the foot reaches forward to land. The rear leg extends backward while in the air because of the strong propelling movement forward and upon landing is swung vigorously ahead into the next lift. The period of suspension in the air and consequent nonsupport is greater than in the run.

B. *Space Design:* Direction, upward, forward; level, elevation greater than with a basic run; path, straight; focus of gaze, forward.

C. *Timing:* Tempo, slower than that of a basic run, relatively the same as that of a walk; intervals, equal. (Because leaps take substantial control and energy, children should not be asked to sustain them in a continuing series.)

D. *Force:* Movement percussive, forceful with strong quality of suspension; contact with floor, strong on takeoff, lighter on landing.

II. Variations and Combinations

Variations in direction and body position in a leap may be made, but most of them are too difficult for children. Leaping is most often combined with running. To gain the proper distance and height for a leap, the momentum offered by one or more preliminary running steps is necessary. Familiar combinations are one run and one leap, where the takeoff into the leap is always on the same foot; and two runs and one leap where the takeoff is on alternate feet. In timing these combinations the run is half as long as the leap (short-long or short-short-long); the accent, or climax of the sequence, is on the start of the leap, that is, on the takeoff into the air (the long beat). It is not on the landing from it, as the landing occurs on the run or runs which start the repetition of the sequence.

Jump

I. Analysis of a Basic Jump

A. *Shape:* A jump carries the body upward in space by lifting it into the air from a takeoff on both feet. The body is suspended somewhat at the highest point of the lift and then released to gravity to drop back to a landing on both feet. The knees and ankles are bent and the feet point forward when on the floor; the knees and ankles are extended and the feet hang downward when in the air. On landing, the weight is transferred very quickly from the toes to the balls of the feet and then to the heels. This sequence is reversed on the takeoff. The arms are bent at the elbows as in the run, and may assist the jump by circling up, out, and down as the lift, suspension, and landing are made.

B. *Space Design:* Direction, upward; level, standing to elevated; dimension of jump, varies with each individual; path, straight upward; focus of gaze, forward.

C. *Timing:* Tempo, moderate, as in a basic walk; intervals, equal. (In a continuing series of jumps the landing on both feet and the takeoff into the air are identical for timing purposes and represent the climax of the movement or the beat from which time intervals are measured.)

D. *Force:* Movement quality, strong, resilient, moderately heavy.

II. Exploring the Jump for Variations

A. *Changes in Shape*—Feet and Legs: With knees straight throughout jump; with landing and takeoff on balls of feet only. Land with feet alternately apart and together, or apart and crossing, or with one foot forward and the other backward. While in the air, kick feet high in back or to either side in back; bend knees up and out to sides; click heels together one or more times or touch soles of feet together; extend legs apart sideward or one forward and the other backward. Jump forward by taking off with one foot and landing on both feet.

Hands and Arms: With arms held still at sides; swinging forward and backward, or from side to side, or in large outward circles; with arms folded or extended in any position; with hands on knees, clasped behind back, clapping upward, or placed on hips; with one arm reaching high above head at height of jump.

B. *Changes in Space Design*—Direction: Adding a forward, backward, sideward, or turning direction to the upward direction.

Level: With knees half bent, with knees fully bent.

Dimension of Jumps: Barely leaving the floor or lifting as high as possible into the air.

C. *Changes in Timing*—Tempo: With slower or faster jumps (bounces).
Intervals: In a pattern of divided and undivided intervals.

D. *Changes in Force*—Contact with floor : With stronger or lighter jumps.

III. Combining Variations

Jump very fast, and then gradually decrease speed through natural timing to slow timing. Reverse sequence.

Combine a little jump with a big jump; combine a definite number of little jumps with half the number of big jumps.

Jump once forward and once backward, or once to one side and once to the other; take one or more jumps in a square, forward, sideward, backward, sideward, always facing forward.

Take off on one foot, click heels in the air to opposite side, and land on both feet.

Jump, making a half turn while in the air; then a full turn.

Combine a jump and a hop and repeat, using alternate feet for the hops.

Jump and land with one foot placed on the floor in front with only the heel touching. Jump again and place the other foot in front in a similar position. This is the *Bleking* step used in many folk dances. It may also be done with the toe instead of the heel of the forward foot touching the floor.

IV. Discovering Movement Concepts

When jumping slowly, one lifts the body higher into the air or the jump covers a greater distance. Similarly, taking big jumps slows down the tempo of the jumps.

When jumping very fast, one has less time to sink to the heels on landing, and therefore a series of fast jumps is made from the balls of the feet with little elevation.

When one jumps high, the arm swing helps lift the body into the air and there is increased knee and ankle action on the landing and takeoff.

When one jumps forward, the knees are bent to lower the center of gravity against the forward momentum.

Hop

I. Analysis of a Basic Hop

A. *Shape:* A hop carries the body upward into space by lifting it into the air from a takeoff on one foot. After a very slight suspension, the body is released to gravity to drop back to the same foot. The knee and ankle of the active leg are bent and the foot points forward when on the floor; the knee and ankle of the active leg are extended and the foot hangs downward when in the air. On landing, the transfer of weight from the toe to the ball of the foot and then to the heel is similar to that of the jump. The free leg is bent under the body so that it makes no contact with the floor.

B. *Space Design:* Direction, upward; level, standing to elevated; dimension of hop, varies with each individual; path, straight upward; focus of gaze, forward.

C. *Timing:* Tempo, moderate, as in a basic walk; intervals, equal. (In a continuing series of hops the landing on one foot and the takeoff into the air from that foot are identical for timing purposes and represent the climax of the movement or the beat from which time intervals are measured.)

D. *Force:* Movement quality percussive, weightier, and less resilient than in a jump; contact with floor, moderately heavy.

II. Exploring the Hop for Variations

A. *Changes in Shape*—Feet and Legs: With free leg bent up high in front or at the side; with free leg extended forward, sideward, or backward. Change to other foot after a definite number of hops on active foot; click heel of active foot to heel of free foot while in the air.

Hands and Arms: With arms folded or extended in any direction; with hands clasped behind back, around knee of free leg, or on hips.

Trunk: With body tilted forward, backward, or sideward toward the active foot.

B. *Changes in Space Design*—Direction: Adding a forward, backward, sideward, or turning direction to the upward direction.

Dimension of Hops: Barely leaving the floor or lifting as high as possible into the air.

C. *Changes in Timing*—Tempo: With slower or faster hops.
Intervals: In a pattern of divided and undivided intervals.

III. Combining Variations

Hop very fast and then gradually decrease speed to natural timing. Reverse sequence.

Hop on one foot, touching toe of other foot diagonally forward on the floor; hop again and lift toe to inside of hopping leg (as in the Highland Fling).

Hop once forward and once backward; hop several times forward on one foot and backward on the other foot; do the same from side to side.

Hop several times to the left side with the right foot, then to the right side with the left foot.

Hop forward several times with the free leg extended forward and then several times with it extended backward.

Hop in place, swinging the free leg forward on one hop and backward on the next.

Hop forward several times on one foot and then on the other, hands clasped behind the back and free leg extended backward.

Hop with the free leg swinging forward and backward. On every other hop clap the hands under it as it swings forward.

IV. Discovering Movement Concepts

When one hops slowly, the body is lifted higher in the air or the hop covers a greater distance. Similarly, with big hops, the tempo of the series of hops is slower.

A series of very fast hops is made from the balls of the feet with little knee action.

It is easier to hop to the right on the right foot than to the left on the right foot.

Balance is more difficult to maintain in the hop than in any other basic movement of locomotion.

Adapted Locomotor Movements

Two ways of traveling from one place to another through space using a base or bases of support other than the feet are the roll and the crawl. These are the first efficient means of locomotion used by the child before he learns to walk and therefore are known to all school-age children. They have various uses in dance, especially when a low level is desired.

Crawl

I. Description

A crawl is a locomotor movement in which the hands and feet or the hands and knees are used as the base for propulsion of the body forward.

II. Exploring the Crawl for Variations

A. *Changes in Shape:* Crawl by moving both hands forward together, then both feet forward together; moving the hand and foot on one side, then the hand and foot on the other side; moving an opposite hand and foot, then the other opposite hand and foot; moving alternate hands alone and dragging body and feet.

B. *Changes in Space Design*—Direction: Crawl forward, backward, sideward.

Level: Approximately the same level is maintained throughout the movement although a base on hands and feet permits a higher shape than on hands and knees. The verb *creep* means to crawl as close to the floor as possible.

Dimension: Some increase or decrease in dimension is possible.

Path: On a curving as well as angular path.

C. *Change in Timing:* Crawl more slowly or quickly than naturally.

D. *Changes in Force:* Crawl smoothly and quietly; ponderously and heavily.

Roll

I. Description

A roll is a locomotor movement in which the prone or supine body is used as the base for propulsion. The body is extended, the arms are stretched overhead, and the roll is made over once, or over and over continuously.

II. Exploring the Roll for Variations

A. *Changes in Shape:* The arms may be bent or extended down at the sides and the head slightly raised to avoid bumping. The upper or lower part of the body may initiate the roll, with the other part following, resulting in a twisted roll.

B. *Changes in Space Design*—Direction: Roll toward left side, toward right side.

Level: The same level is maintained throughout the movement.

Dimension: The same dimension is maintained throughout if the path is straight. Dimension of the upper or lower body is increased if the path is curving.

Path: The roll may describe a circle if the size of roll in the upper or lower part of the body is sufficiently increased and of the opposite part decreased.

C. *Changes in Timing:* Roll very slowly or very quickly.

D. *Changes in Force:* The roll must maintain approximately the same expenditure of force except in relation to its timing.

Using Other Body Parts for Traveling

Besides the total body or the hands and feet or knees, the buttocks and the knees alone may be used as the base for traveling. Children should not be permitted to continue the knee walk for any length of time as this joint is not constructed to use for such weight-bearing.

One can also travel through space by turning forward, backward, or sideward somersaults, by cartwheels, by handsprings, or by walking on the hands. As these are primarily gymnastic feats, they are not analyzed here but may be found in textbooks on movement education or tumbling.

Chapter Preview

Basic Nonlocomotor Movements—bend, stretch, twist, swing

Some Combinations of Basic Movements—push, pull, strike, dodge, rock, sway, lift, turn, sit, fall

> *Description*
> *Exploring the Movement*
> *Examples of Imagery*

Feeling Stretchy

MAX ROBERTSON

9 Nonlocomotor Movements: Basic and Combinations

Many movements used in daily life, in work, play, and dance, do not move the body from place to place. They employ body parts in bendings, twistings, stretchings, swingings, with the feet, legs, lower trunk, or total body length forming a stationary base or moving only enough to retain balance or to give greater force or dimension to the movement. In this book these movements are called *nonlocomotor*, a term which, though negative, serves to differentiate them more clearly from the opposite category, *locomotor*, than does the word *axial* used by some authorities for the same meaning.

Nonlocomotor movements should be used not as a series of exercises or "warm-ups" but as points of departure for exploration and as instruments for creative expression. They serve as excellent leads into dance-making, especially where movement quality or dramatic imagery is involved. Well selected, either alone or combined with locomotor movements, they can also offer the sense of exhilaration which comes from the performance of highly rhythmic movement.

Certain nonlocomotor movements are called basic for the following reasons:

1. The name of the movement describes a characteristic way of using the body, or certain parts of the body.
2. One or more of these movements are present in all movements of body parts, both locomotor and nonlocomotor.
3. They are abstract in the sense that they carry no dramatic meaning unless they are performed for such a purpose.

The *bend, stretch, swing,* and *twist* will be referred to hereafter as *basic nonlocomotor movements.*

Included in this chapter is another group of nonlocomotor movements having a functional or dramatic rather than a mechanical or a kinesiological meaning. Their names describe a way not only of moving the body but of moving it for a specific purpose. They are combinations of the basic non-locomotor movements and are easily identified and used by children in exploring movement for dance purposes. The *push, pull, strike, dodge, rock, sway, lift, turn, sit,* and *fall* are examples of *combinations of basic nonloco-motor movements.*

Basic Nonlocomotor Movements

Bend

I. Description

A bend is a movement in which two adjacent sections of the body are brought closer together. It may occur wherever there is a hinge joint or a ball-and-socket joint. The general direction of a bend as contrasted with a stretch is toward the body center. Only certain ones of all the possible ways of bending are listed below.

II. Exploring the Bend

A. *Shape*—Trunk: (At waist) forward (as in curling the trunk); sideward; backward (slightly).

Neck: Downward, sideward; backward.

Legs: (At knees or hips) forward-upward or sideward-upward (lifting leg); forward-downward or sideward-downward (lowering trunk by bending knees); (at ankles) bending feet upward toward knees or to either side.

Arms: (At elbows) forward-upward; forward-downward; sideward-upward; sideward-downward; (at wrists) upward, downward, sideward.

B. *Space Design*—Direction: As indicated in the description.

Level: Arms, legs, neck, and trunk can be bent in sitting or lying position, as well as standing.

Dimension: Can be slight or as great as the joint will allow.

C. *Timing:* Can be very quick or extremely slow.

D. *Force:* Variety in the amount of force and the way it is employed results in movements which are gentle and relaxed or strong and tense.

III. Examples of Imagery

Mechanical or rag dolls, high-stepping horses, flowers closing their petals, see-saw, the Crooked Man, an accordion, mountaineers, work movements.

Stretch

I. Description

A stretch is a full extension of any part of the body in any possible direction, on a vertical or horizontal plane or any point between.

II. Exploring the Stretch

A. *Shape:* A small part such as a finger or the total body or anything between may be stretched.

B. *Space Design*—Direction: As indicated in the description.
Level: May be taken on any level including an elevation off the floor.
Dimension: The greatest dimension possible for any body part is implied in a stretch.

C. *Timing:* Can be extremely slow or very quick; the latter might be described as a *thrust*.

D. *Force:* This is related to the tempo; a fast stretch takes considerable force and is a sharp, explosive movement; a slow stretch takes less force and is a sustained and somewhat sinuous movement.

III. Examples of Imagery

Airplanes, walking on stilts, climbing ladders, jumping jack, growing things, waking up, picking fruit, shooting baskets.

Twist

I. Description

A twist is a rotation of a part of the body around a long axis. For example, the arm may be twisted at the shoulder, the leg at the hip; the peculiar structure of the spinal column permits twisting of the trunk and head. Rotation in other parts of the body is possible but more limited than in these examples. The general direction of a twist is either clockwise or counterclockwise.

II. Exploring the Twist

A. *Shape*—Arms: (At shoulders, elbows, and wrists) inward rotation; outward rotation.

Legs: (At hips, knees, and ankles) inward rotation; outward rotation.

Trunk: Around to the left; around to right.

Neck: Around to left; around to right.

B. *Space Design*—Direction: As indicated in the description.

Level: Arms, legs, trunk, and neck can be twisted in a sitting or lying position as well as in a standing position.

Dimension: Can be slight or as great as the joint will allow.

C. *Timing:* Can be quick or very slow.

D. *Force:* Variety in the amount of force and the way it is employed results in movements which are gentle and relaxed or strong and tense.

III. Examples of Imagery

Winding a top, the Crooked Man, witches, scarecrows, screwdrivers, snarled rope, wringing a towel.

Swing

I. Description

A swing is an arc or circle around a stationary center. The swinging part is released into gravity with or without impetus, carries up on the opposite side of the arc as far as the propelling power of the drop will take it, hangs for an instant, and then falls back into the gravity pull again. A swing may die out as the dimension of the drop into gravity decreases and hence its propelling power; it may be continued by applying just enough impetus to keep the dimensions of the arcs similar; or it may be increased by applying greater impetus at the beginning of each drop. If the impetus is great enough, the dimension of the arc may be increased to a circle; in other words, the swing, while suspended, tips over and drops back on the opposite side.

One can swing only those parts of the body which are attached to fixed or stationary parts and which are of such a length as to make free swinging possible. Arms can be swung from the shoulders; legs (one at a time) from the hips; and, in a somewhat restricted fashion, the upper trunk from the hips, and the head from the neck.

II. Exploring the Swing

A. *Shape*—One Arm: Sideward (across the front of the body); forward and backward (along the side of the body); in a sideward circle; in a forward and backward circle; in a circle in front of the body and in back of the body (figure eight).

Both Arms: Sideward (arms parallel or in opposition to each other); forward and backward (arms parallel or in opposition to each other); in a sideward circle (arms parallel and starting to the right or left); in opposition to each other and starting down-in and up, or down-out and up; in a forward and backward circle (arms parallel and starting down-forward and up or down-backward and up); in two sideward circles (arms parallel and both arms starting down and around on one side and then down and around on the other side—figure eight); in opposition to each other and both arms starting down-out and around and then down-in and around (two figure eights).

One Leg: Forward and backward; from side to side. The arms swing in opposition to the leg to aid in balance. At first it is sometimes necessary to hang on to something for support.

Trunk: From side to side. Stand in a wide stride; bend the upper trunk forward and to one side, then swing it in pendulum fashion. The arms and head

"We're Reaching to the Sky"

should hang relaxed from the shoulders and move only as they are swung by the motion of the trunk.

Head: From side to side.

B. *Space Design*—Direction: When the arc or circle path of a swing is downward and to the right, its direction is counterclockwise; if to the left, it is clockwise.

Level: The character of the swinging movement makes a standing level necessary except possibly in swinging the head.

Dimension: From a very small arc to as large a one as possible and then into a circle.

C. *Timing:* A swing may be slowed down by increasing its dimension and/or by delaying the suspension of the movement at the top of the arc before it drops back into gravity; it may be quickened somewhat by decreasing its dimension. If the tempo becomes too slow or too fast, however, the movement will lose its swinging character.

D. *Force:* See description of swing.

III. Examples of Imagery

Elephants, the Man on the Flying Trapeze, pendulums, a swing, waterwheels, windmills, bears.

Outline of Some Combinations of Basic Movements

Push

I. Description

A push is used for moving an object from one place to another in space against resistance, without grasping and lifting. Movement is usually made away from the body center, beginning close to the body or in a drawn-in position and extending outward from it. In pushing an object forward at chest level with both hands, the arms are strongly bent with the elbows down; the wrists are extended with the palms forward and spread against the object; the trunk is inclined forward; the feet are in a long forward stride to provide a strong base. Movement starts from this position and continues forward into extension of the arms and a stronger forward bend of the trunk. A push may be prolonged by combining it with a locomotor movement such as a walk.

II. Exploring the Push

A. *Shape:* Push with one or both hands; one or both feet; shoulder or hip; with feet against floor to attain elevation.

B. *Space Design*—Direction: Push forward, downward, sideward, upward.
Level: Push from a standing level; from kneeling on one knee or on both; from sitting squarely, or on either side; from a prone or supine position.
Dimension: Make short, long, or very long pushes.

C. *Timing:* Push very slowly, quickly.

D. *Force:* Make strong, hard pushes; gentle, light pushes.

III. Examples of Imagery

Pushing a swing, a snowball, a balloon, heavy furniture, a plow, an automobile, a grocery cart, a lawn mower, a shovel, a saw; pushing against another person or the floor with hands or feet.

Pull

I. Description

A pull is used to move an object or body part from one place to another against resistance, usually toward the body center and without lifting and carrying. In pulling with the arms from in front, the arms are extended, the hands are closed, the body is bent forward, the knees are slightly bent, and the feet are in a long forward stride to provide a strong base. Movement starts from this position and continues in toward the body until the arms are strongly bent and the body is straightened. A pull may be prolonged by combining it with a locomotor movement such as a backward or sideward walk.

II. Exploring the Pull

A. *Shape:* Pull with both hands; with one hand and the other alternately; pull body or body part up, down, or across; pull an object in back of the body (usually implies a forward locomotor movement).

B. *Space Design*—Direction: Pull from forward, upward, sideward, downward.
Level: Pull from a standing level; from kneeling on one or both knees; from sitting squarely on either side; from a prone position.
Dimension: Make short, long, or very long pulls.

C. *Timing:* Pull very slowly, quickly.

D. *Force:* Make strong, heavy pulls; easy, light pulls.

III. Examples of Imagery

Pulling a rope, a rake, a kite, a bell rope, an anchor, a wagon or sled, a boat, another person, in a tug-of-war.

Strike

I. Description

A strike is a strong, propulsive movement of one or both arms in any direction for the purpose of hitting an object. The arms are generally strongly bent to initiate a strike and they extend with force and speed. The feet are spread toward the object to provide a strong base. The hands may be closed or open. The movement is abruptly stopped at its finish, and there is no follow-through. A throw is similar to a strike except that a preparatory swing is made and there is a follow-through after the release.

II. Exploring the Strike

A. *Shape:* Strike with both arms; with one arm; with one arm and then the other alternately; with either leg (as in a kick).

B. *Space Design*—Direction: Strike forward, upward, downward, sideward.
Level: Strike from a sitting or kneeling level.
Dimension: Strike with a long, medium, or short extension.
Timing and Force: To change the timing and force of a strike to any extent will destroy its character as a striking movement.

III. Examples of Imagery

Boxing, beating against a locked door, playing a bass drum, striking with a hammer, an ax, a bat (a preparatory swing is used when striking with most implements).

Dodge

I. Description

A dodge is any forceful, quick movement of the body for the purpose of avoiding a moving object. Although usually only one movement is made at a time, it may involve many parts of the body working in unison.

II. Exploring the Dodge

A. *Shape:* Dodge with a bend, a twist, a drop, a fall, a stretch, a jump, or a combination of any of these movements.

B. *Space Design*—Direction: Dodge backward, forward, sideward, downward.

Level: Dodge from a standing level, from the knees, from a sitting position.

Dimension: Dodge a small or a large object.

C. *Timing and Force:* To change the timing and force of a dodge to any extent will destroy its character as a dodging movement.

III. Examples of Imagery

Dodging a snowball, a falling object, in traffic, in a game of tag or dodge ball, crossing a crowded playground.

Rock and Sway

I. Description

A rocking movement implies a transfer of weight from one part of the body to another by lifting or rolling. Strong tension is maintained in the body parts; hence balance is suspended and almost lost, then regained by a drop back to the starting point. A sway is similar to a rocking movement except that less force is employed and thus the quality of the movement is changed. The body is easy and relaxed, and therefore there is absence of the feeling of suspension present in the rock.

II. Exploring the Rock and Sway

A. *Shape*—Rock: Standing in a sideward stride or a forward and backward stride, transfer weight from one foot to the other continuously. Sitting with arms clasped around knees and feet off floor, transfer weight from buttocks to feet and back continuously. Lying on back with knees bent up to chest, transfer weight from back to buttocks and feet and on to back continuously. Lying on back with arms stretched overhead, transfer weight from one side to the other continuously.

Sway: Standing in a sideward stride or a forward and backward stride, transfer weight gently from one foot to the other, allowing waist and neck to bend and arms to sway with the movement.

B. *Space Design*—Direction and Level: As indicated in the description.

Dimension: Can be slight or as great as the balance will allow.

C. *Timing:* A rock or sway may be done very slowly if the balance can be maintained. As in the swing, if the tempo becomes too fast, the movement will lose its rocking or swaying character.

D. *Force:* See description of rock and sway.

III. Examples of Rock Imagery

Rocking horses, rocking chairs, bells ringing, pushing a swing, riding the waves, Humpty Dumpty, windshield wipers.

Examples of Sway Imagery

Little trees, reeds, flowers, wheat fields, rocking a baby.

Lift

I. Description

A lift transports an object from one place to another in space, generally from a lower to a higher level. It differs from the push and pull in that the object is carried to the new position. The carry may involve locomotor movement. The character of the movement depends upon the object lifted, but it usually calls for a wide stride and bent knees to provide a strong base. The hands and arms are involved in the lifting process, and the knees straighten to assist the upward movement. A lift is also the process of raising the arms, legs, or any body part from a lower to a higher level.

II. Exploring the Lift

A. *Shape:* Lift with one hand, with both hands; lift either leg.

B. *Space Design*—Direction: Lift from down, up; from one side to the other; from up, down; from forward to back; from back to forward.
Dimension: Lift a little or a long way.

C. *Timing:* Lift very slowly; moderately fast.

D. *Force:* Lift something very heavy; something light.

III. Examples of Imagery

Lifting a heavy stone, a big ball, a chair, a snowball, a log, a Christmas tree, a wheelbarrow, a big balloon, a basket, feet with heavy boots, feathers.

Turn

I. Description

A turn is a movement around an axis—and may be a complete circle or a partial one as in a half- or quarter-turn. It may also refer to a rotation or twist of a body part. In the present context a turn is a movement of the total body all the way around toward right or left until the starting position is reached. It may stop there or be repeated many times.

II. Exploring the Turn

A. *Shape:* Turn the body around in self-space by walking, running, jumping, or hopping; by taking very fast, small steps as in "spinning"; by pivoting on one foot and pushing with the other as in the square dance swing; by turning all the way around while airborne from a jump. Turn on the seat or prone on the floor by pushing around with the feet or hands.

B. *Space Design*—Direction: The direction of the turn itself is always clockwise or counterclockwise. While the turn is being made, the body may progress through space in any direction.

Level: Can be changed from a standing to a sitting or prone turn or progress from low to high as in a spiral.

Dimension: Can be increased somewhat by extending arms and/or either leg sideward on the turn.

C. *Timing:* Turn very slowly by walking or pushing around, or very fast by spinning, jumping, or pivoting around.

D. *Force:* The force in any turn is moderate to very strong.

III. Examples of Imagery

Figure skating, smoke, propellers, revolving doors, tape recorders, tops, corkscrews.

Sit

I. Description

A sit transfers the body from any level to the one in which the weight is supported on the buttocks or thighs. While a sit generally means changing from a standing to a sitting position, a sit can also be made from a prone or a kneeling position.

II. Exploring the Sit

A. *Shape:* There are many ways of sitting down on the floor from a standing level with the assistance of the hands. With a little practice, the following can be done without using the hands. The buttocks should be as close as possible to the floor before one sits backward.

Cross the feet, bend the trunk well forward, bend the knees, and sit. Reverse the process to stand.

Bend the trunk forward and bend the knees until sitting on the heels, extend one leg forward, and sit. Reverse the process to stand.

Stand on one foot and lift the other leg across in back of the knee. Bend the supporting knee, kneel on the outside of the rear leg and sit on the thigh on that side. To sit squarely, center the body weight. Reverse the process to stand.

Stand in a side stride position, facing forward. Turn to the back, allowing the feet to pivot but keeping them in the same stride position. The legs should cross above the knees. Bend the knees, keeping the legs crossed, and allow the rear knee to take the weight on the floor. Sit between the feet. Reverse the process to stand by straightening the knees and turning to face forward again.

B. *Space Design*—Direction: Sit downward from a standing or kneeling level; upward from a prone level; do the same in reverse to stand or lie.

Level: The process of sitting involves a change of level from a standing, kneeling, or prone position to a sitting position.

Dimension: The process of sitting from a standing position is necessarily a movement of larger dimension than is sitting from a kneeling position.

C. *Timing:* Sit down or sit up very quickly, at normal speed, very slowly. Use the same or a different timing to stand or lie.

D. *Force:* Sit down or up suddenly and abruptly or easily and smoothly. Stand or lie in the same way or with a change of movement quality.

III. Examples of Imagery

Ferdinand the Bull, Old King Cole, Raggedy Ann, Indians around a campfire, sliding on a slide.

Fall

I. Description

A fall transfers the body from a standing, kneeling, or sitting position to a lying or partially lying position, either prone, supine, on the side, or any combination of these. Although a fall is generally a sudden movement, it may also be a slow, gradual release to the floor. In either case, the body should be as relaxed as possible.

II. Exploring the Fall[1]

A. *Shape:* There are many ways of lowering the body to a lying or partially lying position on the floor. From a standing position—this involves the greatest distance—the following ways are easiest. For safety's sake, the body should be

---

[1] If the body is relaxed, a young child may fall in many ways without harm.

lowered as close as possible to the floor before the weight is shifted from the feet. Also, care should be taken that joints such as the knee, elbow, and base of the spine do not take the full impact of the body weight. Rather the weight should rest first on the thigh, buttocks, or side of the leg.

To lie face up: Using any of the ways described under "Sit" as a preliminary movement, keep the back rounded and continue backward until lying supine on the floor. Reverse the process to stand.

To lie face down: Stand on one leg, lifting the other leg high in back. As the body tilts forward from the backward leg lift, bend the supporting knee, reach forward and downward with the hands, place them on the floor, and lower the body to a lying position by bending the elbows. To stand again, push back to a kneeling position, turn the toes under and straighten the knees; or roll over on the back, sit up, and regain standing position in any of the ways described under "Sit."

To lie on side: Stand on one leg and lift the other leg across in back of the knee. Bend the supporting knee. Kneel on the outside of the rear leg, sit to that side, and continue sideward movement as body is lowered to the floor. The under arm may extend along the floor to support the head, and the other hand may be placed on the floor in front of the chest to aid in balance. To recover to stand, push up to a side-sitting position, kneel on under knee, and stand.

B. *Space Design*—Direction: Fall forward-downward, backward-downward, sideward-downward, as indicated above.

Level: Falling involves a change of level from a standing, kneeling, or sitting position to a lying or partially lying position.

Dimension: Fall from a sit to a half-reclining position; from a reach-stand or a jump to a full lying position.

C. *Timing:* Fall with a sudden collapse or a slow, gradual release; from a run and stop. Use the same or a different timing to recover to stand or sit.

D. *Force:* Fall with a soft, relaxed motion or a sudden, sharp motion. Stand or sit in the same way or with a change of movement quality.

III. Examples of Imagery

Spinning tops, trees chopped down, falling leaves, rag dolls, bowling pins, snowflakes, clowns, melting snowmen, Humpty Dumpty, Jack and Jill.

Chapter Preview

Methods and Materials

Traditional Basic Dance Steps—gallop, slide, skip, waltz run, step-hop, schottische, two-step, polka, waltz balance, waltz, mazurka

> *Analysis*
> *Variations*
> *Suggested Teaching Procedures*
> *Dancing with Others*

Discovering Dance Steps

> *The Combinations of Walks and Hops*
> *The Dance Steps to Rhythmic Patterns*
> *A Dance Step to Triple Meter*
> *The Waltz Complex*

A Step-Hop Trio

DETROIT PUBLIC SCHOOLS

10 Combining Locomotor Movements into Dance Steps

The traditional dance steps such as the gallop, slide, skip, 3/4 or waltz run, step-hop, schottische, two-step, polka, waltz balance, waltz, and mazurka are combinations of basic locomotor movements performed in a characteristic space and time pattern. Most other commonly used dance steps are variations of these. Many annotated folk dances classified according to their use of these steps may be found in Chapter 26.

Because they are used in so many play activities, the gallop, slide, and skip are easily learned by imitation and may well be part of a child's movement experience before he enters school. Guided exploratory experiences may lead to the discovery of the other dance steps. This problem-solving process is described at the end of the chapter. As most of these steps are used by older children in the learning of folk dances, use of this more creative method will be more successful with them.

Because many of the steps are complex in timing and space pattern and are used mainly in moving with others in formal dance patterns, the outlined suggested teaching procedures are primarily teacher-directed. After demonstration of the step, the movement combination is learned by a logical procedure of movements *starting with those the children already know how to do*. The change of time intervals, accent, floor pattern, or the addition of other movements can then be introduced at the appropriate time.

When used for folk dance purposes, the style of the locomotor movement is usually different. For example, the walk, an ingredient of so many dance steps, has a different shape and dimension. Except in rare cases, the dance walk keeps the weight on the *ball of the foot* rather than starting with a heel contact. The length of the walk and also of the run is *relatively short,* so that the body is carried over the feet at most times and balance is easily maintained. Boys particularly need to be helped to shorten their steps. The basic movement should be reviewed with these things emphasized before other procedures are introduced.

A dance step has been learned when its movement sequence can be performed accurately in the proper timing. Style of movement is, of course, an individual matter. Because of natural gifts, some children always move with more spirit, freedom, and grace than others. However, if all can follow the timing of the step and move in accurate sequence, that is sufficient for successful group dancing.

Methods and Materials

Any sequence used for *direct* teaching of a definite movement pattern, whether it is one of those suggested or any other, should observe certain principles of method.

1. When a new element is added to the original movement, it should be thoroughly grasped before one proceeds with the teaching sequence. A movement may be said to be thoroughly grasped when it can be done automatically, with ease and rhythmic precision, several times in succession by a majority of the class.

2. A simple hand response, such as beating time or clapping, should be made to the timing of the step before it is introduced into locomotor movement. As counts, cue words, or signals for movement, such as "step-hop" or "step-together-step," are used in teaching the step, they *always* should follow the timing, whether or not accompaniment is used.

3. In preliminary practice, the class is given a signal by the teacher to start in unison with the enunciated rhythmic cues. Such a signal as *Ready . . . and!* or *begin!* starts the class on the accent. However, when the step has been learned and can be performed individually by the children, it is important that they have the experience of starting "from the music"—imperative when recordings are used. Here they listen to the music, identify the accents, and begin performing the step on the accented beat. When individuals or partners get out of time or out of accent to the music, they should stop, listen to the music, identify the accents, and begin again.

4. Transference and nontransference of weight need special attention. The free foot should always be free of weight when starting a step. It will not be free if the weight is divided between both feet when beginning a step, at the end of a movement phrase, or during a brief pause. Sharp distinction

should be made between stepping (walking), in which the weight is completely shifted to one foot, and touching, tapping, brushing, slapping, or occasionally stamping, in which the weight is not shifted but remains on the supporting foot while the movement is made with the other foot. The difficulties of many beginning teachers and dancers can be traced to this principle.

5. The dance step should be mastered by at least a majority of the group moving individually before the complexity of performing it with a partner or in a unified group is introduced. Otherwise the procedure is not conducive to a harmonious relationship between partners or to the development of self-confidence on the part of the learner.

6. It will be noted that of the eleven dance steps analyzed, the movement combinations of six are performed to a regular series of pulse beats, in groups of two, three, or four beats with one movement to each beat. The result is even timing. The combinations of the other five (gallop, slide, skip, two-step, polka) break up the pulse beat series into unequal parts, resulting in uneven timing, or a series of rhythmic patterns. See Chapters 13 and 14 for additional information on these timing aspects.

For use with younger children (in order of difficulty): gallop, skip, slide, ¾ run, possibly the step-hop and open polka.

The following steps may be successfully combined with basic movements in short phrases of two or more movements, especially those that can be performed to a series of moderate pulse beats (walking beats or quarter notes). The run is not included in these combinations in order that the pulse beat intervals for the different movements may be identical. Examples which can be used in many different sequences are:

Walk, gallop, skip	Skip, jump, walk
Walk, jump, gallop	Walk, hop, step-hop
Gallop, hop, walk	Skip, slide, polka
Slide, gallop, hop	Walk, jump, step-hop

For use with older children (in order of difficulty): step-hop, schottische, waltz hesitation and balance (open position), two-step and polka (open position), mazurka, two-step (closed position), polka (closed position), waltz step (closed position).

After they have learned them, older children should be encouraged to move freely about the room, combining dance steps in the same timing, as that of the 2/4 and 4/4 pulse beats of step-hop and schottische; the 2/4 patterns of two-step and polka; and the 3/4 pulse beats and accents of the waltz balance, mazurka, waltz hesitation, and waltz step.

A word about the open and closed dance positions is in order here. The open position is a side-by-side position with a partner, with inside hands joined or another such contact.[1] It is used in the waltz balance forward and backward, in the "face-to-face and back-to-back" two-step and polka, and in many other ways in folk and ballroom dance. The closed position is a face-to-face place relationship with a partner, with both hands joined or in variations of the waist-shoulder or social dance positions. The partner is not held in a close embrace, necessary for efficient leading of modern ballroom dance. Partners stand some inches apart; and in the two-step and polka, steps which turn continually, the boy stands somewhat to the left of the girl. In the country dance "swing," the boy, although facing his partner, stands well to his left, so that the right shoulders of the couple are together.

Most folk and country dances that are usable for children consist of one or two of these basic steps put into simple partner or group figures. They can be taught with a maximum of ease and satisfaction and a minimum of routine drill if the basic step is already an integral part of the children's dance repertoire and if workable patterns and figures in which it can be used have already been explored.

Of the eleven dance steps analyzed in the following outlines (which are similar to those used in the preceding chapters), the first five are simple movement combinations. It is conceivable that detailed analyses of their components will confuse rather than clarify. After all, a *gallop* is a walk and a run, with one foot always leading and the other always catching up. A *slide* is a gallop done sideward. A *skip* is a walk and a hop, with the walk taking more time than the hop. A 3/4 *run* is a series of three runs, with a stress on the first one. A *step-hop* is a walk plus a hop and is different from a skip in that both movements are equal in timing.

Nevertheless, those who delve more deeply into the teaching of dance should know exactly how the body moves to produce these steps, and what variations are possible in their performance. Only then will they be able to talk the language of dance movement more intelligently and begin to perceive the infinite abundance of its similarities and differences.

Traditional Basic Dance Steps

Gallop

I. Analysis of the Basic Gallop

A gallop is a combination of a walk and a run.

A. *Space Design:* The walk is taken forward with one foot; this provides the takeoff for the run (from the same foot) which lifts the body into the air. The

---

[1] See Chapter 23 for other place relationships and partner contacts.

landing of the run is made on the other (rear) foot in the place where the walk was taken, not beyond it. The characteristic that makes the gallop different from a free combination of a walk·and a run is this step-together floor pattern.

B. *Timing:* The accent in the gallop is on the walk, which is the takeoff for the run. Actually in a series of gallops the run becomes a sort of preparatory movement adding emphasis to the accent of the walk. When beginning a series of gallops it is easier to begin with the accent, that is, to make the first movement of the series the walk rather than the run.

Because of its walk-run combination, the timing of the gallop is uneven. It is best performed to music in 6/8 meter, with the long and short timing alternated as shown below.

W   R W R   W R W R

(It must be remembered that the notes on which the walk and run appear represent the end of these movements, and the takeoff into the next movement.)

II. Some Variations of the Gallop

A. *Changes in Space Design*—Direction: A gallop may also be done in place, backward, sideward, or turning around.

A sideward gallop is usually what is meant by a slide.

A turning gallop with the leading foot kept in the same place and acting as a pivoting center can lead into the *buzz step* used for swinging partners in certain styles of American country dance. In the buzz step, the run of the gallop becomes a walking push-off into the pivoting center step.

Dimension and Level: A gallop may be done with longer or shorter steps than are commonly used. It may also be done with a low run and a long walking step, which lowers the natural level, or with a high run and a short walking step, which raises the natural level.

B. *Changes in Timing:* If the gallop is high, the run takes the body some distance into the air and therefore uses more time than the walk. If it is low and long, the walk uses more time than the run.

III. Suggested Teaching Procedure for the Gallop

A gallop is best learned by imitation or by moving with another person who can gallop. Join hands with the learner on the side on which he will start the gallop. Then, using the same foot, gallop forward with him, helping him to lift up on the run. Since it is much more difficult to gallop in place or backward than forward, variations in direction should not be attempted when the gallop is first being done.

IV. Galloping with Others

With one other person: One in back of the other, both facing forward, both hands joined, galloping forward or in place.

With two other persons: Two in front and one in back or vice versa, all facing forward, hands joined around a circle, galloping forward or in place.

With three other persons: Two in front and two in back, all facing forward, hands joined around a circle, galloping forward or in place.

Slide

I. Analysis of the Basic Slide

A slide is usually a gallop done sideward. The term *slide* was derived from the movement when it was performed as two walking steps taken sideward in a step-together pattern instead of as a walk and a run. There was no lift of the body from the floor, and the walking steps were taken in a gliding or sliding movement. This kind of slide is no longer characteristic of the slide used by children.

The analysis of the gallop, its uneven timing, and its variations apply as well to the slide, except that the direction is always sideward.

II. Suggested Teaching Procedure for the Slide

Like the gallop, the slide may be learned by imitation or by moving with another person who can slide. Face the person, join both hands, and move sideward with him.

III. Sliding with Others

With one other person: Facing, both hands joined, arms extended toward the other person or sideward, sliding sideward in the line of direction or turning around; one behind the other and facing in the same direction, hands joined and arms extended sideward, sliding sideward in the line of direction.

With many other persons: Hands joined in a circle, facing toward or away from the center, sliding around the circle.

Skip

I. Analysis of the Basic Skip

A skip is a combination of a hop and a walk.

A. *Space Design:* The walk is taken forward with one foot; this provides the takeoff for the hop which lifts the body into the air. The landing is made on the same foot; the other foot then steps forward into the next walk or second skipping step. The hop provides momentum for a strong walking takeoff into the next hop and gives this form of dance locomotion its characteristic lilting quality.

Learning a Polka

B. *Timing:* The accent of the skip is on the walk, the takeoff for the hop and the uneven time pattern of the skip, slide, and gallop is identical.

The basic skip, like the gallop, is best performed to music in 6/8 meter.

W   HW H   W HW H

(It must be remembered that the notes on which the walk and hop appear represent the end of these movements and the takeoff into the next movement.)

II. Some Variations of the Skip

A. *Changes in Shape*—Feet and Legs: Skipping on tiptoe; free knee bent up high in front on the hop; free leg swinging out to the side on the hop; legs crossing in front or in back as the walk is taken.

Arms: Arms folded in front of chest; hands clasped behind back; arms swinging out on one skip, in on the next.

Body Position: Body crouched low; back arched strongly on every other skip (the latter movement combines well with the in-and-out arm swing).

B. *Changes in Space Design*—Direction: A skip may be done backward, sideward, turning around, and in place. When skipping sideward one foot may be brought up to the other in a closed position, or it may cross in front, in back, or alternately in front and back.

Dimension and Level: A skip may be done with longer or shorter steps than are commonly used. It may also be done with a low hop and a long walking step, which lowers the natural level, or with a high hop and a short walking step, which raises the natural level.

C. *Changes in Timing:* If the skip is high, the hop takes the body some distance into the air and therefore uses more time than the walk. If it is low and long, the walk uses more time than the hop.

III. Suggested Teaching Procedure for the Skip

A skip may be learned by imitation or by moving with another person who can skip. Often little children can skip with one foot but not the other. A child can be helped to skip on both feet by having a partner join hands with him on the side on which he cannot hop, so that the partner's lift is communicated. It is much more difficult to skip in place or backward than forward, and therefore variations in direction should not be attempted when the skip is first being tried.

IV. Skipping with Others

With one other person: Skipping forward side by side, with inside hands joined; with hands extended across next person and joined; with arms linked;

with arms around each other's waists. Turning around, facing with both hands joined or hands crossed and joined; with right or left sides together, inside arms linked or inside hands joined.

With two or three other persons: Skipping forward side by side, with inside hands joined; with hands extended across next person and joined; with arms linked; with arms around each other's waists. Turning around, facing around a circle, hands joined; with right or left shoulders toward the center, inside hands joined at the center.

With many other persons: Facing around a circle, hands joined; side by side or one behind the other in a line, hands joined.

¾ Run or Waltz Run

I. Analysis of the Basic 3/4 Run

The 3/4 run is a combination of three runs done to music in 3/4 meter.

A. *Space Design:* A basic 3/4 run is a series of running steps done to rather fast music in 3/4 meter. In the more elaborate version the first run is accented more than the other two because of the following movements: After the third run the body is lifted higher into the air so that the landing into the first run is more accented than in the other two runs; the body leans in the direction of the foot with which the first run is taken. The fact that the accent of the 3/4 run occurs first on one foot and then on the other gives this step its characteristic swaying quality.

B. *Timing:* The 3/4 run is done to the three beats of an accompaniment in 3/4 meter. The three runs have the same relative time value; this makes the intervals in the 3/4 run equal and the timing triple.

The accent of the 3/4 run is on the first run.

R   R   R   R   R   R

II. Some Variations of the 3/4 Run

The most common variation of the 3/4 run is in the direction, which may be backward, turning, or in place. Also, the arms may be extended sideward or swung from side to side.

III. Suggested Teaching Procedures for the 3/4 Run

1. Listen to well-accented music or drumbeats in fast 3/4 meter.
2. Make a hand response to the beats with a downbeat on the first.

3. Run in place to all three beats.
4. Run forward to the accompaniment, keeping in time with the pulse beats. This is a simple version of the 3/4 run and should be mastered before the sideward sway on the accent is added.
5. Sit on the floor and sway from side to side in time to the accents of the accompaniment, somewhat retarded in tempo.
6. Make a hand response to the accents only.
7. With the tempo of the accompaniment still retarded, walk in a zigzag line down the floor, three steps to the right beginning with the right foot, then three steps to the left beginning with the left foot. The pivot toward the new direction occurs on the third step. It is important to keep time to the pulse beats, to accent the first step in the new direction, and to take short steps.
8. Gradually increase the tempo to that of a run. When running, it will be found that a bigger run is necessary to negotiate the turn from one diagonal direction to the other. This affects the accent and sideward sway which characterize the elaborated 3/4 run.
9. Practice it forward, decreasing the extent of the diagonal direction.
10. Try it with a partner and in groups, experimenting with the different formations and directions listed in IV.

IV. Dancing the 3/4 Run with Others

With one other person: Side by side, inside hands joined or arms linked, moving forward.

With two other persons: Side by side, inside hands joined or arms linked; with one in front and two in back or vice versa, facing forward, hands joined around a circle. (See galloping with two or three other persons.)

With many other persons: In a circle, hands joined, facing toward center, moving forward and backward; facing around the circle, moving forward; in a line, side by side or one behind the other, hands joined, moving forward.

Step-Hop

I. Analysis of the Basic Step-Hop

The step-hop is a combination of a walk and a hop, usually performed in a forward direction.

A. *Space Design:* The walk is taken forward with a strongly accented movement; this provides the takeoff for the hop, which is done in place. The free foot in the hop is bent under the body. When the step is repeated, it begins with the alternate foot.

B. *Timing:* The two movements in the step-hop are done to the two beats of an accompaniment in 2/4 meter. The walk and the hop have the same relative time value, making the intervals in the step-hop equal and the timing duple.

The accent in the step-hop is on the walk or step.

W   H   W   H

II. Some Variations of the Step-Hop

A. *Changes in Shape*—Feet and Legs: The walk in a step-hop may be changed to a run, making a more vigorous and springing movement throughout. In this variation the hop as well as the run covers space.

The free leg in a step-hop can be lifted forward, sideward, or backward as the hop is performed; the knee and ankle can be bent up and out to the side, or upward in front; the free leg can be swung forward across the supporting leg. The latter movement is sometimes called the *step-swing* and is similar to the balance used in some types of American country dance.

Arms: The arms can be folded on the chest; the hands clasped behind the back; the arms extended sideward (helpful when lifting the free leg sideward).

Body Position: The back can be arched on each hop with the free leg lifted backward, and the walk taken with a sliding movement forward. This movement is sometimes known as the *slide-hop*.

B. *Changes in Space Design*—Direction: A step-hop may also be done in place, backward, sideward, or turning.

C. *Changes in Timing:* A step-hop can be done to triple time (3/4 meter) in the following ways: Making the step twice as long as the hop, as in step, hold, hop; doing another movement with the free foot between the step and the hop, such as a tap of the toe in front or in back, a brush of the heel forward, a slap backward with the ball of the foot, a kick sideward, and the like. In no case is the weight transferred to the free foot as it takes this extra movement. The step-brush-hop is a variation of the step-hop that is sometimes known as the *Dutch step*.

III. Suggested Teaching Procedures for the Step-Hop

1. Listen to well-accented music or drumbeats in 2/4 meter.
2. Make a hand response with a downbeat on the accents.
3. Stand in place and step on the accent only with one foot and then the other, repeating several times. Lift the free foot well off the floor.
4. Continue stepping on the accent and take the second beat with a slight bounce on the supporting foot as the free foot is lifted.
5. Increase the bounce until it becomes a hop, keeping the step well accented. This is the *step-hop.*

6. Start the step-hop in place and then move forward.
7. Start the step-hop in place and then move backward.
8. Start the step-hop in place and then turn around.
9. While doing the step-hop, experiment with lifting the free leg forward; swinging the free leg across the supporting leg; lifting the free leg directly sideward with a straight knee, and then with a bent knee and flexed ankle; lifting the free foot backward.
10. Try the step-hop with a partner and in groups experimenting with the different ways of moving listed in IV and using step variations. (It is very easy when performing the step-hop to be in time with the music but out of accent with it. Make sure that the step of the step-hop matches the accent in the music.)

IV. Dancing the Step-Hop with Others

With one other person: Side by side, inside hands joined or arms linked, moving forward or backward, using the step-hop or step-swing. Facing, both hands joined, moving in place, turning around, or one moving forward and the other backward with feet on the same side, using the step-hop or step-swing. Facing, both hands joined and arms extended sideward, moving in place or turning around, using feet on the same side and a side lift of leg.

With many other persons: In a circle, hands joined, moving forward and backward; facing in the line of direction and moving around circle. In a line with hands joined, moving forward side by side, using the step-hop or step-swing. In a line one behind the other, with hands joined or one hand on the shoulder of the person in front, moving forward.

Schottische

I. Analysis of the Schottische

The schottische is a combination of three short running steps and a hop, usually performed in a forward direction.

A. *Space Design:* The three runnings steps are taken forward with an accent on the first run. The hop is done on the foot which takes the third run. The free foot on the hop is bent under the body. When the step is repeated, it begins with the alternate foot.

B. *Timing:* The movements are done to an accompaniment in 4/4 meter. The runs and the hop have the same time value, making the intervals in the schottische equal and the timing duple.

The accent is on the first run, with a secondary accent on the third.

R R R H   R R R H

II. Some Variations of the Schottische

A. *Changes in Shape*—Legs: The free leg may be swung forward and across the supporting leg on the hop, as in the step-swing variation of the step-hop. The three running steps may be changed to three walking steps. The walking or running steps may be done in a step-together-step pattern, rather than all three steps being taken directly forward or backward. When progress is sideward, a step-together-step or a step-cross-step pattern may be used, the crossing being made in front or in back.

B. *Changes in Space Design*—Direction: A schottische may also be done in place, backward, sideward, and turning around. The sideward schottische is a common variation.

III. Suggested Teaching Procedures for the Schottische

1. Listen to well-accented music or drumbeats in 4/4 meter.
2. Clap to the first three beats, lifting the hands on the fourth beat.
3. Walk the first three beats in place using the fourth to lift the free foot high off the floor, as step-step-step-lift.
4. Continue walking in place and bounce slightly on the supporting foot as the free foot is lifted high on the fourth beat.
5. Increase the bounce to a hop which lifts the body off the floor on the fourth beat.
6. Add more spring to the first three steps until the walking steps have the quality of a run without elevation.
7. Perform in place and then gradually move forward on the running steps. This is the forward *schottische* step.
8. Perform in place and then gradually move backward, or sideward using a step-together-step or a step-cross-step for the three sideward walks.
9. Swing the free leg forward and across the supporting leg when performing the hop instead of bending it under the body.
10. Try it in combination with step-hops: one schottische and two step-hops, or two schottisches and four step-hops.
11. Try it with a partner and in groups experimenting with the ways of moving listed in IV and using step variations.

IV. Dancing the Schottische with Others

With one other person: Side by side, inside hands joined; inside hands extended across the next person and joined, or inside hands on each other's shoulders or around each other's waists, moving forward, backward, or from side to side. Right or left shoulders together, arms linked or inside hands joined, turning around. Facing, both hands joined, moving in place, turning around, or one moving forward and the other backward, using feet on the same side.

With many other persons: In a circle, hands joined, facing in the line of direction, moving around the circle. In a line side by side, hands joined, moving forward or sideward. In a line one behind the other, with hands joined or one hand on the shoulder of the person in front, moving forward.

Two-Step

I. Analysis of the Basic Two-Step

The two-step is a combination of three walking steps, usually performed in a sideward direction, progress through space being made by body turns.

A. *Space Design:* The first walk is taken sideward, with the outside edge of the foot leading; the position of the feet is open. The second walk brings the feet together into a closed position. The third walk is taken in the same direction as the first, ending the combination in an open position which is held for the fourth beat. In a series of two-steps, progression through space is accomplished by turning the body from side to side. Thus the outside of one foot leads forward on one two-step and the outside of the other on the next. The body may turn to one side and then back to the other (like a hinge), or continually in the same direction (like a top).

B. *Timing:* The two-step is done to one equally divided and one undivided pulse interval in 2/4 meter. The first two walking steps have the same relative timing, and the third is twice as long as the first two.

The accent is on the first walk, with a secondary accent on the third. The word cues are step-together-step-hold, resulting in three movements in uneven timing. Hence the two-step uses a rhythmic pattern rather than a series of pulse beats.

II. Some Variations of the Two-Step

A. *Changes in Shape*—Legs: The first walking step of the two-step may be changed to a run or a spring to the side, the next two steps being taken beside it with the feet kept close to the floor. This is similar to the *single* or *set* used in

English country dancing, particularly when performed in the variation of the natural timing described in the paragraph below.

A similar variation is the *balance* used in some American square and long-ways dance; it is like the English *single* but substitutes a short step sideward for the spring. (Another version of the balance step is like the step-hop and merely lifts the free foot a short distance off the floor with a gentle bounce on the supporting foot.) A balletic derivation of the two-step is the *pas de bas,* in which the second step of the *single* described above is taken in front of the first springing step instead of beside it, finishing with the third step in place.

B. *Changes in Space Design*—Direction: A two-step may be done directly forward, the first step taken each time forward rather than sideward. It may be done backward in the same fashion. The side-to-side direction of the two-step, progress through space being made by a series of body turns, should be considered the natural direction of the two-step, rather than a variation.

C. *Changes in Timing:* The first pulse interval of the two-step may be divided unequally, making the first part twice as long as the second, as in the skip timing.

III. Suggested Teaching Procedures for the Two-Step

1. Listen to music in 2/4 meter.
2. Make a hand response in the two-step pattern to the music, such as clap, clap, clap, hold.
3. Stand and step the pattern in place several times, accenting the first step of the three and making sure there is a pause after the third step.
4. Take the first accented step of the three steps a short distance sideward and the other two steps next to it, making a step-together-step floor pattern. After the hold, repeat to the opposite side.
5. Do this several times from side to side, accenting the first step into the open position, until the step-together-step-hold, step-together-step-hold becomes automatic. This is the *two-step* done in place.
6. Start doing the two-step in place and then gradually move forward by turning the right shoulder and the outside of the right foot diagonally toward the front for the first two-step and repeating with the left shoulder and left foot for the second two-step. Increase the range of these turns until the swing is halfway to the right for one two-step and halfway to the left for the next. This is the *hinge* turn using the two-step. Try doing it the same way moving backward.
7. To practice the hinge turn, stand beside a partner and join inside hands. Starting with the outside feet, take one two-step and at the same time swing the joined hands back and come to a face-to-face position with partner. Follow with another two-step starting with the inside feet and swing the joined hands forward to come to a back-to-back position with partner. Continue face-to-face and back-to-back, using a two-step for each

position and progressing forward with hinge turns. This is the *face-to-face, back-to-back two-step.*

8. Standing alone again, face the front and do a two-step to the left side. Turn a quarter-turn to the right and do a two-step to the right side. Turn again a quarter-turn to the right and do a two-step to the left side. Repeat the turn once again to the right and do one more two-step to the right side. A *square* will have been described facing first the front wall, then the right wall, then the back wall, then the left wall; the quarter-turn each time is to the right. Try starting with the right foot but making quarter-turns to the right in the same way as before. When leading the two-step in the social dance position the boy starts with the left foot and the girl with the right, but both normally make continuous turns to the right clockwise.

9. Do the progression just described, but instead of making quarter-turns to the right, make a half-turn, so that progress is continuous on a straight line instead of turning back on itself as in the square, or swinging from side to side as in the hinge. This is a true spiral or *top* turn that moves continuously clockwise. Space orientation may be difficult at first in learning these turns and it may be well to let the children walk them out before using the two-step as a unit of movement.

10. Dance the two-step alone freely around the room, doing it from side to side in place, with the hinge turn, the square, and the top turn.

11. Try leading a partner in all the ways listed above and in IV.

IV. Dancing the Two-Step with Others

With one other person: Side by side, inside hands joined, starting with outside feet and moving forward in a series of face-to-face, back-to-back turns, swinging joined hands backward for the face-to-face two-step and forward for the back-to-back two-step. Facing, with both hands joined, starting with the feet on the same side, one moving forward and the other backward with a series of diagonal or hinge turns. Facing, with hands on each other's elbows, turning always in the same direction with quarter-turns, forming a square with a two-step on each side. Facing, in waist-shoulder or closed social dance position, moving in all directions with a series of hinge turns and top turns.

Polka

I. Analysis of the Basic Polka

The polka is a combination of a hop and three springy walking steps done on the balls of the feet. It is usually performed sideward.

A. *Space Design:* The hop serves as a preliminary lift for the first walking step; this is taken sideward with the outside edge of the foot leading. The second walk brings the feet together into a closed position. The third walk is taken in the same direction as the first, ending the combination in an open position which is held for part of the fourth count. The space pattern of the three walking steps is identical to that of the two-step. In a series of polka steps, progression through space is accomplished by turning the body from side to side so that the outside of one foot leads forward, then the outside of the other. The turns may be performed in a sequence in which the body turns to one side and then back to the other, or a sequence in which the body turns continually in the same direction. Quarter- or half-turns may be used.

B. *Timing:* The polka is done to one equally divided and one unequally divided pulse interval in 2/4 meter. The first two walking steps have the same relative timing, the third walking step is usually one and one-half times as long as the first two, and the landing of the hop and the takeoff into the first walk is half as long.

Because the accent in the polka falls on the first walking step, and the hop is a means of emphasizing this accent, the hop is actually the beginning of the polka, serving as an anacrusis or upbeat. It bears the same time relationship to the first walking step that the hop does to the walk in the skip, and the run does to the walk in the gallop. It is easier, however, when starting a series of polkas to begin with the accent, that is, to make the first movement a step, rather than a hop. Like the two-step, the polka uses a rhythmic pattern rather than a pulse beat series.

H   W   W   W   H   W   W   W

II. Some Variations of the Polka

A. *Changes in Space Design*—Direction: A polka may be done directly forward—the first step taken forward rather than sideward—or backward. The side-to-side direction of the polka, with progress through space being made by a series of body turns, should be considered the natural direction of the polka, rather than a variation.

B. *Change in Timing:* As in the two-step, the timing of the first and third walking steps may be made identical—twice as long as the timing of the second walking step and the hop. This time pattern is the same as that of a slide plus a skip.

III. Suggested Teaching Procedures for the Polka

A. *For Younger Children*
1. Listen to music for sliding and make a hand response to the beats.
2. Slide around the room, facing the center, with short slides.
3. At any point during the sliding, but without stopping the movement, turn

to face the outside of the room and continue to slide in the same direction. It is important that the turn to the outside be made with a hop which lifts the body off the floor rather than merely a pivot which maintains contact with the floor. Change back to face the center in the same way, still sliding in the same direction. Do this several times at will, until the change from sliding facing in to sliding facing out is made with a good lift off the floor as in a skip.

4. Slide eight times facing in and eight times facing out, turning with a good lift on the eighth step. Accent the first step after the change.

5. Repeat the preceding with three slides, turning with a skip on the fourth step. Then try one complete slide and a skip turn. The latter may be cued as slide-and-change. This is the *polka* performed in the timing described under variations. It is easily learned by children who can slide and skip well. It can be taught to younger children but should not be attempted with partners except possibly in the open face-to-face, back-to-back position.

B. *For Older Children*
1. Listen to polka music in 2/4 meter.
2. With a partner, side by side with inside hands joined, review the face-to-face, back-to-back two-step described in III, 7, under Two-Step.
3. As the clasped hands are swung back and forth in this partner pattern of the two-step, make the swing vigorous enough to lift the body off the sup-

Feeling the Waltz Balance

porting foot which is pivoting for the turn. Make sure that this lift or hop immediately precedes the first step of the combination and is done for the purpose of stressing its accent, not merely a hop at the end of the combination with the same time value as each walking step. This is the *face-to-face, back-to-back polka.*

4. Do the same thing, moving with a partner but not joining hands.
5. Do the polka alone, progressing forward with hinge turns, leading with the right shoulder and then with the left.
6. Do the polka in a square, as described in teaching procedures for the two-step (III, 8, under Two-Step).
7. Do the polka with top turns, as described for the two-step in III, 9.
8. Dance the polka alone, using the hinge turn, the square, and the top turn; when traffic prevents progress through space, do it in place.
9. Try leading a partner in all the ways listed above and in IV.

IV. Dancing the Polka with Others

With one other person: Side by side, with inside hands joined, starting with the outside feet and moving forward in a series of face-to-face, back-to-back turns, swinging joined hands backward for the face-to-face polka and forward for the back-to-back polka. Facing, with both hands joined, starting with the feet on the same side, one moving forward and the other backward with a series of diagonal or hinge turns. Facing, with hands on each other's elbows, turning always in the same direction with quarter-turns, forming a square with a polka on each side. Facing, in waist-shoulder or closed social dance position, moving in all directions with a series of hinge turns, and top turns.

Waltz Balance

I. Analysis of the Basic Waltz Balance

The waltz balance is a combination of three walking steps.

A. *Space Design:* The first walking step is a relatively long step taken either forward or backward; the second step is merely a shifting of the weight onto the ball of the other foot close beside the first step; the third step is another shift of weight onto the ball of the first foot close beside the second step. Only the first step moves backward or forward in space. The other two steps are taken in place beside the first step and high on the balls of the feet.

B. *Timing:* The waltz balance is done to the three beats of an accompaniment in 3/4 meter. The steps have the same time value, so the intervals in the waltz balance are equal and the timing is triple.

The accent in the waltz balance is on the first walking step.

W W W   W W W

II. Some Variations of the Waltz Balance

A. *Changes in Shape*—Arms: The arms may be swung forward and backward as the waltz balances are taken forward and backward; or from side to side as they are taken from side to side.

B. *Changes in Space Design*—Direction: The waltz balance may be performed continuously forward, continuously backward, forward and backward by taking one waltz balance forward and one backward in a continuing sequence, or turning around by turning the body on steps two and three. It may also be performed sideward, taking one waltz balance to one side and the next to the other side.

III. Suggested Teaching Procedures for the Waltz Walk, Waltz Hesitation, and Waltz Balance

1. Listen to waltz music. Sway from side to side on the accents.
2. Make a hand response to all three beats with a downbeat on the accent.
3. Walk continuously in any direction to the beats, taking a slightly longer step on the first but moving ahead on all three. This is the *waltz walk*.
4. Step all three beats in place, using the whole foot for the first step and the balls of the feet for the second and third steps.
5. Step a rather long step forward on the accent only and step backward similarly on the next accent. Continue, bringing the free foot up to the stepping foot without shifting the weight on it. (It is an aid in stepping forward and backward on the accent if hands joined side by side in short lines are swung forward and backward with the steps.) This single step on the accent only is sometimes called the *waltz hesitation*.
6. Step all three beats, stepping forward on the first beat, and stepping the other beats in place on the balls of the feet next to the first step. Repeat the same backward. This is the forward and backward *waltz balance*.
7. Do procedure 6 moving from side to side. This is the sideward waltz balance.
8. Move continuously forward by taking the first step forward, and taking steps two and three in place on the balls of the feet next to the first step. Do the same moving continuously backward.
9. Step on the accents only, maintaining the forward and backward direction but gradually turning in the direction of the forward-going foot.
10. Do procedure 9, stepping all three beats as in the waltz balance, maintaining the forward and backward direction on the first steps but turning on steps two and three. This is the waltz balance turn.

11. Dance the waltz balance forward and backward, continuously forward and backward, and turning around, moving freely about the room.
12. Try it with a partner and a group experimenting with the ways listed in IV.

IV. Dancing the Waltz Balance with Others

With one other person: Side by side, inside hands joined, using forward and backward waltz balances and swinging joined hands forward and backward; or sideward waltz balances, swinging arms from side to side; in closed social dance position, moving forward and backward, continuously forward or continuously backward, or turning around.

With two or more persons: Side by side in a line or circle with inside hands joined, using forward and backward waltz balances and swinging joined hands forward and backward.

Waltz

I. Analysis of the Basic Waltz

The waltz is a combination of three walking steps.

A. *Space Design:* The first walking step is a relatively long one taken either forward or backward and resulting in an open position of the feet. The second step is a short step taken in a sideward direction with the other foot and resulting in a second open position of the feet. The third step, taken with the first foot, brings the feet together, ending the combination in a closed position of the feet. A variation of this space design is necessary when turning around.

B. *Timing:* The waltz is done to three beats of an accompaniment in 3/4 meter. The three walking steps have the same relative time value, making the intervals in the waltz equal and the timing triple.

The accent in the waltz is on the first walking step.

II. Some Variations of the Waltz

A. *Changes in Shape*—Legs: The waltz can be done with a rather decided bend of the knee and a glide into the first step, with a slight sway of the body in the direction of the step. When the tempo of the waltz is increased somewhat, and the steps shortened, this swaying, lilting, down-up-up movement results in the style of waltz known as *Viennese*.

The first walking step may be changed to a light run and the second and third steps performed with such an increased spring that they approach running steps. In this variation the dimension of the steps is considerably decreased, the tempo is considerably increased, and the feet do not necessarily close on the third step. Fast progress through space is made in a series of turns. This style of waltz is known as the *peasant* waltz.

B. *Changes in Space Design*—Direction: A series of waltz steps may be performed forward and backward or continuously forward and continuously backward. Although the first step of the waltz is always taken directly forward or backward, a pivot may be made on the foot as the step is taken so that the second and third steps can move sideward in a new direction. This results in a *waltz turn*.

C. *Changes in Timing:* The natural timing of the waltz is a rather slow triple measure, but the tempo can be increased slightly as in the Viennese waltz, or considerably as in the peasant waltz.

III. Suggested Teaching Procedures for the Waltz

1. Review the teaching procedure for the forward and backward waltz balance.
2. Step forward with a slightly long step on the first beat; then, instead of stepping in place as in the waltz balance, take a short step sideward on the second beat. Then step together in a closed position on the third beat, completely shifting weight on each step. These three steps may be described as forward-side-together. This is the forward waltz step.
3. Step backward with the opposite foot to that used to step forward in procedure 2; take a short step sideward; step together in a closed position. These three steps—backward-side-together—form the backward waltz. The forward and backward waltz performed together make an oblong box pattern on the floor. This is called the *box* waltz.
4. Do the box waltz continuously several times. Start the forward waltz with the left foot and then the right.
5. Do the waltz step moving continuously forward on the first step instead of forward and backward; then continuously backward.
6. Review the waltz balance, turning around. Do the forward and backward waltz steps, turning by using the longer step forward to pivot and the side step and step-together to complete the turn. The turn should be made gradually at first and then with increased dimension.
7. Dance the waltz forward and backward, continuously forward, continuously backward and turning, moving freely about the room.
8. Face a partner, each taking hold of the other's elbows. Dance the waltz in all the above ways, first one way at a time, then combining them.
9. Dance the waltz with a partner in the ways listed in IV.

IV. Dancing the Waltz with Others

With one other person: Facing, in closed social dance or waist-shoulder position, moving forward and backward, continuously forward or continuously backward or turning around. Try variations in timing as in the Viennese and peasant styles.

Mazurka

I. Analysis of the Basic Mazurka

The mazurka is a combination of two springy walking steps and a hop.

A. *Space Design:* In the simplest form of the mazurka, the two walking steps are taken forward and the hop is taken after the second walking step and on the same foot. In the hop the free leg is bent under the body.

B. *Timing:* The mazurka is done to an accompaniment in 3/4 meter.

The two walking steps and the hop have the same relative time value, making the intervals in the mazurka equal and the timing triple.

The accent in the mazurka is on the first walking step, with a characteristic secondary accent on the second walking step.

II. Some Variations of the Mazurka

A. *Changes in Shape*—Legs: Two running steps may be substituted for the walking steps. This is a common variation.

Arms: In the sideward-moving mazurka the arm in the line of direction may be extended in that direction or placed on the leading hip, the other arm being extended overhead.

B. *Changes in Space Design*—Direction: The basic mazurka may be done in place, backward, and turning. In a common variation the body is turned sideward with the shoulder leading in the line of direction. The first walking step is taken sideward, but with the toe rather than the side of the foot leading in the line of direction. The second walking step, which brings the feet together in closed position, is taken with the inside of the second foot leading into the closed position. The second step provides the takeoff for the hop, which, on repetition of the step, leads again into the first walking step and serves to emphasize it. In a more elaborate version the free leg is extended forward with a straight knee as the second step cuts in behind, and then is bent sharply while the hop is taken. This is difficult for children to learn.

III. Suggested Teaching Procedures for the Mazurka

1. Listen to mazurka music.
2. Clap the first and second beats only, accenting the second slightly more than the first; lift the hands on the third beat.
3. Walk in place to the first and second beats, lifting the knee of the free foot on the third beat.
4. Increase the lift on the third count until the lift becomes a bounce and then a hop on the supporting foot.
5. Do the walk-walk-hop in place several times with springy steps; note that the accent always occurs on the same foot. This is the basic *mazurka*.
6. Do the mazurka in place and then forward.
7. Increase the spring of the walking steps until they become runs as in the running variation.
8. Try the mazurka moving backward and turning around.
9. Try it with a partner experimenting with different directions and the turn suggested in IV.
10. Try the sideward-moving variation alone as in II, B; then in the ways listed in IV.

IV. Dancing the Mazurka with Others

With one other person: Using the basic mazurka, with right or left sides together, inside arms linked, and the other arm extended overhead, turning around. Using the sideward-moving mazurka, facing, hands joined away from the line of direction of the step, other hands on hips or extended sideward, starting with the feet on the same side; one in back of the other and facing in the same direction, arms extended sideward and hands joined, starting with the feet on the same side and moving sideward.

With many other persons: In a circle, hands joined, moving around the circle with the basic or sideward-moving mazurka.

Discovering Dance Steps[2]

Children can discover dance steps by exploring movement combinations suggested to them. In this problem-solving activity the components of the steps and their sequential patterns are better recognized and understood than through complete teacher direction and imitation.

As dance steps are almost always used with a musical accompaniment, it

[2] Most of these activities are designed for older children with experience in exploring movement.

is important that a constant pulse beat be kept in mind during the exploration process. The teacher can provide this with a drum or other percussion instrument or can clap or count every now and then to keep the children on the beat. After the step has been discovered and learned by most of the class, it should be correctly identified and danced to suitable music. Often doing the steps to music helps children who may be having difficulty mastering the combination. In every situation children who have discovered the step may help others, if no objection is expressed.

The Combinations of Walks and Hops

The step-hop, mazurka, and schottische can all evolve from the following activities.

Have the children:
1. Walk in place and forward with short, springy steps in time to a moderately quick walking accompaniment.
2. Hop in place and forward on one foot and then the other, changing feet often.
3. Make their own short combination of walks and hops, in place at first, and then forward continuously using only a few of each step.
4. Try to make a combination of walks and hops which fits into *two* counts, with the first count somewhat accented. (Obviously, it can only be one walk and one hop, rather than a hop and a walk, as a hop rarely takes an accent in a dance step.) This is the *step-hop.* It should be explored in place, forward, in all other directions, and turning. (See other variations under Step-Hop in this chapter.)
5. Make a combination of walks and hops which fits into three counts, with the first and second counts somewhat accented. (Several legitimate combinations will be presented, but as the third count is not accented, the walk, walk, hop or *mazurka* will be judged correct, and those who discovered it can help others learn it.)
6. Discover that the mazurka always starts on the same foot, so find ways of changing to the other foot to continue a mazurka series. (Taking three walks in place is the easiest way.)
7. Explore the mazurka alone in place, forward, sideward, and turning a partner with arms linked. (See other variations under Mazurka in this chapter.)
8. Make a combination of walks and hops which fits into *four* counts, with the first and third somewhat accented. (Again legitimate combinations will be presented and should be commended. Some children, however, will have discovered the *schottische,* which is a springy walk, walk, walk, hop,

and all can learn this combination of movements by helping each other.)
9. Explore the schottische in place, forward, sideward, and moving with a partner. (See other variations under Schottische in this chapter.)

The Dance Steps to Rhythmic Patterns

The *two-step* can evolve from the following activities.

Have the children:

1. To four moderately fast walking beats, take three walks in place, *holding* the fourth beat, and repeat this sequence several times. Discover that the rhythmic pattern is quick-quick-slow and that the opposite foot begins each three steps.
2. Try an open-close-open-hold floor pattern. (Open: one foot steps a short distance away; close: the other foot steps up to it transferring weight; open: the first foot steps out again a short distance in the same direction transferring weight, and then *pauses* for a beat.) Discover ways to do the pattern to one side, the other side, forward, backward, diagonally. This is the *two-step*.
3. Fit the open-close-open floor pattern to a quick-quick-slow accompaniment (four moderately quick beats with the fourth one held and silent).
4. Discover how the two-step can be done going forward, side by side with a partner, and starting on the same as well as on opposite feet. (See other variations under Two-Step in this chapter.)

The *forward polka* can evolve from the following activities.

Have the children:

1. Do gallops and skips to a long-short accompaniment, changing from one to the other on impulse without pause.
2. Try to change more often and finally discover how to do one complete gallop followed by one complete skip. Change continuously from one to the other, always leaving the floor on the skip. This is the *forward polka*.
3. Discover ways to do it with a partner, or a trio, moving forward.

The *sideward polka* can evolve from the following activities.

Have the children:

1. Do slides and skips to a long-short accompaniment, changing from one to the other on impulse without pause.
2. Slide counterclockwise with short steps around the room, changing with a half-turn from facing the center to facing the walls of the room. Do this step frequently and without pause. There should be no contact with the floor on the turn.
3. Try taking one complete slide and then turning for the next slide, identify-

ing the turning step as a skip. Discover how to do the slide-and-change pattern continuously around the room. This combination of a slide and a skip with a half-turn is the *sideward polka*.

4. Discover ways to do it with a partner, starting on opposite feet and attaining a face-to-face, back-to-back movement shape. (See other variations under Polka in this chapter.)

A Dance Step to Triple Meter

The *3/4 run* or *waltz run* can evolve from the following activities.

Have the children:

1. Run lightly with short steps in time to a running beat, in place, forward, and in different spatial directions on signal or on their impulse.
2. Do the run to an accompaniment which accents the first of three beats.
3. Run in a zigzag path across the room, changing direction on impulse, but always stepping in the new direction with the foot toward that direction.
4. Try to change the direction of the "zig" and "zag" so that the first run in the new direction coincides with the first accented beat of the three beats. Discover how this is best accomplished (by a pivot into a quarter-turn on the third run). This is the *3/4 run* or *waltz run*.
5. Help others perform the *3/4 run* by joining hands in lines of three or more and dancing it across the room. (See other variations under 3/4 Run in this chapter.)

The Waltz Complex

There are several different waltz steps, but all depend upon four basics which children should understand and experience before being assigned the problem of discovering the steps. (1) All waltz steps are performed in ¾ time of relatively slow speed, except for a few quicker variations. (2) Weight is *always* transferred from one foot to the other in the steps' sequence, which occurs on equally timed beats. (3) The first of the three pulse beats making up the time structure of waltz steps receives an accent in the form of a *slightly* longer walking step. (4) The accented step on the first beat should always move in a forward or backward direction, not sideward.

The Waltz Walk

Have the children:

Keep time to a 3/4 beat (preferably to waltz music) by walking forward or backward in any spatial direction, accenting the first of the three beats with a slightly longer walk. They should discover how and when to change direction so that the accented beat never moves sideward.

The Waltz Hesitation

Have the children:

Walk as before but *only* on the forward or backward accented beat, not stepping on the second and third beat, but keeping the movement continuous. They should discover how to do this, and also how to change direction on successive steps by pivoting.

The Waltz Balance

Have the children:

Walk on all three beats as in the waltz walk, but move forward or backward only on the *first* walk; the other steps must not travel through space. They should discover the resultant floor pattern and how to change direction.

The Box Waltz Step

Have the children:

Walk on all three beats but try to perform them in an open-open-close floor pattern. The first open accented walk must go directly forward and the next accented one directly backward. The second open walk is a shorter sideward one. The children should discover what the third walk must do and the resultant rectangular ("box") floor pattern.

The Waltz Step

Have the children:

Perform the first half of the box waltz step going continuously forward and the second half going continuously backward. They should discover how this is done and also how to turn and still maintain a forward or backward direction on the accented first of the three steps.

Combine all of the waltz steps in an original sequence. (See other variations under Waltz Steps in this chapter.)

Part IV | THE SKILLS OF DANCE RHYTHM

Chapter Preview

Dance Is Not Rhythms

The Sense of Rhythm

Rhythm in Dance and Sports

Rhythm in Dance and Music
> *Pulse Beats*
> *Accents*
> *Rhythmic Patterns*
> *Musical Phrasing*

Presenting Rhythmic Skills

Using a Drum

DESMOND L. KELLY

11 *The Skills of Dance Rhythm: Orientation*

Rhythm demands obedience.[1]

*. . . In dance, just as space cannot be grasped unless limited,
so time must be partitioned and made relative to be understood.
Time is expressed through the rhythm of the human body
as pulse, heartbeat, breath.*[2]

Dance Is Not Rhythms

The term *rhythms* or *rhythmic activity* has been widely used in the last forty years to describe the total dance experience offered to children. To call the dance of children *rhythms* or *rhythmic activity,* however, when we mean more than just that, is to exclude from this area of art expression its principal component. Rhythm is only one aspect of the duality of rhythm and movement making up a broad conception of dance. When this includes sequential designs, audible or silent accompaniment, and the outward expression of inner perceptions which is particularly manifested in dance movement, we come closer to the substance of dance.

The word *rhythm* has been variously defined and has many connotations for all the arts. It may be thought of in one sense as a repetition of like forms among contrasting elements. Sound and silence in music, motion and stillness in dance are the primary substances of rhythmic sequences. Such sequences may be structured or unstructured, as we have seen in Chapter 3. Most of the movements of work, sport, and daily life are unstructured. Contemporary dance considers lack of attention to a structured timing quite legitimate, but exceptions to dance tradition should not be attempted until the tradition is known and has been successfully experienced.

[1] Margaret H'Doubler, quoted in "Extensions of Dance," *Impulse, Annual of Contemporary Dance,* 1969–1970, p. 6.

[2] Geraldine Dimondstein, "Space-Time-Force: An Aesthetic Construct," *Dance—An Art in Academe,* Martin Haberman and Tobie Meisel, eds., New York, Teachers College, 1970, p. 8.

We have said that young children should establish their own personal rhythm and sense of timing, should try out their own "fastness" and "slowness," before attempting to conform to a structured rhythmic sequence imposed from without; that they should be free to devise their own timing when making movement sequences from different catalysts. Not to be lost sight of in the legitimate trend to let everyone "do his own thing" in movement, however, is the fact that accurate response to a series of beats is a primary source of sentient pleasure. A child who finds it difficult to respond to the rhythmic structure of different kinds of music, chants, or poetry, or to order his own movement in a structured timing sequence needs special help. An inadequate "sense of rhythm" may be compared to color blindness in that each limits perceptive responses to only certain aspects of the total environment. A "sense of rhythm" may be developed and refined, and activities to accomplish this purpose, now extensively present in music education, should not be lacking in dance education.

The Sense of Rhythm

Some children are naturally endowed with a highly developed rhythmic sense or ability to respond to a time structure, while in others it may seem to be conspicuously lacking. But to say that a child "has no sense of rhythm," when describing one who never moves in time with the rest of the group, is incorrect. The sense of order and integration derived from pulsation or periodicity gives the child a profound security in a world of confused impulses and stimuli. A movement response to rhythmic structure may be deficient because of poor physical coordination, inadequate kinesthesia, lack of concentration, but it can always be improved by attention to its cause and by practice.

It is necessary, of course, that this training process not be boring and monotonous but offer interest and the satisfaction of accomplishment. Therefore, the part of a dance lesson in which rhythmic response to an accompaniment receives special emphasis should not be too long, and should include rhythmic games and problem-solving which challenge the child's interest in making progress.

To repeat, music and dance have one element in common—rhythmic structure. Therefore, to indicate rhythmic structure in dance, it seems wise to employ musical notation, an efficient system of representing time relationships of musical sounds that has developed over hundreds of years. After children have learned these symbols in music classes, their knowledge may be drawn upon to describe rhythmic relationships in dance. In this part of the book, musical notation is used where appropriate and its application to rhythmic movement is explained.

Rhythm in Dance and Sports

In some sports, such as swimming, skating, and certain track events, movement is employed in a rhythmic sequence similar to that used in dance and depends for its rate of speed upon the individual's body structure and movement proficiency. In skating to music and in synchronized swimming the time sequence is ordered from without. Thus in movement patterns as well as in rhythmic structure these activities become very similar to group dancing. In most sports, however, particularly those in which individuals or groups compete against each other, the rhythmic sequence is interrupted and irregular because each situation in a game or contest is unique and cannot be completely anticipated. In order to fulfill his role the individual must employ the movement pattern that best fits it.

This is not to say that rhythmic movement is not present in these situations. In fact, there is a definite relationship between the rhythm of a movement and the ease and skill of its performance. Witness a fine tennis serve, a football tackle, a pitch in baseball, a golf swing, a lay-up shot in basketball. One of the joys of watching skilled performers in sports (unconscious on the part of most spectators) is derived from the rhythmic quality of individual or group performance.

Rhythm in Dance and Music

Unlike most sports, dance usually employs movement in an ordered time structure, just as most music employs sound. In both, the basis of the structure is mathematical, time being measured by intervals between *beats*. The intervals are short (as in a run or an eighth note), moderate (as in a walk or a quarter note), or long (as in a slow walk or a half note). In a series, however, they must always be equal to each other, and thus they have been compared to the beats of the heart or *pulse*. Intervals between beats may be broken up into parts of two, three, four, or more, as they are in rhythmic patterns. But the pulse beats themselves, as the units of measure, always underlie the movement as they do the music, defining a continuing series of equal intervals.

There must be at least two beats to define an interval in time, one at the beginning and one at the end. In this primary grouping the first beat is stronger than the second. Other groups of three, four, or more are possible, the first beat emphasizing the beginning of the group with an *accent*. Thus groups of beats are measured in twos or threes or more, and the measured beats musically are called *notes*. The time signature in music (2/4, 3/4, etc.) tells, above the line, the number of beats in a measure and, below the line, the kind of note or pulse beat that defines the intervals.

For most purposes, then, dance movement is measured in time just as musical sounds are measured in time. When they are of similar rhythmic structure, dance and music may occur together, one synchronized with the other, one accompanying the other. Dance movement must follow a sequential organization in time whether it is that of music, another sort of rhythmic accompaniment, or the sequence of its own rhythmic form, structured or unstructured.

There follows a description of each of the four aspects of rhythm—pulse beats, accents, rhythmic patterns, musical phrasing—for which activities are described in the next four chapters.

Pulse Beats

The pulse beat is the underlying beat of rhythmic structure repeated continuously to define a series of equal time intervals. A person responds to pulse beats when, in an even series, he taps a foot to music; a metronome ticks the pulse beats as it keeps the tempo of music uniform. Different from the space interval of the inch, however, which never changes in length as a unit of measure, the intervals between pulse beats may be moderate, short, or long. In a continuing series, the amount of time measured by each two beats must be exactly equal to that of the others, unless the tempo of the music is deliberately slowed down or speeded up.

Movement response is made by synchronizing the climax of the movement (such as the contact with the floor in a walk or a jump, or the extension of a thrust) with the exact moment of the beat. The rest of the movement (the preparation or follow-through) must be accurately timed to coincide with the intervals between beats. The response to pulse beats is the simplest of rhythmic responses. A series of finger or foot taps or any other single-unit movement, if done in *time,* are such responses.

Accents

Accents can be described as additional force placed on certain pulse beats of a series. In any grouping of two beats, the first or starting beat receives the accent; if the series is repeated continuously, so does every other *first* beat thereafter. The innate tendency to accent alternate beats in a series relates to heart beat, respiration, and body structure. Hence a continuing series of evenly divided sounds fall into a *strong-weak* sequence.

When accents occur in a regular order, as on the first of every two, three, or four beats, they serve to arrange the beats into equal groups. In music notation these groups of two or three pulse beats or their components are called *measures,* and the number of beats in each measure defines the *meter.* When each measure in a series has two pulse beats, the meter is *duple.* When each has three beats, the meter is *triple.* These are the basic groupings of beats. A derived four-beat group, *quadruple* meter, consists of two groups of two beats, with a strong accent on the first beat and a secondary or less forceful accent on the third.

Besides quadruple meter other combinations used in dance are six beats (two groups of three), five (one group of two and one of three or vice versa), and seven (one group of three and one of four or vice versa).[3] The six-beat combination, ordinarily two groups of three beats in 6/8 time, is in reality a duple meter. It is very useful in children's dance, especially for skips, slides, and gallops. The other combinations are much less common and, like mixed meters and syncopation, are useful in advanced rhythmic activities.

Accents falling at the beginning of each measure are said to be *regular.* When the regular order is temporarily interrupted and accents occur on a normally unaccented or weaker part of the measure, these accents are called *syncopated.* It is important in syncopation that the regular order of accents be established before it is interrupted. In other words, syncopation is effective only in relation to a regular order of accents, so that the syncopated accents are felt against or in conflict with the regular accents. When accompaniment is used, movement may be syncopated against the regular accents of the accompaniment, or the accompaniment may use syncopated accents against the regular accents maintained in the movement.

Movement in which all the force is equalized or sustained, so that there is no recognizable point of additional stress, is rare in children's dance. It may occur in "slow motion" or sustained sequences of relatively short duration. For the most part, in a single unit of movement or in a movement phrase there is a point—at the beginning, middle, or end of a movement—at which added force is applied or released. It may result from the recovery of a temporary loss of balance, from the application of force to begin a push or lift, from the full extension of a stretch, from the release of a swing into gravity, from the drop back to the floor from an elevation above it. The time span of a simple movement phrase is measured from the regular accents which occur at some point in the phrase. In the common dance steps this accent occurs most often at the beginning of the combination.

The problem of accent in rhythmic learning is twofold: to synchronize movement accents with the accents of the accompaniment, and to syncopate

[3] Another seven-beat combination found in some Balkan dances is two groups of two and one of three or vice versa.

movement accents, at least in simple ways, against the accompaniment or against a regular order of one's own. The introductory activities listed in Chapter 13 are designed to develop ability in the first of these responses because, in most of their dance activities both in school and out, children will be using the regular accents of musical accompaniment. To be off the accent when waltzing, doing a polka, or performing an allemande left is almost as unsatisfying as being out of time altogether.

The syncopated response is more difficult. The Advanced Activities in Chapter 13 will help develop it. Since syncopation is used extensively in modern dance and in modern music of all types, it cannot be ignored in rhythmic learning. Furthermore, it lends variety and excitement to dance movement which can be achieved in no other way.

Rhythmic Patterns

The word *pattern* implies variety. A rhythmic pattern results when a series of sounds or movements are so arranged that they are not equal to each other in time. Hence, variety in timing is achieved. When intervals between pulse beats are divided into unequal parts, a pattern occurs—for example, the *long-short* sounds of the skip, slide, and gallop pattern. Actually, the pulse beat interval here is divided into three equal parts, but the first movement takes two of them and the second movement the one that is left. Therefore the best musical accompaniment for these dance steps is the duple meter of a 6/8 measure. The first movement of a skip (the walk) takes two of the eighth notes and the second movement (the hop) the third, with two skips to a measure.

A rhythmic pattern will also occur if a pulse beat interval which is divided into two or three equal parts is followed by an undivided interval. If the divided interval is in two parts, the movement pattern would be two runs and a walk—in musical notation, two eighth notes and a quarter note. The two movement speeds are fast and moderate in a two-to-one relationship, each run being exactly *half as long* as the walk. A three-to-one relationship, or a run one-third as long as the walk, would result if the first divided interval were in three parts, as in a triplet run.

Another common two-speed rhythmic pattern is the result of two pulse beats (two walks) followed by two *tied* beats or two pulse intervals sounded as one (a slow walk). This *twice-as-long* time relationship of slow walk to walk would be notated as two quarter notes and a half note.

Of the dance steps analyzed in Chapter 10, the gallop, slide, skip, two-step, and polka are built on rhythmic patterns; the other dance steps, because they move in even intervals, are built on pulse beats. Unless a single movement is continued in the same way for a length of time, any combination of movements usually results in a pattern, particularly if a pause or a slower movement occurs at the end of a short sequence of movements.

Simple rhythmic patterns use only two speeds—for example, those of a walk and a run. More difficult rhythmic patterns may use three speeds—for example, the walk, the run, and the slow walk. Patterns ending with a walk or a slow walk are more satisfying to perform because they give a feeling of completion. They are also less difficult because it is easier to stop on a slow movement than on a fast one.

Response to rhythmic patterns is more difficult than response to pulse beats and accents because it involves the combination of movements of different speeds in a sequence. However, as soon as one gets beyond the simplest dance activity, such combinations become an inevitable part of dance performance. Some of the very simple patterns, such as the *long-short* pattern used in the skip, the slide, and the gallop, and the *short-short-long* combination of two walks and a slow walk, seem to come easily to children and can be used early in rhythmic development.

Musical Phrasing

A musical phrase is like a language phrase or a sentence. It is at least two measures long and forms a continuous thematic sequence, ending with what is known in musical terms as a cadence or a semicadence. In order that dance movement may change as new musical phrases are introduced or may repeat as old phrases are repeated, the recognition of musical phrasing is part of rhythmic learning. It is especially useful when one is learning and performing folk dances or dance-making to music. Often a phrase length is not arbitrary and may be considered short or long (for example, two or four measures), depending on how it sounds to an individual ear. While much less common than traditional phrases of two and four measures, phrases three, five, and even six measures long are often more interesting to work with in movement.

Traditional music generally uses phrases of equal lengths, although this is not the case with early music or with a great deal of modern music. Music of unequal or irregular phrase lengths often lends itself to dance movement better than does that of equal phrases. Children should become familiar with different types of phrase construction so that this knowledge may be readily employed when they make dances to music and learn traditional dances.

Presenting Rhythmic Skills

There comes a period in the child's development when special emphasis should be placed on *keeping time,* as it is popularly called, but this is not in the nursery school, kindergarten, or even first grade. Children exposed often to an accompaniment so that their movement occurs within it, so to speak, will sooner or later adapt themselves to its rhythm, some sooner than others. Children who find it hard to synchronize their movements with the accompaniment, especially if it departs too far from their natural rhythm, are hindered rather than helped by having their attention called to inaccurate response, by the creation of tensions through continual drill. The surest route to precise rhythmic response is through mastery of free, relaxed, but controlled movement with frequent opportunities to perform it to rhythmic accompaniment.

The activities in the next chapters (except for musical phrasing) are classified as *introductory* and *advanced*. The introductory activities represent elementary accomplishment and are usable at any grade level. The advanced activities involve more difficult rhythmic responses and should be attempted only after the others have been mastered.

The problem in developing rhythmic skill is threefold: to *attend* to the accompaniment; to *identify* the pulse beats, accents, rhythmic pattern, or whatever one is responding to; and to *order* one's movement around it. With children, whose interests as a rule lie in movement for its own sake, motivation may be necessary until the satisfaction of accomplishment is theirs. Gamelike activities in rhythmic response which challenge the child to greater effort are helpful. Playing these games, in order to keep up with the others, a child usually realizes when he is with the accompaniment and when he is not.

So that greater attention may be paid to the accompaniment all sorts of hand and body actions may be used as well as the common one of clapping. Waving the hands, beating the air, shaking the head or shoulders, snapping fingers, tapping the chest, thighs, or another flat body surface, tapping the desk, the chair, or the floor, with both hands together or alternately—all are appropriate responses. An accent and its following weaker beat or beats, or series of successive measures or phrases may be easily differentiated by making the first accented movement "on the body" with one or more slaps or taps, contrasted with the following movements "off the body," as in small pushes, pokes, or wavings in the surrounding space. If children are sitting on the floor, the feet can be raised and tapped. In locomotor movement, a walk in place is easier for children to control than a forward walk, a moderate walk than a slow walk, a gallop or a skip forward than a run, a bounce or small jump than a hop. Once accurate response to a series of beats, accents, or a rhythmic pattern is achieved, children may explore it in other ways, with other movements, in different directions, with a partner, and so on.

The technical terms used in this part of the book, although necessary for the teacher's understanding, need not be used with young children. Words as *walking beat, running beat, skipping beat* will suffice to describe what they are learning. Even such words as *accent, phrase,* and *pattern* may be avoided if they seem too abstract. "Loud and soft beats," "strong movement," "first or second parts of the music," "drum or music signals," are examples of substitutes for some of the technical terms.

Proper accompaniment is of tremendous importance in the development of rhythmic skill. If the accompaniment is not precise in its rhythmic sequence, the movement cannot hope to be. Drums or other percussion instruments, or the many good records now available, will be of great assistance to teachers. In fact, simple beats on a drum are easier for children to attend to than musical selections; there are no complications of rhythmic patterns, melody, or harmony to get in the way of the pulse or accent structure, and besides, by the time they get to school many children have become accustomed to hearing music without attending to it. Background music in supermarkets, incidental music in the movies or on television, and other such experiences in music are partly responsible.

Too much loud drumming, however, especially if it follows an even pulse beat series unadorned by frequent rhythmic patterns, can become so monotonous as to be nerve wracking; the term "drum work" is unfortunately applicable. Also, children are not helped by banging a drum harder and slower. The sound may be changed by using another percussion instrument or a rhythmic record or by keeping the pulse without an accompaniment, through attention to the group response or floor vibrations. Better yet, the children may chant their own accompaniment.

There are many times when movement exploration and invention proceed independently of a rhythmic accompaniment. For rhythmic skill learning, however, movement is always used, even though it may be merely a simple hand response.

Teachers' and children's purposes may vary from lesson to lesson. In one lesson the objective may be to sharpen the rhythmic response to a running beat. While the way in which the run is performed is important it is not the primary purpose of the lesson. In another lesson different ways in which one can run with a partner may be a problem of exploration. Attention to rhythmic response will be only supplementary to the whole procedure.

Such an approach to the teaching of rhythmic skills paves the way for their use in dances. It is a short step from exploring the run with partners to making a dance, using a run as the basic movement. Even though this progression is not always completed, it is fun to run forward with partners in time to an accompaniment and to turn with them on the next phrase of the music. That in itself is a kind of dance, simple though it may be, if children can do it with ease and freedom, at one with the music and a partner as well.

Chapter Preview

Introductory Activities

Advanced Activities

Using Rhythm Sticks

O. R. PETERSON III

12 *Response to Pulse Beats*

The pulse beat is the underlying beat of all rhythmic structure repeated continuously to define a series of equal time intervals.

Introductory Activities

Procedure for Movement

The following movement procedure is suggested for all activities relating to response to pulse beats, because it progresses from small, easily controlled movements, to locomotor movement. In certain activities some of the suggested steps will be omitted. For instance, when doing a skip, slide, or gallop, it is easier to move forward than to move in place. When other responses are suggested, they will be indicated in that place. In general, however, the procedure holds for most activities.

1. Listen to the rhythmic sequences and try to *feel* the sequence of pulse beats.
2. Make a hand response of some kind.
3. Move in place.
4. Move forward.
5. Move in different directions.
6. Move with another person or persons.

Relationship of Notes to Rates of Speed

Single Speeds[a]

Fast Tempo:

run	run	run	run	run	run	run	run
♪	♪	♪	♪	♪	♪	♪	♪

Moderate Tempo:

walk	walk	walk	walk
♩	♩	♩	♩

Slow Tempo:

slow walk	slow walk
♩	♩

Two and Three Speeds Combined[b]

Moderate and Fast:

walk	walk	walk	walk	run	run	run	run	run	run	run	run
♩	♩	♩	♩	♪	♪	♪	♪	♪	♪	♪	♪

Moderate and Slow:

walk	walk	walk	walk	slow walk	slow walk
♩	♩	♩	♩	♩	♩

Moderate, Fast, and Slow:

walk	walk	walk	walk	run	run	run	run	run	run	run	run
♩	♩	♩	♩	♪	♪	♪	♪	♪	♪	♪	♪

walk	walk	walk	walk	slow walk	slow walk
♩	♩	♩	♩	♩	♩

Note: In combining movements of different speeds it is well at first to keep one series of movements equal in total timing to the next as in the above chart. Later the successive series may be unequal in timing, as four walks followed by six or twelve runs instead of eight. When a run is combined with a walk without pause, the tempo of the walk should be moderately slow.

[a] See pp. 185 and 186 for other movements.

[b] See p. 187 for other movement combinations.

Procedure for Accompaniment

To determine a basic walking, running, or slow walking tempo, movement of the group without accompaniment may be perceived and the timing accepted that evolves from the unison movement. A metronome setting, however, is a more effectual means of arriving at an accurate timing. A teacher may borrow a metronome from the music room and practice timing with its help. The metronome setting for a walk for young children should start no lower than 138 with an upward range to 152. When the walk is doubled to a run, however, the basic tempo of the walk should be slower, the run being twice as fast as a range from 128 to 138. The timing of a skip (slide, gallop) should be similar to this slower walk.

With older children an easy walk can be done to a setting of 120 and doubled to a run at this mark or somewhat less. A brisk walk should move the setting to 132 or even 138. A well-known method of timing is to count in continuously even tones "a thousand one, a thousand two, etc.," each thousand being equal to one second and to two normal adult walking steps.

The following procedure ranges from complete rhythmic support of the activity (the accompaniment plays a simultaneous sound for each unit of the movement) to rhythmic opposition to the movement (the accompaniment plays a pattern which is syncopated to the beat of the movement). Syncopated accompaniment should not be attempted until the children are fairly secure in rhythmic performance, and perhaps not until advanced activities are undertaken.

1. Complete and continuous support by the accompaniment.
2. Partial support by the accompaniment (stopping as the movement continues and starting again after a short period).
3. Playing only the regular accents in two-, three-, or four-beat groups.
4. Playing rhythmic patterns (combining short, average, and long intervals in regularly accented sequences).
5. Playing syncopated accents and patterns.

Suggested Movements for a Constant Rate of Speed

These movements are given in each category in order of difficulty. Younger children or beginners would not be able to do them all.

A. Movements in a moderate rate of speed (one movement to each pulse beat).
   1. Make a hand or body response. Standing, tap one foot on the floor a few times, and then change to the other.

2. Walk in place and forward.
3. Skip, gallop forward, or slide sideward (these movements have a preliminary upbeat which may or may not be carried in the accompaniment).
4. Perform nonlocomotor movements such as a bend-stretch, twist-right-left, push-pull.
5. Walk backward and walk turning around.
6. Jump or hop, changing feet after a certain number of hops.
7. Bounce and catch a ball or toss and catch a beanbag.
8. Flick a scarf in any direction.
9. Jump rope in different ways.
10. Make combinations of any of these movements or invent others that fit a moderate tempo.
11. Try any of these movements with a partner or a group.
B. Movements in a slow rate of speed (one movement to each two pulse beats).
  1. Clap, tap, or beat time.
  2. Slow-walk forward.
  3. Sway upper body.
  4. Swing arms and trunk.
  5. Push and pull in any direction.
  6. Twist and straighten any part of the body.
  7. Swing arms, a rope, or a scarf.
  8. Toss or bounce a ball high and then catch it.
  9. Play catch with a partner.
  10. Make combinations of any of these movements or invent others that fit a slow tempo.
  11. Try any of these movements with a partner or a group.
C. Movements in a fast rate of speed (two movements to each pulse beat).
  1. Clap, tap, or beat time.
  2. Run in place and forward.
  3. Bounce in place (small jumps).
  4. Run backward and run turning around.
  5. Tap a small ball continuously against the floor.
  6. Jump rope very fast as in "pepper" jumps.
  7. Invent small movements which fit a fast tempo.
  8. Try running with a partner or a group.

Suggested Movement Series Which Combine Speeds

The gradual acceleration and retard of movement speed is a timing activity which should be used often. However, it is extremely difficult if not impossible to do this and synchronize exactly to similarly accelerating or retarding accompaniments. Only an approximation of the continuously changing timing can be made.

Two, three, or even more speeds can be put together in a series without pause, however, when they relate exactly to the pulse beats. This is a more difficult rhythmic activity than moving at one rate of speed. It should not be attempted until accurate response to the latter has been well established—for many children not until they are eight to ten years old.

When a series of walks is succeeded by a series of runs without a pause, the run must be timed exactly *twice as fast* as the walk. The same rule applies when a jump, a hop, or a leap is used with a run. When a series of walks is succeeded by a series of slow walks without a pause, the slow walk must be timed exactly *twice as slow* as the natural walk. When any movements are combined which naturally or by one's preference have different time intervals, this rule of mathematical time relationship holds. (The 3–1 ratio, resulting in a triplet run when three times as fast, and in a *waltz hesitation* walk when three times as slow, is discussed in the advanced activities. The 4–1 ratio, resulting in a run four times as fast as a natural walk or in a walk four times as slow, is not practical for use with children.)[1]

A. *Moderate* speed alternated with *slow* speed (two speeds).
   1. A series of walks and a series of slow walks.
   2. A series of skips and a series of slow walks.
   3. Two tap steps and one walk.
   4. A short series of pendular swings followed by circular swings.
B. *Moderate* speed alternated with *fast* speed (two speeds).
   1. A series of walks and a series of runs.
   2. A series of jumps and a series of runs.
   3. A series of skips, slides, or gallops and a series of runs.
   4. A series of runs followed by one or two leaps.
C. *Moderate* speed alternated with *fast* and *slow* speeds (three speeds).
   Walks, jumps, skips, gallops, and slides with runs and slow walks may be used in different series and combinations. The moderate movements should be performed at least eight times, the run sixteen times, and the slow walk four times before changing to another movement speed.

Rhythmic Games and Activities

Some of these rhythmic games and others in succeeding chapters depend on movement invention by the children or a child leader. It is assumed that practice in improvising movement will have been part of the dance experi-

---

[1] Many teachers use flash cards successfully as visual aids for rhythmic response. These depict rhythmic relationships in stripes of varying widths and colors which are equated with note values.

ence before children are asked to perform it in a rhythmic sequence, such as synchronizing it to a series of pulse beats, accents, patterns, or phrases. Many kinds of activities for improvisational practice are described in Part II.

Follow the Beats. The teacher, and later a child leader, performs movements to a series of beats in moderate speed. The class imitates each movement, changing when it changes (as in the game Follow the Leader) and keeping the same accurate time. The leader's movement should not change too quickly and may alternate or combine locomotor and nonlocomotor movements. Accompaniment may be percussion or strongly rhythmic music such as "Walking" in Frieda Miller's *Music for Rhythms and Dance*. This is a good game to play in small groups with children taking turns as leaders.

Self-Accompaniment. Half the class stands in place and claps pulse beats as the other half performs them in movement—walking, skipping, galloping, hopping, twisting, bending, pushing, or doing any other locomotor or nonlocomotor movement that fits a moderate pulse. A leader of the moving group may designate the movement to be used, or each may move on his own. Then the process is reversed. The teacher signals the change so that there is no pause when the groups change activities. The object is to keep accurate time to the accompaniment (which should maintain a constant tempo) and to change from moving to accompanying and vice versa quickly and smoothly. Any sound-producing movement which can be done in place, such as snapping fingers, body slaps, tapping of feet, can be used in lieu of clapping.

Traffic Cop. While a child plays walking beats on the drum or a suitable record is played, the teacher or child leader directs the class with arms and hands, using different signals for walking forward, backward, sideward, in place, turning. While signaling is easier if the leader stands in front of the class, it may be done from the center of the room with children moving clockwise or counterclockwise. The arm signals should be large enough for all the class to see. The object is to maintain accurate response to the pulse beats and to follow the direction signals. The leader must be ready to change signals before the class has moved as far as it can in any one direction.

Rhythmic Shapes. For this game, children should have had the experience of exploring movement on different bases of support from a five-point base down to one, and of moving smoothly from one to another. After a moderately slow pulse beat series is set up as accompaniment, the teacher or a chosen leader gives any number signal from one to five. The children assume a body shape on the signaled number of bases of support and at once perform any possible movement in their shape in time to the beat. Presently another number is signaled, and the rhythmic response to the accompaniment is performed on the new number of support bases. After several trials, the teacher or child leader chooses another leader whose performance has been especially well balanced, accurate, and original, and the game continues until all five kinds of body support have been signaled.

Moving Groups I. The class is divided into three groups. After a preliminary clapping trial of the three speeds, one group is assigned walking, another running, and the third slow walking. The three groups, arranged in circles, lines, or, best of all, informally around the room, move *only* when the accompaniment for their movement is played. If the group is in a line or mass formation, a leader is chosen to guide it around the room to avoid traffic mixups, although this guidance is not necessary if children are used to moving around among others. When accompanying, it is well to start with walking and return to it frequently, so that the relationship of twice as fast and twice as slow is precisely maintained. Groups should change movements so that all three speeds are done by each group. A fourth group can be used with a skipping or galloping pattern. The object of the game is to start immediately when one's movement is played, to keep time to it, and to stop immediately when the beat changes. With children who have had experience improvising movement, one, two, or all of the groups may be asked to use nonlocomotor movements to define the long, moderate, or short pulse intervals assigned to them. Although remaining with his group, each child improvises his own nonlocomotor movement.

The Crazy Clock. Children clasp hands together and swing their arms in imitation of the pendulum of a grandfather clock, the tempo of the swing having been set beforehand. At any time during the swinging, the teacher or a child leader calls a number from one to twelve and the children strike that hour. Striking the hour must be done in exactly the same timing as the swing but with some kind of audible movement—series of stamps, walks in place, claps in any direction, slaps of the thighs, or any combination of movement sounds. The swinging pendulum is then resumed without pause in the same timing. Some of the hour signals may be in numerical sequence, but it is more fun if they are not. The timing of the swing should always be moderate to slow in speed. As the tendency in this game is to shorten the intervals and speed up the timing, an accompaniment is indicated for the pendulum swing. This may be provided by a piano or drum or by the children themselves saying "tick-tock" as they swing.

Levels. The class walks forward for eight beats, each child on his own path. On the second group of eight beats everyone makes a change of level downward and comes back again to a standing position, ready to repeat the walks without pause. It is a good idea at first to assign a specific action for the level change, such as touching the floor with both elbows, or the seat, or the chin, or one shoulder, or the top of the head, or the upper back. The object is to lower the body and regain standing position again on exactly the eight beats, no more, no less. Later, children may make their own level changes, and the number of total beats for the two phrases may be decreased or increased. This is a good game to play in two opposing groups, one walking and the other starting with the level change. If the phrase is long enough, the lowering process may start with an extension upward.

Advanced Activities

Using Note Values to Designate Time Intervals

After the children have become familiar with note values in music, these symbols can be used for moderate, short, and long movement intervals. The quarter note used for the walk represents a rhythmic point of departure for the half-as-long eighth note and the twice-as-long half note.

The use of note values is the only efficient and precise way to describe the timing of movements, particularly if the movement intervals are irregular. Teachers should be familiar with the notes used in this chapter, their time relationship to each other,[2] and their use in measures with different time signatures. It is desirable that they be able to read the rhythmic patterns of simple music and to play various patterns on percussion instruments with ease and dispatch.

Quarter Note ♩

The quarter note represents a moderate time interval. Children often call it the walking note because it usually approximates the timing of a natural walk. Many movements adapt themselves to this timing—the jump, hop, leap, and the accented walk of the skip, slide, and gallop, as well as the bend, stretch, push, pull, and short swings.

Eighth Note ♪

The eighth note, exactly half as long as the quarter note, designates a run. It is not easy for children to run rhythmically at a speed faster than the regular time of eighth notes. Few other locomotor movements or dance steps use intervals as short as those in a series of eighth notes except in a combined

[2] See the chart at beginning of this chapter.

pattern with a quarter note (6/8 measure) as in the skip, gallop, and slide, or in the dotted-eighth and sixteenth note pattern of the polka.

Exploration will show that the jump, hop, step-hop, and schottische can be increased in tempo to eighth-note intervals, but that few nonlocomotor movements except those using the hands and head lend themselves to fast performance which is rhythmically controlled.

Half Note ♩

The half note, exactly twice as long as the quarter note, designates a slow walk. Exploration will determine other movements which can be supported by a series of half notes. Most locomotor movements lose their character when slowed down to this extent; but nonlocomotor movements, because they involve the larger movements of the trunk, are naturally timed to a slower series of half notes and in some cases even to whole notes.

Dotted Half Note ♩.

The dotted half note, three times as long as the quarter note (a dot increases a note's time value by one-half), may be used as a slow walk in 3/4 meter or waltz time. This is a good preliminary to learning the waltz balance and waltz steps. It may also be used for nonlocomotor movements.

Whole Note ○

The whole note, four times as long as the quarter note, may be used for a very slow walk, although it is difficult for children to sustain locomotor movement in such slow timing. Certain nonlocomotor movements of large dimension may be adapted to this timing.

Quarter and Eighth Note ♩ ♪

A quarter note followed by an eighth note, expressing a 2–1 ratio, designates the time relationship of walk and hop in the skip, and walk and run in the gallop and slide. This note combination played on an instrument will be recognized by children as the time pattern of these movements.

Triplet ♫

The triplet (eighth note), each note of which is one-third as long as a quarter note, requires a fast run with short steps. To perform triplets efficiently, the pulse beat at the beginning of the three notes must be accented, and because it is the first of the three runs, it occurs on alternate feet. The easiest way to develop a triplet run is to quicken the tempo of a 3/4 run, resulting in a quick controlled coordination of the feet which many children would have difficulty in achieving. The run is the only movement, other than small movements of the hands, that can be performed efficiently to the triplet time of eighth notes. A tied triplet, that is, a triplet in which the first two notes are tied together and the first note has the time value of both, gives a 2–1 time ratio and is sometimes used for skips, slides, or gallops.

A general procedure for the use of accompaniment is described in the introductory section of this chapter. Progress is made in rhythmic acuity when an accompaniment is used for movements which does not completely support them. Performance of the movements suggested for the above notes may become more of a challenge rhythmically if the accompaniment plays (1) a series of different notes from that which the movement is following, such as quarter notes for an eighth-note run, eighth notes for a half-note swing; (2) a series in which several different notes are played in regular or irregular sequences, forming regular or irregular note patterns; (3) a series of patterns containing syncopated accents or measures against which the regular pulse beat of the movement must be maintained. Such accompaniment may be improvised on percussion instruments or on the piano. Music which fulfills these conditions (it is not difficult to find) may also be used as accompaniment.

Rhythmic Games and Activities

Clap and Move. The class walks to quarter notes and claps to half notes at the same time. Then they slow-walk to half notes and clap to quarter notes. At first the two activities are performed with a pause between, but later the changes should be made without pause. A predetermined number of slow-walks and walks may be used at first, such as eight slow-walks and sixteen walks. Later the change from walk to slow-walk and back can be made irregularly when the teacher says *change!* The same game can be played with walks and runs, and the claps can be changed to slaps of the upper leg. A 3–1 ratio of hand to feet movement and vice versa may be used as well as the 2–1 described.

Reverse Ranks. The class walks forward to moderate timing. At the signal *four! three! six!* etc., they walk that number of steps backward in the same timing without accompaniment, then go forward again with a strong accent on the first forward step. Because it is impossible to change direction immediately on the signal, the first number of the signaled count has to be another forward step which shifts the direction from forward to backward and occurs directly after the signal. Signals may be given at irregular intervals; the same number may be given twice in succession if practice is needed. A run may be used, with the reverse taken in place or backward. This game can be played without accompaniment, the class maintaining a unison beat. A speedup in tempo should be avoided.

Line or Circle Clap. The class sits or stands in lines or open or closed circles in groups of from eight to twenty. The teacher sets the tempo for a pattern of two quarter notes and one half note, or quick-quick-slow, on an instrument or by clapping, and gives the signal to begin.

Beginning at either end of the line, open circle or any place in the closed circle, the series is passed along, each child clapping one pattern in turn. The intervals between notes and between patterns which have been set by the leader must be maintained precisely until every child has had a turn. The tempo may be increased in later trials. Other short series of notes may be assigned, such as a measure of four, three, or two quarter notes. The most difficult interval to maintain precisely is that in which each child claps only one note, immediately followed by the child next to him after the appropriate interval.

The interval between claps may be set by the second child in the line rather than the leader. It is well to move children from place to place in the line or circle, particularly those at the beginning and those who find it hard to maintain the timing when it is their turn to clap.

The game is made more difficult by substituting stamping, jumping, or any other audible movement for clapping, or by tossing a beanbag or ball in succession around the group in the exact timing of the sequence.

Calling Numbers.[3] As children move accurately to an accompaniment individually on their own paths with any assigned locomotor movement (walk, run, or dance step), the teacher or leader calls a number from two to eight. As the number is given children may quickly attach themselves to a partner (two) or form a group of the signaled number and proceed with the movement as before. If the signaled number is large (five to eight) they may choose to move in a circle, a single line, or a wheel with right hands joined at the center, rather than abreast. The accompaniment continues as the groups are being formed, and the object of the game is to be among the first to get into an efficient moving formation with the correct number of participants. After a short period, groups or partners are dispersed, and the game begins again with all moving individually with a change of locomotor movement until the next number is called.

---

[3] Calling Numbers and Calling Names are useful in forming random groups and in practicing getting into groups of different numbers.

Traffic Cop

Calling Names. The class walks single file behind a leader in a maze, serpentine, open circle, or free-form line to an accompaniment. A name is called by the teacher, and that person breaks out of the formation followed by everyone who is walking behind him, making another path in the room. The teacher continues to call names, and those persons with their followers make other paths, being careful never to intersect another line. In the initial stages of this game, if the teacher calls the names of children who are short distances from the end of the line (from four to eight places, depending on the size of the group desired) the process does not become confusing.

Once groups of a certain size have been formed they may work together on any problem related to movement exploration or dance-making.

Moving Groups II. This is a more difficult version of Moving Groups I in the Introductory Activities which should be played as review.

After it has been done successfully, the three notes and the pattern with their locomotor counterparts are assigned to each group in a different series, which may start with the half notes (slow walk) and proceed to quarters (walk), quarter-eighths (skip), and eighths (run). Each group starts with a different note (movement) in the series and changes to the next one in its series on the signal *change!* Thus all groups are performing different movements simultaneously, the change from one to the next being made in a definite order. Those moving to half notes may improvise nonlocomotor movement individually or follow an assigned leader who does so in this timing. The accompaniment should start with quarter-note support and return to it at the beginning of each change, but at other times it may support any group which seems to need it. Movement is continuous until each group has performed each note.

Wheel. The children form a wheel of three concentric circles, with space between. The inner circle takes half notes, the next quarter notes, and the outside one eighths. All circles move at once in the same or opposite directions, the accompaniment following different groups in turn. The half-note group may take a high nonlocomotor movement such as rocking with hands joined and extended overhead. Hands may also be joined in the other circles, although performance will be more difficult. Children should change to different circles so that they move to both fast and slow notes, but there always must be fewer children in the inner circles. Several groups may be formed to construct their own wheels.

Step and Clap. To a 16-count sequence of 4 measures of 4/4 meter the following series of walks and claps is taken: 4 walks; 3 walks and 1 clap; 2 walks and 2 claps; 1 walk and 3 claps. This is tried several times, first to a supporting and then to a syncopated accompaniment. Next the series is reversed, starting with 1 walk and 3 claps. A 32-count sequence of 8 measures is then performed starting with either series and reversing it after 16 counts. Note that the beginning and end of the series (4 walks, or 1 walk and 3 claps, depending on the starting pattern) occurs twice in the middle 8 counts when the series is repeated in reverse.

Having mastered the 32-count sequence, children try it in different floor patterns, moving forward and backward or the reverse, or from side to side (more difficult) on each 4 counts. Two groups are then formed, a floor pattern is agreed upon, and the 32-count series are performed simultaneously, but in opposition to each other. That is, one group starts with 4 walks and the other with 1 walk and 3 claps. The total series may be performed three times without pause and the two groups judged for accuracy and precision.

Chapter Preview

Introductory Activities

Procedure for Movement
Procedure for Accompaniment
Regular Accents in Groups of Two, Three,
  and Four Pulse Beats
Rhythmic Games and Activities

Advanced Activities

Syncopated Accents and Mixed Meters
Rhythmic Games .

13 Response to Accents

Rhythmic accents can be described as additional stress placed on certain pulse beats in a series.

Introductory Activities

To help children synchronize rhythmic accents with movement accents is the objective of the procedures and activities discussed in this chapter. The movement accent occurs at the climax of the movement—for example, at the takeoff of a leap, hop, or jump,[1] the release in a throw, the drop in a swing. In music an accent is often preceded by an *up beat* or *anacrusis* which tends to strengthen it. In movement the preparation to perform an accented movement might also be termed an anacrusis. Examples are the lift of the arms before the drop into a swing; the backward lift of a leg before the forward thrust of a kick; the pull back of the arm before a throw. In responding to the accent it is important that this preparation which must precede the movement climax be taken into consideration.

Procedure for Movement

The following movement procedure is in general like that given in Chapter 12, with additions and adaptations which apply particularly to accent response at the beginning of groups of *two, three,* and *four* pulse beats.

A. Listen to an accompaniment in rather slow tempo, recognizing accents and feeling their procession and their relation to the pulse beats. Respond to *all beats in the group* as follows:

[1] In a series of these movements the takeoff and the landing from elevation represent simultaneous accents.

1. Make a hand response by beating sharply downward on the accent and using short light movements for the other pulse beats.
2. Walk in place, then forward to all beats, making a hand response and/or vocalizing on the accent only.
3. Walk forward with a long step on the accent and short steps on the other beats (or beat).
4. Walk in place or forward, stepping on the whole foot for the accent and on tiptoe for the other beats (or beat).
5. Walk forward on each beat, making a strong hand or arm movement on the accent only. (Each child makes his own choice of movement.)
6. Jump in place landing with feet apart sideward on the accent and together on the other beats (or beat).
7. Jump in place, with a big jump on the first beat and bounces on the other beats. (The accent is on the jump landing, and elevation is after the last bounce.)
8. Perform any sequence of movements in place such as a strong lunge, a bend, twist, or push on the accent followed by body slaps, finger snaps, or other small movements on the other beats (or beat). Vocalization may accompany the accents.
9. Step forward on the accent and backward on the other beats, or vice versa.

B. Respond to *accents only* as follows:
   1. Make a response by beating, pushing, slapping, or clapping.
   2. Walk in place, forward, and in any direction.
   3. Jump in any direction, landing on the accent.
   4. Make any strong movement or a combination of movements in a sequence on the accents, freezing the movement until the next accent.

C. Respond to *other beats only* as follows (this gives a sense of syncopation and is the most difficult of the three categories):
   1. Clap, snap fingers, and/or vocalize to the other beats *after* the accent is played. (The accompaniment may continue to play all the beats or it may play only the accents.)
   2. Walk, bounce, or twist in place as in C, 1.
   3. Walk forward or in any other direction as in C, 1.
   4. Perform any other movement or series of movements as in C, 1.

Procedure for Accompaniment

Steps are arranged in order of support of the activity. In steps 1 and 2, complete or almost complete support is given; in step 3 the accompaniment provides only nominal support; in steps 4 and 5, either no support for the accents is given or the accompaniment plays syncopated accents against which the regular accents must be maintained.

1. Play pulse beats in the series of groups being used, with the first beat of each group accented. The accent is stressed by using a louder tone, a different instrument, or the low notes of a piano.
2. Play accents only (such as whole notes, dotted half notes, or half notes).
3. Play patterns with only normal accent stress.
4. Play the other beats only, omitting the accents.
5. Play patterns with syncopated accents on percussion instruments or records.

Regular Accents in Groups of Two, Three, and Four Pulse Beats

Accent on the First Beat of a Group of Four Beats. The four-beat group or 4/4 meter is the easiest for beginning work on accents. In walking or running to the four-beat group the accent always falls on the same foot.

Because of the longer time between accents, movement and accompaniment can exchange the accent and other beats in contrapuntal fashion: (1) the accent is taken in movement without any accompaniment and is followed by the other three beats in the accompaniment; (2) the accent is taken alone by the accompaniment, and the following three beats are taken by the movement.

Accent on the First of a Group of Two Beats. Response to accents of a two-beat group or 2/4 meter presents the problem of a very short time span between them. For some movements, such as walking, this is simple (as in the left-right of marching); combinations of movements or nonlocomotor movements demand a quick response. The contrapuntal exchange of accent and weak beat between accompaniment and movement is a difficult one.

Accent of the First Beat of a Group of Three Beats. The three-beat group or 3/4 meter is harder than the four-beat. In walking or running, the accent falls on alternate feet. Since the time between accents is shorter, response must be quicker. Also, because of the symmetrical structure of the body, a duple grouping is more congenial. However, triple timing has a lilt which is most pleasing to move to, and once its accents are felt, response is rewarding in performance.

Combining Accents of Two- and Four-Beat Groups. Accents of two- and four-beat groups may be combined in equal series, such as two two-beat groups and one four-beat group, or the reverse; or in unequal series, such as one two-beat group and one four-beat group, or the reverse. Combinations of step-hops and schottisches fit such series well.

Because they are in the area of syncopation, combinations of two-beat and three-beat or three-beat and four-beat groups are discussed in the section on advanced activities.

Rhythmic Games and Activities

Squares. Using four-beat groups (4/4 meter) and starting with an accent on the right foot, the children walk forward on the first four beats. Pivoting on the fourth walk, they do a sharp quarter-turn right and walk in that direction for the second four. The right turn is repeated twice more to complete the square. Note that the spatial direction, not the body direction, changes after each four-beat group, and the first step in the new direction is accented.

Changes in body direction as well as spatial direction on each four-beat group may be made by facing forward for the four parts of the square. On the second and fourth four-beat grouping, movement is sideward with step-cross steps; on the third, backward with three steps followed by a touch step. The tempo may be increased to that of a run, and a three- or two-beat grouping may be used, making a much smaller square—obviously a more difficult activity.

Zigzag. Using three-beat groups (3/4 meter) and starting to the right with an accent on the right foot, the children walk diagonally forward on the first three beats. Then, after pivoting on the right foot and facing diagonally left, they take three short walks in that direction for the second three beats. This zigzag pattern continues to the right and then to the left, always with an accent on the first step in the new direction. If the tempo is increased to that of a run, the resulting movement is the 3/4 run.

Follow the Accents. This game is similar to Follow the Beats in Chapter 12. The teacher or a child leader performs strong, sharp nonlocomotor movements on the natural accents of four-beat groups (later three- and even two-beat groups). The tempo should be moderate to slow, and the movement position is frozen through the next three beats. The group must be alert enough to imitate the movements at the moment they are performed, so that the feeling of moving strongly and sharply on the accent only is communicated. The leader faces the same way the group is facing and does not use turns. Thus, group members are not confused by direction changes and can always keep him within view.

Opposing Partners. The class works in twos, each person improvising a single sharp movement on the accents which contrasts in some way to that done by his partner. The type of contrasting movements may be decided upon beforehand. One may stretch upward or outward as the other bends low, push as the other pulls, strike as the other dodges, twist as the other straightens, flatten as the other rounds his body. On the next accent the movement is reversed. This game may also be used with two groups working in opposition, each group member taking an appropriate but not necessarily similar movement on each accent.

Grand Right and Left. Form a single circle, facing partners around the circle, with some space between couples. On the accent of a 3/4 measure grasp partner's right hand and step forward with the right foot. Proceed in the facing direction, passing partners on the right side and taking a step to each of the three beats. Grasp the left hand of the next person on the accent of the second group of three beats. Proceed, passing this person on the left, and grasp the third person's right hand on the third accent. Continue around the circle, joining hands with the oncoming person on the *accent only* of the three beat groups. Each hand grasp should be precisely on the accent and carry a slight downward beat of the hands. Curving in and out of the circle on the walking steps between accents will prevent getting to the new person too soon. Although used infrequently, the triple measure is the most efficient timing for the grand right and left; it fits both the circle spacing and the accents, which alternate on the right and left feet and hands.

Perform the grand right and left as above on the accents of a series of four-beat groups or 4/4 measures. To prevent meeting new persons too soon, leave some space between couples and make a decided curve in and out of the circle. This is a good test of judgment of the dimension of necessary movements in a limited space.

Perform the grand right and left as above on the accents of a series of two-beat groups or 2/4 measures. Here it is necessary to start with the couples closer together and to go directly toward the new person, so that hands may be grasped on every other walking beat.

Advanced Activities

Syncopated Accents and Mixed Meters

In the following activities, movement is made to irregular accents and measures and a feeling of syncopation is developed. *There can be no genuine recognition of and response to syncopated accents until the response to regular accents is well established.* In the foregoing rhythmic activities the children will have had some experience with syncopation if they have performed regular pulse beats and accents to syncopated accompaniment. Now the movement response is syncopated against a regular accompaniment or against a regular series of movements. The accompaniment should be a simple pulse beat series on a drum or strongly accented music that lends itself to syncopated movement.

5/4 and 7/4 Measures and Mixed Measures. Such measures, as well as a series of measures of different metric groups (such as two triple measures followed by one duple measure), will tend to produce asymmetrical movement, besides a feeling of syncopation. Uneven swings, or bends and stretches, or pushes and pulls are nonlocomotor movements which will fit the accents of a single measure of this sort; a combination of swings for triple measures and quick bend-stretches or pull-pushes for duple measures will fit a series of mixed measures. The following locomotor movements are usable and many more may be invented:

1. Do step-hops, with an extra hop or hops for the additional beats, and a change to the other foot on the accents (5/4 is a duple plus a triple measure or the reverse).
2. Jump with one foot forward and the other back on the accent, and bounce in place for the other beats. Change feet with a jump on the next accent.
3. Combine waltz balances with step-hops for a series of triple and duple measures.

Changing Accents Within Eight Beats. The numeral 8 can be divided into three combinations of twos and threes: 3, 3, 2; 2, 3, 3; 3, 2, 3; producing accents on 1, 4, 7; 1, 3, 6; 1, 4, 6. Responding to the accents alone and then to the other beats as well gives a feeling of syncopation as a duple or triple grouping is established and then almost immediately changed to the opposite. Any kind of hand response may be made at first, followed by non-locomotor movements or combinations of duple and triple dance steps—waltz balances or waltz walks with step-hops or two steps, or such a combination as walk, step-hop, walk, step-hop, step-hop.

Reverse Walk and Clap. Start with a simple combination of walks and claps within four counts such as WCCC and, after performing it a few times, reverse it to CWWW. Later change from one to the other after eight or even four counts. Other combinations and their reverse sequences—WWWC, WWCC, or WCWC—may then be constructed. Stamps or small jumps may be substituted for walks, and body slaps or finger snapping for claps.

Mixed Movements to Regular Measures. A combination of movements such as the walk, clap, touch-step or tap, jump, and run may be performed to even beats in regular groups. A jump is a stronger movement accent than a walk, and a walk is stronger than a clap or tap. A single movement to a pulse beat accents that beat more strongly than does a double movement, especially when the latter precedes the former. Hence, in deciding on a combination which will give a syncopated feeling to a regular accompaniment, it is necessary to place the stronger movement accents on the weaker beats. For example, a combination of jump-clap-walk-walk done to a 4/4 measure is a good regular accent or pulse beat activity but gives only a slight feeling of syncopation. If the combination is changed to walk-jump-clap-clap, there is a definite feeling of syncopation. (The jump is a quick one, almost like a fast chug on both feet.)

Some movement combinations for 2/4, 3/4, and 4/4 measures are listed below. Children can make others and do two or more in a series. Initials are used to designate walk, run, jump, tap, and clap. Large letters indicate one movement to each pulse beat. When a run or a quicker clap or tap is used, requiring two movements to one pulse beat, two small letters are used. The coordination demanded by some of these combinations is not easy, and they need to be practiced before they can be performed smoothly and continuously to an accompaniment, which should be strongly rhythmic.

2/4 measures:	WC	rrW	TW
	ccW	CJ	ttW
3/4 measures:	WJC	CTW	TWcc
	rrWC	ttWC	CrrJ
	WJrr	rrWT	ccWJ
4/4 measures:	WJCC	rrWWJ	JJrrW
	WJCT	WJrrW	TWrrW
	rrJccW	WJCtt	ccWrrJ

Moving Accents. In a series of four 4/4 measures, accents may be placed successively on the first beat in the first measure, the second beat in the second measure, the third beat in the third measure, and the fourth beat in the fourth measure. The same scheme may be used in a series of 3/4 measures. The accents will move from the first beat in the first measure to the second beat in the next measure and so on, thus:

| 3/4 measures: | **1** 2 3 1 **2** 3 1 2 **3** 1 2 3 1 2 3 1 2 **3** |
| 4/4 measures: | **1** 2 3 4 1 **2** 3 4 1 2 **3** 4 1 2 3 **4** 1 2 3 4 1 2 **3** 4 |

At first, accents may be clapped, the accompaniment playing the pulse beats. Then they may be clapped, with the feet walking the pulse beats and some support from the accompaniment. Later a combination of jumps for the accents and walks for the other pulse beats, or strong sideward steps on the accents and forward steps on the other pulse beats, may be used.

When the accent series is firmly established, movement is made on the accents only. It might consist of jumps, lunges, strikes, twists, or bends in different directions. This activity may be tried in groups of three or four persons, each one taking a successive accent.

Cumulative Rhythm. The term *cumulative rhythm* describes the pattern of accents resulting when an extra beat or beats is added to each successive one of a series of groups *without a pause between groups*. Often the start is made with a single beat or accent, then another is added so that a two-beat group follows, then a three, and so on; or two beats may be added instead of one so that the progression is from one to three to five and so on; or two or three beats rather than one may be the starting point for adding beats. Beats may be subtracted too. The intervals between accents are always uneven because the groups are of different lengths. Performance of these series will accustom children to accents in an irregular order.

It is best at first to use a short series and to practice adding beats and then subtracting them before combining both activities. Thus 1, 1 2, 1 2 3, 1 2 3 4, and 1 2 3 4, 1 2 3, 1 2, 1 may each be practiced alone before they are combined to make **1, 1 2, 1 2 3, 1 2 3 4, 1 2 3, 1 2, 1.** On repetition of a series which is added and subtracted in this fashion, three single accents will come in succession, i.e, on the last 1, on the 1 beginning the new series, and on the 1 2 in the new series. It is at this point that the most interesting effect of syncopation occurs. Some movements which can be used for cumulative rhythm are as follows:

1. Clap or tap the series of accents on the floor.
2. Walk in place or forward to each beat, taking the accents by claps or by stepping on the whole foot for the accents and on tiptoe for the other beats.
3. Walk forward and backward, changing direction on each new group of beats, as in forward 1, backward 1 2, forward 1 2 3, backward 1 2 3 4, and so on.
4. Use a step for the accents and a hop for the other beats, as in step 1, step-hop 1 2, step-hop-hop 1 2 3, step hop-hop-hop 1 2 3 4, and so on. This combination, if taken up to four beats and down to one, adds up to sixteen beats and gives a good feeling of syncopation when done several times to music in 4/4 meter that lends itself to syncopated movement.
5. Walk from side to side, making a turn toward the free foot to start back in the new direction. Thus, walk to the right with the right foot 1; walk to the left starting left and turning left 1 2; walk in the first direction starting left and turning left 1 2 3; walk in the other direction starting right and turning right 1 2 3 4; walk in the first direction starting right and turning right 1 2 3; walk in the other direction starting left and turning left 1

2; walk in the first direction with the left foot 1. A series that goes up to an even number of beats, such as four or six, finishes facing in the opposite direction from that at the start. A series going up to an odd number of beats, such as three, five, or seven, finishes facing in the same direction as that at the start.

6. Many other locomotor movements, such as the run and skip, as well as nonlocomotor movements may be used with cumulative rhythm. The series may be varied by repeating each group of beats; by doing one kind of movement for the odd numbers and another for the even numbers; by adding a constant movement such as a jump or a three-step turn after each group; by accelerating as the series increases and retarding as it decreases.

Resultant Rhythm. The term *resultant rhythm* describes the pattern of accents resulting when two unequal groups of beats are performed simultaneously. Thus a two- and a three-beat group both start with an accent on the first beat, but their accents do not fall together again until after six beats. During the six beats, the two-beat group accents beats 1, 3, and 5, and the three-beat group accents beats 1 and 4. The combined accent pattern, then, is on 1, 3, 4, and 5. Some examples follow:

Two- and three-beat groups
Two-beat group	1 2 1 2 1 2
Three-beat group	1 2 3 1 2 3
Resultant rhythm	1 2 **3 4 5** 6

Three- and four-beat groups
Three-beat group	1 2 3 1 2 3 1 2 3 1 2 3
Four-beat group	1 2 3 4 1 2 3 4 1 2 3 4
Resultant rhythm	1 2 3 **4 5** 6 **7** 8 **9 10** 11 12

Resultant rhythm means that the accents on one series occur against those of another series. The feeling of syncopation results when one person or group, having established a series, moves against an opposing series in the accompaniment or in another person or group. The accent pattern resulting from both series of accents is syncopated because it establishes one accent series, only to move from it into another.

The two- and three-beat groups are simplest and should be tried first. The three- and four-beat groups are harder because an accent pattern which covers a twelve-beat span is difficult to follow. The three- and five- or the four- and five-beat groups are too complicated for children.

Some ways in which the resultant rhythm of two- and three-beat groups may be used are as follows:

1. Make a hand response to a two-beat group, then a three-beat group,

by hitting the floor or the knees on the accent and clapping softly on the other beat or beats. Change from one to the other on irregular signals.

2. Make the above hand response to a two-beat group against a three-beat group in the accompaniment (2/4 measures against 3/4 measures), or vice versa. Change to synchronize the accents with those in the accompaniment and then change back again. Change both accent groups (in the accompaniment and with hands) and then change back to the original ones. (Changes should be made after six beats or a multiple of six.)

3. Perform a two-part movement (i.e., a step forward and then back or a step-hop) to an accompaniment in 3/4 time. Perform a three-part movement (i.e., a waltz balance or step-hop-hop) to an accompaniment in 2/4 time. Change to synchronize the accents with those of the accompaniment and then change back again. Change both accent groups and then change back to the original ones.

4. Form two groups, one to make the above hand response to two beats, the other to three beats, first with the accompaniment playing unaccented pulse beats, then without accompaniment. Each group changes to the other accent series on irregular signals. The change is made at the beginning of a group of six beats.

5. Form two lines facing each other, one line taking the two-beat group with a two-part movement (i.e., stepping forward and back), the other taking the three-beat group with a three-part movement (i.e., walking three steps forward and then three back). Change to the opposite movement on a signal. Use an accompaniment of unaccented pulse beats and then use no accompaniment. This activity can also be done with a third group between the two lines; this group takes the resultant rhythm. Suggested movement for the "resultant" group follows: Jump on 1, hold 2, step sideward toward the two-beat line on 3, step to the other side toward the three-beat line on 4, step sideward toward the two-beat line again on 5, hold 6. Arm movements may be used to emphasize directions.

6. Form three groups. One group makes a two-beat movement, another a three-beat movement, and the third a movement pattern using the resultant rhythm. Start with any one of the three. Have the other two groups come in one at a time on the appropriate accents, after the preceding movement is established, until all are being done together. The accompaniment of unaccented pulse beats may be stopped after all the groups are going, the movement continuing without accompaniment.

Omitting Beats Within a Group of Beats. When certain beats are omitted within a group of beats, the result is often a syncopated pattern of accents, particularly if more than one beat in succession is omitted. Some kind of movement, locomotor or nonlocomotor or a combination of movements, is invented for each successive beat of a four-, six-, or eight-beat phrase. Then one beat (and the movement used on that beat) is omitted in the sequence so that the preceding movement has twice its original time value, or two beats. After this pattern is successfully accomplished, omitting the movement on two successive or nonsuccessive beats may be tried. It is well to alternate a phrase in which movement is performed to each beat with a phrase in which one or more beats are omitted, at least in the beginning.

At first, this activity can be practiced with a hand response, such as clapping. Then it can be tried with a mixed hand response, such as tapping the knees, chest, or floor as well as the hands together. Then simple locomotor movement such as walking, or nonlocomotor movement such as bend and stretch may be used. Any movement should be definitely pulsed so that there is a precise movement for each beat. The final step is to invent one's own movement combinations to the rhythmic pattern resulting from omitted beats. The uneven five- and seven-beat groups present a more difficult challenge, as do groups of nine or twelve beats with their longer time span. Besides being omitted, single beats may be divided and the movement doubled for greater rhythmic interest.

Miscellaneous Activities for Syncopation. To develop a continuous movement response to the unaccented beat of a two-beat group the following procedure is suggested:

1. Clap the unaccented beat or beats of a familiar piece of music which lends itself to syncopation.
2. Do a toe-heel walk to this music, touching the toe lightly on the accent and dropping the heel on the unaccented or syncopated beat.
3. As the toe-heel walk is done, gradually raise the toe so that it does not touch the floor, contact with the floor being made only on the unaccented beat.
4. Continue lifting the foot forward on the accent and stepping on the unaccented beat.
5. Clap the knee of the lifted foot on the accent and step on the unaccented beat.
6. Alternate stepping on the regular accent and clapping the hands on the unaccented beat, then reverse. Change first on every twelve or sixteen beats and later on every eight beats. At the change there will be two steps or two claps in succession. Accompaniment may be accented pulse beats in two-beat groups or the kind of music described above.
7. Step alternately on the regular accents in a series of eight beats and then on the syncopated accents. The change from regular to syncopated accents may

be made in either of the following ways, the first being simpler than the second:

$$1\,2\,\underline{3}\,4\,\underline{5}\,6\,(\underline{7}\,8\,\underline{1}\,2)\,3\,\underline{4}\,5\,\underline{6}\,7\,\underline{8}\,1\,2\,\underline{3}\,4,\text{ etc.}$$
$$1\,2\,\underline{3}\,4\,\underline{5}\,6\,(\underline{7}\,8\,1\,2)\,3\,\underline{4}\,5\,\underline{6}\,7\,\underline{8}\,1\,2\,\underline{3}\,4,\text{ etc.}$$

Rhythmic Games

Phrases of Five. A sequence of five walks forward, five backward, and five jumps turning in place is practiced, with the first movement of each five accented with the change of direction. The class then divides into three groups or, if it is large, into several divisions of three groups. The first group starts forward and continues the three-part sequence, repeating it at least twice. The second group does the same but begins five counts later, and the third group ten counts later. The result is a canonic sequence similar to the singing of a "round," with the forward, backward, and turning directions maintained as constants.

A greater challenge to the maintenance of accurate pulse beat and accent response is an open or a scattered (instead of a group) formation with each child on his own starting the three five-count phrases as he is assigned. He may move forward or backward in any spatial direction, keeping his own sequence going, and must not be "thrown off" by others moving on different phrases.

Accompaniment should be moderately slow with an accent at the beginning of each five-count phrase. Phrases of seven may also be tried and accents reinforced by clapping, slapping, or vocalizing as children choose.

Combining Dance Steps. The step-hop (two beats), mazurka (three beats), and schottische (four beats) can be combined in several different sequences to a total of nine beats (three measures of 3/4 meter). Because the resulting accents are irregular, the total phrase has a syncopated feeling. These three dance steps can be used in any order to construct a line dance which moves sideward and in place.

Other possibilities: two mazurkas and three step-hops for a total of twelve beats, (three measures of 4/4 meter or six of 2/4); or two schottisches, two mazurkas, and one step-hop; or three step-hops, two mazurkas, and one schottische, both latter combinations for a total of sixteen beats (four measures of 4/4 meter).

Many different hora- or kolo-like dances may be made from such sequences.

Accent Designs. A total number of counts is decided upon (twelve or sixteen is enough to start with, but larger numbers can be attempted later).

The class divides into three groups, and certain counts within the total number are distributed among them in irregular sequence. Each group, working alone, invents *unison movement with everyone in the group facing in the same direction* for these counts, which form a *design of accents* within the total phrase. The movements should be large, sharp, and strong, mostly nonlocomotor, and some of them should be audible (claps, slaps, stamps). Vocalization may also be used at times if it is appropriate to the movement and does not overemphasize a single group.

The first group starts, and the accent designs are performed in sequence. As the counts move from group to group, the nonmoving groups remain frozen in their last shape until it is their turn to move again. An example of a twenty-four count distribution is the following:

First group	1, 2, —9, 10, —15, —17, 18, 19
Second group	5, 6, 7, —13, 14, —16, —23, 24
Third group	3, 4, —8, —11, 12, —20, 21, 22

Many variations of such a distribution may be made for two, three, or four groups. Accompaniment at first should be merely the total series of counts played at a slow tempo. Later more elaborate accompaniments may be used.

Chapter Preview

Introductory Activities
Two-Speed Patterns
Three-Speed Patterns
Rhythmic Games

Advanced Activities
Canon
Rounds
Rhythmic Games

Trying Patterns with a Partner

O. R. PETERSON III

14 Response to Rhythmic Patterns

A rhythmic pattern results when a short sequence of sounds or movements are unequal to each other in timing.

Introductory Activities

The simplest rhythmic patterns to translate into movement besides the gallop, skip, and slide are those that make use of the walk, run, and slow walk, or their equivalent in musical symbols—the quarter note, the eighth note, and the half note. Combinations of these two or three movement speeds within a framework of two-, three-, or four-beat groups (the quarter note or walking beat being used as the group unit) offer varieties of patterns. They may be tried first with a single hand or arm response, then with the feet in place, then forward, and finally in different directions. Once the pattern is reproduced in movement, children may invent combinations of other movements to fit it. For practicing the pattern, however, or a sequence of patterns, the *walk,* its twice-as-fast derivative the *run,* and its twice-as-slow derivative the *slow walk* are best.

Later, a skip or gallop may be used in a pattern if its timing is made equal to that of a simple walk or of one quarter note (as in a tied triplet). Triplet runs, equal to a quarter note in timing, and the very slow walk of the dotted half note or whole note may be used with advanced groups.

In combining movements or notes of different speeds into patterns, two things should be kept in mind. (1) It is easier to perform a pattern which finishes with a relatively slower movement or note (walks after runs, slow walks after walks) unless the pattern is done in a continuous sequence, in which case the end of it is of no special significance. (2) Placing a relatively longer note, particularly a half note, on a beat which does not ordinarily take an accent makes the pattern syncopated and harder to perform. An example in a four-beat group is a quarter note, half note, and quarter note (walk, slow walk, walk). Having the longer movement come on the second beat, which is not an accented beat, makes the pattern syncopated. Such patterns should be avoided with beginners.

Two-Speed Patterns

In a two-beat group the simplest pattern is two runs and a walk or two eighth notes and a quarter note; it is the only one not involving syncopation. Either the runs or the walk may start the sequence. In a four-beat group the simplest pattern is two walks and a slow walk or two quarter notes and a half note. The latter pattern may be lengthened by increasing the number of walks and runs or slow walks proportionately. Thus four runs and two walks make a four-beat group, six runs and three walks a six-beat group, and eight runs and four walks or four walks and two slow walks an eight-beat group.

The walks and runs or walks and slow walks may be arranged in different sequences such as those suggested below, which are listed as far as possible in order of difficulty. (Several of the last ones end with a faster movement; the last one is syncopated.)

Four–Beat Groups (4/4 measures)

Two walks, one slow walk

Two walks, two runs, one walk

Two runs, one walk, two runs, one walk

One walk, two runs, two walks

Two runs, three walks

Four runs, two walks

Six runs, one walk

One walk, four runs, one walk

One slow walk, two walks

Three walks, two runs

Two walks, four runs

One walk, six runs

Two runs, one walk, four runs

Two runs, two walks, two runs

One walk, one slow walk, one walk

Three–Beat Groups (3/4 measures)

One walk, two runs, one walk

Two runs, two walks

Four runs, one walk

Two walks, two runs

Two runs, one walk, two runs

One slow walk, one walk

One walk, one slow walk

Three-Speed Patterns

The slow walk, walk, and run represent three speeds of locomotor movement. They may be combined in various patterns in four-, six-, and eight-beat groups by splitting (doubling) or holding certain of the quarter-note or walking pulse beats, making either runs or slow walks.

The accompaniment, played upon drum, piano, or other instrument, should at first give full support to the pattern, following it exactly. After the pattern is reproduced by the hands and feet, the accompaniment may play only the pulse beats underlying the pattern, or the accents at the beginning of each group.

Four–Beat Groups

Two runs, one walk, one slow walk

One walk, two runs, one slow walk

Six–Beat Groups

Four runs, two walks, one slow walk

Two walks, four runs, one slow walk

Two runs, one walk, two runs, one walk,
one slow walk

Eight–Beat Groups

Four runs, two walks, two slow walks

Two walks, four runs, two walks,
one slow walk

Two walks, four runs, two slow walks

Children may progress to making their own vocal accompaniment. The names of the movement will suffice at first, such as "running, running, walk, walk, stop" for

or "walk, walk, run a little, slow, down" for

The simplest two-speed patterns may be verbalized by such words as *gingerbread, storybook* (two eighth notes, one quarter note), or *lawnmower, wheelbarrow* (the reverse). The children may make sentences or nonsense phrases which may or may not be related to the movement but which are characterized by a definite pattern (*honk, honk, pitter-patter, toot, toot, bang*).

Rhythmic Games

Name Patterns. Certain names of people, when chanted in their ordinary sequence, do not form a pattern: *Betty Johnson* or *Peter Foster*. Names of days, if repeated, do not ordinarily form patterns unless a pause is made on one of the syllables. Such names are good to use when practicing dance steps built on accented pulse beats series rather than rhythmic patterns. *Peter Foster* is excellent accompaniment for two step-hops or a schottische, as *Saturday* is for a waltz balance.

Other names may be chanted in continuously rhythmic patterns derived from the number of syllables, the placing of syllabic accents, and the length of time different syllables are sustained. When moving to these patterns it is best to start with simple ones like *Jennifer* or *Charlie Brown*

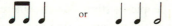

rather than one involving an upbeat or unaccented starting beat as in *Patricia, Marie, Elizabeth*.

It must be remembered that a name may be said in different rhythmic sequences depending upon the length of time different syllables are sustained. For example, *Josephine* can be said with a quarter note for each syllable in a three-beat group

which is merely a series of pulse beats; or it can be said with the last syllable sustained for a half note in a four-beat grouping or for a quarter note in a two-beat grouping

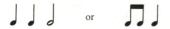

which makes a rhythmic pattern.

Two or more names may be put together to make longer patterns:

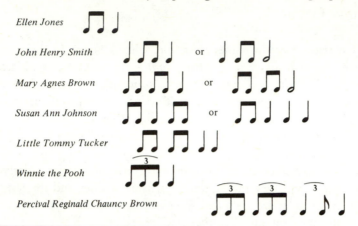

Children may try stepping out their own name patterns, those of others in the class, the teacher's, those of favorite people in stories or elsewhere. A game may be played by having a person or a group clap or step out a name in a certain category and letting the others guess who it is.

Nursery Rhymes. These make splendid patterns to use because their rhythmic sequences have been set by much repetition and therefore are familiar to everyone. It is well to start with the first line only. Then the line can be put into a movement phrase that suggests the words and yet is faithful to the rhythmic pattern. The other lines can be added one at a time. Most nursery rhymes are built on rhythmic patterns rather than continuous pulse beats (although "Peter, Peter, Pumpkin Eater" is an example of the latter). The names of some usable rhymes in order of difficulty follow; children may know many others.

Twinkle, Twinkle Little Star	*One, Two, Buckle My Shoe*
Hot Cross Buns	*Diddle Diddle Dumpling*
Sing a Song of Sixpence	*One, Two, Three O'Leary*
Baa, Baa, Black Sheep	*Tom, Tom, the Piper's Son*
Pussy Cat	*Hickory Dickory Dock*
Ding Dong Bell	*Humpty Dumpty Sat on a Wall*
Pease Porridge Hot	*Little Miss Muffet*
Fe Fi Fo Fum	*Ride a Cock Horse*

The quick sounds, like the sixteenth note for *the* in "Tom, Tom," may be passed over or taken with a hop. "Jack and Jill" works well in a series of skips or gallops, "Humpty Dumpty" with skips and triplet runs. A guessing game may be played with rhymes as well as with names.

Nonsense Phrases. Children can make their own chants for rhythmic patterns with a series of words or vocal sounds that appeal to them, as in "silly" talk like "Rain Makes Applesauce,"[1] or by using tried and true nonsense phrases. A few of the latter from Disney and traditional sources follow: supercalifragilisticexpialadoshus; snuffle-upagus; bibbety, bobbety, boo; abra-cadabra; ibety, bibety, sibety, sab; hocus pocus dominocus; and one of my grandmother's favorites (taken one part at a time), keemo, kīmo, dar-u-o, me-ī, me-o, me-rump, scump, bumpadiddle, willy-willy-wink-scat, sing-song colly-kitcha ki-me-o.

Advanced Activities

Canon

Canon is a form of musical counterpoint in which a short section of music is exactly imitated by the subsequent section or sections. Since the word *canon* implies the use of two or more repeating parts or *voices,* the accompaniment is considered the first voice and the movement the second voice. Thus the first voice (the sound of the rhythmic pattern in the accompaniment) is reproduced exactly and without pause by the second voice (the movement reproducing the rhythmic pattern). Two or more moving groups may be different voices as in *rounds,* which are a form of canon.

Canon may be performed very simply or in a highly complex manner. Four-beat groups (4/4 measures) are the simplest. Three-beat groups (3/4 measures) may be tried later. As noted before, patterns which end in a slow movement (a quarter or half note) are easier to perform.

It is well to use clapping for these activities before stepping them out. Although it is possible and convenient to use a drum as accompaniment for canon, simple melodies improvised on the piano in the desired pattern aid rhythmic memory.

1. The accompaniment plays a 4/4 measure pattern as the children listen. They reproduce it in movement on the second measure as the accompaniment is silent. The accompaniment plays another pattern on the third measure while the children listen. This is then reproduced in movement on the fourth measure as the accompaniment is silent. The same pattern may be

---

[1] Julian Scheer and Marvin Bileck, *Rain Makes Applesauce,* New York, Holiday House, 1964.

repeated if the movement response is not accurate. Eight measures is a sufficient activity duration.

2. The accompaniment plays a 4/4 measure pattern as the children listen. They reproduce it on the second measure as the accompaniment plays four quarter notes (the underlying pulse beats). The children then walk the four quarter notes on the third measure as they listen to the next pattern in the accompaniment. They reproduce this pattern as the accompaniment plays four quarter notes on the fourth measure. Starting with the second measure, movement is now continuous throughout the activity and it is necessary to listen carefully so that the rhythmic memory will accurately reproduce the pattern.

3. The accompaniment plays a series of different patterns which are reproduced in movement one measure later and at the same time that the next pattern is being listened to. Concentration on the accompaniment is essential, and movement reproduction becomes automatic after the pattern is identified, so that complete attention may be given to the next pattern. This activity requires a high degree of rhythmic memory and response and can be made more and more difficult by increasing the complexity of the patterns. For those who have the ability, it is a fascinating kind of rhythmic game.

Four measures make a good beginning phrase. Later, phrases may be lengthened indefinitely.

Rounds

A round is a form of canon; it is as much fun to perform in movement as it is to sing. However, simple movement sequences may be performed as rounds without the necessity of first learning a song. Phrases of Five, a game in Chapter 13 for example, has three equal parts (like three voices) and can be done as a three-voice round with only an accented pulse beat accompaniment.

A round song should first be learned and sung and then its rhythmic pattern stepped out so that everyone does it accurately. For a two- (or four-) voice round the class is divided into two groups. Three- and four-voice rounds may be performed later in three or four groups. Members of each group join hands in a line so that they do not become separated.

The following rounds lend themselves to two- and four-voice treatment (see Chapter 18 for others):

Frère Jacques (Brother John) *Three Blind Mice*
Row, Row, Row Your Boat   *Scotland's Burning*

Rounds which lend themselves to three-voice treatment are:

Sweetly Sings the Donkey   *Lovely Evening*
Where Is John?   *Hey Ho, Nobody at Home*

Rhythmic Games

Echo Game. In the simplest version of canon the accompaniment plays a pattern and the children echo it by moving to it. For older children these may be two-measure patterns in 3/4 or 4/4 meter.

Radio or Morse Code Signals. In this game, an extension of the echo game, the class divides into two or more groups and each group takes the name of a city or a radio station. The accompaniment, which is the home station, plays a pattern (code message). It may be repeated several times before a starting signal is given. The pattern is then picked up and clapped or stepped by each station in turn without pause in a predetermined order. Accurate reception throughout without blurring the pattern or accelerating the tempo indicates that no static is present.

Any station may make a pattern and initiate the message. The patterns must be of one or more 4/4 measure, preferably ending on a quarter or half note. Otherwise it is difficult for the next group to come in promptly at the beginning of the following measure.

This game may also be played with individuals instead of groups receiving and sending messages.

Home Station   Next Station   Next Station

Moving Patterns. As in Moving Accents in Chapter 13, a doubling (two eighth notes) of the single beat or quarter note occurs successively on the first, second, third, and fourth pulse beats of a series of four 4/4 measures. The double or running beats are placed on the first beat of the first measure, second of the second, third of the third, and fourth of the fourth. Once this sequence has been mastered, it is challenging to try it in groups of four abreast, each member moving forward one after the other on his measure. The sequence, with or without accompaniment, is repeated several times, then tried again after group members have changed places.

Threes and Sevens. The sequence of two threes and a seven to a sixteen-beat phrase, with a pause after each three and the seven, is common in folk dances and satisfying to perform by itself.

Try a sequence of three walks forward and a clap, repeated once, and followed by seven walks and a clap, making a total of sixteen quarter-note beats. After this has been mastered, substitute an inaudible hand or body movement for the claps. Then experiment with different directions—forward, backward, forward; or sideward, moving to one side and then the opposite—for each of the two threes and the seven. Then to syncopated accompaniment omit the claps or other movements entirely and merely pause for one beat after each of the threes and the seven. A more difficult sequence is to use one three-step turn to the right, another to the left, and a seven-step turn to the right, revolving twice around and finishing facing forward again. Other movement sequences can be invented by the children.

Rhythmic Conversations. Children work in partners to two different rhythmic patterns of four, six, or eight counts which they have made or have had assigned to them. The second pattern should give a sense of completion or an answer to the first. Each then invents movement to fit his pattern and performs it in turn, freezing the last shape, as though a conversation were being held. If children are adept in movement improvisation, the movements may change each time, or at least increase or decrease in dynamics, becoming forceful or quiet. A constant focus on the other person adds to the fun. This activity can be performed in two small groups as well.

Chapter Preview

Recognizing Musical Phrases

A Procedure for Activities

Rhythmic Games

Activities Integrating Rhythmic Response

A Rhythmic Conversation

15 *Response to Musical Phrasing*

A musical phrase is at least two measures long and forms a continuous thematic sequence, ending with what is known in musical terms as a cadence or a semicadence.

Recognizing Musical Phrases

In any dance composition to music, phrase identification of the music is one of the first important steps so that the movement phrases and those of the music will be allied with each other. Children should recognize that music has a logical temporal structure, with phrase succeeding phrase to make a whole. When listening to music and attending to phrase length, however, teacher and children may not always agree on length of phrases. "In certain songs it is interesting to note that adults are more apt to feel long phrases than are children, who often feel twice the number of phrases that the adults do. When this occurs, the children usually divide each long phrase into two shorter ones. . . . In view of individual differences in musical background, unanimity of responses to phrase length cannot be expected."[1]

Simple and easily understood analogies to musical phrases are rhyme lines such as those in Mother Goose rhymes. "Humpty Dumpty sat on a wall" is readily recognized as a single phrase. "Jack and Jill went up the hill to fetch a pail of water" may be regarded as a single phrase, or as two phrases, *hill* ending the first and *water* the second.

When children are making a dance to music, they should agree on the phrase lengths of the music. When they are learning a dance to music, they should be made aware that movement phrases of a dance sometimes follow long phrases of the music and sometimes short ones.

---

[1] Robert E. and Vernice T. Nye, *Music in the Elementary School,* 3rd ed., Prentice-Hall, Englewood Cliffs, N.J., 1970, p. 468.

It is also important that children learn to identify identical phrases, that is, phrases which are repeated identically or almost identically in the musical sequence. As far as possible in the following games and activities, identical phrases should be treated as such; the same series of movements should be performed to them with perhaps only a change of direction, or the same person or group may perform different movements.

The activities proposed in this chapter are not classified as introductory and advanced, because progress into more advanced activity depends upon the phrasing complexity of the music selected for analysis. Music in duple or triple timing which can be easily divided into two or four phrases, each consisting of two or four measures, is the simplest kind. Response may be made later to phrases that are less symmetrically balanced. Of more advanced phrasing construction is music with two or four phrases of three measures each; with three, five, or six phrases; with phrases of unequal length.

A Procedure for Activities

In the following procedure it is neither necessary nor desirable to repeat all the activities with each new piece of music, because after some practice in listening and responding, phrases are easily identified.

1. Listen to all the music, attending to its quality and its division into parts.
2. Identify phrases as they are played separately.
3. Move arms in response to phrases either from one side to the other, or up, across, and down on each phrase. There should be a definite change of direction of the arm movement at the beginning of each phrase.
4. Clap the accent at the beginning of each phrase.
5. Use a walk, movement up-down, or another suitable locomotor or nonlocomotor movement changing the direction sharply at the beginning of a new phrase.
6. Using any suitable locomotor movement forward, and movement in place such as hand movements, turns, swings, or bounces, change from forward movement to movement in place on successive phrases and repeat identical movement on identical phrases.
7. Move as above in two groups, one group moving to the first phrase, the other to the second, and so on. Do the same with a partner.
8. Move in two groups, each group alternating locomotor and nonlocomotor movements on successive phrases so that one group is moving through space as the other moves in place. Movement may be decided upon beforehand or improvised by a leader whom each group follows.

9. Move in several groups, each with a leader, to music which has been heard and analyzed. Each leader is responsible for improvising new movement (locomotor or nonlocomotor) or at least changing the direction or level of the movement at the beginning of each new phrase. The group follows the leader's movements as accurately as possible, staying behind him as he steers a course around the other groups. As the music used will be familiar, leaders should use identical movements for identical phrases or a variation of the same movement.

Rhythmic Games

Leading Phrases.   A leader, at first the teacher, faces the group. A simple means of locomotion is decided upon (walking, running, skipping, or sliding) and the music is played. The leader signals a change of direction for the group on each phrase. Signals are pointing for sideward right or left, pushing for backward, beckoning for forward, pushing downward for movement in place, circling hand a few times for turning around. The leader may choose any direction pattern, trying to balance it as well as possible and giving the new signal just before the beginning of the new phrase. Children make good leaders after some experience in responding to phrasing. (See Traffic Cop in Chapter 12.)

Copy Cat.   The class divides into twos, the partners facing each other. One partner makes a series of movements to the first phrase of the music. The other partner imitates these movements on the second phrase while the first one watches to check accuracy. The first partner makes a new series of movements on the third phrase, which his partner imitates on the fourth. Movements should be improvised and may consist of movements of arms, legs, and head while sitting on the floor; nonlocomotor movements standing in place; or locomotor movements in different directions. Suitable music for this game should have some repetition of melody or rhythmic pattern in alternate phrases.

Answer Me.   This game is played like Copy Cat except that, instead of imitating his partner, the second person invents movements of his own to answer his partner's movement phrase. Phrases are alternated between partners as before, and the music should have a different melody or rhythmic pattern on alternate phrases. The game can also be played in two groups, each following a leader's movements. The spontaneous movement invention often achieves grotesque and humorous effects. (See Rhythmic Conversation in Chapter 14.)

The Phrase Game. The leader, using a simple song, assigns for each phrase specific movements which fit the words, at least rhythmically, and which are performed throughout the phrase. Such movements might be any of the basic locomotor movements or simple dance steps, the nonlocomotor movements of swinging, swaying, rocking, pushing, pulling, stretching, turning, or miscellaneous movements such as clapping, slapping, tapping. Identical phrases should use identical movement.

As the song is sung by half the class, the other half performs the movement assigned to each phrase. Each child does the movement in his own way, varying direction, dimension, and level as he desires. The timing and dynamic quality of the movement are dictated by the music.

The group may then choose specific movements for each phrase selecting the most appropriate movement to use among those performed. From here it is a short step to making a formal spatial arrangement of such movements so that a group dance to the song is the result.

Activities Integrating Rhythmic Response

The following activities use all four types of rhythmic response (to beat, accent, pattern, and phrase) simultaneously and therefore should be attempted only after children have mastered introductory activities in each area.

Music in Motion. Chants, descants, and countermelodies to the melodic line of songs may present a rhythmic challenge in movement. Groups of children can move to these song parts while other groups sing them. Two songs sung together may be the accompaniment for two movement interpretations performed simultaneously. Simple rounds which can be used in this fashion are "Three Blind Mice" combined with either "Row Your Boat" or "Are You Sleeping."[2] Children in the fourth and fifth grades begin to do this kind of simple part singing in music classes. The same children could use some of these suitable songs to build rhythmic movement which could be performed in the several parts in which the songs are sung.

Visualizing Music. Music with well-marked phrases (preferably a familiar song) is chosen. Its rhythmic patterns should be simple, consisting of runs and walks, or runs, walks, and skips. The children listen to the music, identifying *pulse beats, accents, patterns,* and *phrasing.* They divide

---

[2] For other examples, see Nye, ibid., p. 387.

into four groups, and each group invents movements to fit one of the above rhythmic responses which has been assigned to it. Locomotor, nonlocomotor, or a combination of both is in order. The rhythmic pattern need not be followed exactly, but the predominant pattern should be used. Then, as the music is sung or played, all four groups perform their movements simultaneously. The groups can then be placed in a harmonious and balanced spatial design. Children should change from group to group and should be given an opportunity to see the movement of the four groups by having half of each group watch at one time.

Orchestra Leader. The children sit on the floor close together in three or more groups. Each group is assigned a note—a whole note, a half, a quarter, an eighth, or combinations such as a dotted eighth note and a sixteenth or two eighth notes and a quarter note. The leader faces the group and beats a 4/4 measure, using a slow tempo and repeating it several times. He then constructs a four- or eight-measure phrase by pointing to a different group for each measure; the group responds by clapping its assigned note throughout the measure. Leaders must give a strong signal just before the accent at the beginning of a new measure so that the new group can come in on time. They may point to a group which has already been used or to the same group for two measures. The tempo first designated by the leader must be maintained throughout the phrase. The rhythmic sequence of the phrase can be appraised by the children. It will be found that phrases are more satisfying if they finish on the slower notes (half and whole notes).

Part V | MAKING DANCES

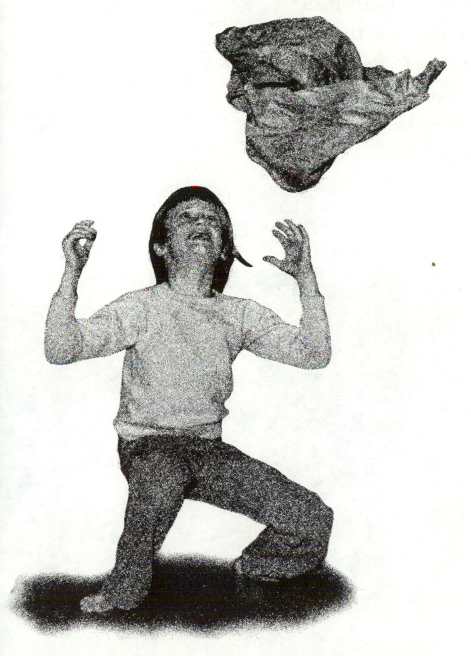

Chapter Preview

Listening for the Right Sound

IRVING BERG

16 Making Dances: Orientation

Adults can make it possible or impossible for children to be creative. If the shackles or binders are too tight, atrophy sets in; if there are no restraints, the child may fly off into space; but if they exist in the right amount . . . a spark of genius may show up in a classroom, or a gymnasium.[1]

Dance as a living art depends upon creating new forms which have artistic validity. All the forms that exist today on the concert stage, in theaters, in community halls and auditoriums, on village greens or parks, in school gymnasiums, in ballrooms or public dance places have at one time or another been made by a person or by persons dancing together. The new form may have been motivated by a particular fancy or belief, by dissatisfaction with old forms in a modern setting, by the desire to achieve something spectacular or novel in movement, or by an urge to express an aesthetically significant movement experience. Whatever the creative purpose, whether noble, genuine, worthy, or unworthy, a different form came into existence, to be seen or to be danced.

Values of Dance-Making

One of the great values of dance in the education of children comes from the experience of making their own forms to express, to communicate, to enjoy. Each child is unique in his individualism and in his environment. He needs a chance to say what he is, how he feels, what his world means to him. He

[1] *People Make Ideas Happen, The Story of Creativity in HPER,* Washington, D.C., AAHPER, 1971, p. 41.

should be helped to perceive his relationship to his group, to have the satisfaction, when working with others, of contributing to a whole.

Participation in dance-making then, is every child's due and depends in
great part upon the teacher's ability to free children for creative endeavor.
Willingly or unwillingly, children will follow imposed patterns of thought
or action if that is their meager and constant fare. On the other hand, they
will think for themselves, make for themselves, if the opportunity is present
and the way is cleared.

Gardner Murphy makes the following statement "We know from
watching children in progressive schools that the desire to create must be
almost universal, and that almost everyone has some measure of originality
which stems from his fresh perception of life and experience, and from the
uniqueness of his own fantasy when he is free to share it. Fantasy ideas are
as much a function of a healthy, active mental life as motor achievements
and skills are of healthy muscles."[2]

What Is a Child's Dance?

If dance as play and dance as art are to achieve status in the school community, there must be clarity in terminology lest everyone be bogged down
again in the nomenclature of *rhythms, rhythmics,* and *rhythmical activities.*

A piece of music or a musical composition implies some arrangement of
notes into a form, simple or complex. In the same way *a dance* (or *a dance
study,* a more accurate term for the creative product of children) must be
more than the act of moving to a rhythmic accompaniment, however
creative the moving. It must have contrast or variety, and temporal form
demands that it possess a beginning, a middle, and an end. It may indeed
have only two parts in the sequence, as it often does with young children;
but in the change from one movement to the other, variety is present and the
beginning of a form is achieved. Form is the essential element that distin-
guishes *a dance* from exploratory, improvisational, or merely rhythmic
movement.

The Process of Dance-Making

Where do ideas for dances come from? From many sources: experience from
life itself, music, drama, legend, history, psychology, literature, ritual, religion,
folklore, social conditions, fantasy; and from such vague promptings as moods,

---

2 Gardner Murphy, *Personality*, New York, Harper & Row, 1947, pp. 453–454.

impressions. And special interests, such as technical aspects of a theory of movements, comment on styles of dances or other arts, theatrical effects, or even abstract sources: line, color, shape, dynamics, rhythm. It is probably rare for a choreographer deliberately to make a choice of a theme by rational means. He is more likely to be seized by an enthusiasm which wells up from the subconscious and demands to be born. All the thinking comes, or should, following the initial seizure, when decisions should be made by reason. Is this theme the kind of child who will make a dance—or should he be put out for adoption by an author, a painter or a psychologist? If he is to be mine, how shall he be clothed and educated and made to speak of my glorious vision? These considerations involve all the resources of choreographic craft.[3]

These words were written by the late Doris Humphrey, one of the great choreographers of this century. She is speaking to mature dancers, not to teachers of children. But much of what she says speaks also to them.

What does one need to make a dance? Oneself, to be sure, and a certain amount of space to move around in. Chiefly, though, one needs an idea, a purpose, an intention which is conscious and voluntary. With children it may be motivated by the teacher. There is only one precaution to consider. The dance must grow out of movement, its purpose or intention must be centered in movement, or its idea or theme must have movement potential. These potentialities for movement expression may sometimes not be obvious to the unimaginative. Children often see legitimate movement possibilities in subject matter which many adults would reject. It stands to reason, however, that there are hosts of ideas, concepts, theories, doctrines, opinions which should be left to other means of human expression, for they could not possibly be communicated by movement alone.

What is involved in making a dance? Planning, experimenting, replanning, selecting, eliminating, appraising—for the making of a dance is a task of construction. How may one describe the process of dance-making? What role does the teacher play? What preparation must she make for it and how does she carry it through? Unfortunately, there is no standard formula. The method is implicit in the interaction within the group and between the group and the teacher. The stronger the teacher's direction and the greater her influence, less and less does the dance become a product of the children. If, on the other hand, she merely says, "Now, everyone make a dance," many children lost in a sea of possibilities will get nowhere.

When a child or a group of children make a dance which is legitimately theirs, it means that they, more than the teacher, have decided what shall go into it, have drawn upon their repertoire of movements or invented new ones,

[3] Doris Humphrey, *The Art of Making Dances,* New York, Rinehart, 1959, p. 32.

and have put them into some kind of form. Hundreds of other children may have come upon exactly the same thing before. For this child, for these children, it is new and it is theirs.

The dearth of dance-making or of related creativity in dance in our schools is due in part to the complexity of the teacher's role. It is so much easier to teach a dance and be done with it. Here the process is logical, neat, circumscribed, pat. However, the process of making dances brings three things to the child's development which are not provided in nearly so great a degree in other aspects of the dance program. One is the opportunity for his expression of selfhood, the deepening of his perception of himself in the context of his group. The second is the challenge, using himself as a medium for expression, to solve a movement problem which calls upon his intellectual and imaginative as well as his physical powers. The third relates to the making of group dances and is implicit in the social interaction in which each member makes his special contribution to group activity.

Catching a Mood

O. R. PETERSON III

Helping Children Make Dance Studies

The teacher's role in any creative activity is to set the stage, to establish an environment in which decisions as to progress can be made smoothly. What creative problem is stated depends upon the approach to composition selected, a decision made by teachers and children together before actual work begins.

After the stage is set or the problem accepted come discussion and planning, evaluation of progress, discovery of movements which *work* and elimination of those which do not, structuring of the sequence of parts, selection of the accompaniment if the approach does not include it, performance of the dance, and sometimes audience appraisal.

In the early grades, dance studies will be solos; that is, each child will work out his own individually. Young children are not yet ready for the give-and-take of group creative endeavor, are still unable to perceive themselves as contributing members of a group. When classes are small enough, each may make his own study irrespective of studies made by others, even though the approach to the problem to be solved will generally be the same for all. The teacher helps the slow ones to get started; offers suggestions to others who are getting off the track; calls a halt when productive creativity slows down; helps the children to evaluate their own and others' progress and final product. The same process takes place when the children have reached enough social maturity for two or three to work together.

When large classes are working on studies from the approach of imagery or dramatic idea, another kind of procedure may be somewhat less creative but more practical. After the dance idea is decided on, movement experimentation is engaged in by everyone and a sequence decided upon which all will follow. The teacher first leads the discussion on the idea (it may be one she has suggested) and later helps the children decide what the sequence of action will be. She is careful to encourage individual variation of dance expression within the limits imposed by the similar sequence so that each child makes his own rather than imitating another's.

With older children, groups of four to eight are excellent units for dance-making. It is well to have a group chairman through whom suggestions clear and who keeps the others moving along on the dance sequence. The teacher helps with the general plan, circulates from group to group, is available when help is needed, offers suggestions when an impasse is reached or progress seems blocked, and leads the discussion of the class evaluation of progress and performance.

When the whole class works together to make a group dance study, the teacher assumes the role of leader. This can be an excellent group project, provided the teacher keeps in abeyance her own ideas as to how the dance should be made and offers suggestions only when others which the children have made are judged unsatisfactory by them.

It is as hard to define the precise limits of teacher guidance in the area of dance-making as it is to say how much direction she should offer in any other creative field or even in leading a classroom discussion. A good teacher is so sensitive to children and to situations that she knows when to keep hands off and when a few words will provide new impetus for action. A teacher who dominates the children's ideas and remakes them into patterns more satisfying to herself may produce more interesting dances. But she should not fool herself. Her creative ability is being exercised, not the children's.

Accompaniment[4]

The best accompaniment for a dance that starts from an image or a dramatic idea is improvised live, on the spot, and preferably with the children's participation. Percussion instruments of various types, a piano, or voice sounds can be used.

Vocalizing often has the virtue of causing the movement to come alive, especially if the child invents his own appropriate vocalizing as he moves, so that the sound seems to arise from the movement itself. Onomatopoetic words (*buzz, tick, plop, hiss, boo, bang, lull*) as well as suitable abstract sounds are effective. Clapping, slapping, or striking different parts of the body is also perfectly legitimate. An autoharp is a useful instrument, and playing directly on the strings of the piano (after first removing the front) affords unusual sound effects.

The following percussion and toy instruments have been used successfully for dance accompaniment:

Bells	Harmonicas	Tambourines
Castanets	Kazoos	Temple blocks
Chimes	Ocarinas	Tone blocks
Coconut shells	Ratchets	Toy accordions
Cymbals	Rattles	Toy flutes
Drums	Rhythm sticks	Triangles
Finger cymbals	Sand blocks	Glass wind-bells
Gongs	Slide whistles	Wood-blocks
		Xylophones

[4] See also Chapter 4.

Next to the piano, drums[5] are most useful for improvised sounds. They may be struck with the hand, knuckles, fingers, fingernails, drumsticks, a brush, or hard or soft beaters. The face of the drum can produce different tones as the center and then the edges are struck. The side of the drum struck with the wooden part of the beater produces a sound similar to that of a wood-block. For maximum effect gongs, triangles, cymbals, and xylophones should be suspended from a stout cord when struck.

Accompanying instruments are best classified by the sounds they make. A well-equipped dance room should have one or two of each type. Gongs and good xylophones are fairly expensive but very useful. Drums, rattles, water bottles, and rhythm sticks can be made at home or at school. Kazoos, slide whistles, ratchets, and other toy instruments are relatively inexpensive.

Clear, tonal sounds with some resonance: drums struck with a soft beater or with the hands.

Deeply pitched, sustained, ringing sounds with much resonance: gongs swung and struck with a soft beater.

Metallic, ringing, high-pitched sounds: triangles, bells, chimes, water bottles, cymbals.

Lightly ringing, tinkling sounds: glass wind-bells, finger cymbals, triangles tapped lightly, jingle bells.

Sharp, hard, sudden, staccato sounds: rhythm sticks, ratchets, single bars of a xylophone struck sharply.

Sharp, staccato, hollow sounds: wood-blocks, temple blocks, drums struck with a hard beater, tambourines struck with the hand.

A succession of light, quick sounds: rattles, maracas, tambourines shaken, drums struck with the fingernails, a stick drawn lightly across the bars of a xylophone.

Soft, clinging, swishing sounds: drums played with a wire brush, rattles swung in an arc.

Crashing, roaring sounds: gongs or large cymbals struck sharply with a hard beater, large cymbals clashed together.

[5] For drum-making instructions and other helpful information about instruments and how to use them, see Emma Sheehy, *Children Discover Music and Dance,* New York, Teachers College, 1968, chap. 5, or Pia Gilbert and Aileene Lockhart, *Music for the Modern Dance,* Dubuque, Iowa, Brown, 1961, chap. 4.

Clanging, harsh, persistent sounds: triangles struck continuously on the inside of the bars, a hard beater drawn firmly back and forth over a few bars of a xylophone, a bell shaken vigorously, gongs or cymbals struck continuously with a hard beater, ratchets turned continuously.

Scratchy, scraping sounds: a wood-block or drum rubbed with sandpaper, grooved gourds, sand blocks.

Sounds moving quickly from low to high pitch and vice versa: a slide whistle, a beater drawn quickly over successive bars of a xylophone (glissando).

Buzzing or low monotonous sounds: humming into a kazoo, drumming on a drum with the fingers.

Musical sounds of various types: harmonicas, ocarinas, toy flutes, toy accordions.

In *Art for Teachers of Children,* Chandler Montgomery devotes most of Chapter 9 to "Found Sounds"—sound-making objects that are not any of the conventional musical instruments "because [the latter] by their strong associations, . . . tend to dominate and to narrow the field of listening."[6] Experiments with spoken or "found" sounds, with "junk instruments" which imaginative children can construct in the art room or at home offer new and interesting potentials for dance accompaniment.

For teachers who have an accompanist, who can play the piano them- selves, or who prefer to use composed music, references for musical selections are suggested in Chapter 20. Most of them adapt themselves to varied use. A piece titled "Falling Leaves" might do equally well for a dance about snowflakes or clouds; one called "Elephants," for giants or bears. It is hoped that the accompanying pianist will gradually attempt to improvise such descriptive music rather than depending solely upon the notated page.

Approaches to Dance-Making

An approach to dance-making might be considered the catalyst which sets the creative process in motion. There are many such catalysts, some idea- tional, interpretive, and dramatic, others representing the solution of move- ment and rhythmic problems or the translation into movement of the structure and quality of a piece of music. That a person may start in one way and end with a different kind of dance entirely is, of course, one of the hazards and delights of any kind of creative endeavor.

---

[6] Chandler Montgomery, *Art for Teachers of Children,* Columbus, Ohio, Merrill, 1968.

If a beginning is made from an idea, a poem, a song, or music which is distinctly descriptive, the dance product will have a dramatic flavor, conveying some semblance of the content of whatever gave it its initial impetus. If a beginning is made through movement itself, through investigation, invention, problem-solving, or an attempt to find appropriate movement for the formal structure of a piece of music, the result, although expressive, will be more abstract and lack the literal or emotional meaning of the first approach.

In the following chapters five approaches are described and materials and references given for each. In the first three, the materials appropriate for younger and older children are separated. Each chapter suggests procedures as well as materials, although detailed discussion of procedures will be found in Chapter 17. Among these approaches the teacher should find many which will stimulate her to embark with her children upon the creative enterprise of making dances.

Chapter Preview

With Younger Children

Leads into Dance-Making: Contrasts and Combinations
Making the Dance Study
Procedure for Dance Studies of Similar Sequence
Units of Dance Images

With Older Children

Leads into Dance-Making: Contrasts and Combinations
Ideas for Dance Studies
Making the Dance Study

Witches and Such

DETROIT PUBLIC SCHOOLS

17 *Approach from Imagery and Idea*

. . . The dancer connects his inner world with his body to find a new reality . . . the awareness of the artistic self can be found not only through the development of superior technical equipment, but also by exploring the dancer's imaginative life.[1]

With Younger Children

For younger children particularly, the approach to dance-making from an image or an idea—making a dance *about something*—seems to be the most useful because children identify readily with many kinds of animate and inanimate objects, giving them human impulses and rhythmic vitality. Whatever is being interpreted, however, should employ large rather than small movements. Refined gestures or pantomimic sequences that are rhythmically unstructured should be deemphasized unless they can be exaggerated in dimension or executed in a rhythmic sequence. Children will willingly forgo some of the literal aspects of a subject's activity in favor of getting on with its more energetic functions.

Leads into Dance-Making: Contrasts and Combinations

Chapter 6 suggested a number of images for movement exploration. Here there need be no formal arrangement of movements into a dance sequence except for a starting position and a finishing one. The benefits and

---

[1] Joseph Gifford, "Some Aspects of Movement Education," paper read at the annual meeting of the American Dance Guild, New York, N.Y., June 1969.

joys of experimenting are more important at this age than putting movements together into a dance study. Sometimes, however, a sequence happens
spontaneously when children are improvising to imagery as in the following:
The rag doll, after dancing, falls down; the kite gets stuck in a tree and
shakes in the wind; the pony changes from a gallop to a walk as he goes
back to the barn.

In such simple combinations of actions, usually contrasting in time,
space, force, shape, or movement and stillness, a simple dance form begins to
evolve. The sequence sets one movement against another, making each more
vivid and meaningful. For example:

CONTRASTS

A tornado and a breeze
Goblins and ghosts
An elf and a giant
A wooden doll and a rag doll
A grasshopper and a snake
The Three Bears
An alarm clock and a cuckoo clock
Toast in a toaster and popcorn in a popper
Flopsie Mopsy and Elegant Ellen
A cactus plant and a flower petal
Big Bird and Cookie Monster ("Sesame Street")

Many images suggest a sequence of events, involving contrasting movements. For example:

CONTRASTING SEQUENCES

An egg carefully broken and then scrambled
An elastic slowly stretched and then snapped
The echo of a shout
Climbing a steep hill and running down the other side
Lifting a heavy weight, carrying it, and then putting it down
A piece of paper blown hither and yon and then into a quiet place
Floating balloons which either pop and fly into pieces or gradually leak into a
    collapse
Flickering flames which change into softly curling and drifting smoke
Heavy surf succeeded by gentle lapping on the shore
Clothes hanging on the line, blown by the wind, which disengages one, then an-
    other clothespin and blows the clothes against the fence

A parachute jumper whose movement is fast and direct until the pulling of the
    cord makes it slow and floating
Rockets to the moon and moonbeams
A violent storm followed by a peaceful rainbow

and even

> 'Twas the night before Christmas
>   and all through the house
> Not a creature was stirring, not
>   even a mouse,
> When out on the lawn there arose
>   such a clatter,
> I sprang from my bed to see
>   what was the matter.

Children's literature and nature supply ideas of the metamorphosis of
one kind of being into another and perhaps still another. They have their
counterparts in movement.

METAMORPHOSES

Beauty and the Beast	*Caterpillar into moth*
Cinderella	*Egg into bird*
King Midas's Daughter	*Seed into flower*
The Ugly Duckling	*Tadpole into frog*

Making the Dance Study

Since young children cannot yet work cooperatively as a group efficiently
without the guidance of the teacher, they work as individuals for the most
part, and there are two procedures that may be followed. Everyone can make
his own study, or all the children can jointly decide upon one dance sequence, within which each child is free to make his own movement
interpretation.

When a solo is made in which the sequence of parts is similar for all, the
accompaniment too can be similar. There will still be much opportunity for
individual variety in movement expression. The children decide on the
sequence of parts after the movements associated with the idea have been
discussed and explored. They also decide what type of accompaniment best
fits each movement. Thus, it is everyone's dance, although each child may
dance it in his own way.

A large group making a solo dance of similar sequence will proceed more or less as follows:

1. Idea for dance is decided upon (Jack Frost)
2. Discussion of idea
    a. How it looks
    b. How it moves
    c. What it does
3. Movement experimentation on basis of discussion
4. Review of discussion on basis of experimentation
5. Further movement experimentation, if necessary
6. Selection of parts best fitted for dance, and elimination of others
7. Planning of dance sequence
8. Planning of accompaniment
9. Trial of dance
10. Evaluation and replanning, if necessary
11. Further trials
12. Performance for peers (half of class performs for the other half)
13. Evaluation of performances (optional)

In a smaller group of children each child may, at least some of the time, make his own dance study, possibly on a different subject to a different accompaniment. Although a single idea may inspire all of the compositions, after preliminary discussion each child chooses from among several subjects related to the controlling theme or unit—Halloween, Christmas toys, the circus, and so on. Personal themes adapt themselves well to this kind of dance-making. A dream, a birthday dance, contrasting sequences or metamorphoses like those suggested earlier in the chapter are good for such individual interpretations.

The teacher assists each small choreographer, offering suggestions when inventiveness ebbs (but not insisting that they be followed), keeping the dance within the bounds of the idea chosen, and acting as accompanist if accompaniment is called for.

Such a procedure offers more opportunity for individual creativity than the one in which the group together makes many of the suggestions and decisions. Unless the class is quite small, however, there is rarely time for each child's dance to be seen and appraised—for the shy child probably a desirable situation. The process, not the product, is what is important at this level. If half of the group performs for the rest, daring invention or at least variations from the obvious in movement will be noted by children and teacher alike. The problem of a common accompaniment is solved if dances are made to a recording of descriptive music, a song, a poem, or percussion or vocal sounds chosen by the child. An alert teacher will always be able to

Procedure for Dance Studies of Similar Sequence

Idea	Differentiation of Parts in Idea (Discussion by Children and Teacher)	Experimentation with Movement (Children)	Structuring the Sequence (Children with Some Guidance by Teacher)	Choosing the Accompaniment (Children)	Dance About Jack Frost (A-B-A-C-A-D-E-A)
Jack Frost	How he looks	Bright, spry, little, mischievous, perky	Appears with characteristic locomotor movement	Triangle tapped lightly	A (20–30 fast beats)
	How he moves	Quickly, quietly, slyly (light runs, toes turned in or out, knees up high in front or side, hands held up in front or behind back or on hips, or on top of head to make a pointed cap, etc.; sometimes slower creeping movements)	Paints leaves	Rattles shaken softly	B (10–15 slow and fast beats)
			Moves on	Triangle	A (15–20 fast beats)
			Paints window pictures	Short and long glissandos on xylophone	C (15–20 slow and fast beats)
	What he does	Comes out at night, slowly, then faster / Paints the leaves (swings, reaches, bends, some fast, some slower) / Makes funny pictures on windows / Makes the sidewalks slippery (sweeps rime on them) / Does a funny little jig dance when he gets through working / Runs away when the sun comes up / (Suggestions not used in dance: pinching people's fingers and toes, melting when the sun comes up)	Moves on	Triangle	A (10–15 fast beats)
			Sweeps sidewalks and fields with rime	Brush on drum	D (10–15 slow beats)
			Is amused by what he has done and laughs and dances about	Single bars struck on xylophone in quick, random series	E (20–30 fast beats)
			Runs off at sunrise	Triangle	A (10–15 fast beats)

note particular studies in progress that will please and inspire the other children if performed for them. If she is also a wise teacher, she will know which children need to dance for the others in order to develop status, security, and creativity as members of the group.

Units of Dance Images

Often a classroom teacher finds it desirable to integrate children's activities in literature, music, art, dramatics, and dance around a single theme, suggested by children's interests or a particular unit of work. Many stories lend themselves to dance and creative dramatics. As has been said before, a very thin line exists, particularly with younger children, between these two areas.

The following pages offer lists of (1) stories enjoyed by children related to the overall theme, (2) images or ideas about which children may wish to dance, and (3) movement clues in the words of young children who have used them in this fashion. In no sense do these clues exhaust the possibilities for creative movement either in the subjects or in the units themselves. Children will suggest many new ones and many variations on the old.

Poems which may be used in the same way as the suggested stories will be found in Chapter 19.

The Seasons

Autumn

STORIES

Autumn Harvest	Alvin Tresselt
Georgie the Ghost	Robert Bright
Georgie's Halloween	Robert Bright
House of Four Seasons, The	Roger A. Duvoisin
Littlest Witch, The	Jeanne Massey
Mr. Apple's Family	Jean McDevitt
Proud Pumpkin	Nora Unwin
Thanksgiving Story, The	Alice Dalgliesh
Wooble, the Witch Cat	Mary Calhoun

Unit: Early Fall

Leaves Falling
They drift down.
They flutter.
They fall softly into a quiet place.

Leaves Blown by the Wind
They whirl around.
They fly down the street.
They hide under the bushes.

Birds Flying South
Sometimes they fly alone and sometimes they fly together for company. They stop to rest on branches and ponds.

Unit: Halloween

The Good Witch
She rides up in the clouds on her broomstick.
She sweeps cobwebs out of the sky.
She waves her wand to make wishes come true.

Goblins
They have big black wings.
Their faces look like witches.
They fly very fast.

Scarecrows
Their clothes flutter when the wind blows.
When they dance they take stiff crooked steps.

The Black Cat
He is proud and slinky.
He walks on the fence and howls.

Jack-o'-Lanterns
They roll their heads and blink their eyes.

They scare you at windows.
They would do a funny dance.

The Wicked Witch
She is humpbacked and scary-looking.
She walks with a limp.
She hunts for toads and snakes to stir into her cauldron.
She weaves magic spells.

Ghosts
They are tall and wispy.
They float around.
They sway and swoop.
Suddenly they are gone.

Bats
They fly at night.
They swoop down from trees and rafters.
In the daytime they sleep with their heads hanging down.

Unit: Thanksgiving

Pilgrims
They hunt in the woods with their guns for wild turkeys.
They bring them home for their Thanksgiving dinner.
They all walk to church together every Sunday.

Going to Grandmother's
Over the river and through the woods.

Turkeys
(See Animal Units)

Indians
(See Out West Unit)

Winter

STORIES
Appolonia's Valentine   Katherine Milhous
Babar and Father Christmas   Jean de Brunhoff
Brownies—It's Christmas   Gladys L. Adshead

I Like Winter	Lois Lenski
Nutcracker, The	Warren Chappell
Rackety-Packety House	Frances Hodgson Burnett
Snow Birthday	Helen Kay
Snow Party, The	Beatrice S. de Regniers
Steadfast Tin Soldier, The	Hans Christian Andersen
Torten's Christmas Secret	Maurice Dolbier
Tree That Trimmed Itself, The	Carolyn Bailey

Unit: Christmas Things

Reindeer
They are swift and light.
They shake their horns and paw the ground.
They bring Santa Claus from his house to ours.

Bells
They make a ringing sound.
You can pull them with a rope.
They die away.

Candles
They flicker and dance at the window.
They melt into little puddles.

The Christmas Tree
Children who live near the woods can cut down their own.
We carry ours home from a big vacant lot.

Unit: Christmas Toys

Jack-in-the-Box
He hides in the box when the cover is on.
When it's open he pops out with a funny smile waving his arms.
You have to push him back in because he hates to go.

Mechanical Dolls
You have to wind them up.
They walk with stiff jerky steps.

Rag Dolls, Puppets, Marionettes
They are floppy things with funny faces.
They swing and bend all around when they dance.
Sometimes they fall down.

Balls
They bounce low and fast or high and slow.
They roll away.

Tops
We wind them up with string or a key.
They whirl very fast at first, then slow down and fall over.

Rocking Horses
They swing back and forth.
They stop to let a new rider on.

Toy Instruments
We can play little drums or big drums.
We can play a trumpet or a flute.

Toy Animals
(See Animal Units)

Bicycles, Trains, Airplanes
(See Transportation Unit)

Unit: Winter Things

Jack Frost
He is a spry little elf.
He pinches our fingers and toes and runs away.
He paints funny pictures on the windows.

Snowflakes
They are soft and dreamy.
Sometimes they whirl in the wind.
They lie on the ground to keep the plants warm.

The Snowman
He would do a clumsy dance.
At first he is big and fat.
The sun makes him very small.

Playing in the Snow
We can shovel it in big piles.
We can build a snowman.
We can make snowballs and knock him down.
We can have a snow fight with our snowballs.

Snowshoes
You have to walk wide apart with stiff feet.
Sometimes you have to shake off the snow on your snowshoes.

Skating
We can skate forward or backward.
We can do fancy steps.
We can skate with a partner or in a long line.

Sleigh Ride
Sometimes a team of horses pulls the sleigh.
It moves quietly over the snow.

Spring

STORIES

Bear Who Saw the Spring, The	Karla Kuskin
Easter Bunny That Overslept, The	Priscilla and Otto Friedrich
Egg Tree, The	Katherine Milhous
Follow the Wind	Alvin Tresselt
Growing Story, The	Ruth Krauss
Hi, Mr. Robin	Alvin Tresselt
Nicest Time of the Year, The	Zhenya Gay
Raindrop Splash	Alvin Tresselt
When the Root Children Wake Up	Helen Dean Fisk

Unit: March

The Wind
It blows hard and soft.
It can make us run fast or we can put our arms out and float along.

Kites
A kite can sail very high.
Sometimes it gets stuck in a tree.

Windmills
Windmills have arms that swing when the wind blows.
One person can make a little windmill and two can make a big windmill.

Unit: April

Raindrops
They pitter-patter all around.
They splash on the walks, but they sink
  deep in the ground.

April Fool's Dance
You would do a silly, laughing dance
  on April Fool's Day.

Easter Basket
Bunnies ⎫
Ducks ⎪
Chickens ⎬ (See Animal Units)
Roosters ⎭

Birds Making Nests
(See Animal Units)

Unit: May

Flowers Growing
Flowers have different faces.
Their buds uncurl.
They nod at you from their beds.

Walking in the Woods
The path winds through the trees.

We can jump over little brooks.
Sometimes we have to go across on
  stepping stones.

*Animals and Insects Come Out of Their
  Winter Homes*
(See Animal Units)

Summer

STORIES
Boats on the River, The   Marjorie Flack
Bojabi Tree, The   Edith Rickert
Brown Cow Farm   Dahlow Ipcar
Little Sailboat, The   Lois Lenski
Nu Dang and His Kite   Jacqueline Ayer
Through the Trees   Karla Kuskin

Unit: Boats

Sailboats
They have big white wings that float
  and dip.
The wind blows them fast or slow.

Rowboats
One person can row alone, two persons
  can row side by side, or you can
  have a crew.

Canoes
You dip in your paddle and pull.
Sometimes you have to carry your canoe
  over your head.

Tugboats
They work hard, pulling big boats.
They chug-chug.

Unit: The Playground

Swings
Back and forth.

Seesaw
Up and down.

The Slide
Climb up.
Slide down.
And run around.

The Merry-Go-Round
'Round and 'round and up and down.

Walking on Stilts
High and stiff.

Jumping Rope
Jump and skip and turn.

Hopscotch
Hop and stop.

Roller-Skating
Slide and turn.

Playing Ball
Bounce and catch.
Toss and catch.

Rolling Hoops
Over and around.

Playing with Balloons
Tap and lift.
Bounce and pop.

Nature Around Us

STORIES

A Tree Is Nice	Janice May Udrey
Goodbye Thunderstorm	Dorothy Marino
In the Forest	Marie Hall Ets
Johnny Mapleleaf	Alvin Tresselt
Moon Jumpers, The	Janice May Udrey
Storm Book, The	Charlotte Zolotow

The Sun
It comes up slowly and shines on all of us.
It moves slowly across the sky.
It sinks in the west and is gone until tomorrow.

Clouds
White clouds float across the sky.
Sometimes dark storm clouds move very fast.

Stars
Perhaps they are dancing when they twinkle.
Sometimes they fall through the sky and are gone.

Lightning
It flashes very fast.
It goes zigzag.

Trees
In big trees only the branches sway and shake in the wind.

Little trees bend and twist to get away from the storm.

Growing Things
You can see them getting taller and taller.
In the fall they get tired and go back into the ground to sleep.

The Moon
The moon is like a big balloon.
Sometimes her face is round and jolly and sometimes it's sharp and pointed.
It's like floating to walk up there.

Wind
(See Unit on March under Spring)

Rain
(See Unit on April under Spring)

Animals and Other Live Things

STORIES

And To Think That I Saw It on Mulberry Street	Dr. Seuss
Andy and the Lion	James Daugherty
Ask Mr. Bear	Marjorie Flack
Babar	Jean de Brunhoff
Bambi	Felix Salter
Curious George	Hans A. Rey
Five Little Monkeys	Juliet Kepes
If I Ran the Zoo	Dr. Seuss
I Like Animals	Dahlov Ipcar
Johnny Crow's Garden	Leslie L. Brooke
Little Bear	Else H. Minarik
Look!	Zhenya Gay
Make Way for Ducklings	Robert McCloskey
Millions of Cats	Wanda Gag
Sphinx, the Story of a Caterpillar	Robert McClung
Story of Ping, The	Marjorie Flack
Tall Grass Zoo, The	Winifred and Cecil Lubell
Timothy Turtle	Alice Davis
Ugly Duckling, The	Hans Christian Andersen
What Horse Is It?	Anna Pistorius
Where Is the Bunny?	Ruth Carroll
Whirlybird, The	Dimitri Varley

Unit: Our Pets

Our Dog
He runs to meet me.
He can do tricks.

Our Kitten
She creeps up and then she pounces.
She humps her back and hisses.
She washes herself.

Our Pony
He can trot and he can gallop.
He nudges me with his nose when he
    wants sugar.

Our White Mice
They creep and scamper.
They nibble at their food.

Our Bunny
He jumps with his front legs and his
    hind legs.
He wrinkles his face when he eats.
He has long floppy ears.

Our Canary or Our Bird
He jumps about in his cage.
He cocks his head at me and talks or
    sings.
When I let him out he flies a little way
    and then hops back.

Our Baby
I rock her to sleep and then tiptoe away
    so she will not wake up.

Unit: Animals at the Zoo

Bears
They are slow and clumsy.
They look around for food.
Lots of times they just lie down and sleep.

Monkeys
They run with their hands touching the ground.
They scratch themselves.
They play tricks.

Camels
Their heads swing when they walk.
They are humpbacked.
They kneel down to rest.

Elephants
They have a long swinging trunk.
Their legs are heavy.
They like peanuts.

Lions and Tigers
They prowl back and forth in their cages.
They raise up their heads when they roar.

Seals
They have long heavy tails that drag.
They catch fish in their mouths.
Sometimes they lie on their backs and flap their flippers.

Ostriches
Their legs are long and their necks are long.
They run with their feet up high.

Kangaroos
Sometimes they run and sometimes they take big jumps.

Unit: Animals on the Farm

Farm Horses
They pull plows and big wagons.

Little Chickens and Hens
They run fast to get corn to eat.
They scratch the ground for food.

Roosters
They have a jerky walk.
They cock their heads to look at you.
They flap their wings and say cock-a-doodle-doo.

Ducks and Geese
They waddle.
They swim in the pond.
They duck their heads to get a worm.

Lambs
They jump around and play in the fields.
Then they stop and stare at you.

Donkeys and Mules
They can kick.
Sometimes they carry packs.

Turkeys
They are very proud and strut around.
They spread their feathers wide.
They say gobble-gobble.

Goats
They like to eat.
Sometimes they butt at you.

Unit: Insects

Spiders
They weave big webs to catch their food and wait in the center.
They have so many legs.

Bees
They fly from flower to flower to gather honey.
They have little wings which move very fast.

Ants
They carry big loads of food and build their houses.
Sometimes they crawl in lines.

Grasshoppers and Crickets
They jump and jump.
Sometimes they sit still and sing.

Caterpillars and Worms
They hump themselves to crawl.

To look at you they raise up their heads and wave them around.

Butterflies and Moths
They move their wings slowly up and down.
When they stop on a flower sometimes their wings close over their heads.

Unit: Animals of the Woods and Fields

Frogs and Toads
They jump with their long back legs.
Sometimes they rest on a stone and catch flies to eat.

Turtles
They walk slowly under their shells.
When they are frightened they pull in their heads. .

Squirrels
They run very fast and stop quickly.
They gather nuts and hold them in their paws when they sit up to eat.
They scamper up trees.

Groundhog
He digs himself out of his winter home to look for his shadow.

Rabbits
(See Our Pets Unit)

Birds
They fly in the air and jump along branches.
They build nests.
They pull up worms to feed their children.

Field Mice
(See Our Pets Unit)

Butterflies
(See Insects Unit)

Bees
(See Insects Unit)

The Circus

STORIES
Bambino the Clown
Circus Baby, The
Circus Ruckus

Happy Lion, The
Madeline and the Gypsies
Wait for William

Georges Schreiber
Maud Petersham
William Lipkind and Nicolas Mordvinoff
Louise Fatio
Ludwig Bemelmans
Marjorie Flack

Unit: Circus Animals

Dancing Bears
They dance on their big hind legs.

Lions and Tigers
In their cages they balance themselves on big balls.

When their trainer cracks his whip they climb up on boxes and roar.
(See Animals at the Zoo Unit)

Elephants
They can climb on each other's backs.
When they walk in a line they hold on with their trunks and tails.

Dancing Ponies
Their hoofs step just in time to the music.
They can bow, too.

Seals
They balance balls on their noses and flap their flippers.
(See Animals at the Zoo Unit)

High-Stepping and Prancing Horses
Circus horses are very proud of their beautiful harnesses.
Sometimes they do tricks, like galloping over a fence.

Monkeys
(See Animals at the Zoo Unit)

Unit: The Circus Parade

Motorcycle Cop
He clears the track.

The Band
They wear capes and march very straight.

Animals in the Parade
(See Circus Animals Unit)

Clowns
They have very funny faces and shapes.
Some of them walk on stilts to be tall.
They do funny tricks.
Sometimes they fall down.

Unit: The Circus Performance

Chariot Race
The best horses make the chariot team.
The driver must be strong.

Tightrope Walkers
It is hard to balance yourself.
If you are very good you can jump or kneel or stand on one foot.
When you have done a hard trick you run back to your platform and bow.

Jugglers
You have to keep your eyes on the things you are juggling.
A good juggler can kneel or sit down while he juggles.
He can pass things under his legs or behind his back.

The Animal Trainer
He holds up a chair and cracks a whip to make the animals do their tricks.

Transportation

STORIES
Blaze   Clarence W. Anderson
Camel Who Took a Walk, The   Jack Tworkov
Choo Choo: The Story of a Little Engine Who Ran Away   Virginia Lee Burton

Horse That Lived Upstairs, The   Phyllis McGinley
Little Airplane, The   Lois Lenski
Little Auto, The   Lois Lenski

Little Engine That Could, The   Piper Watty
Little Toot   Hardie Gramatky
Little Train, The   Lois Lenski
Loopy   Hardie Gramatky
Maybelle, the Cable Car   Virginia Lee Burton
Mr. Penny's Race Horse   Marie Hall Ets
Sparky   Hardie Gramatky
World Full of Horses   Dahlov Ipcar

Automobiles
We have to stop at stop streets and red lights.
We must be careful to stay on our own side of the road.

Motorcycles
You can go fast if you steer carefully.

Trains
We can take tiny chug-chug steps.
Our arms are the pistons that make us go.
A strong engine can pull cars behind it.
Sometimes trains go through tunnels.
We slow down when we come to the station.

Bicycles
You have to mount first.
Then you pedal around and around.

Boats
(See Unit on Boats)

Airplanes
The propellers spin for contact.
They zoom into the air.
They bank their wings when they go around a curve.
A good pilot makes a smooth landing.
If our plane gets into trouble, we can parachute down.

Horseback
Horses can walk, trot, and gallop.
A proud horse holds his head high.

Snowshoes
(See Winter Unit)

Elephants
(See Animals at the Zoo Unit)

Camels
(See Animals at the Zoo Unit)

Skates
(See Winter Unit)

Occupations and Community Helpers

STORIES
I Want to Be a Farmer   Carla Greene
I Want to Be a Fireman   Carla Greene
I Want to Be a Policeman   Carla Greene
Little Fire Engine, The   Lois Lenski
Mike Mulligan and the Steam Shovel Virginia Lee Burton
Nobody Listens to Andrew   Elizabeth Guilefoile
Wake Up Farm   Alvin Tresselt

The Fireman
He slides down the pole when the fire bell sounds.
He can carry the hose up a ladder and shoot water through a window.

Sometimes he has to chop out burning things.

The Farmer
In the spring he plows the fields.

In the summer he pitches hay.
In the fall he binds up the cornstalks.

The Traffic Policeman
He tells us when to cross the street.
Sometimes he blows a whistle when it's
time to change.

The Postman
We like to see him come.
Sometimes he has to carry heavy packs
of mail.

The Builders
Sometimes they run a steam shovel.
Sometimes they carry bricks or lumber.
Sometimes they hammer and pound.
Sometimes they paint and paper.

The Repair Man
He fixes the TV.
He fixes the car.
He fixes the plumbing.
He fixes the broken window.

The Bus Driver
He has to drive carefully.
He has to stop often to let people on
and off.

Out West

STORIES

Brave Cowboy, The	Joan Anglund
Brave Cowboy Bill	Kathryn and Byron Jackson
Cowboy Small	Lois Lenski
Cowboy Tommy	Sanford Towsey
Little Owl Indian	Hettie B. Beatty
Little Wild Horse	Hettie B. Beatty
Mighty Hunter, The	Berta Hader
One Little Indian	Grace Moon

Cowboys
They always ride horses to get to another place.
They lasso cattle and pull them in to be
branded.

Bucking Bronco
He can hump his back so that you fall
right off.
He kicks his legs way up high.
Sometimes he shies sideward.

Indians
They hunted for game in the woods.
They used to shoot with bows and
arrows.
They paddled canoes and carried them
across land.
They rode Indian ponies.
Sometimes they danced around their
campfire.

Storybook Characters

STORIES

A Baker's Dozen	Mary Gould Davis
Alice in Wonderland	Lewis Carroll
Candle Light Stories	Virginia Hutchinson
Chimney Corner Stories	Virginia Hutchinson
Fireside Stories	Virginia Hutchinson

Golden Treasury of Myths and Legends, The	Anne Terry White (Golden Press)
Once Upon a Time	Rose Dobbs
Peter Pan	James Barrie
Read Me Another Story	Barbara Cooney
Rootabaga Stories	Carl Sandburg
Tall Book of Nursery Tales, The	Harper & Row
Tanglewood Tales	Nathaniel Hawthorne
Three Billy Goats Gruff, The	Peter C. Asbjørnsen

Fairies and Elves
Fairies dance in the moonlight.
They wave their wands to make wishes come true.
Elves are boy fairies.
They help poor people and others who are in trouble.

Giants
Giants are as tall as a tree and take great big steps.
Sometimes they carry clubs to kill animals for their dinner.

Brownies, Dwarfs, Gnomes, Leprechauns
They are funny little men who work in the woods.
Some gnomes work in caves in the mountains.
Sometimes they have fun playing tricks on people.

Witches, Goblins, and Trolls
(See Unit on Halloween and "Character" Movement in Chapter 6.)

Television and Comic-Book Characters

From "Sesame Street": Big Bird, Cooky Monster, Mr. Snuffle Upagus, Oscar, etc.
From *Peanuts:* Charlie Brown, Linus, Lucy, Snoopy, etc.
From Disney Features: Donald Duck, Mickey Mouse, Pluto, Mr. Moose, etc.

Books of General Interest to Young and Older Dance-Makers

A Hole Is to Dig	Ruth Krauss and Maurice Sendak
A Fly Went By	Mike McClintock
All My Shoes Come in Twos	Mary Ann and Norman Hoberman
Do you Move as I Do?	Helen Borten
Dress Up and Let's Have a Party	Remy Charlip
Happy Day, The	Ruth Krauss
Herman McGregor's World	Miriam Schlein
I'll Be You and You Be Me	Ruth Krauss
Of Course, You're a Horse	Ruth S. Radlauer
Shapes	Miriam Schlein

With Older Children

In some interpretations of dance ideas there are two possibilities in the role-playing children do. One may become the thing itself (a ball, a swing, a pony, the wind), as young children often do; or one may be the agent which reacts to it, manipulates it, relates to it in one way or another. The latter response, being a dramatic interpretation rather than dramatic play, is the more mature identification with the role. To an older child, a human or near-human character, perhaps, or an animal that "moves and talks like a man," is acceptable for dance material, but the bus itself, or the plane, or the train, or the horse—no. It is not that his qualities of imagination have deteriorated, but his relationship toward these things has changed.

Leads into Dance-Making: Contrasts and Combinations

When dance-making experiences are being planned for older children, materials should be presented which in their opinion could not possibly be considered childish. Chapter 6 presents many images and dramatic situations for older as well as younger children's dance-making. These are the lists of activities under *Do* and perhaps *Feel,* some of the sensory sources for movements, "Character" movement, and "As If" situations. Exploration of these areas of subject matter often serves as the point of departure into sequential combinations of actions to which temporal and spatial principles of form may be applied.

Also, sequences made up of from three to six words which offer contrasting but related movement qualities lead rather quickly into dance studies. As in the Movement Word Game in Chapter 5, children improvise to the words as they are given slowly by a leader. Then, working alone or in small groups, they put their movement into a sequential form which has dramatic overtones. Some obvious word sequences are: tired, nightmare, waken; or curious, scared, dash, hide. Children can make their own word combinations and then perform the movement sequence for other groups to guess.

Work with contrasting movement may be done individually, with

Movement like a Whisper

Movement like a Shout

partners, or in groups. Boys, especially, enjoy opposing a partner in movement which suggests conflict. Movements of aggression—strike, punch, thrust, slap, lunge, kick, slash, poke, thump—may be paired by an opposing type—flinch, shrink, dodge, turn, recoil, retreat. Such opposing movements lend themselves to group as well as partner treatment, with two groups reacting spontaneously to the other's movements, but retaining group identity.

Other movement contrasts for individual or partner use are suggested by a contrasting pair of words (whisper-shout; gravel-glass; yawn-snore; yellow-purple; devil-saint) or of different styles of meeting and parting (Hello-Goodbye; Hi—See you; How do you do—So glad to have met you) or, with experienced classes, of positive and negative feelings (agitated-relieved; angry-regretful; timid-eager; strange-familiar; hope-disappointment).

Ideas for Dance Studies

The following lists are of movements of work and play which can be made rhythmical in performance, of characters and things with which the older child can identify, and of possible titles for dance studies. After experimenting with them, children work with a chosen idea alone, in partners, or in groups. They make a combination of movement parts into a whole action sequence; contrast one movement with other movements in the same category; compose a group design of one or more movements; or, choosing several movements in the category, make an overall spatial design, each individual, couple, or group using one specific movement.

Performing rhythmical play and sports activities: Jumping rope, rolling hoops, playing catch, playing hopscotch, flying kites, skating, bicycling, paddling canoes, rowing in a crew.

Performing rhythmical movements of building and construction: Sawing, hammering, digging, lifting and carrying, painting, mixing and pouring plaster and cement, laying bricks, riveting, planing, sanding.

Performing other rhythmical work movements: Chopping trees, cutting kindling, mowing lawns, pitching hay, hoeing potatoes, driving horses, carrying a canoe, rowing a boat, carrying a pack, swabbing decks, signaling with flags, blowing up balls, roping a steer, shearing sheep, swatting flies.

Performing assembly-line movements: Operating a punch press, riveting, welding, tightening bolts.

Personifying machine actions with swings, strikes, pushes, pulls: Stamping, crushing, screwing, drilling, scooping, striking, grinding, magnetizing.

Ecological themes: Smog, litter removal, water pollution, tree planting, recycling paper, glass, metal.

Transforming into robotlike movements: Characters at a meeting, a party, a shopping expedition, a sports event.

Circus characters: Clowns, ringmaster, animal trainer, tightrope walker, tumblers and acrobats, jugglers, fire-eater, Strong Man.

Storybook characters: Raggedy Ann, Johnny Appleseed, Paul Bunyan, Tom Sawyer, Huck Finn, the Tin Woodman, the Cowardly Lion, Pinocchio the Puppet, Tweedledum and Tweedledee, the Seven Dwarfs, Gulliver, the Ancient Mariner, Ali Baba, Aladdin, Alice in Wonderland, Dorothy in the Land of Oz.

Historical people: Indians, Pilgrims, cowboys, pioneers, Paul Revere, Robin Hood, John Henry, Paul Bunyan.

Legendary characters: Wizards, sorcerers, soothsayers, misers, oracles, imps, angels, sirens, monsters, the Chimera, the Jabberwock, golliwogs, giants, gargoyles, witches.

Fantastic creatures: Visitors from Mars, from outer space, from distant galaxies, flying-saucer pilots, the Loch Ness Monster, the Abominable Snowman, robots, poltergeists, a blob.

Miscellaneous modern characters: Cheerleaders, drum majors, boxers, rodeo riders, astronauts, pilots.

Reproducing spectators' movements: Watching a parade, a football game, a tennis match, a boxing match, building construction.

Reproducing supermarket shoppers' movements: The gossips, the comparative shoppers, the speedy ones, the exasperated ones, the searchers, the checkout lines, the naughty child, the bored cashier.

POSSIBLE DANCE STUDY TITLES FOR OLDER CHILDREN

Airs and Graces
Cause and Consequence
Fabulous Friday, Morbid Monday
Gremlins, Grinches, and Ghouls
Hexes and Jinxes
Mostly Like Flight
Rumor Runs Rampant
Sentimental Swooners

Making the Dance Study

Most older children seem to do their best composing of dances when working with others, perhaps with only a partner or with several children. The goal is set by the total group or by each small group individually, and the responsibility for achieving it satisfactorily and within a reasonable time serves as a cohesive factor in the group process.

The teacher is the resource person in this process. When asked to do so, she provides audience reaction, consultation service, criticism of work in progress, ideas for improving form or content, help with accompaniment, even aid with performance if an extra person is needed. In the interaction between teacher and class each inspires the other, and much of her own creativeness is released.

The term *working group* is used to designate any number of persons, from two to approximately eight, who join forces to make a dance. A group of more than eight becomes unwieldy, is apt to break up into smaller groups, and needs a strong leader to keep it moving ahead. For this reason, when large group dances are made, as when the whole class cooperates on a composition, it is best for the teacher to act as leader.

Dances which evolve from an idea are meant to communicate that idea. Therefore group dances particularly should be planned in a dance space with definite boundaries and a front, back, and sides. Composition is made easier if all those watching sit in one specified place toward which movement is projected. The dance space, then, resembles a stage, with the spectators in front and a defined space for the performance into and out of which entrances and exits are made. (See Using the Dance Space in Chapter 21.)

To thus formalize the dance setting is not necessary or even desirable for the solo dances or duets of young children. With older children who are making group dance studies, particularly studies that are more than an abstract manipulation of movement, introduction of the traditional setting is fitting and proper. In folk dances and other dances designed for participation rather than communication, the spatial form may consist only of movement around and in and out of a circle, but the sequence of parts may be long and somewhat involved. When the spatial form of a dance study is more complex, the sequential form may be relatively simple or may match it in complexity.

In any event, older children should grow in the knowledge of how part follows part in dances, and how they combine in an ordered and unified whole; of how varied formations and group designs in space add interest and effectiveness. They should recognize and use such simple sequences as two part (A B), three part (A B A or A B C), and rondo (A B A C A or A B A C A B A).

It is probably less tedious to make all the machine dances, circus dances, or the like during only a few working periods. After ideas or titles have been discussed and decided upon, working groups are formed on the basis of choice of idea. That the groups may be unevenly divided or that more than one dance is made on the same subject is immaterial.

The following sequence of steps is typical for making dances in small working groups. Some of the steps listed may not be used, others may be substituted, and the order may be quite different from that in the outline.

1. Class discussion and decision on idea (or ideas) for dances. (Examples; one idea, clowns; several ideas, characters at a football game, such as cheerleaders, drum majors, spectators, referees, and linesmen).

2. General discussion of the characteristic movements of the subject chosen which also offer possibilities for dance.

3. Division into working groups:
   a. If only one subject is used, the division is made on the basis of peer choice.
   b. If several subjects are used, the division is made on the basis of choice of subject (and also partly peer choice).

4. Assignment of a working space to each group, indicating the front (where the others will view the dance).

5. When the group is fairly large (five to eight), selection of a leader through whom suggestions clear and who is responsible for keeping group activity moving toward the goal.

6. Group activity which will include some of the following (the order depends upon many factors: chance, one member's inventiveness, a burst of energy in a certain direction, possession of a particular percussion instrument, or the wandering path of the Muse herself!):
   a. Experimentation by each member with characteristic movements; evaluation of usable movements by group.
   b. Discussion, trial, and decision on which movements will be used, and how (in unison, two or more simultaneously, in succession, in opposition, etc.).
   c. Discussion, trial, and decision on how many times and at what tempo each movement will be done (counting helps to keep the group moving together rhythmically and to decide how long a part should be).
   d. Discussion, trial, and decision on a beginning spatial form (circle, semicircle, line or lines, mass group, open-order group, etc.).
   e. Discussion, trial, and decision on other forms which may evolve from the beginning form.
   f. Discussion, trial, and decision on the sequential form (two parts: A B; three parts: A B A or A B C; etc.).
   g. Discussion, trial, and decision on how the dance shall begin (with or without an entrance) and end (with or without an exit).
   h. Selection of accompaniment and assignment of group members to play it (a vocal chorus, one or several percussion instruments, a certain kind of musical sound and beat played on the piano, if one is available, a recording or perhaps part of more than one recording).
   i. Practice of the completed dance so that each member can perform his part well.

7. Performance and evaluation of work in progress if the dances cannot be completed by the end of the working period. (It is a good idea, when dances are fairly long, to include this step in any case).

8. Continuation of the composition with possible reworking of the parts completed on the basis of the evaluation and suggestions.

9. Performance of the completed dances for the rest of the class.

10. If the dances are to be performed for a larger audience than the immediate class, the group may wish to do further evaluation, reworking, and practice for maximum effectiveness.

Chapter Preview

Using Songs for Dance-Making

With Younger Children

Action Songs, Singing Games, Movement Songs and Dance Songs
Movement and Dance Songs from School Music Books
Supplementary Songbooks

With Older Children

Dance Songs from School Music Books
More Dance Songs
Supplementary Songbooks
Songs on Records

18 *Approach from Songs*

Shoo, fly, don't bother me, for I belong to somebody,
I feel, I feel, I feel like a morning star.

—American Dance Song

One of the easiest and most popular ways for children to make a dance is from a song approach. Song was the traditional accompaniment for much of early European folk dance from which most of the folk and country dances of this country derive. Beautiful songs from Israel, Latin America, and from Asian and African countries are beginning to appear in children's song books. Children gain a broader international perspective by singing them and dancing to them.

If the music teacher is also the dance teacher, she can provide her children with the opportunity to make and dance a song whenever they learn a new one which seems to have that appeal. Some music teachers are reluctant to allow children to sing and dance at the same time because the breathlessness which accompanies vigorous movement interferes with voice quality. An easy remedy is to have half the class or those watching sing the song. "It will be noticed how much the vitality of the singing by a chorus group is increased when it . . . provides the accompaniment for a moving group in action."[1]

Using Songs for Dance-Making

Creative activity is channeled in two ways by a song accompaniment. The quality of the movement and the sequential form of the dance study must follow that of the music. The idea or meaning of the dance must approxi-

[1] Ann Driver, *Music and Movement*, London, Oxford University Press, 1966, p. 11.

mate to a certain degree the words of the song. These limitations make composing easier in that there are fewer decisions to be rendered before work can proceed.

When composing dances to songs, beginners often attempt a too literal interpretation of the words. It is the spirit rather than the words that should be maintained. The song words that are most important to the meaning, that evoke rhythmic movement, are the ones to include in the dance sequence. Often an otherwise usable dance song has a line which expresses an intellectual idea impossible to interpret in movement. Certain kinds of meditation, reflection, deliberation, contemplation—in fact, abstract ideas of any kind—are difficult to express in dance language. Such ideas can simply be passed over, or locomotor or nonlocomotor movements which have no particular meaning in the total sequence can be used.

Many songs in school music books suggest movement in one way or another. Published by leading music publishing houses, these books relate music to painting, poetry, and "movement," a word often used in lieu of "dance." If the music teacher and the dance teacher have like values regarding the creative process, coordinated activity between them can result in the learning of songs which are catalysts for dance-making. Conversely, the construction of dance studies for which a percussion, instrumental, or "sound" accompaniment might be composed will expand the creative talents of children in the music class.

With Younger Children

Songs useful for younger children's dance may be put into the following categories:

Action Songs and Singing Games. Movement for the most part is imitative and noncreative. *Action songs* provide auditory cues from their words, which tell what to do, and visual cues from the actions of a leader or the teacher. Often eliciting nonlocomotor movements of hands, head, feet, etc., they help young children to identify a sequence of body parts.[2] These songs, although limited in creative scope, provide group movement experiences rarely present when young children are exploring or improvising. Such unison rhythmic and movement responses not only are enjoyable but afford

---

[2] Such a song in "pop" rhythm may be found in Edna Doll and Mary Jarman Nelson, *Rhythms Today,* Morristown, N.J., Silver Burdett, 1965, p. 178.

security and new movement experiences for the child who is shy or who shows little movement inventiveness.

Many *singing games* derive from folk material from the past, some even celebrating ancient rituals. "Ring-Around-Rosy," "Round and Round the Village," and "London Bridge" are examples of the latter sort. Later ones, like "Bluebird" and "Looby Loo," evoke movement sequences which are usually exact interpretations of the words. Most singing games require some kind of formation, usually a circle, but often free locomotor movement in a counterclockwise direction is an adequate substitute. Many singing games for younger children are listed in Chapter 26, and identified by "word dramatization" under "Remarks."

Movement Songs. This designation refers to songs which, although dancelike, offer only one or two movement ideas. They differ from action songs in that there is usually more locomotor movement involved and a freer interpretation of the words is possible. They are useful for younger children's improvisation. The movement described is usually that of an animal, a toy, things of nature or special seasons. "Pony Song," "Elephants," "Slish, Slosh," and "Over the River and Through the Woods" are examples of movement songs, as are many of the songs to nursery rhymes.

Dance Songs. Useful mostly for older children, dance songs offer a sequence of action ideas which may be structured into a dance study with the song as accompaniment. Some such songs offer more of a story than do the simpler movement songs; others tell little of specific action but use nonsense words and syllables. Thus a free interpretation is possible, and children can follow their own ideas of what the words suggest. Examples of dance songs for younger children are "The Old Gray Cat" and "Les Petites Marionnettes."

It must be realized that the difference between *dancing* and doing a *dance* with younger children is very slight and relatively unimportant. A child may change from angular to curving paths in one of the movement songs so that his interpretation actually approximates a dance sequence; or he may want to do nothing but run around to a song about the wind.

The following school song books with selected references for younger children's movement and dance songs are from only two companies among several which provide school music books. All of the song book series have been compiled by well qualified teachers of music, so a teacher will find similar songs for dance in any one her school may use.

In order to avoid duplication of song items, the selected books from different song book series have been listed alphabetically and given key numbers. The number (or numbers) of the book in which the song appears follows the song title. This is true of the song lists for both younger and older children.

Movement and Dance Songs from School Music Books

KEY

(1) American Book Co., *New Dimensions in Music: Music for Early Childhood*, New York, N.Y., 1970.
(2) Silver Burdett Co., *Making Music Your Own: Kindergarten Book*, Morristown, N.J., 1971.

American Folk or Traditional Songs

Allee Allee O, The* (2)
Bow Belinda* (1)
Down by the Station (1)
Giddy-up Little Horses (2)
Go Tell Aunt Rhody* (2)
Jim Along Josie* (2)
Jimmy Crack Corn* (2)
Jingle at the Window, Tideo* (2)

Little Bird, Little Bird* (2)
Make a Pretty Motion (2)
Old Brass Wagon* (1)
Old Gray Cat, The (2)
Over the River and Thru the Woods (2)
Paw Paw Patch* (1)
Skip to My Lou* (2)
Yankee Doodle (1, 2)

Songs from Other Ethnic Sources

Autumn Leaves (1, 2) German
Friends (2) Dutch
Joyous Chanukah* (2) Hebrew
Les Petites Marionettes (1, 2) French
Merry Go Round (1) Jamaican
Michael, Row the Boat Ashore* (1) Afro-American
Pony Song, The (1) German
Ram Sam Sam, A* (1) Moroccan
Rig a Jig Jig (1) English

Slish, Slosh (1) Finnish
Snail, The (2) French
There's Just One Boy in the Ring (1) Jamaican
This Old Man* (1) English
Ti-Ri-Lin (1) Mexican
Valentine Dance (1) German
We Wish You a Merry Christmas (1, 2) English

Other Movement and Dance Songs

Bunny (1)
Busy (2)
Elephants (2)

Fire Song (1)
Hakof (1)
Hokey Pokey* (1)

*These songs can be used as well with older children.

I'm a Very Fine Turkey (2)
Jingle Bells* (1)
Jump (1)
Let's Go Walking (2)
North Wind, The (2)
Old King Cole* (1)
One Elephant (1)
Put Your Finger in the Air (1)

Shoes (1)
Train Is A-Coming, The (1)
Walk to School (2)
Walking with the New Math (1)
Weather Song (2)
What Shall We Do? (2)
Whoosh! The Jet Goes By (1)
Witch Rides, The (2)

Supplementary Songbooks

ABELSON, MARION, and BAILEY, CHARITY, *Playtime with Music,* New York, Liveright, 1967.

ASSOCIATION FOR CHILDHOOD EDUCATION INTERNATIONAL, *Songs Children Like—Folk Songs from Many Lands,* 3615 Wisconsin Ave., N.W., Washington, D.C., 1958.

COLEMAN, SATIS W., and THORN, ALICE G., *Singing Time* (1929), *Another Singing Time* (1937), *A New Singing Time* (1952), New York, Day.

GARSON, EUGENIA, ed., *The Laura Ingalls Wilder Songbook,* New York, Harper & Row, 1968.

GLASS, PAUL, and SINGER, LOUIS C., *Songs of Field and Mountain Folk,* New York, Grosset & Dunlap, 1969.

LANDECK, BEATRICE, *More Songs to Grow On,* New York, E. B. Marks, 1954.

SEEGER, RUTH CRAWFORD, *Animal Folk Songs for Children,* New York, Doubleday, 1950.

WINN, MARIE, ed., *What Shall We Do and Allee Galloo!,* New York, Harper & Row, 1970.

With Older Children

The song approach to dance-making is most profitable to use with older children, provided some exploration of movement and musical forms is part of their background. The form of the song offers a framework upon which movement interpretation may be constructed. The essential quality of the song should be reproduced rather than a literal or mimed duplication of the words. Word phrases or lines which are repeated in the song should be repeated in their respective movement sections—if not identically, at least in not too great a variation of the original treatment. A repeated melody with different words, however, may depart considerably from its original movement statement. Thus in a verse-chorus type of song, or two-part form

("Yankee Doodle," "Oh Susanna," "Jingle Bells"), each repetition of the chorus (the same words sung to the same music) will use at least portions of the same movement material used in the first chorus. Successive verses, however, each having different words even though similar music, may be quite different in movement and form. It is not necessary to try to dance to all verses of a song. Only the ones that lend themselves best to dance-making should be used.

Rounds may be used for dance-making as a single short song is, or they may be danced as rounds are usually sung. The only problem is space. The direction of the movement of one group must not be such that it interferes with the movement another group is doing at the same time to another part of the song. A quick way of making a dance to a round is to assign one line of the song, with the direction in which the movement must go, to each group or voice of the round. The first line of "Scotland's Burning," for example, might be done moving forward, the second line in place or from side to side, the third line moving backward, and the fourth line turning around. Each of four groups would make the movement for one of these lines; the four parts would be put together, possibly with minor adjustments; all four groups would learn the entire dance and then perform it and sing it as a round.

Dance Songs from School Music Books

KEY
(3) Allyn and Bacon, Inc., *This Is Music for Today,* Book II, Boston, Mass., 1971.
(4) Ginn and Company, *The Magic of Music,* Book II, Boston, Mass., 1970.

American Folk and Traditional Songs

Allee, Allee O, The (3, 4)
All the Pretty Little Horses (3)
Bye'm Bye (3, 4)
Doktar Eisenbart (3)
Jenny Jenkins (3)
Jingle at the Window (3, 4)

Jingle Bells (3)
Paw Paw Patch, The (3)
Sandy Land (3)
Skip to My Lou (4)
Slumber Boat, The (4)
Yankee Doodle (4)

Songs from Other Ethnic Sources

Bingo (3) English
Carpenter, The (3) Brazilian
Chiapenacas (4) Mexican
Clocks and Watches (3) German

Come, My Friends and Dance (3) German
Dance in a Circle (4) Italian
Dance, My Top (4) French-Canadian

THOMAS HALSTED

A Dance to a Spiritual (1)

A Dance to a Spiritual (2)

THOMAS HALSTED

Deck the Halls (3) English
Frère Jacques (3) French
Hanukkah (3) Jewish
Here Comes Bi-Ba Butzemann (3)
  German
On the Bridge at Avignon (4) French
Puppet Show, The (4) Dutch

Rain-Dance Song (4) Zuni Indian
Rig-a-Jig-Jig (3) English
Seasons, The (3) English
Snow Is Falling (3) German
This Old Man (3) English
We Wish You a Merry Christmas (3, 4) English

Other Dance Songs

All Day My Hands Keep Moving (3)
Animals in the Zoo (3)
Balloons (3, 4)
Clouds (4)
Have You Heard the Wind? (3, 4)
I Think It's So (3)

If You're Happy (3)
Mail Myself to You (3)
My Old Dan (3)
There Was an Old Witch (3)
Three Clouds (3)

More Dance Songs[3]

American Folk and Traditional Songs

Arkansas Traveler
Blow the Man Down
Can't You Dance the Polka
Casey Jones
Clementine
Daisy, Daisy
Dogie Song
Goodbye, My Lover, Goodbye
Good Night, Ladies
It Ain't Gonna' Rain
I've Been Workin' on the Railroad

K-K-K-Katy
Lil' Liza Jane
Old Gray Mare, The
Polly Wolly Doodle
Reuben and Rachel
She'll Be Comin' Round the Mountain
Turkey in the Straw
When Johnny Comes Marching Home
When the Saints Go Marching In
Yeo Heave-Ho

Spirituals and Christmas Songs

Ain't Gonna Grieve No More
All God's Chillun Got Shoes
Amen
As I Sat on a Sunny Bank
Christmas Eve Is Here
Dame, Get Up and Bake Your Pies
Dry Bones
Deck the Halls
Elijah Rock
Great Day

Here We Come A-Caroling
Here We Come A-Wassailing
Jingle Bells
Little David, Play on Your Harp
Old Ark's A-Moverin', The
Patapan
Rocka My Soul
Twelve Days of Christmas, The
Wassail, Wassail
We've Been a While a-Wandering

[3] These may be found in many community song booklets.

Rounds

A-Hunting We Will Go	*Hey Ho, Nobody Home*
Christmas Is Coming	*Kookaburra*
Clock, The	*Little Tom Tinker*
Come Follow	*Lovely Evening*
Donkey, The	*Merrily Merrily*
Ducks on a Pond	*Row, Row, Row Your Boat*
Frère Jacques	*Scotland's Burning*
Get Acquainted	*Three Blind Mice*

Contemporary Songs

There are many good contemporary songs which offer possibilities for older children's dance-making. Some of the best are those songs from stage or filmed musicals which involve children in their plots. "Oliver" and "The Sound of Music" are good examples. Many of the Disney songs lend themselves to dance-making. Consultation with the music teacher is desirable to discover those that are approved and suitable for dances. New sources for children's songs are the popular television programs—for younger children, "Sesame Street"; for older children, "Zoom."

Supplementary Songbooks

ATTAWAY, WILLIAM, *Hear America Singing,* New York, Lion Press, 1967.

BONI, MARGARET BRADFORD, and LLOYD, NORMAN, *Fireside Book of Favorite American Songs,* New York, Simon & Schuster, 1952.

BONI, MARGARET BRADFORD, and LLOYD, NORMAN, *Fireside Book of Folk Songs,* New York, Simon & Schuster, 1947.

BRAND, OSCAR, *Singing Holidays: The Calendar in Folk Song,* New York, Knopf, 1957.

CARMER, CARL, *America Sings,* New York, Knopf, 1942.

COOPERATIVE RECREATION SERVICE, Delaware, Ohio. Inexpensive paperback pamphlets of a variety of folk and novelty songs.

DETROIT PUBLIC SCHOOLS, *Afro-America Sings,* Board of Education of the City of Detroit, 1971.

EHRET, WALTER, *Gather Round,* The Complete Community Song Book, New York, Frank Music Corp.

EISENSTEIN, JUDITH, and PRENSKY, FRIEDA, *Songs of Childhood,* New York, United Synagogue of America, 1955.

LANDECK, BEATRICE, *Echoes of Africa in Folk Songs of the Americas,* New York, McKay, 1969.

LLOYD, NORMAN, and LLOYD, RUTH, *American Heritage Song Book*. New York, Heritage, 1969.

LOMAX, ALAN, *Folk Songs of North America*, New York, Doubleday, 1960.

NOBLE, T. TERTIUS, *A Round of Carols*, New York, Henry Z. Walck, 1935.

Songs on Records

Some records of children's songs are childlike and of good quality; others are coy, "jazzed up," or slightly saccharine. One must depend on reputable vocalists and folk singers, and certain companies (Folkways, for example) for records that preserve the quality of the recorded songs. Usable records representing a variety of styles are the following:

Activity Songs, sung by Marcia Berman, B204, Rhythms Productions Records, Cheviot Corp., Box 34485, Los Angeles, Cal., 90034.

American Folksay, Vols. 1, 2, and 3, "Ballads and Dances," sung by Woody Guthrie, Pete Seeger, Josh White, Tom Glazer, and others, Educational Record Sales, 157 Chambers St., New York, N.Y. 10007.

American Folk Songs for Children and *Folk Songs for Young People,* sung by Pete Seeger, Folkways F17601, FG7532.

And One and Two, sung by Ella Jenkins, Folkways FC7544.

Birds, Beasts, Bugs and Little Fishes and *Birds, Beasts, Bugs and Bigger Fishes,* sung by Pete Seeger, Folkways FC7610, FC7611.

Folk Songs, sung by Odetta, RCA LSP 2643.

Follow the Sunset, sung by Charity Bailey, Folkways FC7406.

Forty-five Songs Children Love to Sing, RCA CAS 1038 (e).

Hans Christian Andersen and *Tubby the Tuba,* sung by Danny Kaye, Bowmar 45.8479.

Mother Goose Songs, sung by Frank Luther, Decca 78357.

Music Time, sung by Charity Bailey, Folkways FC7307.

Negro Folk Songs for Young People, sung by Huddie Ledbetter, Folkways FC7533.

1, 2, 3 and a Zing, Zing, Zing (street songs and games of New York children), Folkways FC 7003.

Parsley, Sage, Rosemary, and Thyme, songs by Paul Simon and Art Garfunkel (includes "Feeling Groovy"), Columbia CS9363.

Songs from Sesame Street, RCA CAS 1127.

Songs to Grow On, Vols. I, II, III, sung by Woody Guthrie, Folkways FC7675, 7020, 7027.

The Little White Duck and Other Children's Favorites, sung by Burl Ives, Harmony 14507.

Wonderful Fantasy of Walt Disney, RCA CXS 9014.

World's Greatest Children's Songs, RCA Records, Educational Dept., 1133 Avenue of the Americas, New York, N.Y. 10036.

Chapter Preview

Using Rhymes and Poetry for Dance-Making

With Younger Children
Leads into Dance-Making
Dance Poems

With Younger and Older Children
Putting Movement Words into Sequences

With Older Children
Leads into Dance-Making
Dance Poems

Poetic Image: "Sharp Silver Flames Spinning Up"

O. R. PETERSON III

19 *Approach from Words*

*Not that I find any hatred here in our new kind of school
. . . I find quarrelsomeness, discontent, unwillingness and
rudeness . . . but I do not sense hatred. . . . But I don't sense
love here, either. What's happened to the dynamics of feeling;
where is the third dimension?*[1]

Verbal and vocal accompaniments for dance are not new. Primitive dance
was often accompanied by rhythmic chanting and shouting. The choruses of
the great Greek tragedies were spoken and danced together, the movement
reinforcing the emotional impact of the memorable words.

The chanted rhyme of the square dance caller is an example of verbalizing as dance accompaniment. There may be a fiddle or so in the background, but that is merely to keep the beat. The accents, phrases—the larger
rhythms—are the caller's responsibility. The dancers respond only on his
signal, and the way they dance often depends on the lustiness and gaiety of
his calls.

Children have long used simple chants for games and counting-out
rhymes. Much less has been done with words as motivation or accompaniment for dance, but they offer rich material for movement exploration. (See
the Movement Word Game, Chapter 5, and Sensory Sources for Movement
Invention: Auditory, Chapter 6.)

---

[1] Sylvia Ashton-Warner, *Spearpoint,* New York, Knopf, 1972, p. 31.

Using Rhymes and Poetry for Dance-Making

Jingles, slogans, and rhymes are excellent accompaniment for dance move-ment, being in themselves rhythmic and often suggesting action in their words. Nursery rhymes, counting-out rhymes, and nonsense rhymes are often learned at home or in preschool and kindergarten. Mother Goose rhymes usually suggest dramatic action—by a single figure, as in "Tom, Tom, the Piper's Son"; by two characters, as in "Little Miss Muffet" and the spider; by several, as in "Sing a Song of Sixpence."

Even more interesting for dance interpretation are poems, some written in definite metrical lines or verses, and others, unrhymed and of freer rhythmic construction, allowing for irregular movement phrases. On the whole, a poem offers opportunity for less arbitrary interpretation for dance-making than does a song. The sequences of words into verse, even of metri-cally rhymed stanzas, can be made more flexible as accompaniment by pauses, by repeating certain lines, by slowing down or speeding up for emphasis.

Most authorities believe that children's appreciation of poetry involves more than merely reading, understanding, and memorizing. A poem be-comes significant and is remembered when it catches the child's interest through its rhythmic and expressive verbal portrayal.[2] A teacher using this approach should be sure not only of the movement potential of the poem but also of its appeal to the children who are to dance it. Offering a choice from among several poems for interpretation may be desirable.

It is not always necessary for the rhymes or poetry to provide the accompaniment for the dance movement. Many poems with excellent dance potential may be difficult to fit to movement phrases because they are too long, are too short, or have too many or too few poetic images. In that case the poem or certain images from it may be used as subject matter, content, dramatic idea, or point of departure for the dance rather than as the accom-paniment. Any rhyme or poem, whether or not it provides appropriate accompaniment, may be used in this fashion. First the poem is read and reread so that the children understand its meaning. Then working alone or in groups they structure dance studies reflecting the meaning in movement. The dances may be unaccompanied, or music or sound effects can be impro-vised for them. Such use of poetry will appeal more to older than to younger

---

[2] Choral speaking or verse speaking is an effective aid which combines well with dance movement.

children, as the rhythmic drive and dramatic stimulation of the recited words are not present in the dance performance.

For younger children, half the charm in a poem is its measured rhythm—its rhymed words which give it a feeling of movement. The meaning of the words is of secondary interest. Older children, however, whose developing intellectual powers demand deeper probing into the meaning of word symbols, will often prefer a more freely structured poem or even a prose selection for dance-making.

If the dancers so desire and the meaning of the poem is not destroyed by interspersed pauses, they can continue in their movements beyond the actual spoken word. The meaning of word phrases or even single words can be extended by movement which continues in the silence after they are spoken. The dance actually creates a new rhythmic sequence built upon the flow of

Poetic Image: "Seagulls Squabble Over Scraps"

O. R. PETERSON III

Poetic Image: "Drenched in Gray Sadness"

words and movement intermingled, sometimes occurring together, sometimes either alone.

Examples of poems of a definite metered structure are "The Light-Hearted Fairy," "Mrs. Peck-Pigeon," and "Swing Song" for younger children; "The Peppery Man" and "Afternoon on a Hill" for older children. Here the accompanied movement will follow or relate rhythmically to the meter and accents of the words. Varying the tempo will allow time for movements suggested by the words.

Other poems are irregular in timing and lack periodicity of beats. This should be observed in their reading. To a certain extent, therefore, children may determine their own timing and manipulate it as they wish. Examples are "Lawn Mower" and "Brown and Furry" for younger children; "Fog" and "The Mysterious Cat" for older children.

Sometimes only certain stanzas of dance poems are usable, as the first stanza of "Rabbits" and the first two stanzas of "Cat" in *Sung Under the Silver Umbrella*. Poems that tell about some kind of movement are excellent choices for dances. Not good choices are poems that describe how something smells, tastes, or sounds, rather than how it moves; that tell of meditations, aspirations, reflections, contemplations; that are several stanzas long; that contain abstract ideas too complicated to express in movement.

A poem is used as accompaniment for dance-making much as a song is. The first reading by the narrator (usually the teacher) will determine the variations in tempo, quality, or rhythmic structure which are desirable for movement phrasing. The children will then invent movement to follow the rhythmic sequence and the expressive quality of the spoken words. When children recite their own poems as they make their dance studies, however, they may follow their own ideas as to how the poem should be said, and hence how the sequence of movements should be made to interpret it. Older children will be able and probably will prefer to compose their dances to poems in this fashion.

With Younger Children

Leads into Dance-Making

A characteristic activity of very young children is the continued repetition of words in rhythmic sequence, often without meaning to anyone but themselves. It is probably not happenstance that one of the first words many babies learn is "Bow-wow," combining as it does rhymed sounds in a duple grouping. Preschool children often accompany play activities with their own chanted verbal improvisations, and at times the words they use to name toys or pets or imaginary companions have a rhythmic flavor.

Teachers should freely explore the use of sounds and words as accompaniment for the dance activities for younger children. Rhythmic response improves if the accompaniment is their own.

Sounds of animals: Bow-wow, me-ow, purr-rr, quackety-quack, peep-peep, cheep-cheep, cut-cut-cut-cudaw-cut, cock-a-doodle-doo, gobble-gobble, baa-baa, moo-oo, clippety-clop, buzz-zz, to-whit-to-whoo, bob-o-link, coo-coo-coo, bob-white, whip-poor-will.

Sounds of things: Ding-dong, honk-honk, toot-toot, choo-choo, clickety-clack, chug-chug, tick-tock, cuck-oo, ting-a-ling, bang-bang, boom-boom, pitter-patter, woo-oo-oo, rat-a-tat-tat, ack-ack-ack.

Sounds of activity: Giddy-ap, whoa-oa, hippety-hop, see-saw, rock-a-bye, tra-la-la, rap-tap-tap, ha-ha-ha.

Nonsense syllables: Higgledy-piggledy, tiddledy-i-o, fiddle-de-dee, jiggedy-jig, bumpety-bumpety-bump, deedle-deedle-dumpling, hickory-dickory-dock.

Selling calls: Pea-nuts, pop-corn, hot-dogs, ham-burgers, ice-cream, balloons, ice-cold-pop, yum-yum-yummy.

Words of greeting and farewell: Hello, hi-there, yoo-hoo, how-do-you-do, how-are-you, Happy birthday, Merry Christmas, Happy New Year, good-bye, so-long, be-seeing-you, fare-thee-well.

Our own sounds: Clicks and clucks, giggles, growls, hisses, sighs, sh——, squeals, swishes, whines, yells, ohs, and ahs used as a sympathetic questioning or scolding utterance.

Offering something more in the way of content, and hence sequence of movement, are the rhymes and jingles from Mother Goose and other sources.[3] There is a wealth of material here for both younger and older children to translate into dance movements.

The following younger children's dance poems are from collections or anthologies rather than volumes by a single author. The first volume, *Miracles,* is a collection of children's own poetry.

Dance Poems

From *Miracles—Poems by Children of the English-Speaking World,* collected by Richard Lewis, New York, Simon & Schuster, 1966.

Creep	Linda Kershaw	Age 10
Flying Sea, The	Roger Mortimer	Age 7
I feel relaxed and still (first line)	Karen Anderson	Age 7
I Love the World	Paul Wollner	Age 7
My Feelings	Paul Thompson	Age 6
Rain	Adrian Keith Smith	Age 4
Splish Splosh	Stefan Martul	Age 7
Trees	Susan Forman	Age 7
Wind was bringing me to school, The	James Snyder	Age 6

From *Story and Verse for Children,* selected and edited by Miriam Blanton Huber, New York, Macmillan, 1966.

Busy Carpenters	James S. Tippett	*Dancing*	Eleanor Farjeon
Cat	Mary Britton Miller	*Halloween*	Harry Behn
Caterpillar, The	Christina G. Rossetti	*Kangaroo, The*	Elizabeth Coatsworth

[3] See Charles Cousley, *Figgie Hobbin,* London, Macmillan, 1971; Louis Untermeyer, *The Golden Book of Fun and Nonsense,* New York, Western, 1970; Carl Withers, ed., *I Saw a Rocket Walk a Mile: Nonsense Tales, Chants and Songs from Many Lands,* New York, Holt, Rinehart & Winston, 1965.

Little Star	Jane Taylor	*Thanksgiving Day*	Lydia Maria Child
Merry Go Round	Dorothy W. Baruch	*White Window, The*	James Stephens
Moonlight	Maud E. Uschold	*Who Has Seen the Wind?*	Christina G. Rossetti
Mrs. Peck-Pigeon	Eleanor Farjeon	*Wind, The*	Robert Louis Stevenson
Night Was Creeping	James Stephens	*Wings and Wheels*	Nancy Byrd Turner
Rabbit, The	Edith King	*Woodpecker, The*	Elizabeth Madox Roberts
Skyscrapers	Rachel Field		
Some One	Walter de la Mare		
Squirrel, The	Author Unknown		

From *Sung Under the Silver Umbrella,* poems for young children selected by the Literature Committee of the Association for Childhood Education, New York, Macmillan, 1972.

Brown and Furry	Christina G. Rossetti	*Lawn-Mower*	Dorothy W. Baruch
Cat	Dorothy W. Baruch	*Light-Hearted Fairy, The*	Author Unknown
Cat	Mary Britton Miller	*Little Wind*	Kate Greenaway
Conversation	Anne Robinson	*Merry Go Round*	Dorothy W. Baruch
Corn-Grinding Song (Butterflies)	Natalie Curtis, tr.	*Mrs. Peck-Pigeon*	Eleanor Farjeon
Crescent Moon	Elizabeth Madox Roberts	*Rabbits*	Dorothy W. Baruch
Different Bicycles	Dorothy W. Baruch	*Squirrel, The*	Author Unknown
Down! Down!	Eleanor Farjeon	*Stop-Go*	Dorothy W. Baruch
Envoi	Algernon Charles Swinburne	*Swing, The*	Robert Louis Stevenson
Fly Away	Christina G. Rossetti	*White Window, The*	James Stephens
		Who Has Seen the Wind?	Christina G. Rossetti

From *Lets'-Read-Together Poems,* an anthology of verse for choral reading selected by Helen A. Brown and Harry J. Heltman, New York, Harper & Row, 1949.

Boots, Boots, Boots	Leroy F. Jackson	*My Funny Umbrella*	Alice Wilkins
Cover	Frances M. Frost	*My Kite*	Barbara and Beatrice Brown
Crescent Moon	Elizabeth Madox Roberts	*My Shadow*	Robert Louis Stevenson
Funny the Way Different Cars Start	Dorothy W. Baruch	*Playing Leaves, The*	Oro Clayton Moore
Galoshes	Rhoda W. Bacmeister	*Pop Corn Song*	Nancy Byrd Turner
Jack Frost	Author Unknown	*Rabbit, The*	Edith King
Merry Go Round	Dorothy W. Baruch	*Rabbits*	Dorothy W. Baruch
Milkman's Horse, The	Author Unknown	*Robin*	Tom Robinson
Mrs. Peck-Pigeon	Eleanor Farjeon	*Seesaw*	Evelyn Beyer
		Skyscrapers	Rachel Field

| Snow | Alice Wilkins | White Window, | |
| Squirrel, The | Author Unknown | The | James Stephens |

From *Favorite Poems Old and New,* selected by Helen Ferris, New York, Doubleday, 1957. (Many usable poems in this large collection have already been listed and are not repeated here.)

Back and Forth	Lucy Sprague Mitchell
Hey! My Pony!	Eleanor Farjeon
Holding Hands	Lenore M. Link
Little Black Bug	Margaret Wise Brown
Little Jumping Girls	Kate Greenaway
Little Turtle, The	Vachel Lindsay
Puzzled Centipede, The	Author Unknown
Song of the Train	David McCord
Swing Song	William Allingham
Tugs	James S. Tippett
White Butterflies	Algernon Charles Swinburne

With Younger and Older Children

While the following activity is more useful for older children for word interpretation into movement, in its simpler form (only two or three words employed) it will be enjoyed by younger children as well. As preliminary improvisational practice The Movement Word Game in Chapter 5 should be played. Improvised movement in response to a movement word signal leads to the discovery of different ways of interpreting the word in nonverbal fashion and deepens awareness of the many meanings a single word may have.

Putting Movement Words into Sequences

In the following lists of words, the participle form rather than the verb form is used. The former suggests ongoing action while the latter often suggests a single movement only. When the words are put into a sequential form, their movement interpretation, although it may be performed in a variety of ways, must be continuous.

Younger children may first choose one locomotor and one nonlocomotor word (the selection offered may be less extensive) to perform in a movement phrase. In the beginning the teacher signals the change from one word to the other and back again. Then three words are chosen and tried in the same way.

Later, younger children may choose their own contrasting words and make individual sequences in their own timing and length of movement phrase. Or partners can use the same two or three words and phrase duration but move in opposition to each other. Suggestions for older children follow the movement word listings.

Locomotor

Basic Movement Words

walking, running, leaping, jumping, hopping

Evolving Dance Steps

galloping, skipping, sliding, etc.

Descriptive Locomotor Words

crawling	pouncing
creeping	prancing
darting	rolling
dashing	sailing
floating	spinning
flying	stamping
gliding	swooping
pattering	tramping

(cartwheeling, knee walking, seat walking, somersaulting, and other athletic actions may be used if they can be performed by many in the class)

Nonlocomotor

Basic Movement Words

bending, stretching, twisting, swinging

Descriptive Nonlocomotor Words

collapsing	rising
curling	rocking
dodging	shaking
expanding	shivering
exploding	sinking
flopping	sitting
grabbing	slapping
jerking	squirming
leaning	striking
lifting	swaying
pointing	tapping
poking	thrusting
pulling	touching
pushing	turning
quivering	wriggling
reaching	writhing

Older children may put together three to six words of their own choice, including some of both kinds. Ways of using them in a sequential study follow:

1. The duration and tempo of the movements are the children's choice; each should be performed long enough to be recognized as a distinct part of the total.

2. There should be a logical movement transition or "flow" from one word to the next, without a pause, unless a period of stillness is planned as

part of the whole. Children may change their choice of words if transitions seem difficult or forced.

3. Variations in the sequences are made by changing the order of the movements, changing their duration from longer or shorter to the reverse, or changing the size or level of the movement. The variations should not alter the word's meaning. Accompaniment is not necessary unless the child wishes to vocalize his own. After completion of a sequence, however, an appropriate percussion accompaniment may be played by a partner.

4. Children may find other movement words for this activity. An extension of this use of words to elicit variety of movement is to add a list of adverbs which are then selected to modify the movement words: reaching timidly, jumping quickly, pouncing angrily, rolling roughly, walking carefully, etc.

5. This activity, at first an individual one, may be done in twos or threes in several ways. One of two or three persons chooses two movement words, one of which is nonlocomotor. Functioning as a unit in a specific space, the children attempt to make their movements contrast with each other but also relate, so that the study is recognized as a duet or trio.

Using three or more of the same chosen words, those working together perform them in unison, but with individual variations in treatment or interpretation. If the duration of each movement is identical, they may follow each other in succession, as in round singing; or each participant may choose his own sequence, performing it individually but relating it to the others' movement in a spatial design.

In any series of movements which children put together, they should be made conscious of its beginning, developing, and finishing. A definite neutral starting shape should be taken before movement begins. The teacher may have to use cues or signals for word changes, especially for the sequence to end. Children often become so involved in their own movement that they continue, oblivious that others have finished. Or they may not know quite how to affect a conclusion. The following word signals suggested on earlier pages may help:

1. For a sudden ending, in which the final movement shape is held and maintained on the sharp signal "Freeze," "Stop," "Hold."

2. For a gradual ending, in which the child makes his own finish to the sequence, attaining his final shape in space in a few seconds after the quiet signal "Put a period to the phrase," "Bring it to a conclusion," "Bring it to a stillness," or "Make your ending now."

With Older Children

Leads into Dance-Making

Cheers. Cheerleading is a good example of movement in a rhymed and/or rhythmic sequence to accompany a vociferous chant. Both boys and girls enjoy making vigorous movements to accompany their school cheers or the cheers of a high school or college with which they are familiar. Often they may invent their own cheers.

Slogans. Television slogans are another field for rhythmic word accompaniment. Because of the often exaggerated sentiments expressed, older children enjoy treating them humorously or satirically in movement. An assignment to bring in well-known slogans which advertise commercial products and to make movement sequences to illustrate them, either individually or in groups, can provide much fun.

Older children also enjoy experimenting with movement to some of the sounds and words listed on page 284. This might develop into a comic dance made to an accompaniment of nonsense syllables or one's own sounds; a vendor's dance with "Peanuts, popcorn, hamburgers, and pop!" as its supporting rhythmic sequence; a greeting dance examining the difference between "Hello" or "Hi" and "How do you do."

A related kind of movement experimentation with words consists of the use of single words (see Chapter 6 under Auditory) or short phrases ("Come here," "Go away," "Excuse me," "Let me go") enunciated in different timing, dynamics and modulation, or number of repetitions. This again extends awareness of how the voice's expression may change word meaning and hence the accompanying movement.

Proverbs. As nursery rhymes suggest action sequences to younger children, proverbs may serve the same purpose with older ones. The meaning of these terse popular sayings should be discussed in the total group, and one or more of them chosen as subjects. Small groups can be given a short time to illustrate the proverb in movement. It is desirable but not necessary that all in the group perform, as long as each tries to contribute an idea for the sequence. The following proverbs lend themselves to such treatment:

A bird in the hand is worth two in the bush.
A new broom sweeps clean.
Birds of a feather flock together.

Don't cry over spilt milk.
Look before you leap.
Pride goeth before a fall.
When the cat's away, the mice will play.

Poetic Images. In preparation for dance-making to a complete poem older children may be asked to improvise to single poetic images suggested by the teacher. Children who have experienced continuous movement to single words describing states of being or feeling should be able to cope improvisationally with poetic images such as the following:

sharp silver flames spinning up
crippled grass bent oddly
drenched in gray sadness
seagulls squabble over scraps
snowflake blossom drifting
silence hanging in the dark air
fragile lace against the winter sky[4]

and "My Feelings" a poem by six-year-old Paul Thompson:

I am fainty
I am fizzy
I am floppy.

Dance Poems

Of the poems for older children listed below, some express more mature poetic ideas than others and may not be appropriate for all groups to attempt to put into dance form. Many children are deeply responsive to poetry because it touches inner emotions and aspirations and it would perhaps be intrusive to ask them to make these known to their peers through movement interpretation. Therefore, at first it is best to try objective or humorous poems, such as "Swift Things Are Beautiful" by Elizabeth Coatsworth, "Jabberwocky" by Lewis Carroll, or "Witches" by Linden in *Miracles*. A free choice of poems on which to work should be given; and as certain children try the more subjective ones, others will be encouraged to do so, too.

[4] These phrases and the poem are from *Miracles—Poems by Children of the English-Speaking World,* collected by Richard Lewis, New York, Simon & Schuster, 1966. Copyright © 1966, by Richard Lewis. Reprinted by permission of Simon and Schuster.

Children often like to compose their own jingles or rhymed verses about events, people, or characters they know, their hopes and ambitions, and a multitude of other subjects, some humorous, others serious. Those which lend themselves to movement interpretation may be used for dance-making.

From *Miracles—Poems by Children of the English-Speaking World*, collected by Richard Lewis, New York, Simon & Schuster, 1966.

Breeze	Marie Hourigan	Age 11
Concrete Mixer, The	Timothy Langley	Age 11
Dancing	Alex M	Age 10
Fickle Wind, The	Cindy Schonhaut	Age 8
Fire	Pat Taylor	Age 13
Morning Mist, The (first line)	Geeta Mohanty	Age 13
Sparrows	Anne Fyfe	Age 11
When spring comes (first line)	Michael Patrick	Age 10
Whoops a Daisy	Teddy Carr	Age 8
Winter	John Constant	Age 10
Witches	Linden	Age 10

From *Story and Verse for Children*, selected and edited by Miriam Blanton Huber, Macmillan, New York, 1966.

Afternoon on a Hill	Edna St. Vincent Millay	*Lobster Quadrille* *Mysterious Cat, The*	Lewis Carroll
Falling Star, The	Sara Teasdale		Vachel Lindsay
Fog	Carl Sandburg	*Skating*	Herbert Asquith
Hills	Hilda Conkling	*Swift Things Are Beautiful*	Elizabeth Coatsworth
Indian Summer Day on a Prairie	Vachel Lindsay	*Velvet Shoes*	Elinor Wylie

From *An Inheritance of Poetry*, collected and arranged by Gladys L. Adshead and Annis Duff, Boston, Houghton Mifflin, 1948.

Almanac	Fiona Macleod	*"Over Hill Over Dale"*	William Shakespeare
April Showers	James Stephens		
Cargoes	John Masefield	*Prayer to the Dark Bird*	Traditional: Navajo Indian
Counting-Out Rhyme	Traditional: English	*Rune of the Peat Fire, The*	Traditional: from the Gaelic
For a Mocking Voice	Eleanor Farjeon	*Silent Snake, The*	Author Unknown
Green Grow the Rushes, O	Traditional: English	*"Through the House Give Glimmering Light"*	
Merry Are the Bells	Traditional: English		William Shakespeare
Months, The	Christina G. Rossetti		

From *All the Silver Pennies,* edited by Blanche Jennings Thompson, New York, Macmillan, 1967.

African Dance	Langston Hughes	*Potatoes' Dance*	Vachel Lindsay
Caravans	Hal Borland	*Spirit of the*	
Cargoes	John Masefield	*Birch, The*	Arthur Ketchum
Fog	Carl Sandburg	*Velvet Shoes*	Elinor Wylie
Fog, the Magician	Melville Cane	*Welcome to the*	
Irish	Edward J. O'Brien	*New Year*	Eleanor Farjeon
Mysterious Cat,		*Wind Is a Cat*	Ethel Romig Fuller
The	Vachel Lindsay		

From *Sung Under the Silver Umbrella,* poems for young children selected by the Literature Committee of the Association for Childhood Education, New York, Macmillan, 1972.

City of Falling		*Sea Bird to the*	
Leaves, The	Amy Lowell	*Wave, The*	Padraic Colum
Dirge for a		*Snow Toward*	
Righteous Kitten	Vachel Lindsay	*Evening*	Melville Cane
Fog	Carl Sandburg		

From *The Speech Choir,* American poetry and English ballads for choral reading, by Marjorie Gullan, New York, Harper & Row, 1937.

Jazz Fantasia	Carl Sandburg	*Rain Chant*	Natalie Curtis
Johnny at the Fair	Traditional		Burlin, tr.
King of the Yellow		*Robin-a-Thrush*	English Ballad
Butterflies, The	Vachel Lindsay	*Swift Things Are*	Elizabeth Coats-
Pioneers, Oh		*Beautiful*	worth
Pioneers	Walt Whitman	*Tide Rises, The*	Henry Wadsworth
Pirate Don Durke			Longfellow
of Dowdee	Mildred Plew Meigs		

From *The Dream Keeper* by Langston Hughes, New York, Knopf, 1945.

African Dance	*Long Trip*
Autumn Thought	*Walkers with the Dawn*
Dream Variation	*Youth*
Homesick Blues	

From *Early Moon* by Carl Sandburg, New York, Harcourt Brace Jovanovich, 1939.

Good Night	*Summer Stars*
Jazz Fantasia	*Sunsets*
Sea-Wash	

From *Wind Song* by Carl Sandburg, New York, Harcourt Brace Jovanovich, 1960.

Lines Written for Gene Kelly to Dance to
Night
Summer Grass

From *Poems 1923–1954* by e. e. cummings, New York, Harcourt Brace Jovanovich, 1954.

in just-spring	*little tree*
hist whist	*who knows if the moon's*

A few selections from *Haiku. Series I—Seventeen Syllable Poems* (the tiny verse-form in which Japanese poets have been working for hundreds of years), Mt. Vernon, N.Y., Peter Pauper Press, 1956 (first lines).

Arise from Sleep,		*My Two Plum*	
Old Cat	Issa	*Trees*	Buson
A Single Cricket	Anon.	*You Turn and*	
Butterfly Asleep	Buson	*Suddenly*	Onitsura
Good Evening,			
Breeze	Issa		

From *A Crocodile Has Me by the Leg,* African poems edited by Leonard W. Doob, New York, Walker, 1966.

Coo-coo-roo of the Girls
Dance of the Animals
Praise Song for a Drummer
Song of Young Men Working in Gold Mines

From *Favorite Poems Old and New,* selected by Helen Ferris, New York, Doubleday, 1957. (Many usable poems in this large collection have already been listed and are not repeated here.)

City	Langston Hughes	*Skyscrapers*	Rachel Field
Halloween	Harry Behn	*Sun, The*	John Drinkwater
Jabberwocky	Lewis Carroll	*Tired Tim*	Walter de la Mare
Paul Bunyon	Arthur Bouninot	*When Young*	
People	Lois Lanski	*Melissa Sweeps*	Nancy Byrd Turner
Peppery Man, The	Arthur Macy		
Ride-by-Nights,			
The	Walter de la Mare		

Chapter Preview

Using Music for Dance-Making

With Younger and Older Children
    Leads into Dance-Making

Music for Older Children
    Music for the Piano
    Records from Classical to Modern
    Electronic Records
    Miscellaneous Records

20 *Approach from Music*

*Drama, dance, and music are important elements in the
development of the growing child, as food, shelter and clothing
are necessary material elements of his existence. The arts
should be the source of a child's education, not a superfluous
frill attached for status symbol later in life.*[1]

A time-honored method of composing dances is to start with a favorite
musical selection and then arrange steps and movements to fit the structure
and quality of the music. Contemporary concert dance may depart notably
from this custom by having the musical accompaniment composed either
after a dance was made or during the choreographic process. Even contemporary dance artists, however, often use the traditional method and
compose to a piece of music which appeals to them.

This approach to dance-making for children is excellent, but there is one
obstacle which is sometimes insurmountable—the accompanist! Even though
simple music is selected, an accompanist who is constantly available to help
analyze the musical structure and to play parts of it for improvisation,
experimentation, or practice is a rarity.

More and more records now fill this need, and several are listed at the
end of this chapter and in Chapter 29. To avoid having the record wear out,
a tape recorder is most helpful. This technological aid also makes other types
of accompaniment possible (the singing of children in the music room,
choral speaking in literature, making a collage of sounds), and its use in
modern schools is increasing.

Activity must be channeled if the dance and the music are to belong to

---

[1] Olga Maynard, *Children and Dance and Music,* New York, Scribner, 1968, p. 188.

each other and the music is to be more than merely a background for the movement. The dance should reproduce in movement not only the quality of the music but its structure—that is, its timing and its sequence of parts. The dance should obviously be related to pulsation and accents, whether moving with them or against them in syncopation. A movement phrase should parallel a musical phrase, not begin in the middle of one and finish in the middle of another. When a melodic phrase differs considerably from the one preceding it, the movement should show a similar change. Likewise, musical phrases which are repeated identically or almost identically should be reproduced in movement which is not radically different from that of the original phrase, though it may vary somewhat.

It is important, then, to listen to the music carefully. Its quality will be determined by such things as the kind of melody, harmony, dynamics, tempo, and accentuation. Listening to the music for its structure will allow one to determine its arrangement in phrases and sections. The form of the music may be charted (as, for example, A B C) to make it easier to remember and to simplify the stages of composing.

Children may work individually, in couples, or in groups. The procedures are similar to those described in Chapter 17. However, from time to time the music should be played, on demand from the working groups or otherwise, so that the children may check their progress with it.

With Younger and Older Children

Leads into Dance-Making

Becoming sensitive to environmental sounds, natural or man-made, is important for the dance education of children, as it is for their musical education. Even more important is their developing sensitivity to musical sounds, reacting to their dynamics, pitch, duration, tone. Such obvious adjectives as *heavy, light, loud, soft, high, low* may not be as meaningful or as dancelike to them as *bang-y, scary, wispy, sleepy, tinkly.* Children should not be asked to go much beyond such a general description of music. Asking them whether they liked it, what it reminds them of, and the like may force the inarticulate to invent answers just to please the teacher.

Percussion instruments are most useful for relating sound to movement. After the children have discussed *how* a gong sounds—or a wood-block, a triangle, a rattle—they may experiment with movement that looks and feels like the sound. With children who have a meager background in movement expression this is a rewarding catalyst. In their concentration on reproducing the sound with body action, movements result which would not otherwise have been attempted.

The piano may not be as stimulating at first because its sounds are so familiar. Percussion instruments are novel and fun and the children them-

"Spring Has Sprung" (1)

"Spring Has Sprung" (2)

selves can play them. The familiar ones can be augmented by some of those listed in Chapter 16. One instrument can be used alone, the children having several trials at producing movement which is congenial to its sound. Later, instruments giving contrasting sounds may follow in a sequence, so that a change from one movement quality to another is made and then perhaps repeated. A gong and a wood-block provide a strong contrast, as do a slide whistle and a rattle.

With very simple improvisational abilities, the teacher can use the piano in the same way, for it is the richest single instrument for the production of musical sound. Sometimes children who play other instruments (flute, recorder, accordion, violin, or a brass instrument) may be invited to accompany movement experimentation as well as finished dances.

Other sounds which lend themselves to movement interpretation are city sounds such as the wail of a siren, the intermittent ring of an alarm clock, the roar of a jet plane, the sounds of construction machines. The sounds of birds and insects, the crackle and snap of a bonfire, the sighing of the wind in the trees belong to the country, and some city children may not be familiar with them. Sound-effects records may be successfully used for dance improvisation from this approach.[2]

Music for Older Children

In most school music books the teacher's editions contain "Music for Listening," available in albums of records related to the series, which in some cases could be used for dance composition. In a school having closely related dance and music programs the children themselves may convey their desire to make a dance to a selection they have heard in the music room. A tape recorder in this situation is of great value in bringing the music to the dance room.

Music of folk songs is often excellent for dances. Their structure is usually simple and suggests locomotor movement with which most children are comfortable. In albums of folk dance there are always some that for various reasons will never be taught. What could be a better use for this folk music than to have several groups make their own dances to it?

The following music references range from classic to modern. The first section classifies a book of simple piano pieces and suggests other books.

2 See p. 424.

Then come records, some of short pieces, some of children's classics. If a piece is too long, one section, carefully extracted, may be used without damaging the continuity of the whole.

Electronic music represents an important segment of today's music and can provide a stimulating "sound landscape" for creative movement. In the final miscellaneous section only one composer of jazz music is included; this style, while fun to dance to, is generally too complicated for children's dance-making.

Records have been chosen for their simplicity of arrangement (piano rather than symphony, if possible) and for the fact that the second side sometimes includes other selections on the list, or pieces not listed which nevertheless might be interesting for children to hear.

Teachers should be reminded: (1) that children are not conditioned to the more traditional harmonic and rhythmic structures of music and do not react unfavorably to dissonance and mixed meters, as do many adults; and (2) that although some of the references may seem overly familiar—even hackneyed—to children's ears they are fresh and new.

Music for the Piano

As few dance classes are blessed with an accompanist, certain selections in only one book of piano music have been categorized according to the quality of the music. (*Phrasing* after a composition means that there is some departure from the common four- or eight-measure phrase construction, possibly only an extension of the final phrase.) A few books from other publishers, recommended by the head of a music school, are listed at the end of this section.

Easy Classics to Moderns, Vol. 17 of Music for Millions Series, Consolidated Music Publishers, 33 W. 60th St., New York, N.Y. 10023.

Gay, Lively, Locomotor

Andante	Mozart	*First Miniature*	Bartok
Circle Dance	Villa-Lobos	*Fourth Ländler*	Schubert
Dance with Me		*Hunting Song*	Schumann
(phrasing)	Volkmann	*March*	J. S. Bach
Ecossaise in G	Beethoven	*March*	Gurlitt
First Country		*On Tiptoes*	Bertini
Dance	Beethoven	*Peasant Song*	
First Ecossaise	Schubert	(phrasing)	Mendelssohn

Ride, Ride	Kabalevsky	Two Austrian	
Russian Folk Song	Beethoven	Folk Themes	Czerny
Soldiers March	Schumann	Wild Horsemen	Schumann

Slow, Swinging, Flowing, Quiet

A Farewell	Purcell	Larghetto	
Constants		(phrasing)	Stravinsky
(phrasing)	Villa-Lobos	Lento (phrasing)	Stravinsky
Cradle Song	Kullak	Lullaby	Kirnberger
Evening in the		Melody	Khachaturian
Meadow		Minuet (Gm)	J. S. Bach
(phrasing)	Rebikoff	Minuet	Telemann
Fifth Miniature		Old French Song	Tchaikovsky
(phrasing)	Bartok	Rondino	Rameau
First Ländler	Schubert	Sixth Miniature	
German Dance	Beethoven	(phrasing)	Bartok
German Song	Tchaikovsky	The Reaper's Song	Schumann
Humming	Kabalevsky	Waltz	Schubert

Strong, Sharp, Staccato, Rhythmic

Arabesque		Musette	J. S. Bach
(phrasing)	Burgmuller	Playing Soldiers	Rebikoff
A Regal Dance	Turk	Promenade	
Burleske	Mozart	(phrasing)	Gretchaninoff
Carnival	Couperin	Second and Third	
Chit Chat		Short Canons	Kunz
(canonic)	Kabalevsky	The Clock	Kullak
Fourth Miniature	Bartok	Third Country	
Gavotte and		Dance	Beethoven
Variation	Handel	Trumpet Tune	Purcell
Le Petit Rien	Couperin	Waltz	Kabalevsky
Little March	Kabalevsky		

SUPPLEMENTARY BOOKS OF PIANO MUSIC

A Little Treasure of Folk Songs and Dances: One and Two, selected and arranged
by Cecily Lambert, New York, Heritage Music Publications.

Fifty-seven Piano Pieces Children Like to Play, New York, Schirmer.

From Bach to Bartok, selected and edited by Denes Agay, New York, Witmark.

More Easy Classics to Moderns, compiled and edited by Denes Agay, New York,
Consolidated Music Publishers.

Records from Classical to Modern

(Many of these are also available on tapes.)

ANDERSON, LEROY, *Music of Leroy Anderson,* RCA LSC 5006 (includes "Jazz Pizzicato," "Fiddle Faddle," "Syncopated Clock")

BARTOK, BELA, *For Children,* Vols. 1 and 2, 3 Vox SVBX 5426, 3 Vox SVBX 5427

BARTOK, BELA, *Mikrokosmos,* 3 Vox SVBX 5425

BIZET, GEORGES, *Jeux d'enfants (Children's Games),* Odyssey 32160334

COLGRASS, MICHAEL, *As Quiet As,* RCA LSC 3001

COPLAND, AARON, *Billy the Kid,* Columbia MX 6175 (excerpts from *Billy the Kid;* "Hoe-Down" from *Rodeo*)

DEBUSSY, CLAUDE, *Children's Corner Suite,* RCA LSC 3090 (Piano); Turnabout 34166 (Piano)

DEBUSSY, CLAUDE, *Clair de Lune* (from *Suite Bergamasque*), RCA LSC 3090

GOULD, MORTON, *American Salute,* Turnabout 34459 (plus Siegmeister's *Western Suite,* Robertson's *Punch and Judy Overture,* etc.)

GROFÉ, FERDE, *Grand Canyon Suite,* Mercury MCR 4-95003 (plus *Mississippi Suite*)

HOLST, GUSTAV, *The Planets,* Angel S 36420

KHACHATURIAN, ARAM, *Gayne Ballet Suite,* Columbia MX 7018 (plus Tchaikovsky's *Nutcracker*)

MOZART, WOLFGANG AMADEUS, *Contradance in F Major* from the Divertimento No. 8, Phillips 6500-002

SAINT-SAENS, CAMILLE, *Carnival of the Animals,* Columbia MX 6368 (plus *Young Person's Guide to the Orchestra*); London 6187 (plus *Peter and the Wolf*); Angel S 36421 (plus Poulenc's *Animaux*)

SAINT-SAENS, CAMILLE, *Danse Macabre,* RCA LSC 3314 (plus Dukas's *Sorcerer's Apprentice;* Grieg's *Peer Gynt Suite No. 1,* Rimsky-Korsakov's *Flight of the Bumblebee,* etc.)

SCHULLER, GUNTHER, *Seven Studies on Themes of Paul Klee,* RCA LSC 2879

SHOSTAKOVICH, DMITRI, *Polka* from the *Age of Gold* Ballet Suite, RCA LSC 3133

SIEGMEISTER, ELIE, *Western Suite,* Turnabout 34459 (plus Gould's *American Salute,* Robertson's *Punch and Judy Overture,* etc.)

STRAVINSKY, IGOR, *Suite No. 2* (March, Waltz, Polka, Galop), Columbia M 31729

VAUGHAN WILLIAMS, RALPH, *English Folk Songs Suite,* Mercury 90388 (plus Grainger's *Hill Song No. 2;* Holst's *Suites*)

VILLA-LOBOS, HEITOR, *Little Train of the Calpira,* Everest 3243

Electronic Records

CARLOS, WALTER, *The Well-Tempered Synthesizer*, DEL 9

Electronic Record with Four Composers, Turnabout 34004

HYMAN, DICK, *Moog-Electric Eclectics*, Command S 938

Moog Synthesizer, *Switched on Bach*, Columbia MX 7194

Nonesuch Guide to Electronic Music, Nonesuch 2 HC 73018

PERRY-KINGSLEY, *The "In" Sound from Way-Out*, available from The Dancer's Shop, Children's Music Center, 5373 W. Pico Blvd., Los Angeles, Calif. 90019

Miscellaneous Records

Bernstein Conducts for Young People, Columbia D3S 785 (three-record set includes *Peter and the Wolf, The Nutcracker, Carnival of the Animals, Danse Macabre, Young People's Guide to the Orchestra, Sorcerer's Apprentice*)

BRUBECK, DAVE, *Time Out*, Columbia CS 8192 (especially "Take Five" and "Blue Rondo" with their unusual rhythms)

Children's Concert Series, The Franson Corp., 225 Park Avenue South, New York, N.Y. 10003. Several records are issued in this series, all 78 rpm, and reasonably priced. These are recommended:
9011 *Flight of the Bumblebee* (Rimsky-Korsakov) and *Dance from Orpheus* (Offenbach)
9013 *The Swan* (Saint-Saens) and the March from *The Love of the Three Oranges* (Prokofiev)
9015 March of the *Toreadors* (Bizet) and *First Hungarian Dance* (Brahms)

COLEMAN, JOHN, *Music for Contemporary Dance* (piano) (little jumps, light steps, vibratory walk, irregular meter), Hoctor Records HLP 3047

DEBEOCK, EVELYN LOHOEFER, *Music for Movement Expression*, AR 615, and *Progressions* (piano and percussion). Both of these records have pieces in a variety of styles useful for older children as well as adults. Available from Educational Activities Records, Freeport, N.Y. 11520.

MALAMENT, SARAH, *Improvisations for Modern Dance* (Series II) (9 beat; 5 beat; 5 and 3 beat; hoedown; adagio; jazz), 3215 Netherlands Ave., New York, N.Y. 10063.

MILLER, FRIEDA, *Records for Dance*, Albums I and III (piano) (short pieces intended for technique but useful for dance studies, as many have definite form with contrasting sections), 131 Bayview Ave., Northport, N.Y. 11768

Music for Dance Rhythms, Folkways FC 7673 (41 short piano pieces in various tempos and moods)

OLATUNJI, *Drums of Passion,* Columbia CS 8210

Sounds of New Music, Folkways FX 6160

The Swingle Singers, *Bach's Greatest Hits,* Phillips 600-097 and *Going Baroque,* Phillips PHS 600-126

Chapter Preview

With Younger Children

Leads into Dance-Making

With Older Children

Leads into Dance-Making: Contrasts and Combinations
Some Leads Involving Shape, Space, Time, and Force
Typical Dance-Making Problems
Using the Dance Space

Using a Constant Focus

21 *Approach from Dance Movement*

The difference between seeing a line as a static, accomplished fact and seeing it as the movement of a point is the difference between seeing product and seeing process.[1]

The making of dances from dance movement is one that leads naturally and logically from the exploration and manipulation of movement and from its use in rhythm-oriented activities. It becomes the solving of a problem in sequential form, having no relation, at least at the outset, to imagery, dramatic motivation, or accompaniment. How movement may be put together to make a satisfying sequence in time and space is the goal, a direct and nonsubjective one.

Sometimes the studies made from this approach—individually, in couples, or in groups—are merely agreeable and exhilarating movement combinations, contrasted and balanced one against the other, with a beginning, a middle, and an end characterizing the total form. Sometimes, however, a combination evokes overtones which, if deemed appropriate, may be carried beyond the mere arrangement of movements into the realm of expressive communication.

With Younger Children
Leads into Dance-Making

In the process of exploring movement and trying it in different ways young children often discover that it can resemble something they have seen

[1] Chandler Montgomery, *Art for Teachers of Children*, Columbus, Ohio, Merrill, 1968, p. 83.

or felt or read about. This can lead into doing whatever the movement suggests and often a sequence of movements results. This does not mean however, that the exploration of movement for its own sake should not be a meaningful and initial part of their dance program. Combining action words into a sequence can help make them aware of sequential form, of the effect of the juxtaposition of movements, of the importance of transition.

Sequences of basic locomotor movements and simple dance steps are a familiar part of most dance lessons at this age level, and structuring them as

A Design for Two

DETROIT PUBLIC SCHOOLS

to direction and duration offers a good lead into dance-making. Skipping, jumping, and sliding, or walking, hopping, and galloping may each be done in a different direction or with a turn, and in equal or unequal phrases. After help from the teacher, the children can make their own locomotor sequences and plot their own phrasing and directional changes. Actually, a young child makes his version of a dance study when from a beginning (a starting shape) he moves through one or two contrasting movements and stops in a finishing shape. A movement study may use a locomotor movement as the first and third parts with a nonlocomotor movement in between, or the reverse (an A B A form). The series of phrases may be of the same or of contrasting qualities, fast or slow, low or high, strong or soft. Such simple constructs (call them mini-dances) are well within the abilities of most younger children.

With Older Children

With older children the approach from the use of dance skills is rewarding whenever the investigation of movement and rhythm leads naturally to the solution of a movement or rhythmic problem in dance form. Divorced from emotional or dramatic overtones, this experimentation becomes a kind of game in which one sees how he alone or with a partner or group can manipulate or invent movement to achieve the stated goal. When several children are working together, cooperation is essential if anything worth while is to be produced. For the teacher this process of problem-solving is excellent for observing her children. During a work period, those who need help because of shyness, overaggressiveness, poor work habits, or inability to get along with others are easily identified.

Leads into Dance-Making: Contrasts and Combinations

A start is made with the simple contrasts afforded by technical movement factors: dimension, level, tempo, force. Any invented movement pattern, performed in a contrasted sequence, shows the beginning of sequential form. Some contrasting movement ideas not previously listed are the following: flexible-rigid; jagged-smooth; slippery-sticky; weightless-weighty; energetic-lazy; stare-search; on the floor-in the air; move-freeze.

Combining movement phrases into sequences helps older children to become aware of movement flow, of smooth transitions, of necessary variations in force, use of space and duration of the phrases, and of ways to build toward a climax or effective conclusion. Their interest will be aroused by changes in timing from sustained to sudden, by the repetition of certain movements but not others, by the use of asymmetrical design.

The use of movement words to initiate sequences is explained in Chapter 19. After a few trials children will prefer to make their own word sequences, but the following examples may serve to initiate action. Each sequence should start in a neutral shape and finish in a concluding one. They all may be performed more than once.

Turn, freeze, collapse, twist, stretch

Lie, sit, rise, swing, turn

Reach, drop, rise, run, twist

Roll, curl, explode, spin, drop

Jump, lean, twist, fall, sit

Some Leads Involving Shape, Space, Time, and Force

The following activities are suggested for children who understand the concepts involved and who have explored them with a variety of movements. For the most part, the first activities in a series are the simplest and may progress from individual to partner or group action.

CONCEPTS OF **Shape**

A.

1. Keeping arms, hands, legs, and feet relatively still, move the trunk and head, using different levels and directions, bending, extending, and twisting.
2. Keeping trunk relatively still, move arms and hands and/or legs and feet in many ways as above.
3. Change after a short time from trunk movements to peripheral movements and back again.
4. Add vocal sounds to the sequence for trunk or peripheral movements, but not always for both.

B.

1. Assume a place-shape in which the predominant interest is in vertical body lines.
2. Change to a shape in which the predominant interest is in horizontal body lines. (This will usually involve a change of level.)

3. Continue changing from vertical to horizontal shapes with sudden and gradual changes in the timing of the transitional movement.
4. Choose several shapes and one's own timing sequence when going from one to another.
5. Try as a group project, relating shapes to a group design and keeping to a fairly slow unison timing.

C.

1. Assume an asymmetrical shape on any level, one hand or arm in contact with the body and the other extended upward or outward. Start moving in any way suggested by this design, changing shapes continuously and freely and freezing at any time on impulse for a few seconds. Then continue movement, letting the held shape suggest a new sequence.
2. Spatial, quality, and timing variations should characterize these movements.

A Design for Three

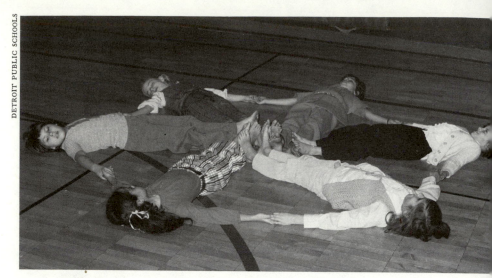

A Design for Many

CONCEPTS OF **Space**—DIRECTION

A.

1. Make a straight-line floor pattern with locomotor movements which travel forward and backward.
2. Make a circular floor pattern with locomotor movements which travel forward, backward, and sideward.
3. Make a square floor pattern using four different locomotor movements in three body directions, one on each side of the square.
4. Combine two of the above in a contrasting sequence.

B.

1. Perform a square floor pattern with an equal number of walks on each side of the square, facing continuously forward. Movement progresses forward, sideward, backward, and sideward, in any chosen order, body and spatial direction being changed on each repetition of the counts.
2. Transfer the square pattern to a single straight line, maintaining the changes in body direction but keeping to a constant spatial direction (always moving in one line of direction). Alternate 1 and 2.

CONCEPTS OF **Space**—LEVEL

A.

1. Explore locomotor movements which are airborne (above the floor with an instant of nonsupport): run, jump, hop, leap, gallop, skip. Emphasize movement upward rather than distance forward.
2. Explore locomotor movements which stay close to the floor, such as low walks or lunges, rolls, or somersaults.

3. With a partner, design a floor pattern which uses high movements contrasted with low movements. They may be performed one after another or together, and both partners should have a chance to do both kinds.

B.

1. Choose a body part (the head, the seat, one hand, one elbow) and move from a low shape on the floor to a high standing one with that part leading or starting the movement.
2. Change to another body part to start the return to the low shape.
3. Repeat the sequence, starting the movement each time with a different part.

C.

1. Choose any four lying and sitting shapes; move slowly and efficiently from one to another in sequence.
2. Do step 1 with four kneeling and standing shapes.
3. Choose at least six shapes from at least three levels, and move from one to another using a variety of transitional movements.
4. Make a sequence of these shapes in which the transitional movements show changes in timing from slow to fast and a short freeze when each succeeding shape is attained.

CONCEPTS OF **Space**—DIMENSION

A.

1. Start with any two movements involving hands and arms alone that have directional contrast (up-down, out-in, forward-backward, side to side). Perform in as small a dimension as possible and in slow timing.
2. Gradually increase the size of the movements (but not the timing) until they become very large, involving the total body and possibly locomotor movement.
3. Reverse the series from the large to the small and bring to a conclusion.
4. Start with large movements, gradually decrease to small, back to large, and freeze in a large shape.

B.

1. Using one or both arms and the total body, describe large curving movements in self-space in various directions and levels.
2. Do the same with smaller, straight, angled movements.
3. Combine the large curving and small straight movements in a sequence and repeat, improvising different movements on each repetition.
4. Try the same dimensional activity, but make the straight, angled movements large and the curving movements small.
5. Try either sequence moving through space, using curved and straight paths.

CONCEPT OF **Space**—PATH

A.

1. Move in straight lines on the floor (square, triangle, zigzag, forward, backward, sideward, diagonally) with walks, runs, hops, or jumps.
2. Move in curved lines (arcs, circles, figure eights, serpentines, spirals) with skips, gallops, or slides.
3. Make a sequence changing from one to the other and back again.

B.

1. Using a forward walk or run, move in a zigzag or serpentine path across the floor, approximately six feet in each spatial direction.
2. Move slowly toward one wall, quickly toward the other, using any two kinds of locomotor movement.
3. Move forward toward one wall, sideward toward the other with any two kinds of locomotor movement.
4. Move heavily toward one wall on a low level, lightly toward the other on a high level.
5. On each change of spatial direction move in a different way, using variations in body direction, level, timing, force, and type of locomotor movement.

CONCEPTS OF **Space**—FOCUS

A.

1. Focus on a body part (foot, knee, hand, elbow) and maintain a constant gaze as it leads into a variety of improvised nonlocomotor movements.
2. Suddenly change focus and movement lead and continue as above.

B.

1. Improvise movement through space on any path or direction but maintain a constant focus on a spot on a wall, on the floor, on a prop, on a pretend audience, or on another person who is also moving. Freeze movement on impulse and change focus.
2. In twos, focus on each other continually, moving sometimes near, sometimes a short distance away, with any movement on any movement path. After a bit, drop focus and freeze movement to finish.

C.

1. In any high shape, focus strongly upward with a constant or wandering gaze.
2. Move quickly or slowly to the floor, or into any low shape, maintaining upward focus.
3. Focus quickly or slowly downward and freeze in the low position.
4. Recover in own timing and move through space into a high shape with an upward focus. Repeat sequence.

D.

1. In small groups, follow a leader who improvises nonlocomotor movements with focus changes from constant to wandering to dual, near or far, up or down, varying timing on each change.
2. Add locomotor movement, with changes in direction, to group focusing as in step 1.
3. Change leaders, so all can improvise.

CONCEPTS OF **Time**—RATE OF SPEED

A.

1. Walk on own path, either very fast or very slow. Change suddenly to the other speed.
2. Add to the two changes of speed a sudden freeze from either speed on impulse for two or three seconds. Then resume fast or slow walk.
3. Combine the three activities in any random series.

B.

1. Walk on any path, starting at a slow speed. Gradually accelerate to a natural walk, a fast walk, a natural run, and a fast run, and make a sudden stop.
2. Starting with a fast run, retard speed gradually to a natural run, a fast walk, a natural walk, a slow walk, and a gradual stop.
3. Combine 1 and 2, but without a stop at the height of the top speed. Movement continues from slow to fast and back to slow until it stops.

C.

Use changes of timing described in A and B with nonlocomotor movements. Children will find others besides the following suggested ones. (It should be noted that the change from slow to fast timing often reduces the dimension of certain nonlocomotor movements considerably.)

1. A series of slow touches with both or alternate hands, on thighs, shoulders, sides, top of head, or a combination of body parts, which accelerates into very fast touches and then retards.
2. A slow bend and stretch of both knees accelerating to a series of fast bounces and then retarding.
3. A knee lifting and lowering into a pressing of the foot into the floor which accelerates to a fast series of stamps and then retards.
4. A relaxed, shaking movement of the arms which, adding tension, accelerates into vibratory movement and then retards.
5. A slow turn which accelerates into a fast spin and then retards.

D.

1. Follow a piece of fast music by improvising fast movements to it.
2. Do the same to a piece of slow music with slow movements.

3. Now try the slow movements to the fast music and the fast movements to the slow music.
4. Finish the sequence by returning to movements in the same timing as the accompaniment.

E.

1. Perform a series of slow movements and follow them with a phrase of quick movements.
2. Provide a vocal accompaniment of long-drawn-out sounds or tones for the slow movements, but do the quick movements in silence.
3. Do the slow movements in silence but accompany the quick movements with quick, sharp sounds or tones.
4. Vocalize for both slow and fast movements, but not continuously. Let the sounds form their own intermittent time pattern, sometimes accompanying the movements, sometimes not.

CONCEPTS OF **Force**

A.

1. Touch hands together with varying degrees of force in movements suggested by: clap, slap, stroke, press, rub, caress, scrub, tap, brush, scratch, smooth.
2. Using one hand and an arm, the head, torso, thigh, or a leg, try movements suggested by the above words.
3. Explore the space all around self-space including the floor by pressing, pushing, poking, or punching strongly, and touching, smoothing, tapping, or stroking lightly.
4. Change from one force quality to another. For example, use a strong hard movement on surrounding space and a light, soft movement to touch oneself. Reverse to a light touch on surrounding space and forceful touch on torso, thigh, or arm.

B.

1. Perform any familiar phrase of locomotor and/or nonlocomotor movements with the body in as complete a state of tension as possible.
2. Try it with the body as relaxed as possible.
3. Intersperse tension with relaxation in a sequence.

C.

1. After having explored the six qualities of movement (sustained, percussive, suspended, swinging, vibratory, collapsing), choose any two and contrast one with the other. Perform each movement long enough to establish its "feeling" before changing to another.
2. Perform three movement qualities in a sequence, using both nonlocomotor and locomotor movements and different durations of time for each.

3. Try above in a group of three or four, each one performing his own movement phrase but relating to the others where possible.

Typical Dance-Making Problems

The problems below are for children who have previously experienced or are at present working on the particular materials dealt with in each problem.

Accompaniment will be omitted or improvised for the ensuing dance studies unless suitable music is available or is part of the problem. The teacher may play pulse beats on a drum if she is told the tempo and the number of counts in each phrase of movement. Better still, members of the group may do a percussion accompaniment. Having been part of the composing process, they know the dance better than an outsider. Sometimes the dancers may accompany themselves on small instruments with which they can move, or through vocalization appropriate to the movement.

When there are numerous dances to be seen, children can count the time structure for themselves, with perhaps the help of a drum. Many dances based on rhythmic problems may be seen first in this way and a more elaborate accompaniment planned if the study justifies it.

The following dance problems may be simplified by eliminating elements, changed by substituting elements, or used merely to formulate new problems.

Movement-Oriented Problems

For a more complete explanation of terms, see Chapter 3. Children decide on their own time structure for these dance studies, or the teacher may assign the total number of counts or the number for each movement phrase. The word *dance* has been used throughout as it has more meaning for children than does *dance study*.

FOR ONE OR TWO

1. Make a dance using a movement phrase containing both locomotor and nonlocomotor movements in which the main element is variation in speed from very slow to very fast.
2. Make a dance starting with a very small movement at a sitting or prone level. Gradually increase the dimension of the movement until a standing level and locomotor movement are involved. The sequence may suddenly or gradually decrease to the original dimension.

3. Make a dance in which swaying, soft pushing, or quiet walking are gradually done more and more forcefully until their quality is entirely changed. Then change suddenly back to the soft, light movements.
4. Make a dance using a combination of walks of different speeds and directions, with changes in focus of gaze and sudden freezes into immobility.
5. Make a dance using walks, jumps, and claps in different speeds and directions; use a sit at some place in the sequence.
6. Make a dance which combines a collapse, a stretch, a sway, and a turn, each performed any number of times and in any sequence.
7. Make a dance in which the interest is in the contrast between curving, rounded movement and sharply angled movement and between symmetrical and asymmetrical design.
8. Make a dance in which a constant focus on hand, foot, arm, or leg will initiate a variety of movements as the gaze follows the moving body part. At times contrast suddenly with a wandering focus.
9. Make a dance for two persons which starts with a constant focus on each other but no physical contact, develops into the opposite (some type of contact with a focus away), and changes back again.
10. Make a dance in which physical contact with a partner makes slow-motion nonlocomotor movement possible. Release contact and reproduce the partner movement individually, possibly changing speed.
11. Make a dance using a push and/or pull, changing level at least once, and combining with walking steps of different speeds.
12. Make a partner dance, using a skip and a slide, with movements which go forward, backward, away from and toward each other, and which turn around.
13. Make a partner dance, using combinations of the step-hop and schottische, involving at least three different place relationships and contacts with the partner.
14. Make a dance with an inanimate object such as a small prop, at times manipulating the object in different ways and at times ignoring it.
15. Make a partner dance using the polka to move through space, alternating with different walks, stamps, turns, and claps in one place, partners facing each other. Use any contact or place relationship.
16. Make a partner dance using a strike and dodge combined with low-level walks, fast runs, and falls.

FOR A GROUP

1. Make a dance with a circle as its main formation, using both walks and runs.
2. Make a dance in which two groups alternate, one moving in place on any level with swings, claps, and turns, the other moving through space with

any locomotor movement. All should join in unison at a certain time or times during the dance.

3. Make a dance in a line, inventing a sideward locomotor pattern of jumps, hops, and grapevine walks, and a forward-and-backward pattern of walks, runs, and stamps. Take the line into a snail and then a circle.

4. Make a dance using a lift, carry, and place, combined with slow and fast walks and different levels.

5. Make a dance in threes or fours using any dance step in 3/4 meter (waltz, waltz balance, mazurka, 3/4 run) which involves lines, circles, and winding under arches.

6. Make a dance in two groups using locomotor and nonlocomotor movement, in which differences in tempo and dimension are the main factors and are contrasted either simultaneously or sequentially.

7. Make a dance starting in a mass group in contact with each other in different shapes on a very low level. Gradually a tight group on a standing level is achieved. One by one dancers spin off to finish in individual shapes. Coming together again in slow motion, the group eventually returns to the starting position or another group shape.

8. Make a dance in which hoops are used as props and ways in which they can be manipulated are explored. Unison, succession, and opposition should be used.

Rhythm-Oriented Problems

For a more complete explanation of terms, see Part IV. It is expected that any type of movement which children may invent will be used to translate these problems into dance forms. One or more persons may work with them.

1. Make a dance following the beats of an assigned rhythmic pattern or one arrived at through a name pattern, a nursery rhyme, or a simple melody. Alternate the pattern at times with its underlying pulse beats or accents. Use any locomotor or nonlocomotor movements in a simple floor pattern.

2. Make a dance using three or four of the numbers in an address or telephone number to portray the movement phrases, with a strong accent at the beginning of each number. A pause for an assigned number of beats with an agreed-upon movement such as a turn or a sit may be used after the completion of each number or movement phrase.

3. Make a dance with three or four persons or groups in which movement succession is used in certain places during the sequence; that is, each person or group performs a movement one after the other successively, and then all return to unison movement again.

4. Make a dance using assigned accents in a group of eight beats alternating

regularly or irregularly with the natural accents. (Example: assigned 1, 4, 7; regular 1, 3, 5, 7, or 1, 5.)

5. Make a dance assigning one line of a three- or four-voice round to each of three or four groups. Assign a direction or level to each group, so that when the entire round is performed the groups will not collide. Have one group use the pulse beats of its line as the rhythmic structure for its movements, another the accents of its line, another the rhythmic pattern, and the fourth (if a four-voice round is used) a continuous movement representing the phrasing of its line. Perform in unison first, one line after the other, and then as a round.

6. Make a dance as above, but using six, eight, or ten rather slow beats for each group rather than the lines of a round song. Each group will invent its own rhythmic sequence against the background of the slow pulse beats and make a movement sequence in an assigned direction or level to fit it. When the total sequence is performed in unison, slight alterations may be necessary for a transition from one part to the next, as well as for variety in the total rhythmic structure. Perform in unison and then as a round.

7. Make a dance using cumulative rhythm in two opposing groups. Counts may accumulate by ones, twos, or threes and then decrease in the same order. Each count may also be repeated. After each number a constant interval of counts such as a two, three, or four may be used. Each new group of counts should change direction or level so that it is easily identified.

8. Make a dance using resultant rhythm. Two groups use the natural accents in a two- or three-beat grouping within six beats. These may be interchanged at any time with the resultant accent pattern (1, 3, 4, 5). Or one group may be assigned the two grouping, another the three grouping, and a third the resultant pattern. Accents should be strongly and perhaps audibly indicated so that they are noticeable when the three groups perform their movements together.

Using the Dance Space

It is through the solution of such dance problems as the above that children become conscious of the many ways in which their dance space may be used for arranging movement in a satisfying and suitable form. This in itself is a kind of problem that is definitely related to all dance-making, particularly with older children. Whether the space is used in too symmetrical or asymmetrical a fashion, whether maximum use is made of it, whether the same group formation is exploited to a monotonous degree or new and interesting ways of moving through the dance space are discovered—these factors all relate to space principles.

The following principles cover only certain common aspects of the use of space in dance-making. Experienced choreographers sometimes deliberately depart from some of them. Children need first to understand the rule before they can understand the exception to it.

1. The most important place in the dance space is the center, toward the front rather than the back. The important parts of the dance should take place there, and its beginning, end, and climax should relate to this center place, though not necessarily happen there.

2. Effective use of the main parts of the dance space should be made; one or two parts of it should not be used exclusively. This rule should be interpreted with some flexibility, for it stands to reason that certain relatively unimportant parts of the space may not be used at all.

3. Although a symmetrical arrangement is often the most satisfying to beginners, they should be made aware of the surprise and unexpectedness of asymmetry. It is more interesting to upset the balance of a space divided into halves by moving three persons in one half and two in the other; to do a movement twice to one side and only once to the other; or in some other way to keep the observers from anticipating the next part of the dance.

4. When one is in the dance space and facing the audience, "stage right" is always to one's right; "stage left," to one's left; "up stage," toward the back of the dance space; and "down stage," toward the front.

5. Space is used more effectively if one does not always face the front and move only forward, backward, or sideward. Different body facings, turns, curved and diagonal lines of movement add interest and variety.

6. Besides circles, lines, and squares, movement may occur in semicircles, zigzags, serpentines, triangles, diagonals, and other formations, paths, and patterns. Or a group may move together in close contact, possibly supporting each other, or with only hands joined, or with no contact at all.

7. The center space (center stage) should not be left vacant for any appreciable time while movement goes on at either side, because the vision of those watching is split and they cannot see the dance as a whole. But it is sometimes interesting to have all the movement occur on one side and then on another part of the stage.

8. Too many different movements should not occur in the dance space at the same time without having the dancers soon move in unison or come together in a unified group, because those watching see only parts and not the whole of the dance.

9. Not everyone needs to move in the dance space all the time. One or more persons or a whole group may remain frozen in a dance position while others move, or they may leave the dance space and return later.

Part VI | *LEARNING DANCES*

Chapter Preview

22 *Learning Dances: Orientation*

Every teacher who studies child development knows that there is a fundamental relation between these three factors: a child's ability to control his body with skill and grace; his feelings about himself as a learner; and the development of his intellectual processes. If we put this triangular relationship into pedagogical language, we can say that the development of psychomotor skills is intimately interwoven with the development of affective sensitivity and cognitive power.[1]

Learning the dances of their elders has been part of the process of growing up for children in innumerable cultures, both primitive and civilized. Often the acceptance of the young adolescent into the tribe depended upon his knowledge of and skill in performing certain tribal dances at the initiation ceremony. An important part of the education of a young European gentleman during the Renaissance and for several centuries thereafter was learning the dances which were fashionable at court at the time. The sons and daughters of peasants and pioneers learned the dances of their communities by observing, imitating, and participating in village gatherings and festivals, corn-husking bees, barn dances, and other occasions when their parents gathered together to celebrate.

Most children today are denied these experiences. When celebrations or festivals occur, there are professionals to provide the dancing; the children watch from the bleachers or balconies or see it on the television screen. The rich heritage of dance patterns of other peoples and other times come to them only in their school experiences or in community groups which use

---

[1] Elizabeth Wilson, "Problems of Balance in Curriculum Change," *Dance—An Art in Academe*, New York, Teachers College, 1970, p. 84.

dance as part of their recreational program. If these dances are to have meaning and value for children, they must be taught so that the color, spontaneity, and fun of their original form are preserved. They must be taught easily and efficiently so that the entire dance configuration is quickly grasped. Finally, if they are folk dances they must be taught so that their identity is not lost, so that there is some relationship to the cultural heritage of which they are a part.

The Process of Learning Dances

The teaching of a dance which is already prescribed, in which a certain order of movement must be followed if the form of the whole is to be maintained, is of necessity a teacher-directed and hence a rather formal procedure. This is the kind of dance teaching that is traditional wherever dance is part of the school curriculum. Usually the greatest number of books in the school dance

Nebesko Kolo

THOMAS HALSTED

library are those that contain descriptions of dances to be taught. Many of them, particularly the courses of study, describe dances to be learned in certain grades, the assumption being that all the children in any particular grade have the same backgrounds, skills, interests, and dance readiness.

Modern educational theory holds that efficient learning takes place only when the child is involved in the total process, when he both gives and receives, when his learning purposes reside in himself, not in the teacher. For this reason dances (selected with the child's interests and background in mind) should be taught so that he contributes to the learning process with the skills he already has and the figures and formations he may already have explored, and with his recognition of the new arrangements of movement which the dance offers as a challenge. He will want to know other things about these dances, too—where they came from, who danced them before, why and when, how they are different from other dances he knows, and how alike they are. Finally, dancing the dance should be fun, something he returns to with pleasure, just as he does to the games he knows and likes to play.

Program Pressures

Too often selection of dances is made not with the children in mind but because of pressure brought to bear upon the teacher. The school play needs a harvest dance; the supervisor wants a Mexican dance for the state convention; the Parent-Teacher Association would like a minuet for its February meeting; the committee for the School Carnival thinks it would be "cute" to have the second-graders do a square dance in costume. In their violation of all that is known about children's aptitudes and interests, some of the requests are ridiculous. Yet the teacher feels that she must cooperate. Because the time is short (there is hardly *ever* time for the children to make their own dance), she flies to available references, finds something that will do, sells it to her class on the basis of their being in the performance, and begins the long process of drill. A good dance teacher will avoid this by providing as much audience education as possible (this may include the principal and fellow teachers) and by refusing to teach material which is meaningless, artificial, or in bad taste.

For the teacher's as well as the children's sake, dances chosen for children to learn should be closely related to their interests and their degree of movement skill, and particularly they should be childlike and not adultlike dances. More specific criteria for the selection of dances are listed in a following chapter. It is sufficient to say here that the dance itself should be the motivating factor because it catches the child's interest, is satisfying for him to learn, and is pleasing to perform. If occasionally it has to be performed in connection with some project or other, this should always remain a secondary consideration.

A Repertoire of Dance Skills

In the interests of integrating the dance program as well as of teaching efficiently, learning of dances should be based upon dance skills already mastered by the children. For instance, a dance in which the schottische is the basic step should not be taught until the children know how to do the schottische step in all the ways demanded by the dance. This is not a violation of the *whole-part* method, for the schottische is a *whole* in itself, satisfying to perform in many directions, with a partner or a group, before it is woven into a formal dance. In fact, the figures and formations used in most schottische dances may be discovered by the children themselves if they are allowed to explore its possibilities as a dance step.

Often certain dances use a step in one or two directions only. In that case, the dance can be taught when the learning of the step has progressed that far. Even though a step has presumably been learned, a review should be given before proceeding to a dance based upon it, so that the sequence of the parts of the dance will not be interrupted by practice of the step. Reference to Chapter 10 will suggest how these steps may be taught efficiently and with emphasis on the children's exploration of the many ways in which they are used in *learned* dances.

Acceptable Teaching Procedures

There are easy and hard ways to learn dances, logical and illogical procedures, shortcuts and long sessions of distressing drill. A sensible teacher uses good techniques to make the experience enjoyable and meaningful for the children. Chapter 24 discusses these procedures in detail. The essentials appear here in miniature:

The use of wisdom and discretion in choosing dances that will "work" for a particular class (e.g., one having boy-girl antagonisms, one new to the folk dance experience, or one with a meager dance skill background).

The assurance that children can travel around the room in ways demanded by the dance before they are obliged to do it with partners or in groups.

The demonstration of the dance sequences and the dance figures with the assistance of members of the class. Because some children learn more quickly through visual means than by verbal analysis, it is occasionally a challenge to see how many can learn a foot pattern merely by seeing it demonstrated a few times.

The direction of the class through the movements or figures as quickly and efficiently as possible, the children helping each other with certain parts when necessary.

The performance of the dance at least twice without pause so that the transition into the repetition is smooth.

The children's evaluation of their progress in learning it. Parts that give trouble can then be isolated and practiced separately.

The review of the dance for practice of the skills involved as well as for fun, so that it becomes a satisfying part of a repertoire of dances.

Dances taught and used in this fashion can be as popular as games. They are harder to teach, it is true, for they involve all the children in action and demand as much from one as from another, as games often do not. But they offer the salutary effects of group cooperation, the benefits of unison rhythmic movement, and, within certain limits, unselfconscious expressiveness in the use of the body.

Chapter Preview

Components of Folk Dances

Outline for Exploration
Number of Persons Dancing Together
Their Place Relationship
Type of Contact with Other Persons
Direction of Movement
Type of Movement

Dancing with One Other Person

Dancing with Two or Three Other Persons

Dancing with Many Other Persons

With Many Others

THOMAS HALSTED

23 Exploring Ways of Dancing with Others

Experimentation with and discovery of ways of moving with others, especially in locomotor-oriented recreational dance, kindles in children an awareness of the importance of making adjustments in their own movement if the combination is to function harmoniously. In this chapter, dancing with others implies for the most part rhythmic locomotor movements by two or more persons in physical contact with each other which is the basis of recreational dance in most countries. Problems are created as soon as one person joins hands with another and tries to match the space design, timing, and force of the other's movement. A child must master the locomotor movement alone before trying to adapt it to that of another person or persons—especially if there are variations in space design. It is, of course, possible to dance with a partner or a group without physical contact. If such dances are recreational in nature, the same principles apply as are suggested in the following material.

Components of Folk Dances

Recreational dances which involve more than one person moving together in unified or related fashion must be differentiated from the theatrical dance seen so often on television today. The latter is usually a solo dance done by several dancers in unison, with little interrelationship. Interest lies in the complex movement routines and how well the dancers can reproduce them identically.

Traditional or contemporary folk dances involve more than one person in the dance who are specifically related to one another. Such dances have three basic components:

1. the *dance step* or steps, locomotor in nature, used alone or in combinations (examples: schottische, waltz, skip);
2. the *dance figures* or movement designs performed by two or more persons in unison or interacting, usually in a sequence of such figures (examples: with two persons, do-si-do; with three persons, passing under arches; with more than three, forward and back in a circle);
3. the *dance formation* or the group arrangement, usually the same throughout, but sometimes changing during the progress of the dance (examples: circle, line or lines, square set).

Some line dances, especially the currently popular Middle Eastern *kolos* and *horas,* often move in a series of somewhat complex step combinations performed repeatedly in lieu of dance figures. On the other hand, many square dances, using only a brisk walking step throughout, take the dancers through an intricate series of couples and group figures.

Outline for Exploration

Some of the ways a specific dance step may be used in dancing with others are given in Chapter 10 after the analysis of the step. Here we take many other conditions of partner and group dancing into account and classify methods in which children may explore them.

Number of Persons Dancing Together

Two persons may dance together as a couple or as partners, three as a trio, four most often as two couples, and more than four in single or double lines, square sets, single or double closed circles, or single open circles. These formations are traditional in almost all types of recreational dance. Other conditions of movement are often determined by the number of persons dancing together.

Their Place Relationship

Two persons may dance together side by side, facing in the same or opposite directions; facing each other squarely; standing back to back. When

With Two Others

a boy and a girl stand or move together side by side as partners, the boy is traditionally to the *left* of the girl.

Three or four persons may dance together side by side, facing in the same direction; facing toward a common center or with backs to a common center; with right or left sides together toward a common center; one behind the other, facing in the same direction; one or two in front and two in back or vice versa, facing in the same direction; two facing the opposite two.

Many persons may dance together in a single or double circle or an arc, facing in or out; in a line one behind the other, facing in the same direction; in a line side by side, facing in the same direction.

Type of Contact with Other Persons

Couples or groups move together most easily if they are joined in some fashion. One person may join another (or others) by taking hands, by linking arms, by placing hands on the other's hips or shoulders, by putting arms around the other's waist or shoulders. When these positions are indicated on the listing below, the following words have these specific meanings: *Inside* means the foot, hand, arm, hip, or shoulder toward the other person or persons (usually the boy's right, the girl's left if moving forward counterclockwise). *Outside* means the foot, hand, arm, hip, or shoulder away from the other person or persons (the boy's left and the girl's right if moving forward counterclockwise). *Same* refers to the side directly across. *Opposite* refers to the side diagonally across.

With One Other

Direction of Movement

One may move forward, backward, sideward, or turning around, depending on the place relationship of the persons moving and the type of contact between them. Certain movements adapt themselves more readily to certain directions than to others. A slide is the easiest way to move continuously sideward. A mazurka is an efficient sideward movement, but harder to perform than the slide. The walk, run, skip, and similar steps, if used in their natural form when progressing sideward, require the body to be turned somewhat in the line of direction so that the step is actually done forward rather than sideward. Most dance steps are difficult for children to perform in a backward direction until they have had considerable practice.

While most locomotor movements are done most easily forward, the two-step and polka move sideward in their natural forms. When using these in a forward direction, therefore, a slight turn of the body away from the leading foot makes performance easier.

When two facing persons turn, or when a boy turns a girl partner who is facing him, the direction of the turn is *clockwise*[1] unless otherwise indicated, regardless of the type of contact, except if left hands are joined or left arms linked. When many persons are moving forward around the room or in a circle (as in the *promenade* in American country dance), the direction is traditionally *counterclockwise*.

Type of Movement

The most suitable basic locomotor movements and dance steps for certain of the group arrangements and for the direction of the movement are suggested in order of difficulty. However, a simple movement used to turn around is easier to perform than a more difficult step taken forward. The walk and run may be used widely with almost any number of persons, place relationship, or type of contact. The dance steps are more limited in their application. Several steps are suggested for each place relationship, but some will adapt better than others to the contact and direction indicated.

Except as they are combined with other movements, the jump, hop, and leap are not very easy to use in dancing with others. Because of the expenditure of energy they demand, it is hard to repeat them for any length of time; moreover, to control their performance to coincide with that of others calls

[1] This is not meant to apply to ballroom dance, although even here a clockwise turn is easier to lead.

for considerable skill. One exception, described in variations of the jump in Chapter 8 is the *Bleking* step, which is used extensively in European folk dances.

Dancing with One Other Person

Side by Side, Facing in the Same Direction

Contact

Inside hands joined.
Inside arms linked.
Right hands and left hands joined (arms crossed).
Inside arms around each other's waists.
Inside hands on each other's inside shoulders.
Right hands joined in back across girl's shoulders, left hands joined in front.
Boy's inside arm around girl's waist, her inside hand on his inside shoulder, outside hands on hips.
Open social dance position, i.e., boy's inside arm around girl's waist, her inside hand on his shoulder, outside hands joined in front, both facing forward as far as possible.

Direction and Movement

Forward: walk, gallop, skip, run, 3/4 run, step-hop, schottische, waltz balance.
Sideward or side-to-side: slide, mazurka, schottische, two-step, polka.
Backward: walk, run, skip, 3/4 run, step-hop, schottische, waltz balance.
Turning—girl moves forward and boy backward to turn around: walk, run, skip, 3/4 run, step-hop, schottische.

Facing Each Other

Contact

Both hands joined in front.
Both hands joined and extended sideward.
Both opposite hands joined.
Hands on same side joined, others extended sideward or on hips.
Boy's hands at girl's waist, her hands on boy's shoulders (this is the waist-shoulder position).
Closed social dance position, i.e., boy's right arm around girl's waist with his hand at the center of her back, her left hand on his shoulder, other hands joined and extended sideward.

Direction and Movement

Sideward or side-to-side: slide, step-hop, schottische, mazurka, two-step, polka.
Turning: walk, slide, skip, run, jump, step-hop, schottische, two-step, polka, waltz balance, waltz.
Forward and backward—one moving forward and the other backward: walk, skip, 3/4 run, step-hop, schottische, two-step, polka, waltz balance, waltz.

Side by Side, Facing in Opposite Directions

Contact	Direction and Movement
Inside hands joined. Inside arms linked. Both hands grasped across in front. Both hands grasped across in back. Inside hand on outside hip of partner, outside hand on own hip or held high. Left reverse social dance position, i.e., right shoulders together, boy's right hand at outside of girl's waist, her left hand on his right shoulder, other hands joined and extended sideward (the common position for the swing in American country dance).	Turning around: walk, skip, run, 3/4 run, step-hop, schottische, mazurka, buzz step—see gallop variations. Sideward: slide. Forward and backward—one moving forward and the other backward: walk, skip, 3/4 run, step-hop, schottische.

One Behind the Other, Both Facing Forward

Contact	Direction and Movement
Both hands joined. Both hands joined and extended sideward (used only for sideward movements). One or both of rear person's hands on shoulders of person in front. Hands of rear person at waist of person in front. (Because of proximity to partner, this and the preceding should be used only with very simple movements.)	Forward: walk, gallop, skip, run, 3/4 run, step-hop, schottische. Sideward or side-to-side: slide, step-hop, schottische, mazurka.

Back to Back

Contact	Direction and Movement
Both hands joined and extended sideward. Hands joined on same side in line of direction; others extended sideward or on hip.	Sideward: slide, mazurka. Side-to-side: step-hop.

Dancing with Two or Three Other Persons

Side by Side, Facing in the Same Direction

Contact

Inside hands joined.
Inside arms linked.
Inside arms around each other's waists.
Inside hands on each other's inside shoulders.
Hands of middle person joined in front or back with outside hands of outside persons; their inside hands joined in front or back with each other. (Because of proximity to each other, all but the first contact should be used only with simple movements.)

Direction and Movement

Forward: walk, gallop, skip, run, 3/4 run, step-hop, schottische, waltz balance.
Backward: walk, run, skip, 3/4 run, step-hop, schottische, waltz balance.
Sideward or side-to-side: slide, schottische.
Turning—one outside person acts as pivot and the others wheel around him; middle person acts as pivot, one outside moves forward, the other backward: walk, run, skip, 3/4 run, step-hop, schottische.

Facing into a Circle

Contact

Hands joined.

Direction and Movement

Around circle: walk, slide, skip, run, jump, 3/4 run, step-hop, schottische, mazurka.

One or Two in Front and Two in Back, or Vice Versa, All Facing Forward

Contact

Hands joined around in a closed circle.

Direction and Movement

Forward: walk, gallop, skip, run, 3/4 run, step-hop, schottische.

With Right or Left Sides Toward the Center

Contact

Inside hands joined together in a star.

Direction and Movement

Forward around circle: walk, skip, run, step-hop, schottische, two-step, polka, mazurka.

One Behind the Other, All Facing Forward

Contact

Hands joined as though side by side.
Hands joined on alternate sides.
One hand on same shoulder of person

Direction and Movement

Forward: walk, gallop, skip, run, 3/4 run, step-hop, schottische.
Sideward: slide, mazurka.

in front. (Because of proximity to each other, this should be used only with simple movements).

With Backs Toward the Center (Circle)

Contact	Direction and Movement
Hands joined.	Around circle: walk, slide.

Dancing with Many Other Persons

Side by Side in Circle

Contact

Hands joined.
Hands on shoulders of persons on either side.
Hands joined with those of second person away, behind back of next persons (*basket* formation).

Direction and Movement

Around circle with first contact: slide, walk, skip, run, 3/4 run, step-hop, schottische, mazurka, two-step, polka.

Forward and backward with first contact: walk, polka, skip, gallop, run, 3/4 run, step-hop, two-step, polka, waltz balance.

Around circle with second or third contact: walk, slide, buzz step.

Side by Side, All Facing Forward

Contact

Inside hands joined.
Inside arms linked.
Arms around each other's waists.
Hands joined, in front or behind back of next persons, with those of second persons away.

Direction and Movement

Forward and backward with first contact: walk, skip, run, 3/4 run, step-hop, schottische, two-step, polka, waltz balance.

Forward and backward with second, third, or fourth contact: walk, skip, step-hop, schottische, waltz balance.

One Behind the Other, All Facing Forward

Contact

Hands joined as though side by side.
Hands joined on alternate sides.
One hand on same shoulder of person in front.

Direction and Movement

Forward with first or second contact: walk, gallop, skip, run, 3/4 run, step-hop, schottische.

Sideward with first or second contact: slide, mazurka.

Forward with third contact: walk, gallop, run with short steps.

Chapter Preview

Swinging with a Buzz Step

THOMAS HALSTED

24 Teaching Dances

Children should be able to learn a dance with a minimum amount of formal instruction, preferably not more than one or two lessons. If it takes longer, the teacher has not made a clear, logical presentation or the dance is too difficult for the present ability of the class or for some other reason is a poor choice. If the children know the basic steps and have been allowed to explore steps patterns and ways of moving with others, only the arrangement of parts, incidental figures, and the music of the dance will be new to them.

Preliminary Discussion

If a dance is worthy of being taught, more should be known about it than merely the form in which its parts are arranged. With younger children where formal dances are a relatively small part of the total dance experience, and knowledge of other times and countries is limited, the name of the dance and what it is about is a sufficient introduction. Older children, however, should be acquainted with its name,[1] and who the people were who made it and danced it. Something about their culture and when and why they danced that way is pertinent to the discussion, especially if it can relate to study of the country. Visual material, even library references may enrich the presentation of the dance.

This preliminary discussion should not become so involved however, that the actual learning of the dance is an anticlimax, rather than central to the activity. The short folk dances and mixers which are appropriate for

---

[1] It is important if the dance is from a non-English-speaking country that the title be accurately pronounced. Most good references give this information.

children should not require an elaborate presentation for their appreciation. Participation in the dance itself, if it is agreeable and engaging, is sufficient. Often understanding of its cultural significance is more meaningful after the dance is learned and enjoyed.

Preliminary Teaching

An important first step in the teaching of a dance is to hear the accompanying music. During a short listening period the music is played through once for attention to its general quality and again for identification of particular phrases and perhaps accents if they are especially important in the performance of the dance. As parts of the dance are learned, they should be tried with the particular section of the music to which they belong.

With a partner dance, it is well to teach as much of it as possible to the children individually, before the complexity of performing it with a partner is added. The preliminary teaching can best be done in open-order formation, with the class all facing in the same direction and moving back and forth or from side to side or informally around the room. The basic step is reviewed with the dance music in the different directions and ways it will be used. Traditionally this teaching has been done in a large circle. However, trying to distinguish between right and left or to learn sideward-moving steps or turns in a circle is difficult and confusing for two reasons: first, the opposite side of the circle must move in the opposite direction; and second, the teacher must have her back to part of the class most of the time. Consequently, informal open-order grouping with identical facing is preferred.

Excellent for children are dances of the kolo or hora type. They are vigorous dances, done without partners in a closed or open circle and are merely a repeated sequence of locomotor movements: walks, hops, jumps, taps, body turns, usually done sideward or sometimes into the center and out (forward and backward). If children have had exploratory experiences with locomotor movements, especially in making their own combinations, they learn these dances readily. The combination of movements can be taught in open-order formation. For example, the Greek *Kritikos* or *Miserlou,* as it is popularly called because of the music usually used for its accompaniment, seems difficult when performed in a circle because of its swinging body turns. Actually the footwork is simple, being a series of weight changes in duple timing as follows: step-hold-tap-hold, step-step-step-hold, step-step-step-hold, step-step-step-hold. After this combination has been learned in place, it will be much simpler to teach the sideward and diagonally forward and backward floor pattern of the dance with the curving sweep of the foot after the tap. The final step in the procedure would be to get into the circle formation and to perform the combination together with hands joined.

If a partner dance is performed in square or longways sets and the interest lies in the dance figures rather than the dance steps, as in the American square or contra dances, many of the figures can be taught in a large double circle before the children are scattered in small *set* groups around the room. Partner turns and swings, do-si-do, allemande left and right, promenade, ladies chain, right and left through, right and left hand star, circle four, circle left and right and forward and back, grand right and left, are all common dance figures which are more easily learned in one large circle than in sets. In this way the teacher can see immediately where difficulties are encountered and can straighten them out.

The Demonstration

Children, and anyone else for that matter, learn movement patterns more easily if they are presented to them through visual as well as auditory imagery. It is, moreover, good motivation to see what the dance *looks like* and how one should appear when he performs it.

The demonstration should first be given *up to time,* that is, in the regular tempo and preferably with the music. It may then be repeated, if necessary, very slowly—without music, and with a verbal explanation of the movements. It is important to remember that words or counts used instead of music to accompany the movements must be spoken in the *identical rhythmic sequence* with which the movements are done to the music. Intervals between counts or beats may be increased, but the rhythmic relationship of part to part must be preserved. Thus, the word or count cues when given slowly must be the same as if the music were played in the same slow tempo. However, the rate of speed should be increased as soon as possible to the correct tempo of the dance, so that the children will get the *feel* of performing it that way.

With the children following the teacher's direction and trying the movements she has demonstrated and explained, it may be helpful if she continues to move with them for a while. If the movement involves a forward or backward direction or a turn, she should face the way they are facing. If the direction is sideward she may face them, but she must remember to move in the same direction in which they move—her right for their left, and vice versa. The adaptation will be easier for her and the directions easier for the children to understand if she uses visual imagery instead of saying *right* or *left.* The arms and hands can indicate the foot which starts the movement, the direction of a line or a circle or a turn, or the wall toward which movement is to be made.

Cuing the Movements and Sequence

It is sound procedure for the teacher to cue movements and figures with spoken words or at least with rhythmic counts as the dance progresses. Such one-syllable words as *walk* or *step, close, hold, hop, turn, run, tap, touch, stamp, heel, toe, jump,* and such directional words as *side, forward, back, right, left,* are helpful in establishing step sequences if cued at the same time the movement is done. As children hear them pronounced by the teacher, they can say them, too, thus in a sense telling themselves what movement to make. The teacher should verbalize in this fashion directly after the starting signal or after the record's introductory phrase, so the children start dancing in the correct rhythmic pattern.

Sequences of parts are hard for children to remember until a dance has been repeated a few times. A helpful teacher will be ready with the proper cue for the next figure in time for the children to perform it at the beginning of its musical phrase. Instead of being given simultaneously with the movement performance, as noted above, the word cues for sequential dance figures are given near the end of the previous figure. Thus memories are jogged and dancers forewarned. After the steps are mastered and the sequence of figures is memorized to the music, such cuing is superfluous.

Many dances use songs for accompaniment which cue the figures by their words. For this reason, they are generally easier for children to learn. If the song is not familiar, it may be possible to draw upon the services of the music teacher so that too much time is not borrowed from the dance period to learn it. When records of songs are used, the song may, of course, be learned from the record.

A logical way of presenting a dance which has several parts is to perform parts one and two together after learning them, before proceeding to part three. If the dance is not long and complicated, however, constant review of parts learned when each new part is added is wasteful of time. It is better for the children to grasp the total sequence as quickly as possible. The successful transition from one part to the next will be accomplished by subsequent performances and by cue directions from the teacher.

Counting and Signaling

Indicating the number of times a movement occurred was once thought to be poor educational practice. The children were supposed to get all cues solely from recognizing them in the music. But when a teacher must work

The Bleking Step for Jibi-Di

from a recording of the music, that approach is not practical. If the children have good basic dance skills, it will not impair their musical growth to tell them that the dance takes sixteen slides to the left or four steps forward and back rather than taking time to let them listen to the music and figure out when one part finishes and the next begins. As they dance it through several times to the music, counts are soon forgotten anyway, and rhythmic response is directly to the music.

Many dance descriptions, when stating the number of times a movement is to be performed, make no provision in time for the fact that a change of direction or of position must be made to start the next phrase. Thus, *eight slides to the left,* if literally translated into eight complete slides, would make it impossible to start back to the right for the next eight slides. Actually what it means is seven slides and a step to the left, so that the right foot is free to start in the new direction. The teacher must be alert to such small discrepancies in dance descriptions, so that the children will have time to make the proper transition to the next part of the dance.

When a group must start moving simultaneously without a musical cue, a starting signal is indicated. This is commonly given by the teacher and serves for both the class and the accompanist, if any. The class is alerted by a preliminary word such as *Ready,* followed by a short pause and then the signal word, preferably *And! Go* or *Begin* may also be used, but the former is associated with game-playing, and the latter, having two syllables, is not as easy to pronounce in an incisive fashion. As stated before, it is highly desirable to cue or count in time with the accents or pulse beats of the music for a short time after the signal word, to help the class swing into the rhythm of the music. (Also useful are several counts "for nothing" before beginning a movement—a starting device of contemporary dancers.)

Most good folk dance recordings have a few introductory measures before the music for the dance begins. They require alert listening so that movement can begin on the first accent of the dance proper. If the record lacks an introduction, children can listen to the first section of the music once through and begin dancing on its repetition. The experience of starting *from the music* rather than from a signal is important and should be part of the procedure of teaching a dance step. Social dance demands that the man start leading the fox-trot, waltz, or similar steps in this fashion. Children should learn to listen to the accents of the music and *swing into* the step in accurate timing.

Performing the Dance

Even though all the fine details have not been quite mastered, it is desirable that children have the experience of "going through" a dance as soon as possible. This, of course, does not mean trying it out if they are so poorly prepared that performing it becomes a farce. Children are nervous and unhappy when their lack of skill is evident not only to themselves but to others. The result, if not chaos, is usually strong dislike of that dance and a negative attitude toward future dance lessons.

If the dance comes out right and feels good with the music in spite of small mistakes, it is encouraging to see how repetition helps to correct them. In line dances the slow ones, feeling the rhythmic swing of the group, gradually manage to shift weight when they should. In mixers, even if both partners are on the wrong foot, successive partners will eventually correct them. This is an important point to remember because a dance can become boring if it is continually interrupted to correct the few "with two left feet."

After once through and a pause for evaluation and suggestions, and perhaps further practice, a dance should be repeated twice through; if the children are ready for it, more than that. The transition into the repetition may need special assistance, particularly if a change of partners is involved. Sometimes children are so busy remembering the sequence they forget how the dance began. To get the true feeling of a dance sequence and to benefit physiologically from the vigor of its movement, successive performances without pause are indicated.

Some recorded accompaniment, however, repeats the dance sequence over and over to the point of exhaustion or at least boredom. When children begin to lose control of their movement so that it no longer has zest and precision, they are probably breathless and tired. An alert teacher will stop the music before that point.

The Taking of Partners

One source of many boys' unwillingness to participate in dance is the fact that they must often dance with a girl. This reluctance is considerably lessened if boys and girls have profitable, happy dance experiences together from the time they enter school. It is also not nearly so prevalent if boys and girls play games together, rather than being separated from each other for all their school play activities after the second or third grade.

A teacher who is not acquainted with their background in dance or their attitudes about partner selection should spend the early dance periods on basic skills and testing the ability of the class on movement inventiveness and rhythmic response.[2] The first dances to be learned might be those which do not demand partners or in which boys can dance with boys and girls with girls. Of the latter, Jessie Polka, Greensleeves, Noriu Miego, Ten Pretty Girls (call it Hold That Line!) are suggestions. A great many line dances popular today are examples of the former. Of course, in these circle, open circle, or line formations a solid concentration of one sex together should be avoided. After the step combinations have been learned in open order, a scattering of boys and girls throughout the formation is easily achieved. Later when boys discover that girls have good footwork, sometimes superior to their own, a pairing of sexes into couples is more acceptable to them.

Some partner dances emphasize a group rather than a partner relationship. All individual mixers are examples of circle group dances, and many simple square and longways dances are of this type. Trios deemphasize the single boy-girl relationship, as, to a lesser extent, do dances for two couples. If a teacher will search out appropriate dances, the necessity of taking a partner, almost universally disliked by boys (and many girls) at a certain age, can be postponed indefinitely.

Even if it is carefully planned and supervised, the process of choosing partners can cause embarrassment for some of the boys and deep-down hurt feelings for the girls who are the last to be chosen or who are left out entirely. There are mechanical ways of getting partners, of course, and they can be used for variety at times. A free choice by the boys, however (and occasionally by the girls), is to be preferred, because in our society it is the accepted method of pairing off when a dancing partner is needed. The class should understand that when a free choice is offered, it is made quickly. If certain children hesitate too long, their free choice is forfeited and the teacher assigns a partner to them. When the process of getting partners raises prob-

2 See Chapter 27.

lems, it should always be discussed with the class and certain points emphasized. A boy in inviting a girl to dance is not asking her for a date but
merely to match her skill with his for a short time. It improves everyone's
dance skill to learn to adjust to many types of dancers, not just one or two.
Finally, any treatise on popularity will stress a friendly and helpful manner
with everyone, not just a favored few.

The individual or single mixer dance is a boon and should be used as
often as possible. Here it is of little importance who the first partner happens
to be, for many changes to others occur in the course of the dance. The first
partner, then, may be taken with little exercise of choice—*whoever is nearest
to you* or *the opposite girl* and the like.

When there is completely free choice, the choosing should be conducted
in a businesslike and unostentatious manner and as quickly as possible.
Those left without partners should be paired off quietly, girl with girl or boy
with boy if there are extra ones, so that they are not made conspicuous. A
wise teacher will not force a boy to dance with a girl (or vice versa) when it
is obvious that the experience will be unpleasant. If too much antagonism is
present in partner dances, other dance experiences are in order until attitudes
change. If the dance period is enjoyable, interesting, and challenging, the
children will soon be willing to cooperate in trying a dance with partners.

Boys should never be asked to approach a girl in class, make a bow, and
offer an arm to her. It is enough to ask them to walk, stand, or sit by the girl
of their choice or to take her hand and draw her into the circle, without
making any more formal overtures.

It is also undesirable to have *permanent* partners, either assigned or
acquired by free choice. Children should be encouraged to dance with many
partners, not with just one. Girls should accept graciously the first boy who
asks them. "Today let's take a partner you have not danced with in a long
time" is a good preliminary to the choosing process.

A few suggestions for choosing partners follow. The first three involve
mechanical ways; the others embody free choice and may be considered
more desirable for that reason.

1. If in the gymnasium assigned floor spaces are used where children sit to
   change shoes, boys and girls may be placed in alternate lines. Then they
   may take the person opposite them for a partner.
2. Boys and girls form separate lines according to height on either side of the
   room. Then they walk to music until the lines meet and proceed down the
   center in twos.
3. Boys form a circle and girls form another outside it. They take the opposite
   person for a partner and walk around the circle as the music begins. A
   gamelike activity may be made by having circles move to the music in
   opposite directions. When the music stops, each person takes his opposite's

hand as quickly as possible. Those who are not successful in getting a partner go to the center (often called the "lost and found" place), pair off boy with girl, and rejoin the circle when the music starts again.

The game Brothers may be retitled Partners and played as follows: In a double circle each boy starts out with a girl whom he has acquired in one of the mechanical ways suggested. When the music or a drum plays, or on a signal, he leaves his partner and walks around the circle in the opposite direction. When the music or drum stops, or on another signal, both boys and girls dash to get back to their partners again. The last couple to make it goes to the center until another couple is declared last. After two or three play-throughs, the boys move up one place. When the partners reunite, contact and place relationships may be changed to offer variety to the game: "Join both hands," "Link right arms," "Stand back to back," "Sit facing each other." This is a good game for getting boys and girls used to a partner before attempting partner dances.

4. Children move informally around the room to any type of accompaniment. The accompaniment stops, and before it starts again each boy must be walking with a girl partner. Those not quick enough go to the center of the room and find a partner there. Because everyone is moving, those who have no partner are less noticeable.

5. As the accompaniment plays, the children walk around the room choosing partners as they go, those not immediately successful moving to the center and raising hands to indicate the fact that they are still alone. Within a reasonably short time the accompaniment stops, and all who have not made their own choice are paired off by the teacher.

6. If children are accustomed to sitting in random spaces on the dance floor, the boys may rise on a signal and quickly sit beside the partner they choose. The teacher should step in to help with choices after a very short time so that the girls left sitting alone are not conspicuous.

7. A class social committee may be made up of leaders who are good dancers and have some social sensitivity. These students assist others to find partners and make it a practice to dance with many different persons, particularly those who need help. The personnel of such a committee should be changed from time to time so that the good dancers are not penalized by having to dance too often with poor ones.

During mixer dances, when the mixing is accomplished by a grand right and left or by two circles moving in opposite directions, there will be times when a few children, by chance, are left without partners. They should be instructed to move quickly to the "lost and found" place and raise their hands high, so that they can be seen by other children who have been left out. Each pair then rejoins the circle at any point so that the repetition of the dance is not delayed.

In many classes there will be an extra girl or boy who because of awkwardness, greater age or size, or for other reasons is often left out when a free choice of partners is made. If an extra teacher or adult is available, she can sometimes fill in with this child. A teacher may appeal to the more cooperative and socially sensitive members of her class to choose the person occasionally without putting an undue burden upon them or making it appear that they have been asked to do so. The extra person should always be included in the process of learning the dance in any way possible, perhaps by attending to the recording machine or stating his opinion about the way the dance is being performed, or designating couples who dance it particularly well. In any case, he should watch the sequence of the dance carefully, so that he may replace someone and have a chance to dance it before the period is over.

In classes having more boys than girls, or vice versa, it is occasionally a good idea to ask a few of the boys or girls who are good dancers to stay out of the dance proper in order to make numbers more even. Those who need it most, then get the experience of dancing with a partner of the opposite sex. The good dancers can act as assistants to the teacher, perhaps by taking those who need help off to the side for extra practice in executing a step. Classes unequally divided as to sex always present a problem when partner dances are being learned. Such classes might well use partnerless dances or those that are performed in groups of three. Many of the suggested ways of getting partners are easily adapted to forming trios. It should be understood that the center person in the trio will be a boy or a girl depending upon which sex has fewer dancers. There is nothing objectionable, of course, in having three boys or girls dancing together.

Forming Sets

Folk and country dances not danced informally around the room in couples or in groups of three or four are danced in circles, open circles (as in the kolo and hora dances), or square and longways sets. The single or double circle is the easiest formation to make and the one most common in folk dance. Individual and trio mixer dances are almost always done in circles. Circle dances may also be couple mixers, although this type of mixer is more frequently found in square or longways (contra) dances.

The forming of square or longways sets should be done as simply and quickly as possible so that the dancing may proceed. An efficient way to form squares is to use a *grand march*,[3] or a walk with partners, down the

3 See Jane A. Harris, Ann Pitman, and Marlyn S. Waller, *Dance A While*, 4th ed., Minneapolis, Burgess, 1968, p. 347.

center in twos, fours, and then eights. When the eights are spaced across the floor, they are stopped and each eight persons or four couples form a square in an assigned place.

For longways sets, the couples walking around the room are separated into groups of six or eight couples, each group moving from the edge of the room and into its place in turn. Because many longways dances engage only one or two couples at a time while the others wait their turn, the lines should be as short as possible; six couples is a good number.

If children are at all self-directing, the quickest way is to allow them to make their own sets. After partners are obtained, the formation of the set, if it is new to the class, is demonstrated by the teacher with one group of children. The others then form sets around the room, sitting down when their set is complete, or raising their hands to indicate the number of couples needed to complete it. The teacher helps to arrange the incomplete sets. Couples left over after the sets are formed can try the figures that can be done with the number they have. They should be given a chance to dance in a complete set before the period ends.

Two games that are of assistance in helping children learn to arrange themselves in different formations are Calling Numbers (see Chapter 12) and Move-Stop-Listen-Go.

The title explains the action in Move-Stop-Listen-Go. The class divides into groups of at least nine, and one child in each group is given an identifying object: a piece of colored paper, a large cardboard number, a small percussion instrument, or even a ball if it can be carried in one hand. The children then leave their groups and move freely about the room on individual paths. They use an assigned type of locomotor movement and keep in time to a drum, or other percussive or recorded accompaniment. When the accompaniment ceases or on the spoken signal *Stop!* they all stop and the child with the identifying object raises it above his head. The teacher then names a certain formation—a line, a single or double circle, a square, two lines facing, or trios. On her signal *Go!* they run (without colliding) to their group leader, make the desired formation around or in front of him as the case may be, and sit down as directed by the leader when it is complete. If leaders are too close together when the stop signal is given, they should move apart quickly. The first group to move into the signaled formation in good form is given a point, and the game proceeds. As the children move around the room again, the first leader passes his object unobtrusively to another group member, so that its presence is not known to the rest. This game helps to orient both younger and older children into the different group formations required by dances.

Chapter Preview

Greensleeves

THOMAS HALSTED

25 *Selecting Dances*

Of all the types of dances meant to be taught to children, those of most value are folk and country dances. They are vigorous, sociable, and gay. They offer the child, first, unison movement with another child or a group of children, and second, experience with styles of dance movement performed by groups of people in different sections of this country and other countries.

A teacher, knowing the interests and abilities of her classes, is the best judge of the dances they can learn quickly and enjoy performing. She should not, however, allow her personal inclination toward a particular culture to influence unduly her choice of dances. Older children especially should experience a variety of types of folk dance. A course of study with prescribed dances for certain grades should be used as no more than a guide to possible content.

For Younger Children

To younger children, knowledge that a dance represents a particular country is unimportant. They like simple, lively dances which have dramatic significance provided perhaps by a song, as in that body of dance material known as *singing games*. They should not be asked to perform movements that are slow and controlled or that demand much attention to footwork. For instance, the 3/4 run may be used advisedly if they have learned to run in time to music. The waltz step, however—even the waltz balance and the dances using it—and most dance steps except the skip, slide, and perhaps the step-hop are for older children. Sometimes the basic step of a dance is simple enough, as is the walk, run, and skip used in American square dances, but their figures, because of the complexity of their orientation to other dancers and to changing space environments, are not suitable for younger children.

Many of the early singing dances are done in a circle, even though to join hands and move rhythmically in a circle is a difficult skill for young children. Unless a joined-hands circle is necessary for the action (as in "in and out the window" dances), a circle can be approximated without joined hands, and movement can proceed counterclockwise without having the children stay side by side or one behind the other. Such dances as Gallant Ship and Sally Go Round the Moon can be done with the children moving vigorously around and then sinking slowly or quickly to the floor. Looby Loo is quite possible to do as a solo dance. In fact, it is a good idea to try dances like Did You Ever See a Lassie and Go Round the Mountain with everyone doing a movement of his own at the same time. Later, a Lassie or Laddie can be singled out to stand in the center and have all the others imitate him. Children then have a chance to invent their movements without

Dancing a Hora

THOMAS HALSTED

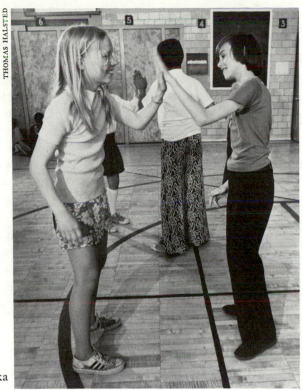

Pattycake Polka

pressure or to copy those of someone else. Thus they will be ready with a movement when chosen to be "it."

Many singing games involve choosing a partner, a replacement, or someone else to join one in the ring. Although none of the stigma attached to this process by older children may be present, it sometimes demands special attention. A child may find it hard to decide on one among many, or he has to search around for his friends, or, if he is timid, a free choice of another person, especially of another sex as is sometimes demanded, is a somewhat aggressive and distasteful act. Consequently delay occurs, and the action of the dance never does catch up with the progress of the song. A teacher can remedy the situation by starting the choosing at the first line of the verse instead of at the end where it is usually supposed to occur, by suggesting that "it" shut his eyes and point, or by making the choice herself if "it" is too reluctant. She should caution the class that choosing someone is not an exercise in judgment but merely a chance to give a classmate an opportunity to play an active part. Any way that song dances can be made easier to learn and more fun to perform is legitimate for a teacher to use. The word *game* in their classification identifies them as a play activity, and they should be treated as such.

Very young children are too individual to conform for long to the rules inherent in learning any group dance, even a simple singing game. Action songs, however, calling for specific movements, together with demonstrated cues from a leader, offer security for the timid, and rhythmic and movement satisfaction for the active. Songs that tell children to "clap your hands, tap your feet, nod your heads, shake your hands, turn around, skip along," etc. are found in most early music books.

It is a temptation for the traditional teacher who loves order in the classroom and believes she is not creative, to confine dance activities to action songs and singing games with their unison and simultaneous responses to musical or verbal cues. Yet a dance program that consists solely of "Bluebird," "Oats, Peas, Beans," "Ach Ja," and the like is completely inadequate. Such dances are valuable and fun to teach once in a while for a change from individualized activity and to help children achieve a feeling of group unity. But they should be only supplementary to a wide variety of exploratory, expressive dance lessons.

Some Criteria for Selecting Dances for Older Children

The selection of a folk or country dance for older children should be undertaken most carefully. It should be made not because it is listed in some course of study for that particular grade, or because it is needed for the school operetta, or even because the teacher herself likes it. More fundamental principles should be kept in mind:

1. Can the children perform the basic step used in the dance in time to the music and in all the ways necessary for its use; or will drill on the step be likely to interrupt the progress of learning the dance?
2. Can the dance be learned quickly, so that its whole configuration can be grasped by the children at one time; or is it long and involved, with successive parts which take several dance lessons to learn, so that the children's feeling of accomplishment is retarded, and everyone, including the teacher, becomes bored with the process?
3. Are the successive parts short, so that movements must be continually changed; or are they long enough so that there is time to remember what comes next?
4. Does the dance allow lively and informal movement; or is it constrained and overprecise, employing small, controlled foot patterns?

Ve' David

Changing Notated Dances

Some teachers feel that a notated dance is never to be changed but must be translated and taught precisely as written so that its authenticity as part of the folk culture of a particular group will remain pure and unsullied. This attitude prevails in spite of the fact that descriptions of dances made by collectors differ, just as the words and melodies of folk songs never achieve exact uniformity in the several published volumes in which they may be found. A slight alteration or the elimination of part of a notated dance often makes an otherwise unsuitable one easy to learn and fun to perform. Of course, the teacher must make changes carefully, so that the original pattern of the dance will not be distorted and the music will come out right. But a modicum of movement inventiveness and the ability to count the measures in the music are all that is needed. It is better that folk dances be danced and enjoyed than abandoned or disliked, if a small change which does not alter their essential pattern and style will make the difference. Examples of such changes are the following:

1. Some dances start out well enough but become intricate in their several parts. Perhaps the first part is enough to teach. How many of us attempt to remember all the verses of a folk ballad?
2. Dances using the polka may call for difficult partner-turns around the edge of a circle. A skipping turn in place or a face-to-face, back-to-back polka forward can be substituted.
3. Many dances call for a circle when nothing in the dance pattern makes a circle necessary or even desirable. How much easier to dance it informally around the room with one's partner or group instead of trying to follow the line of a circle!
4. Many dances can be performed to music different from that traditionally assigned to them. Songs which all the children know may be used at times for dances whose patterns they happen to fit. For instance, during the Christmas season Csebogar might be danced to "Jingle Bells," Pattycake Polka to "Here Comes Santa Claus," and Susan's Gavotte to "Deck the Halls."
5. In dances which call for bows and underarm turns a handshake or partner clapping or turning oneself around is much easier. The teacher might ask, "What ways of turning would fit this music?" Common sense and some inventiveness can expand the children's repertoire of dances readily learned and performed again and again.

Ethnic and National Dances

An ethnic group is a group of people who are racially or historically related and have a common and distinctive culture. While European countries from which most of our folk dance literature is derived are included in this definition, it now has special reference to Afro-Americans, American Indians, Mexican-Americans, and Oriental groups. Although we have been teaching pseudo-Indian dances for many years in our schools, only recently has there been scholarly effort to investigate authentic American Indian dances and to make them available for study and possible use. One difficulty lies in the fact that many of these dances are not performed for social recreation but are ritualistic or ceremonial dances done only by certain members of the group for particular purposes and on special occasions. Consequently, use by outsiders for entertainment or recreation is frowned upon, as well it might be.

Folk dance in ethnic cultures is that part of the dance heritage in which all participate, and which is usually performed for fun on social occasions. It is thus simpler and demands less skill than do the more serious dances of religious and ceremonial significance or those in which physical ability is especially exploited. Hence it can be adapted more readily to children's learning.

The so-called ethnic or national dances, also part of the total dance culture, have been developed for audience viewing by skilled dancers using ethnic music and movement style. Most of these dances are too difficult for children to learn without tedious drill. Consequently, the Highland Fling of Scotland, the Hambo of Sweden, the Jarabe Tapatio of Mexico should be left for older and more expert feet. Sometimes in a homogeneous community of foreign background the children's strong motivation to learn their own ethnic dances overcomes the difficulties. In such a case a wise teacher will draw upon community resources or ask for help from the children who know the dances.

Athletic and Character[1] Dances

Certain dances composed by teachers or other individuals are called, for want of a better name, character dances. Some, because of their use of athletic stunts, may bear that designation. Being unprotected by the sanctity of tradition, the steps may be adapted at will to fit the needs of a particular group. Unless the dance must serve a particular purpose, the best so-called character dances may be those made by the children themselves about historic and literary characters that interest them.

Fad Dances

Older children, especially those approaching the teens, will be interested in trying out "fad" dance patterns, especially if a popular jazz or rock record is played and improvisation is called for. A basic beat is usually taken in the feet with a touch and step or a single or double bounce or vibration which changes the weight from foot to foot. Flexed ankles and knees and arm movements from side to side or forward and back emphasize the weight change. Isolated movements of the head, shoulders, hips, and knees are difficult to perform. They are quite beyond most elementary school children, who look somewhat awkward trying them. They may attempt to follow the

[1] This bears no relationship to "character dancing," which area of dance training belongs exclusively to the realm of classical ballet.

larger movements, however, interspersing them with jumps, taps, and claps. While such fad dance improvisations and their sequential patterns to "pop" music may be tried for fun once in a while, they should never monopolize the dance experiences of older children.

Children's Own Dances

Having learned a dance or dances of a particular country, children may want to make their own dance using a folk tune or song of that country.[2] A different formation may be tried, the arrangement of figures changed, or a different step introduced.

A useful way to lead into such creative activity is to teach all but the last eight, twelve, or sixteen counts of a not too familiar folk dance, or one which the teacher herself has made. The class, in couples, trios, or larger groups, are asked to invent the final section. The most interesting one is selected, learned by everyone, and then compared with that in the dance description.

Schottisches combined with step-hops are basic to many couple dances. Given a lively schottische piece, two persons new to dance-making can often come up with a creditable series of figures. Combinations of slow walks, touch steps, two-steps, and jumps done to strongly rhythmic syncopated music might produce a solo sequence that will also work as a group dance in unison. Or a series of steps (grapevine walks, jumps, hops, toe taps, claps, runs, etc.) can be danced sideward in a circle or line in a sixteen-count phrase of suitable music. The sequence should resemble that of a hora or kolo, and after each group has demonstrated its sequence, the combination with the most appeal may be taught to the others and danced by everyone together.

Reading Dance Descriptions

The interpretation of the written description of a dance, particularly an unfamiliar one, requires the teacher to have some knowledge of musical structure—at least if the music is included in the directions. A good plan is to look at the music first (the top line is usually sufficient), noting the time signature, the phrasing, and the number of measures in each phrase. The pulse beats, accents, and finally the rhythmic patterns should then be counted

2 See Chapter 18.

out. Now familiar with the rhythmic accompaniment, the teacher can turn her attention to the description of the movements and how they are related to it.

If a record is being used and music itself is not available for perusal, the problem is somewhat different. An important first step is listening to the record for phrasing and accents, attending to the tempo, and noting identical and contrasting phrases. Counting measures in each phrase by finding where the accents fall is the next step. The teacher, with this understanding of the accompaniment, may then work out the sequence of the dance from the written description and put the movements and accompaniment together.

Some folk dance records have vocal directions with a person calling out instructions for learning the dance. For the most part, the teacher's instructions are much to be preferred. Such records may assist the teacher in learning the dance herself if it is unfamiliar, but experience seems to indicate that recorded instructions are often confusing and difficult for a class to follow.

The accurate reading and reproducing of dance descriptions should be a part of the training of a dance specialist or of any physical education teacher or recreation leader who expects to be involved in teaching folk dance. To misread the directions, to teach steps faster or slower than is correct, or to mistake the accents of a movement sequence can result in utter confusion, or at best in an unsatisfactory dance interpretation.

In most of the references for folk and country dances in this section, the relation of the dance movements to the music is carefully noted. In some the measures are numbered for easier reading. No attempt to present the dance should be made until the teacher knows exactly how each part is performed to the music and how much of the music it uses. The dances listed in Chapter 26 have been chosen because of their simplicity, variety, and general interest. None are of more than moderate difficulty, and many would fall into the easy classification. Learning a number of dances which can be quickly grasped and which are "catchy" is challenging to most boys and girls.

Chapter Preview

Explanation of Dance Annotations

Alphabetical Index of Dances

Annotated References
Dances for Younger Children
Dances for Older Children

Notes on Records and Folk Dance Record Companies

Supplementary Materials
Books
Ethnic Records Recommended for African and American
Indian Dance
Periodicals
Films

26 *Annotated Dances, Classifications, and References*

Explanation of Dance Annotations

In this chapter many folk dances are classified according to the *basic step* or, in some cases, the step most difficult to perform. Other information includes the *country* or source from which the dance derives, the type of *formation* used *with or without partners,* a few *remarks* which may be helpful in making the selection or recalling the dance, and the *references* for its description. One list is for younger children and one for older children. The *American* mixers or progressive dances are listed separately, and the way in which partners change is indicated. Because changing partners is always a little complicated, these dances are reserved for older children. A separate listing is also given for *American square dances* and *longways* or *contra dances.* Of the contra dances, only those are included in which all couples are active; of the square dances, only those which have singing calls and in which the figures are not complex. The more advanced American square dances for which a caller is needed are more appropriate for adolescents and adults.

American Indian dances require such special style and skill for authentic reproduction that they have not been included. If they are needed for special projects or programs, a few relatively simple ones may be found in reference 11. Other more extensive Indian steps and dances are available for teachers who may need them for special projects.[1]

Insofar as complete authenticity is possible, most of the dances listed are authentic folk material. In the few instances where the source is unknown, the source of the folk music or song used as accompaniment is given under derivation.

---

[1] John L. Squires and Robert E. McLean, *American Indian Dances,* New York, Ronald, 1963. William K. Powers, *Here Is Your Hobby: Indian Dancing and Costumes,* New York, Putnam, 1966.

An explanation of the terms used follows:

Circle, open, lines, square, contra or longways, open circle refer to the formation used. A *contra* or longways formation is one of partners facing each other in two parallel lines as in the Virginia Reel. An *open circle* is one in which all but two persons join hands, one of these two being the leader.

Extras means that a circle is used with one or more extra children in the center.

Open means that the dance may be performed in informal or open formation any place on the floor.

Couples or *partners* means that two people dance together, preferably a boy and a girl.

Groups of three means that a boy dances with two girls, or the opposite, making a trio.

Mixer dances are those in which the persons dancing together change with each repetition of the dance. Most common are the ones in which *individual dancers* change their partners. In *couple mixers* two couples who have been dancing together move on to repeat the dance with other couples. In *trio mixers* two trios who have been dancing together move on to repeat the dance with another trio, or one of the three dancers (usually the center one) in a single trio leaves his group and moves ahead to repeat the dance with another group.

Closed position is noted when it is desirable that it be used. It means the face-to-face waist-shoulder position or the closed social dance position with one's partner described in Chapter 23.

When dances with different titles are grouped together, it means that they are identical, almost identical, or slightly different versions of the same dance. Detailed directions for teaching all the dance steps used for classification purposes are found in Chapter 10. The following alphabetical list will help to locate the dances in the annotated section.

Alphabetical Index of Dances

Title[2]	Basic Step or Type
Ach Ja	Walk
A-Hunting We Will Go*	Skip, etc.
Alabama Girl	Skip, etc.
Alley Cat	Walk
Alunelul	Walk

[2] An asterisk after the title indicates that the dance is for younger children.

Apat-Apat (Na Avu)	Walk
At Va Ani	Walk
Bingo	Walk
Black Nag, The	Slide
Bleking	Step-hop
Bluebird*	Walk
Bow Belinda (Ginny Crack Corn)	Skip, etc.
Bunny Hop	Step-hop
Captain Jinks	Mixer
Captain Jinks	Square
Carousel*	Skip, etc.
Chapanecas (Mexican Waltz)	Waltz
Cherkessia	Walk
Chester Schottische	Schottische
Chimes of Dunkirk	Skip
Circassian Circle	Mixer
Circle Hopak	Walk
Climbing Up the Mountain (Go Round the Mountain)*	Walk
Come Let Us Be Joyful	Skip, etc.
Come, My Love	Mixer
Cotton-Eyed Jo	Mixer
Crested Hen	Step-hop
Csebogar	Skip, etc.
Czardas	Two-step
Darling Nellie Gray	Square
Debka (Horra Arabi)	Walk
Did You Ever See a Lassie*	Skip, etc.
Donegal Country Dance	Skip, etc.
Doudlebska Polka	Polka
Ersko Kolo	Schottische
Far Northland, The (Road to the Isles)	Schottische
Five Little Chickadees*	Run
Four in a Boat	Skip, etc.
Gallant Ship*	Skip, etc.
Galopede	Skip
Ginny Crack Corn (Bow Belinda)	Skip, etc.
Girl I Left Behind Me, The	Square
Glow Worm	Mixer
Good-Night, Ladies	Mixer
Go Round the Mountain (Climbing up the Mountain; Rise, Sugar, Rise)*	Walk, etc.
Grand March, The	Walk
Greensleeves	Walk
Gustaf's Skoal	Skip, etc.
Hansel and Gretel (Let Your Feet Go Tap)*	Skip, etc.

Hatter, The	Step-hop
Heel and Toe Polka	Polka
Highland Schottische	Schottische
Hinky Dinky Parley-Voo	Square
Hi Ya	Square
Hokey Pokey	Walk
Hold That Line (Ten Pretty Girls)	Walk
Hop Mor Anika (Hop, Mother Anika)	Polka
Hop, Mother Anika (Hop Mor Anika)	Polka
Horra (Hora)	Schottische
Horra Arabi (Debka)	Walk
Hot Time in the Old Town	Square
How Do You Do	Skip, etc.
How Do You Do, My Partner*	Skip
Irish Washerwoman, The	Mixer
I Should Like to Go to Shetland*	Walk, etc.
Jessie Polka	Polka
Jibi-Di, Jibi-Da	Two-step
Jingle Bells	Mixer
Jugo	Run
Kaca	Run
Kalvelis	Polka
Koroboushka	Schottische
Kritikos (Miserlou)	Walk
Kuma Echa	Schottische
La Cucaracha	Run
La Raspa	Run
Let Your Feet Go Tap (Hansel and Gretel)	Skip, etc.
Life on the Ocean Wave (Two Head Gents Cross Over)	Square
Lili Marlene (Susan's Gavotte)	Two-step
Little Man in a Fix	Waltz
Looby Loo*	Skip, etc.
Lott Ist Tod	Polka
Makazice	Walk
Ma Navu	Walk
Mayim	Run
Mexican Waltz (Chapanecas)	Waltz
Milanova Kolo	Schottische
Miserlou (Kritikos)	Walk
Muffin Man, The*	Walk, etc.
Na Avu (Apat-Apat)	Walk
Nebesko Kolo	Two-step
Nixie Polka*	Run
Noble Duke of York	Skip, etc.

Noriu Miego	Walk
Northern Lights	Square
Norwegian Mountain March	Run
Oats, Peas, Beans and Barley*	Walk, etc.
Oh, Johnny	Square
Oh Susanna	Mixer
Oklahoma Mixer	Mixer
Old Time Schottische	Schottische
On the Bridge of Avignon*	Skip, etc.
Pass the Left-Hand Lady Under	Square
Patch Tanz	Walk
Pattycake Polka	Mixer
Paw Paw Patch	Skip, etc.
Pease Porridge Hot*	Skip, etc.
Polka Zu Dreien	Polka
Pop Goes the Weasel	Square
Put Your Little Foot	
(*Varsouvianna*)	Waltz
Red River Valley	Walk
Red River Valley	Square
Rheinlander Schottische	Schottische
Rig-a-Jig-Jig*	Skip, etc.
Rise, Sugar, Rise (Go Round the	
Mountain)*	Walk
Road to the Isles (Far Northland,	
The)	Schottische
Round and Round the Village*	Walk
Rumunjsko (Rumonsko Kolo)	Step-hop
Rumonsko Kolo (Rumunjsko)	Step-hop
Rye Waltz	Waltz
Sally Go Round the Moon*	Skip, etc.
Salty Dog Rag	Schottische
Savila Se Bela Loza	Run
Schottische for Four	Schottische
Sekerecka	Two-step
Seljancica (Serbian Kolo)	Schottische
Sellinger's Round	Run
Serbian Kolo (Seljancica)	Schottische
Setnja	Step-hop
Seven Jumps	Step-hop
Seven Steps	Run
Shake Them 'Simmons Down	
(*'Simmons*)	Mixer
Shibolet Bassadet	Step-hop
Shoemaker's Dance*	Skip
Shoo Fly	Mixer
Sicilian Circle	Walk
Sicilian Tarantella	Step-hop

'Simmons (Shake Them 'Simmons Down)	Mixer
Sing a Song of Sixpence*	Walk, etc.
Skating Away	Skip, etc.
Snail, The*	Walk
Spanish Circle (Waltz, The)	Waltz
Susan's Gavotte (Lili Marlene)	Two-step
Swiss Changing Dance	Schottische
Tancuj	Schottische
Tanko Bushi	Walk
Ten Little Indians*	Skip, etc.
Tennessee Wig Walk	Mixer
Ten Pretty Girls (Hold That Line)	Walk
Teton Mountain Stomp	Two-step
This Is the Way the Lady Rides	Walk
Thread Follows the Needle, The*	Walk
Troika	Run
Tropanka	Step-hop
Twelfth Street Rag	Walk
Two Head Gents Cross Over (Life on the Ocean Wave)	Square
Varsouvianna (Put Your Little Foot)	Waltz
Varsovienne	Waltz
Ve' David	Waltz
Veleta Waltz	Waltz
Virginia Reel	Contra
Waltz, The (Spanish Circle)	Waltz
We Won't Go Home Until Morning	Skip
Wheat, The	Skip, etc.
When Johnny Comes Marching Home	Square

Annotated References

Of the thirty references for folk dance descriptions given in the second edition of this book only four are still in print. The following books are all recommended, and most have been published in the past ten years. Their emphasis is international, with much more interest than has been evident in the past in the line or open circle dances of eastern Europe. These kolos and horas are done without partners (demanded by most of the dances of the British Isles, Germany, and the Scandinavian countries). They are a welcome departure from that tradition and a welcome addition to elementary school folk dance materials.

The fact that dance records today usually include printed descriptions of the dances included, and in some cases verbal instructions on how to dance them, may account for the fact that fewer collections of folk dances are being published and the older ones[3] are no longer in demand. Mass instruction by a disembodied voice, however, emerging from a machine, takes automation a step too far, in the opinion of this author. Let the teacher do the teaching. She can read the directions as well as the voice of the expert and can adapt them to her children's abilities.

Another reason for using a book to obtain dance directions authored by a folk dance teacher or specialist is that it usually includes something about the history, educational values, and cultural characteristics of this body of dance material. The teacher thus becomes aware that learning a folk dance is more than performing specific movements to thirty-two beats of a record. It is part of a universal cultural tradition in which all children should be able to take part.

1. BELIAJUS, VYTAUTAS FINADAR, *Merrily Dance,* Delaware, Ohio, Cooperative Recreation Service, Inc.

    This small, inexpensive pamphlet, containing dances selected by a leading authority on folk dance, is included because it is his only collection now in print. Music is included and a record reference for each dance. Directions are clear and accurate.

2. CZARNOWSKI, LUCILLE K., *Folk Dance Teaching Cues,* Palo Alto, Calif., National Press, 1961.

    One third of this book by a well-known specialist is devoted to fundamentals and progressions for teaching. While many of the dances are difficult for children, the directions for all are clearly detailed, both piano and record references are given, and for a majority of the dances there is some background information.

3. FARWELL, JANE, *Folk Dances for Fun,* Delaware, Ohio, Cooperative Recreation Service, Inc.

    This is another small and inexpensive pamphlet containing many usable dances. Music and record references are included, and brief but clear directions.

4. GILBERT, CECILE, *International Folk Dance at a Glance,* Minneapolis, Burgess, 1969.

    This book contains dances of international variety and extremely clear directional charts devised by the author. By means of counts, small arrows and one-syllable words, and clearly indicated directions, she has made sure that even a beginner can read and understand the notations. Background in-

---

[3] It is hoped that libraries will carefully guard such series as those of Elizabeth Burchenal, for example, in the interest of future research in ethnic dance.

formation, record references, and stylized sketches of the formations and place relationships are also useful.

5. HARRIS, JANE A., PITTMAN, ANNE, and WALLER, MARLYN S., *Dance A While,* 4th ed., Minneapolis, Burgess, 1968.

This voluminous book might almost be considered an encyclopedia of recreational dance. Western square dance, New England contras, round dance, and social dance are examined as to history and fundamentals, and many dances of each type are carefully described. The section on international folk dance and the one on mixers contain dances suitable for children. Music and record references are included.

6. JENSEN, MARY BEE, and JENSEN, CLAYNE R., *Beginning Folk Dancing,* Belmont, Calif., Wadsworth, 1966.

Designed for college classes as one of a series on "sports" skills, this booklet offers a brief background on values, history, and basic skills and describes two dozen folk dances, many of them simple enough for children. Record references are included.

7. KIRKELL, MIRIAM, and SHAFFNIT, IRMA, *Partners All—Places All!* New York, Dutton, 1949.

This is an excellent book for elementary schools. It contains mixers, squares, and couple dances both American and European, each described in detail and related to its accompaniment, whether song, music, or call. A few squares may be too hard for elementary schools. Music and record references are included.

8. KRAUS, RICHARD, *Folk and Square Dance and Singing Games for Elementary Schools,* Englewood Cliffs, N.J., Prentice-Hall, 1966.

This soft-cover "pocket guide" contains well-selected games and folk dances specifically for the elementary grades. Some of the singing games described for younger children are difficult to find in other references. The treble line of music and record references are given. Mr. Kraus is an authority on recreational dance.

9. KRAUS, RICHARD, *Folk Dancing,* New York, Macmillan, 1962.

This is a comprehensive, authoritative guide to folk dance teaching. The dances, carefully described, are divided into categories: circle dances without partners, couple dances, dances for three, partner-changing dances, etc. With a few exceptions all are usable for older elementary school children and a few for younger. Record references are included.

10. KRAUS, RICHARD, *Square Dances of Today,* New York, Ronald, 1950.

In addition to many singing squares suitable for older children, this book contains simple mixers, longways, and circle dances. Music (no records) is included, and diagrams, descriptions, and teaching theory attest to Mr. Kraus's reputation.

11. LASALLE, DOROTHY, *Rhythms and Dances for Elementary Schools,* rev. ed., New York, Ronald, 1951.

Originally a course of study in dance for the Detroit Public Schools and used successfully for years, this book includes dances from many countries for all ages. Some are from collections which are no longer available. An introductory section has excellent piano music for basic locomotor and non-locomotor movements, dance steps, and movement combinations. The dances are arranged according to degree of difficulty, and the descriptions are accurate and easily interpreted. Music is included for all the dances but record references are not.

12. LIDSTER, MIRIAM D., and TAMBURINI, DOROTHY H., *Folk Dance Progressions,* Belmont, Calif., Wadsworth, 1965.

This comprehensive and scholarly volume can be considered "a source book of international folk dances," as the Preface states. Cultural areas specifically covered are the Balkans, Israel, Scandinavia, and the Philippines, but other dances are included as well. All are categorized according to basic step patterns and are meticulously described. Appendix contains information on folk dance leaders and an extensive bibliography of folk dance and folk lore books. While intended primarily for students beyond the elementary level, many of the dances are simple enough for children. Record references are included, but no music.

13. MYNATT, CONSTANCE V., and KAIMAN, BERNARD D., *Folk Dancing for Students and Teachers,* Dubuque, Iowa, Brown, 1968.

This relatively inexpensive soft-cover book classifies into "easy to learn" and "moderately easy to learn" a number of nonpartner dances, couple dances, and dances for three or more. "What to do with the feet, . . . the hands, . . . and the people" are briefly but adequately described. Teaching method is less adequate and applies to the teaching of adults more than children. Dance movements are carefully described, but number of counts for each movement are not always clear. Record references are given, and dances are classified in Appendix by nationality and basic step.

14. SPIESMAN, MILDRED C., *Folk Dancing,* Philadelphia, Saunders, 1970.

This booklet, one of a series on physical activities, contains helpful material on folk dance teaching as well as a selection of dances classified according to the basic step and arranged according to difficulty. Dance directions are carefully given and include record references. Lack of an index of the dances makes finding them a bit difficult.

15. VICK, MARIE, and COX, ROSANN M., *A Collection of Dances for Children,* Minneapolis, Burgess, 1970.

This is a card catalogue of a great number of dances for younger and older children which can, of course, be removed from the file for teaching purposes and then replaced. It is also useful because the teacher may note on the back of the card anything she wishes to remember after trying it out. The directions are easy to interpret, but there are some inaccuracies which will undoubtedly be corrected in a later edition. No music, but record references are given.

16. WAKEFIELD, ELEANOR ELY, *Folk Dancing in America,* New York, J. Lowell Pratt, 1966.

After three chapters on history and teaching, the dances are organized in chapters on "Our Colonial Heritage," "Westward Expansion," and "The Twentieth Century." In the latter chapter, dances brought to America from European cultures are described. Directions are clear, and the Appendix grades all dances according to easy, moderate, and difficult to perform. Record references are included, but no music.

17. *World Wide Games and Dances,* International Council on Health, Physical Education and Recreation, 1201 16th St., N.W., Washington, D.C. 20036, 1967.

Many of the dances in this attractive little book are unfamiliar, and some of the easiest ones are singing games. All are titled in their native language, and the choice is truly international. The treble line of music is included, but no record references. A pronunciation guide would be helpful.

Notes on Records and Folk Dance Record Companies

In most of the annotated folk dance reference books, preferred records are listed. The three that have no such listing (Kraus, No. 10, LaSalle, No. 11, and World Wide, No. 17) supply printed music for each dance. It should be remembered that for many American dances, unless they use a characteristic song, the stated accompaniment is not the only one possible. Any good schottische of similar phrasing can be used for such dances as Old Time Schottische, Chester Schottische, or Rheinlander, and a good, popular syncopated tune for Bunny Hop and Salty Dog Rag. The same is true for such walking dances as Greensleeves and Ten Pretty Girls, and for two-step and polka dances like Susan's Gavotte and Jessie Polka. Most longways and square dances (without singing calls) use any lively fiddle tune in 2/4 or 6/8 meter. It is necessary, of course, to try the piece out first to see whether it fits the dance sequence in terms of both its musical structure and its dynamics.

Dances for Younger Children

Dance	Derivation	Formation	Remarks	References[a]
Dances Based on the Walk and/or Skip				
Bluebird	American	Circle; no partners	Word dramatization; bluebirds go in and out through circle arches	11
Did You Ever See a Lassie	American	Circle with extra; no partners	Partial word dramatization; group imitation of extra person's movements during second part of song	11, 15
Go Round the Mountain (Climbing Up the Mountain, Rise, Sugar, Rise)	American	Circle with extra; no partners	Partial word dramatization; imitation of center person	8, 15
I Should Like to Go to Shetland	English	Circle with extras	Word dramatization; partner choosing; gallop	11
Muffin Man	English	Circle with extras; no partners	Partial word dramatization; partner choosing; skip	8, 11
Oats, Peas, Beans and Barley Grow	English	Circle or open; partners	Word dramatization; partner choosing; skip	11, 15
Round and Round the Village	English	Circle with extras; no partners	Word dramatization; partner choosing; skip	11, 15
Sing a Song of Sixpence	English	Circle with extras; no partners	Word dramatization; partner choosing; skip	11, 15
Skating Away	American	Circle with extras; no partners	Partial word dramatization; choosing replacements; star figure	8, 10
Snail, The	American	Open circle; no partners	Word dramatization; circle winding in and out like a snail	11

[a] See pp. 366–370 for key to references.

Dances for Younger Children (Continued)

Dance	Derivation	Formation	Remarks	References
This Is the Way the Lady Rides	English	Open; no partners	Trotting run and gallop used for gentleman's and messenger's rides. Tempo of song should adapt to movement	8, 9, 11
Thread Follows the Needle, The	American	Line; no partners	Leader "sews" up line by going through arches, one after another; seam is "ripped" by turning under arms	11, 15
Dances Based on the Skip, Slide, or Run				
A-Hunting We Will Go	English	Longways	A simple longways dance with sliding down center by each couple in turn	11, 15, 17
Carousel	Swedish	Circle; no partners	Dramatization of a merry-go-round; starts with sideward walk (step-together), ends with fast slide; joined hands may prove difficult	8, 9, 11, 15, 17
Chimes of Dunkirk	French	Circle or open	Word dramatization and turn partner; skip around circle in second part	8, 9, 11, 15
Five Little Chickadees	English	Circle with five extras; no partners	Word dramatization; one by one the children in the center fly to the circle and everyone flies around it	8, 11
Gallant Ship	English	Circle or open; no partners	Sliding or skipping around and sinking slowly to the bottom of the sea	8, 11
Hansel and Gretel (Let Your Feet Go Tap)	German	Line or open; partners	Word dramatization; foot tapping and clapping, heel and toe touch	11, 15

How Do You Do, My Partner	Swedish	Partners, open formation	Word dramatization in first part, then partners skipping; can be done as mixer	8, 15
Looby Loo	English	Circle; no partners	Word dramatization with skipping interlude; dance is about taking a bath on Saturday night	11, 15
Nixie Polka	Danish	Circle with extra; no partners	Bleking step and running in a line; extra person is Nixie, who charms people and makes them follow him	8, 11, 15
On the Bridge of Avignon	French	Circle; partners	Word dramatization; interludes of pantomime with skipping	11, 15
Pease Porridge Hot	English	Circle or open; partners	Traditional clapping pattern followed by sliding or skipping	8
Rig-a-Jig-Jig	American	Circle with extra; no partners	Extra chooses partner, then each chooses, and so on until all are chosen	9
Sally Go Round the Moon	English	Circle or open; no partners	Skip without joining hands; fall down fast on bump	8, 11
Shoemaker's Dance	Danish	Circle or open; partners	Word dramatization in first part; skip with partner in second part; could be danced without partners	8, 9, 15
Ten Little Indians	American	Circle; no partners	Word dramatization of numbers; improvised "Indian" dancing	15

Dances for Older Children

Dance	Derivation	Formation	Remarks	References
		Dances Based on the Walk		
Ach Ja	German	Circle; partners	Sideward walk (step-together); bowing; may be danced as mixer	8, 15
Alley Cat	American	Open; no partners	Touch steps, clap and jump; once facing each wall	13
Alunelul	Rumanian	Circle; no partners	Sideward cross steps; stamping; somewhat similar to "Tropanka"	2, 4, 6, 9, 12, 13
Apat-Apat (Na Avu)	Philippine	Circle; partners; mixer	In a series of four walking-step phrases, partners move forward, backward, turn, and then walk to new partner	12, 13, 17
At Va Ani	Israeli	Circle; no partners	Slow lyrical dance, using brushes, sideward cross steps, and a turn	4
Cherkessia	Israeli	Open circle; no partners	Grapevine and sideward cross steps, step-hop, buzz steps; repeating chorus	5, 9, 13
Circle Hopak	Armenian-Ukrainian	Single circle; partners	A simplified Hopak; stamping, sideward cross-walk, run and clap; buzz step swing	9
Debka Hora (Horra Arabi)	Palestinian	Circle or open; no partners	Toe taps; side cross-walks and jumps	1
Grand March, The	American	Partners or single lines of boys and girls	Meeting partners; marching in twos, fours, and eights; several other line figures	5, 10

Dance	Nationality	Formation	Description	References
Greensleeves	English	Open or circle; two couples	Four-hand star; walking backward under arches ("turning sleeves inside out")	3, 5, 8, 9, 15
Hokey Pokey	English	Circle; no partners	Slower, more sophisticated version of "Looby Loo"	5
Makazice	Serbian	Line or open circle; no partners	Sideward cross step; simple jump series in part 3	4
Ma Navu	Israeli	Circle; no partners	Uses point or touch steps and rocking forward and back; quiet dance	4, 12
Miserlou (Kritikos)	Greek	Circle; open circle or lines; no partners	Slow touch step; grapevine, and two-step forward and back with swinging body turns	4, 5, 6, 9, 15, 16
Noriu Miego	Lithuanian	Groups of four; no partners	Bleking steps, clapping; star figure; dance may get progressively faster; may also be danced in circle with joined hands	9, 15
Patch Tanz	Jewish	Circle; partners; mixer	Slow walk around circle; forward and back and turning partners; clapping	1
Red River Valley	American	Groups of three in circle; trio mixer	Walk in threes; circle left and right; star figure; do-si-do; side persons change	3, 5, 7
Sicilian Circle	American	Couples in circle; couple mixer	Uses square dance figures, right and left, ladies chain; references give slightly different versions	10, 11, 14, 15
Tanko Bushi	Japanese	Lines; no partners	Coal miners' dance with pantomime of digging, throwing, pushing cart; clapping	15

375

Dances for Older Children (Continued)

Dance	Derivation	Formation	Remarks	References
Ten Pretty Girls (Hold That Line)	American	Lines; no partners	Touch step, side cross step and forward walk; may be done alone or side by side in line	3, 5, 7, 9, 15, 16
Twelfth Street Rag	American	Open; no partners	Strutting and touch steps; "Charleston" combination; jumps and clapping	13
Ve' David	Israeli	Circle; partners; mixer	Clapping; buzz step swing; similar to Oh Susanna mixer	4, 9, 13
Dances Based on the Skip or Slide				
Alabama Girl	American	Longways; partners	Uses reel figure as in "Virginia Reel" but omits preliminary figures; good lead-up for that dance	1, 5, 7, 10
Black Nag, The	English	Sets of three couples; longways	English figures of forward and back, siding and arming; a "cast-off" could be substituted for the last "hey for three"	9, 12, 13, 15
Bow Belinda (Ginny Crack Corn)	American	Contra; partners	Employs "Virginia Reel" figures except for reel; good lead-up for that dance	7, 8, 10, 15
Come, Let Us Be Joyful	German	Circle; groups of three; trio mixer	Walk; has center person swing right and left partners as in "The Wheat"	9, 11, 15
Csebogar	Hungarian	Circle; partners	Step-together used; skip may be substituted for Hungarian turn	9, 11, 15
Donegal Country Dance	Irish	Circle; partners	Sliding and balance steps; running turn and promenade	11

Galopede	English	Longways; partners	Crossover, swing, first couple turns down center; linked arms rather than two-hand swing preferable	6, 9
Gustaf's Skoal	Swedish	Square; partners	Forward and back; couples skipping through arches; skipping turn	8, 9, 11, 15
How Do You Do	American	Circle; partners; couple mixer	Uses simple country dance figures; shake hands with opposites to say "how do you do"	11
Noble Duke of York	English	Longways; partners	First couple swings down center; cast off	8, 10
Paw Paw Patch	American	Longways; partners	Partial word dramatization; cast off	15, 16
Virginia Reel (Sir Roger de Coverley)	English-American	Longways; partners	Head and foot couples do first figures; head couple reels down set; cast off; some references move all couples at once for first figures	4, 8, 9, 10, 11, 15, 16
We Won't Go Home Until Morning	English	Longways; partners	Walking, skipping, clapping; circle four and star figures	11
Wheat, The	Czech	Open or circle; groups of three	Walk; center turns right and left partners; center may progress if danced in circle	9

Dances Based on the Run and the 3/4 Run

Jugo	Rumanian	Circle; no partners	Schottische, toe taps; third part uses continuous side-cross runs	4, 13
La Cucaracha	Mexican-American	Open; partners	Combination of two-step with two stamps used in first part; 3/4 run forward and turning	11
La Raspa	Southwest American	Open; partners	Step similar to bleking but with feet kept on floor; walking and running turns	4, 5, 7, 8, 9, 15, 16, 17

Dances for Older Children (*Continued*)

Dance	Derivation	Formation	Remarks	References
Mayim	Israeli	Circle; no partners	Cross grapevine run; movement into center as "Mayim" (which means water) is sung; tapping, clapping, hopping	4, 5, 6, 13, 16
Norwegian Mountain March	Danish	Open; groups of three	One person in front and two behind; second figure of dance has interesting turns under joined arms; imitation of a guide taking travelers up a mountain and through tunnels	9, 11, 15
Savila Se Bela Loza	Serbian	Open circle or line; no partners	Runs in part 1; sideward schottische in part 2	13
Sellinger's Round	English	Circle; partners	English figures of sliding, doubling, siding, arming; repeated chorus figures using "set and turn single"	9, 11
Seven Steps	Austrian	Circle or open; partners	Run forward, backward, and turning	7, 9
Troika	Russian	Circle or open; groups of three	Side person runs under arches made by other two; troika means three horses abreast	4, 5, 9, 11, 13, 14, 15
Dances Based on the Step-Hop and Schottische				
Bleking	Swedish	Open; partners	Bleking step pattern followed by a step-hop turn	9, 11, 15
Bunny Hop	American	Line; no partners	Touch step with forward and backward jumps	5

Chester Schottische	American	Circle; groups of three; trio mixer	Toe touch and walk; two schottisches and four step-hops	10, 13
Crested Hen, The	Danish	Open; groups of three	Circle three; second figure uses winding under arms as in "Troika"	11, 13, 15, 17
Ersko Kolo	Yugo-slavian	Circle; no partners	Sideward cross-walk; stamping	2, 5, 8, 9, 11, 14
Hatter, The	Danish	Circle of four couples; partners	Several figures used, including grand right and left and men's and women's basket with buzz step; clapping and stamping	9, 11, 15
Highland Schottische, The	Scottish	Circle; partners; mixer	Toe touch and lift of the "Highland Fling" is used; linked-arm turns; dancers may progress to new partners	4, 11
Horra (Hora)	Balkan	Circle or open circle; no partners	One sideward schottische and one step-hop repeated continuously; one of the simplest of the horas. Although this dance is now considered to be the national dance of Israel its use of variations of a schottische and step-hop combination can be found in other Middle Eastern dances	4, 5, 8, 9, 13, 15, 17
Koroboushka	Russian	Circle; partners; mixer	"Hungarian break step" cross-apart-together, used at end of first part. Three-step turn can replace schottische in second part	2, 4, 5, 6, 9, 13, 15, 16
Kuma Echa	Israeli	Circle; no partners	Grapevine walk; forward and backward run; stamping	9, 12, 13, 15

Dances for Older Children (Continued)

Dance	Derivation	Formation	Remarks	References
Milanova Kolo	Yugo-slavian	Circle; no partners	Sideward cross-walk; schottische variation	2, 9, 12, 15
Old Time Schottische	American	Open; partners	Two schottisches and four step-hops in several simple figure variations	5
Rheinlander Schottische	German	Open; partners	Two schottisches and four step-hops used in a simple backward and forward space pattern	11, 16
Road to the Isles (The Far Northland)	Scottish	Open; partners	Heel touch and side cross-walk; schottische with quick turns	2, 4, 5, 7, 9, 14, 16
Rumonsko Kolo (Rumunjsko)	Rumanian	Open circle; no partners	Step-hop, schottische; rocking and stamping (two references use same step in reverse order)	4, 5, 12
Salty Dog Rag	American	Open or circle; partners	Variations of two schottisches and four step-hops sequence throughout. Lively "pop" style music	4, 8, 13
Schottische for Four	American	Open; two couples	Hands joined in square, all facing forward; lead couple drops inside hands and circles around behind second couple for repeat of dance	5
Seljancica (Serbian Kolo)	Yugo-slavian	Circle, open circle or lines, no partners	Three different versions of this kolo-type dance, each increasing in difficulty; four schottisches, four step-hops, and running steps used	5, 7, 9, 12, 13, 16
Setnja	Serbian	Line with arms linked; no partners	First part uses slow-slow-quick-quick-slow walk; second part faster with step-hops	2, 4, 12, 13, 16

Seven Jumps	Danish	Circle; no partners	Accumulative "jumps," such as lifting knees, kneeling, etc., alternated with a circle step-hop; variations in the tempo of the "jumps" add to the fun	8, 9, 11, 15
Shibolet Bassadet	Israeli	Circle; no partners	Dance celebrates ripening of sheaves of barley; dancers face in and out of circle; step-hop forward and backward	12, 13
Sicilian Tarantella	Italian	Two couples	Run used for forward and back, linked-arm turns, do-si-do; skip for left and right hand star; clapping, finger snapping; tambourines may be used by girls	8, 11
Swiss Changing Dance	Swiss	Circle; partners; mixer	Two sideward schottisches and four step-hops turning; boy progresses forward to new partner	11
Tancuj	Czech	Circle or line; partners	Sideward schottische and a running turn with linked arms	15
Tropanka	Bulgarian	Circle; no partners	Run, step-swing, and stamping without weight	9, 14, 15

Dances Based on the Two-Step and Polka

Czardas	Hungarian	Open; partners	Two-step with heel click or heel touch; turn with walk, bend walk, or Hungarian partner turn	11
Doudlebska Polka (Czech Polka)	Czech	Circle; partners; mixer	Walk, clapping pattern for men; women polka around circle to new partner; face-to-face and back-to-back polka may be used in part A	2, 3, 4, 5, 6, 9, 12, 13, 14, 16

Dances for Older Children (Continued)

Dance	Derivation	Formation	Remarks	References
Heel and Toe Polka	American	Open; partners	Heel and toe followed by a polka in closed position; continuous polka turns in second part	16
Hop, Mother Anika Hop Mor Anika	Swedish	Circle or open; partners	Walk; skip; clapping pattern; polka face-to-face and back-to-back	11, 15
Jessie Polka	American	Open; partners or more	Toe and heel taps in eight-count pattern followed by forward two-steps or polkas; may be done by several in line formations	4, 5, 9, 15
Jibi-Di, Jibi-Da	French	Circle or open; no partners	Two-step combined with a step-hop, swinging foot forward and backward; bleking step	8, 9, 15
Kalvelis	Lithuanian	Circle; partners	Polka used around in single circle, forward and back, in grand right and left, and in closed position, each followed by a chorus of clapping and linked-arm turns	1, 4, 6, 7, 9, 13, 14
Lott Ist Tod	Swedish	Double circle; partners	Slow and quick slides; face-to-face and back-to-back polka or even a skip will simplify second part	9
Nebesko Kolo	Yugo-slavian	Open circle or lines; no partners	Stepping forward and back and two-step balance in place	4, 9, 13
Polka Zu Dreien	German	Circle or open; groups of three	Heel and toe and forward polka; star and circle of three	2, 4, 9

Sekerecka	Czech	Open; partners	Two-step used with one moving forward and the other backward; bleking step and running turn	11
Susan's Gavotte (*Lili Marlene*)	American	Circle; partners; mixer	Walk and slide; step swing; two-step face-to-face and back-to-back or in closed position	5, 9, 13, 15
Tantoli	Swedish	Circle or open; partners	Heel-and-toe polka; fast step-hop turn	11, 15
Teton Mountain Stomp	American	Circle or open; partners	Uses closed and right and left reverse social dance positions; side walk and stamp	5, 9, 13, 15

Dances Based on the Waltz, Waltz Balance, and Mazurka

Kaca	Czech	Circle; partners; mixer	Waltz balance forward and back; grand right and left with 3/4 run	11
Little Man in a Fix	Danish	Open; two couples; couple mixer	Couples turn in wheel and women run under arches; fast waltz in closed position or waltz balance in open position	4, 5, 9, 11, 15
Mexican Waltz (*Chapanecas*)	Southwest American	Circle or open; partners; mixer	Step-swing in 3/4 meter; waltz balance; waltz in closed position; clapping pattern	10, 16
Rye Waltz, The	American	Circle or open; partners	Heel-toe and slide alternated with waltz in closed position; music changes from duple to triple meter	7
Spanish Circle (*Waltz, The*)	American	Circle or open; two couples	Cross over, star, right and left figures; waltz in closed position; possible couple mixer	5, 9, 15

Dance	Derivation	Formation	Remarks	References
Varsouvianna	American	Open; partners	The American version of the varsovienne, often called *Put Your Little Foot*, differs somewhat from the Scandinavian; it has been elaborated into many different figures and regional styles	5, 9, 13, 14, 15, 16
Varsovienne	Swedish	Open; partners	The varsovienne uses a variation of the mazurka combined with waltz steps; there are other almost identical Scandinavian versions	4, 5, 9, 13, 14
Veleta Waltz	American	Open; partners	Waltz walk and step-draw in open position alternated with waltz in closed position	5

Individual American Mixers[a]

Dance	Formation	Partners Change By	References
Bingo	Circle; partners	Grand right and left	10, 11, 15
Captain Jinks	Circle; partners	Boy takes corner lady (similar to the square dance except it is done in circle)	7, 8, 11, 15
Circassian Circle	Circle; partners	Boy swinging corner lady	2, 3, 9

[a] These dances are based on the walk, but occasionally use the slide or skip. Couple and trio mixers, some of European origin, will be found under dances based on the walk, skip, schottische, polka, and waltz.

For other individual mixers see: *Ach Ja* (German), *Highland Schottische* (Scottish), *Kaca* (Czech), *Patch Tanz* (Jewish), *Susan's Gavotte* (American), *Swiss Changing Dance* (Swiss). (Almost any partner circle dance may be danced as a mixer with some adjustment at the end of the dance.)

Come, My Love	Circle; partners	Boys and girls moving around circle in opposite directions	10
Cotton-Eyed Jo	Circle; partners	Grand right and left	6, 9, 13, 15
Glow Worm	Circle; partners	Boy and girl moving one place to their right	9, 15
Good-Night, Ladies	Circle; partners	Boy and girl moving on to left several times and shaking hands with each new person met	7, 15
Irish Washerwoman, The	Circle; partners	Boy promenading corner lady	5, 7
Jingle Bells	Circle; partners	Boy moving on to next girl	15
Oklahoma Mixer	Circle; partners	Boy turning girl to face new partner	2, 9, 15, 16
Oh Susanna	Circle; partners	Grand right and left	7, 8, 9, 10, 15, 16
Patrycake Polka	Circle; partners	Boy and girl moving one place to their left	3, 5, 10, 15, 17
Shake Them 'Simmons Down	Circle; partners	Boy promenading corner lady	1, 11
Shoo Fly	Circle; partners	Boy putting partner on his left after swing	7, 10, 11, 15, 16
Tennessee Wig Walk	Circle; partners	Turning partner with "wig walk" and moving on to new partner	5, 8, 13

American Country Dances: Square Dances with Singing Calls

Name	Some of the Figures	References
Captain Jinks (square)	Do-si-do; allemande left and right; balance, swing, and promenade	8, 10
Darling Nellie Gray	Allemande left and grand right and left; promenade; circle four; right hand over and left hand back with opposite	8, 10
Girl I Left Behind Me, The	Balance and swing; allemande left and grand right and left	11
Hi Ya	Couples separate and promenade outside the set; swing	7

Dances for Older Children (*Continued*)

Name	Some of the Figures	References
Hinky, Dinky, Parley-Voo	Do-si-do; allemande left and grand right and left; also allemande right in first version	8, 10
Hot Time in the Old Town	Allemande left and right; grand right and left; girls to center, boys promenade around; do-si-do	5, 8, 10
Two Head Gents Cross Over (Life on the Ocean Wave)	Two head gents (or head ladies) cross over; swing; promenade (ladies grand chain in "break" may be omitted)	7, 8, 10
Northern Lights	Look at Northern Lights; clapping; swing; allemande left and grand right and left	7
Oh, Johnny	Allemande left, do-si-do, swing, and promenade	3; 5
Pass the Left-Hand Lady Under	Forming threes on sides; forward six and single men do-si-do; left-hand lady under the arch; swing; promenade	10
Pop Goes the Weasel	Circle, swing, and promenade; first girl (and then first boy) visits and is "popped" under arch by other couple	8, 15
Red River Valley (Square)	Allemande left and grand right and left; circle four; swing; promenade	10
When Johnny Comes Marching Home	Head couples forward and sides divide; star, swing	7

American Country Dances: Contra Dances (Longways) *See Dances Based on Skip*

Alabama Girl   *Paw Paw Patch*
Bow Belinda   *Virginia Reel*
Galopede   *We Won't Go Home Until*
Noble Duke of York   *Morning*

Folk Dance Record Companies[4]

Bowmar, 622 Rodier Dr., Glendale, Calif. 91201

Dancecraft, Canadian F.D.S. Audio Visual, 185 Spadina Ave., Toronto 2B, Ontario, Canada

Educational Activities, Freeport, N.Y. 11520 (includes World of Fun and Honor Your Partner records)

Educational Dance, P.O. Box 6062, Bridgeport, Conn. 06611

Festival, 161 Turk St., San Francisco, Calif. 94102

Folk Dancer, Box 201, Flushing, N.Y. 11352

Hoctor, 115 Manhattan Ave., Waldwick, N.J. 07463

Imperial, 127 N. Western Ave., Los Angeles, Calif. 90004

Kismet, 227 E. 14th St., New York, N.Y. 10003

MacGregor, 728 S. Western Ave., Hollywood, Calif. 90005

RCA Records, Educational Dept., 1133 Avenue of the Americas, New York, N.Y. 10036

Rhythms Productions, Cheviot Corp., Box 34485, Los Angeles, Calif. 90034

Tikva International Record Industries, 32 Oxford St., Lynn, Mass. 01901 (especially for Middle East folk dance)

Windsor, 5530 Rosemead Blvd., Temple City, Calif. 91780

Worldtone (Folk Music International), 56-40 187th St., Flushing, N.Y. 11365.

Supplementary Materials

Books

Bambra, Audrey, and Muriel Webster, *Teaching Folk Dancing,* B. T. Batsford, 4 Fitzhardinge St., London, England

Berk, Fred, *Ha-Rikud—The Jewish Dance,* Union of American Hebrew Congregations, 1972

Ellfeldt, Lois, *Folk Dance,* Dubuque, Iowa, Brown, 1969

Joukowsky, Anatol M., *The Teaching of Ethnic Dance,* New York, J. Lowell Pratt, 1965

Ethnic Records Recommended for African and American Indian Dance

African Dances and Games, S & R Records 2000A, 2000B, 1607 Broadway, New York, N.Y. 10019 (for older children, "Ampe," "Adenkum," "Adawe," and the rhythm game "Passing the Stone" could be used). Music and instructions.

[4] These companies will send catalogues to schools upon request.

African Heritage Dances, Educational Activities Records No. AR 36, P.O. Box 392, Freeport, N.Y. 11520. Music and instructions.

Authentic Indian Dances and Folklore, Educational Activities Records No. 9070 (see above address). Accompaniment and manual of instructions.

Periodicals

"Let's Dance," Folk Dance Federation of California, 1604 Felton St., San Francisco, Calif. 94134.

"New York Folk Dance News," 777 Foster Ave., Brooklyn, N.Y. 11230.

"Viltis—A Folklore Magazine," V. F. Beliajus, P.O. Box 1226, Denver, Colo. 80201.

Films

Folk Dance Today, Bailey Film Associates, 11559 Santa Monica Blvd., Los Angeles, Calif. 90025. 16 mm film, 16 min., color, sound. (Recommended for children.)

Information about references for other ethnic films may be found on p. 427.

Part VII | AIDS TO DANCE TEACHING

Chapter Preview

**Conditions for Movement and Rhythmic
Skill Attainment**

Suggested Standards

For Grades 1 and 2 (after two years of dance)

For Grades 3 and 4 (after four years of dance)

For Grades 5 and 6 (after six years of dance)

27 Suggested Standards for Certain Dance Skills

Children appear to have different ways of learning to gallop. Most seem to introduce a galloping step into their running or as an emphasis on the strong beat of the music. Only later do they learn the basic movement of throwing the weight on to the forward foot when galloping. . . . Skipping enters later than galloping into a child's motor repertory. At four years of age only a few children are able to skip; . . . while at six years nearly all children have learned this basic step.[1]

Many teachers feel the need for certain standards of performance with which to measure children's progress in acquiring dance skills and their own skill in teaching them. The developing of these skills should not take preference over the important experiences of exploring movement and of making and learning dances. In fact, many of the skills included here should evolve from an efficient program of movement exploration.

The skills included are those that can easily be checked for adequacy of performance. For that reason they consist almost entirely of basic locomotor movements, dance steps, and rhythmic responses using such movements. The child's mastery and use of other body skills, his inventiveness and imagination in the use of movement elude such standards as are set forth here. So many variables are present that competent evaluation of a child's ability depends, for the most part, upon a teacher's keen observation and aesthetic sensitivity. On the other hand, a child can either perform a simple schottische in time to the music, or he cannot, and needs help.

---

[1] Marian E. Breckenridge and E. Lee Vincent, *Child Development,* 5th ed., Philadelphia, Saunders, 1965, p. 236.

Conditions for Movement and Rhythmic Skill Attainment

Certain conditions should be obtained if children are to reach the performance levels listed on the following pages with sufficient time as well to carry on the creative aspects of the dance curriculum:

A room large enough so that children can move with freedom.

Percussion instruments and/or a piano, for improvised accompaniment; possibly a metronome, if one is available.

A recording machine, for accompaniment.

At least two dance periods weekly, preferably on two successive days.

A period of at least twenty-five to thirty-five minutes.

A class of no more than thirty children unless an assisting teacher is present.

While grade level is an artificial measuring stick and has not been used in this book, it is still the classification system of most of our schools. The standards are based on what most children, under the stated circumstances, should be able to do at the end of the second grade (after two years), and at the end of the fourth grade (after four years), and at the end of the sixth grade (after six years). A great many skills are listed. For measuring achievement only a few from each group need to be used. It should be kept in mind that standards for grade levels describe only a certain degree of group accomplishment. Some children will be able to do more advanced movement, some perhaps substantially less. Also, movement style is understandably not considered.

Standards under *movement skills* include a variety of locomotor movements. However, only basic locomotor movements, the skip, slide, and gallop dance steps, and a few nonlocomotor movements are included under *rhythmic skills*, because rhythmic accuracy, if achieved in these movements, generally carries over to the more complicated ones.

As with all skill learning, certain coordinations of movement which are easily achieved in the lower grades may become more difficult as children grow older because of their uneven physiological development. Teachers should keep this fact in mind when applying these performance standards at the upper-grade levels.

For Grades 1 and 2 (after two years of dance)

After two years of dance children have made good progress if they can perform the following movements well and make the following rhythmic responses accurately. Through exploration and improvisation and the learning of simple dance forms, they will have had many other dance experiences which will aid performance immeasurably.

Movement Skills

Basic Locomotor Movements

Walk

Basic walk

VARIATIONS

In space design

Changes in direction: in place; backward; sideward (step-together); turning around

Changes in level: on tiptoe; with knees half bent; with knees fully bent

Changes in dimension: steps shorter than natural; steps longer than natural

In timing

Changes in tempo: steps faster than natural; steps slower than natural

In shape

Simple variations such as: knees bent up high in front; body bent forward; hands on knees; arms high over head

In walking with others

With one other: side by side, inside hands joined, walking forward; facing, both hands joined, walking around in a small circle

With two others: side by side, inside hands joined, walking forward; in a circle, hands joined, walking around circle

With many others: in a circle, hands joined, walking around circle; in a line with one child leading, hands joined, walking forward

Run

Basic run

VARIATIONS

In space design

Changes in direction: in place, turning around

In shape
   Simple variations such as: knees bent up high in front; arms extended
      forward or backward
In running with others
   With one other: side by side, inside hands joined, running forward

Jump

Basic jump
   VARIATIONS
   In space design
      Changes in direction: forward; turning around
      Changes in level: knees fully bent; knees half bent
   In shape
      Simple variations such as: landing with feet alternately apart and to-
         gether; swinging arms out and in as feet jump apart and together

Hop

Basic hop
   VARIATIONS
   In space design
      Changes in direction: forward; turning around
   In shape
      Simple variations such as: changing from one foot to the other after a
         certain number of hops; with arm on side of hopping foot extended
         sideward

Dance Steps

Gallop

Basic gallop
   VARIATIONS
   In galloping with others
      With one other: side by side, inside hands joined, galloping forward; one
         in back of other, both facing forward, both hands joined, galloping
         forward
      With two others: one in front and two in back, or vice versa, all facing
         forward, hands joined, galloping forward

Slide

Basic slide
   VARIATIONS
   In sliding with others
      With one other: facing, both hands joined, arms extended toward other
         person or extended sideward, sliding sideward

Skip

Basic skip
> VARIATIONS
> In space design
>> Changes in direction: turning around
> In skipping with others
>> With one other: side by side, inside hands joined, skipping forward; side by side, inside hands crossed and joined with outside hands, skipping forward; right or left hands joined, skipping in small circles; facing, both hands joined, skipping in small circle
>> With two or three others: side by side, inside hands joined, skipping forward; in circle, hands joined, skipping around circle; in line, one child leading, hands joined, skipping forward

Rhythmic Skills

Pulse Beats

Response to successive beats with moderate intervals (quarter-note beats)
> Moving alone
>> Walking in place, forward, turning around
>> Jumping in place
>> Hopping in place
>> Galloping forward
>> Skipping forward, turning around
>> Sliding sideward
>> Combining any two of the above movements without a pause between
> Moving with others
>> With one other: side by side, inside hands joined, walking forward, skipping forward; facing, both hands joined, walking around a small circle
>> With two others: side by side, inside hands joined, walking forward
>> With many others: in a circle, hands joined, walking around the circle

Response to successive beats with short intervals (eighth-note beats)
> Moving alone
>> Running in place, forward
>> Jumping (small jumps) in place
> Moving with one other
>> Side by side, inside hands joined, running forward

Response to successive beats with long intervals (half-note beats)
> Moving alone
>> Slow walking in place, forward
>> Swinging parallel arms from side to side

Swaying body from side to side
Pushing both arms forward and pulling back
Combining any two of the above movements without a pause between
Rhythmic games
Self-Accompaniment, Follow the Beats, Moving Groups I

Musical Phrasing

Response to two-phrase selections
Move forward on first phrase, stand and clap pulse beats on second, and continue
Move forward on first phrase, move in place on second, and continue
Walk forward on first phrase, jump, skip, slide, or gallop on second, and continue
Rhythmic games
Leading Phrases

Rhythmic Patterns

Response to two-speed patterns
Combining two runs and a walk
Combining two walks and a slow walk
Combining two walks, two runs, and a walk
Rhythmic games
Echo Game (with very simple patterns), Name Patterns (Examples: Santa Claus, Mary Ann Parker, Little Tommy Tucker)

Accents

Formal response to accents should probably not be given until the third grade.

For Grades 3 and 4 (after four years of dance)

After four years of dance children have made good progress if, in addition to the skills acquired in Grades 1 and 2, they can perform the following movements well and make the following rhythmic responses accurately.

Movement Skills

Basic Locomotor Movements

Walk

VARIATIONS
In space design
Changes in direction: sideward, crossing feet in front or in back

In shape
> Variations such as: legs crossing on every step; legs kicking up in front; arms held in any position; arms swinging in any direction

In walking with others
> With one other: side by side, arms linked, walking forward; one behind the other, both facing forward, one hand on shoulder of person in front
>
> With two others: side by side, arms linked, walking forward
>
> With three others: right or left side toward center, and right or left hands joined in the center, walking around (star formation)
>
> With many others: in circle, hands joined, walk forward toward the center and backward from the center

Run

VARIATIONS

In space design
> Changes in direction: backward
>
> Changes in level: crouching low
>
> Changes in dimension: steps shorter than natural; steps longer than natural

In shape
> Variations such as: legs kicking up in front or back; arms held in any position

In running with others
> With one other: facing, both hands joined, running around in small circle; right or left sides together, right or left elbows linked, running around in circle
>
> With two others: one in front and two in back, or vice versa, all facing forward with hands joined, running forward
>
> With many others: in circle, hands joined, running around circle

Jump

VARIATIONS

In space design
> Changes in direction: backward; sideward
>
> Changes in dimension and timing: jumping close to floor (fast tempo); jumping high into the air (slower tempo)

In shape
> Variations such as: landing with one foot forward and the other backward, and vice versa; landing with feet alternately apart and crossing; clapping on every other jump; swinging parallel arms from side to side or forward and back

In jumping with others
> With one other: side by side, inside hands joined, jumping forward; facing, both hands joined, jumping around in small circle

Hop

VARIATIONS
In space design
> Changes in direction: sideward; backward

In shape
> Variations such as: lifting free leg forward or sideward, or knee bent up in front; arms folded in front of chest or hands clasped behind back

Dance Steps

Gallop

VARIATIONS
In shape
> Variations such as: clapping thighs as feet gallop; swinging one arm overhead (lassoing)

In galloping with others
> With two or three others: side by side, facing forward, arms linked, galloping forward and wheeling in half circles or circles

Slide

VARIATIONS
In space design
> Changes in facing: sliding once with one side forward and then again with other side forward, continuing in same direction (simple polka)

In shape
> Variations such as: extending arms sideward; clapping on each slide

In sliding with others
> With one other: side by side, inside hands joined, sliding face to face and back to back (polka with hinge turn)
> With many others: in a circle, hands joined, sliding around circle in both directions

Skip

VARIATIONS
In space design
> Changes in level, dimension, and timing: crouching low; skipping high

In shape
> Variations such as: arms folded on chest or behind back; clapping on
> each skip

In skipping with others
> With one other: right or left arms linked, skipping around in small circle
> With many others: in circle, hands joined, skipping around circle in both
> directions; in line, with one child leading, hands joined, skipping
> forward

3/4 Run (simple version) and *Variations*

Some of the variations in direction and in dancing with others suggested for
the simple version of this step in Chapter 10

Step-Hop and *Variations*

Some of the variations in direction suggested for this step in Chapter 10
> VARIATIONS IN DANCING WITH OTHERS
> With one other: side by side, inside hands joined, moving forward or
> backward; facing, both hands joined, moving in place, turning
> around, or one moving forward and the other backward
> With many others: in circle, hands joined, moving around circle in both
> directions and forward and backward

Schottische and *Variations*

Some of the variations in direction suggested for this step in Chapter 10
> VARIATIONS IN DANCING WITH OTHERS
> With one other: side by side, inside hands joined, moving forward;
> facing, both hands joined, turning around; right or left arms linked,
> turning around

Waltz Balance and *Variations*

> VARIATIONS IN DIRECTION
> One balance taken forward, one backward, and repeated continuously
> VARIATIONS IN DANCING WITH OTHERS
> With one or more other persons: side by side, inside hands joined,
> balancing forward and backward

Rhythmic Skills

Pulse Beats

Response to successive beats of different intervals without pause
> Moving alone
> Combine walking and running in even phrases

Combine walking and slow walking in even phrases

Combine walking, running, walking, and slow walking in even phrases

Response to successive beats with moderate intervals (quarter-note beats)

Moving alone

Walking backward, sideward

Jumping forward, turning around

Hopping forward, turning around

Moving with others

With one other: side by side, inside arms linked, walking, skipping, or galloping forward; facing, both hands joined, skipping, sliding, or jumping in a small circle; with right or left arms linked, walking or skipping in a small circle; facing, both hands joined, walking sideward (step-together), sliding sideward; one in back of other, both facing forward, hands joined, galloping forward; side by side, inside hands joined, sliding face to face and back to back (polka with hinge turn)

With two others: side by side, inside hands joined or arms linked, walking, skipping, or galloping forward; one in back and two in front, or vice versa, all facing forward, hands joined, skipping or galloping forward; in circle, hands joined, skipping or sliding around circle; in line with one child leading, hands joined, walking, skipping, or galloping forward

With many others: in circle, hands joined, skipping or sliding around circle; in line, with one child leading, hands joined, walking forward; in line, side by side, hands joined, walking forward and backward

Response to successive beats with short intervals (eighth-note beats)

Moving alone

Running backward; turning around

Jumping (small jumps) forward, backward, turning around

Moving with others

With one other: facing, hands joined, running in small circle; with right or left arms linked, running in small circle

With two others: side by side, arms linked, running forward

With many others: in circle, hands joined, running around circle

Response to successive beats with long intervals (half-note or dotted half-note beats)

Moving alone

Slow walking backward; sideward (step-together or crossing feet); turning around

Moving with others

With one other: facing, both hands joined, slow walking sideward (step-together); turning around

With many others: in circle, hands joined, slow walking sideward (step-together); in line, side by side, hands joined, slow walking forward and backward

Rhythmic games

Levels, the Crazy Clock

Accents

Response to accent only, in a group of four beats

By making a hand response (beat downward or clap)

By jumping, walking, or performing a nonlocomotor movement

Response to accent only in a group of two beats as above

Response to accent only in a group of three beats as above

Rhythmic games

Square, Zigzag

Rhythmic Patterns

Response to two-speed patterns

Combinations of walks and runs within a four-beat group; within a three-beat group (see Chapter 14)

Rhythmic games

Name Patterns (simple ones), Nursery Rhymes (simple first lines), Echo Game

Musical Phrasing

Response to four-phrase selections

Alternating forward movement with movement in place on successive phrases

Moving in two groups, one group on first phrase, other group on second, and so on

Response to four-phrase selections with two of the four phrases identical

Using appropriate locomotor movement forward for the identical phrases, and a nonlocomotor movement or a turn around for the other two

Using four directions with changing locomotor movements to define the four phrases

Rhythmic games

Copy Cat, Answer Me

For Grades 5 and 6 (after six years of dance)

After six years of dance children should be able to perform, in addition to the skills achieved in Grades 1–4, many of the activities listed in Part III, experienced through either exploration or direct instruction, and at least the introductory activities in Part IV.

Movement Skills

Basic Locomotor Movements

Walk

VARIATIONS

In space design

Changes in direction: sideward, feet crossing alternately in front and in back (grapevine walk); change facing from forward to backward, sideward, and turning around, while continuing in same direction

In shape

Variations such as: knees bent up at sides; legs kicking up at sides; both arms swinging parallel or in opposition in any direction

In walking with others

With one other: side by side, in open social dance position, walking forward; right sides together in social dance position, walking around (turning)

Run

VARIATIONS

In space design

Change in direction: sideward, crossing feet in front or in back; change facing from forward to backward while continuing in same direction

Changes in dimension, level, timing, and force: doing several continuous leaps using slower timing, greater elevation from the floor, and longer steps than are used in the run; combining a leap with one or two preparatory runs in a continuous sequence

In shape

Variations such as: crossing legs on each step; bending knees up at sides; bending body sharply forward or backward

In running with others

With one other: right or left sides together, inside hands on outside hip of partner, running around (turning)

With two or three others: side by side, arms linked, running forward and wheeling in half circles or circles

With many others: in circles, hands joined, running around circle and forward and back in circle; in line with one person leading, hands joined, running forward

Jump

VARIATIONS

In space design

Changes in direction: with half and full turns while in the air

Changes in dimension, level, timing, and force: combining a certain number of quick jumps with half that number of slow jumps; combining a fast jump with a slow jump (uneven intervals); gradually retarding quick jumps to slower jumps, and vice versa

In shape

Variations such as: extending legs sideward while in air; clicking heels together while in air; arms swinging in outward circles or forward and backward

Hop

VARIATIONS

In shape

Variations such as: holding free foot sideward or backward; swinging free leg backward on one hop and forward on the next; folding arms around knee of free leg

Dance Steps

3/4 Run, Step-hop, Schottische

Variations in direction and dancing with others suggested for these steps in Chapter 10 and not included in the material for Grades 3 and 4

Two-Step, Polka, Waltz, Mazurka, and Their Variations

Some of the variations in direction and dancing with others suggested for these steps in Chapter 10

Rhythmic Skills

Pulse Beats

Response to successive beats of different intervals without pause

Moving alone

Combining several locomotor movements, including a run, in phrases of unequal length (example: 6 skips, 12 runs, 4 walks, 4 slow walks)

Moving from a slow walk to a run (four times as fast) without pause, and vice versa

Moving with others
> With one other: in at least three different place relationships and three different contacts combining two locomotor movements of different intervals (walk and run, slow walk and skip, etc.)
> With many others: in circle or open circle, hands joined, combining a slow walk, a walk, and a run

Rhythmic games
> Moving Groups II, Clap and Move

Accents

Doing any learned dance step accurately on the accent by listening to the music and starting without a verbal signal

Response to accents in a group of three beats
> Doing a grand right and left, joining hands on the first beat of a group of three beats

Response to other beats only (accent played by accompaniment) in a group of four beats
> Walking or bouncing in place or improvising nonlocomotor movements
> Walking forward

Response to accents in a series of unequal groups
> Making a movement response to accents in groups of two and four, two and three, three and four
> Doing a simple version of Cumulative Rhythm (see p. 204)

Rhythmic games
> Phrases of Five

Rhythmic Patterns

Response to three-speed patterns
> Doing combinations of walks, runs, and slow walks within four-, six-, and eight-beat groups (see Chapter 14)

Canon
> Doing the simplest version accurately (see Chapter 14)

Step a song
> Stepping out the rhythmic pattern of a round or a short simple song

Rhythmic games
> Canon I, Threes and Sevens

Musical Phrasing

Response to music of conventional phrasing
> Moving in two groups as described in No. 9 of the procedure for activities in Chapter 15

Response to music with an unconventional number of phrases such as three or

five, and to music with phrases of unequal length, using any of the simpler
procedures for activity listed in Chapter 15

Rhythmic games

The Phrase Game

A Jumping Classroom

Chapter Preview

Some Teaching Problems

Boys with Girls
Negative Attitudes
Noise
Child Demonstrators
Unit Conclusions
Rates of Progress

School Performances

Participation of Children
Costumes
Interruption of Regular Schedules
Audiences

DETROIT PUBLIC SCHOOLS

Active and Alert

28 *Problems and Performances*

Some Teaching Problems

Boys with Girls

Studies of human growth and development show that boys and girls differ in velocity and rhythm of growth. Most girls are more mature physiologically than boys of the same age. Therefore, their dance movement performance may be superior to that of the boys in their classes. If boys are to like dance, it is essential that competition between them and girls be avoided. Actually today, the activity interests of boys and girls are drawing closer together, and dances and dance themes which have appeal for them both are not hard to find. In any case, it is more important that girls make and learn dances in company with boys than that they learn more complicated movement patterns of their own by themselves.

While boys undoubtedly enjoy movements of force and aggression, our newer concepts of the masculine role in human society point to the importance of experiences in delicate, soft, fine, pliant movement as well. Also, modern girls like the strong free movements of work and play, of characters and events as much as boys do.

Negative Attitudes

A special problem is presented by children who have a negative attitude toward dance. This attitude may be the result of unfortunate past experiences, or the prejudiced opinions of elders, or the fact that dancing is forbidden by some religious groups in the community. The teacher should proceed with caution in such situations. Although substituting for the word dance such terms as *rhythms, rhythmic activities, rhythmic play* is distasteful to this author, it may be necessary when the word *dance* is in disfavor. But the teacher must know she is indulging in camouflage.

The dance activities chosen should be as unlike the children's preconceived ideas of dance as possible. Self-testing activities for rhythmic skills, simple movement games, exploration of nonlocomotor movements, especially those related to work and sports, and movements made to school cheers are examples. Vigorous and challenging nonpartner dances may be tried. Dancing with a partner of the opposite sex should be postponed until the class shows readiness for it.

Pointing out identical movement elements in dance and sports often helps to stimulate the interest of the boys in the group. The similarity of pivots and turns in dance and sports, of the two-step to the shift in basketball, of arm swings to the pitcher's warm-up, of leaping to hurdling, of the necessity in both dance and games for quick changes in direction are obvious examples. Of course, if there is a respected male teacher who can and will give his enthusiastic support to dance as a virile and rewarding activity, the battle is won. And to judge from the following quotation, the change in attitude is occurring more quickly than could be hoped.

> As recently as a decade ago, the world of modern dance and ballet was the exclusive preserve of a relatively small group of *aficionados*. The mere appearance on a stage of a dancer in tights—especially a male dancer—was enough to make a captive audience squirm. The prospect of such a spectacle kept the public away in droves and condemned dancers to appear for starvation wages in tiny recital halls. Today dance has become the hottest ticket in town from coast to coast, and not just in the sophisticated big cities. Even on college campuses, home grounds of the counterculture with its electric-guitar anthems, dance concerts are outselling rock concerts.[1]

Noise

One by-product of creative work in dance with children is noise. Teachers who are only happy when children sit, stand, or move in orderly lines, who will allow a child to be heard only when permission is granted, will have great difficulty teaching creative dance. The process of exploring

[1] World Progress Report, *World Magazine,* Vol. 2, No. 7, March 27, 1973, p. 4.

and manipulating movement cannot be carried on in lines or circles, nor can the enthusiasm of sharing new discoveries, knowledge, ideas be continually frustrated by having to raise hands and wait for permission to speak.

When groups work together there will be much talk, even some argument, and the instruments used for accompaniment will often be banged on with complete disregard for other persons. An experienced teacher soon learns to distinguish between work noise and noise for its own sake. She never worries about the former. When argument interferes with others' progress or when a group reaches an impasse, she may step in and help, after observing for a sufficient time to be sure that adult direction is needed. Even here it is probably better to let children learn for themselves that a group goal is rarely achieved without compromise.

An After-School Group Rehearsing

THOMAS HALSTED

Child Demonstrators

When working in any of the arts, a teacher is naturally inclined to be charmed by the creative talent of a particular child. When children are exploring movement or making dances, she will perhaps call too often on one child to demonstrate for the others. The rest of the children, who also wish to please the teacher, are then likely to imitate the chosen one rather than to draw upon their own creative powers. When demonstration is part of her procedure, the sensitive teacher will call on several children to demonstrate different interpretations. With a large number of things to choose from, a child will find imitation much more difficult. On the other hand, seeing many successful efforts demonstrated may stimulate his inventive faculties and make it possible for him to carry out his own ideas more successfully than before.

Unit Conclusions

When a particular unit in dance-making or -learning is begun, a natural conclusion is an informal program of some kind after the unit materials have been sufficiently explored. The dances which have achieved some success may be shown in a simple program sequence to class members, to other children who have similar interests in dance, or possibly to invited guests. For such a program, titles that come quickly to mind are "A Circus Parade or Performance," "Halloween Happenings," "Masks and Motions," "New and Old Song Dances," "Around the World in 60 Minutes," "Circles and Squares," "Our Favorite Characters," "Human Shapes, Moving and Still," "Moon Journey," "Aids to Ecology," "A Haiku Happening," "A Seasonal Celebration." Children enjoy inventing such project titles. The dances may well be part of a larger project involving other curriculum experiences. In that case their performance will be part of the conclusion of the project.

Rates of Progress

A word to the teacher who wants her class to make rapid progress and to have a great many dance experiences as soon as possible. The creative process, like the mills of the gods, grinds slowly. Children do not all produce at the same rate. Some will still be exploring movement while others are making sequences with it. All should be allowed to develop at their own rate, and they will if the atmosphere is relaxed and free, with each child secure in the knowledge that his contribution is important in the whole process. Children cannot be forced into things for which they are not ready. The wise teacher starts with the children where they are, carefully assesses their interests and abilities, and proceeds to build dance experiences with and for them.

School Performances

From time to time, older children are called upon to show dances they have made or learned to people other than their peers. Because it is a performing art, dance is a favorite part of the program when parents visit or when an auditorium performance, a school play, a demonstration, or an operetta is given. Requests for dance programs from administrators or parents are sometimes so extravagant and so contrary to good educational practice as to make the dance teacher's burden heavy. The teacher, who should be considered the authority in the matter, must then tactfully try to educate parents and others as to what is and what is not good dance education. Otherwise

A Costumed Trio

IRVING BERG

children will be exploited for their entertainment value and the dance program will be lost in a morass of practice and drill on dances which may have no relation to the children's interests or abilities. An equally unsound alternative is to permit a few children whose parents can afford dance lessons to represent the school's dance activities. An honest school performance must illustrate what all the children are doing.

It is highly questionable whether younger children should participate in public performances. Often the values that may be imparted are apt to be detrimental. For them it is much better if audiences (preferably small groups) observe a lesson taught in its natural setting with no embellishments or special effects.

For older children, however, performing for an audience which includes parents and friends can be a memorable event. Showing one's abilities to sympathetic and uncritical eyes is a test of one's mettle and adds immeasurably to self-esteem and confidence. There is always the chance that nervousness may impair performance, but an understanding audience is indulgent and rarely makes comparisons.

The children, however, should be consulted about what they will take part in; and unless a definite assignment must be given they should be allowed to choose. If it is at all feasible, programs should be based upon dances the children have already composed or learned. When a new dance must be taught for a program, it should be chosen first because it is right for the children who are to learn it and only secondarily because it is right for the program.

Participation of Children

Children who are left out of a program instead of being chosen to perform are likely to be hurt. Every effort should be made to have all the children take part. If that is impossible because of space or for other reasons, two performances should be arranged so that all may participate either actively or "backstage." Children who are not dancing should be made to feel an important part of the project by assuming the responsibility for the many other learning experiences that attend any kind of public performance: printing programs, making posters, taking care of props, working with costumes, changing recordings or tapes, or acting as announcers. They should have special mention, either on the printed program or by having their names called as they "take a bow."

Sometimes if the dance teacher is enthusiastic and industrious, an after-

or before-school group of children may meet weekly for additional experiences in creative dance or folk dance. Anyone interested may be included, or the group may be formed initially by special invitation of the more skillful children. Such special classes are commendable, always providing that a child who wants very much to be included is allowed to join, unless there is an excellent reason why he should not. If the group becomes competitive and cliquish, its educational values diminish and it should be discontinued.

Special dance groups stimulate interest in dance just as intergroup games do for an athletic program. They also provide standards of dance skill which other children may wish to emulate if opportunity is occasionally given to see them perform. They may be used, of course, for any special school programs without interrupting the total school schedule.

The understanding and appreciation of audiences for dance begins in such small ways within the dance class and the school itself. They can be augmented by bulletin boards or exhibit case displays of dance pictures;[2] by films if they are provided by the Board of Education or if the school can afford to rent them; and possibly by lecture-demonstrations presented by dance groups from nearby high schools or colleges or from a particular ethnic community. Even semiprofessional and professional dance companies, touring in cities or college communities, will sometimes do "lec-dems" in selected elementary schools.[3]

Costumes

Costumes[4] for school performances should be kept at a minimum. They fulfill their function best when they are simple and inexpensive and take little time to make. A paper hat or a sash or a simple cape which children can make in school during an art or home economics class is just as effective as a complete outfit. If the costume is left to parents, certain children will be overdressed at the expense of others unless identical costumes are planned for all. It is essential that a simple pattern and a sample of inexpensive and easily obtained material be provided for them. The teacher should always deter-

[2] Children love to see pictures of themselves and their friends in dance performances. With the excellent cameras available today, picture exhibits can stimulate interest in the total dance program.

[3] Federally funded projects such as Impact and Artists in the Schools as well as state arts councils and the National Endowment for the Arts are making such programs possible in certain parts of the country.

[4] See Barbara Berk, *The First Book of Costume and Make-up*, New York, F. Watts, 1954.

mine first whether the parents can afford the money or time necessary to costume their children. Working mothers or those who lack sewing experience may politely refuse, in which case a child can be made extremely unhappy and insecure. This author has too often seen elaborate costumes used as a substitute for good dancing and has wondered how many harassed mothers and teachers and unhappy children there were behind the scenes.

Interruption of Regular Schedules

Every effort should be made to keep the performance from disrupting the regular program of school activities. Before any large-scale affair gets under way, the school personnel should seriously consider whether the values which accrue will be equal to the teachers' loss of time, effort, and often disposition, and the children's loss of participation in other classes. Overstimulation of the performers should be avoided as much as possible. There is a natural excitement in taking part in a performance. If the importance of the occasion is overemphasized, apprehension and nervous tension may result. While a good performance should certainly be everyone's goal, insistence on the kind of perfection that is attainable with children only after hours of tiresome drill will destroy their spontaneity and naturalness. If a calm, good-humored, and encouraging atmosphere prevails throughout the preparation, the experience will be happier for all.

Audiences

Sometimes insensitive or at least thoughtless adults will embarrass children by laughing heartily at a mistake or at something else not meant to be funny. The principal or a teacher in charge should give some tactful suggestions to an audience watching a children's performance so that the young participants will not be hurt or confused by audience reaction. Inexperienced children should be prepared in subtle ways so that they will not become traumatic or forgetful. Usually an intelligent audience is sympathetic to the efforts of children and teachers alike and receives them with respect and admiration.

Entered into with suitable planning which involves the children rather than merely uses them, these performances can be a significant stimulant for the total dance program as well as a notable occasion for the dancer. The opportunity to demonstrate one's ability to others is a strong motivating force and, if wisely used, may help to break down prejudices and negative attitudes toward dance. Once the child has indicated his willingness to give the project a try, it will influence his future efforts if it proves to be a happy and exhilarating experience.

Bringing It to a Stillness

DESMOND L. KELLY

Chapter Preview

Selecting and Playing Dance Music

References for Recordings

Dance Music
Music with Narration, Instructions, or Songs
Records of Sounds, Rhythmic Structure,
    and Certain Ethnic Styles
Some Distributors of Educational Records

References for Films

For Teachers' Viewing
For Children's Viewing

29 Resources for Music and Films

It was once thought that the inability to play the piano or the lack of an accompanist made dance teaching inconceivable. This was before technology provided excellent dance records and tapes, and before the era of modern dance made percussion instruments legitimate for accompaniment. There are many records designed for children's dance, descriptive of imagery, qualities of movement, or merely rhythmic accompaniment. Narration of some sort may be part of these records. Some are excellent and delightful for children to experiment with. Others lack musical value to a greater or lesser degree. If a teacher feels somewhat inadequate in judging useful records, materials in this chapter may be helpful.

Selecting and Playing Dance Music[1]

Music to accompany rhythmic skills and most *learned* dances, whether on records or piano should be well accented, with a crisp, even slightly staccato touch and little or no pedal. This does not mean that each accent should be forceful to the point of monotony. Accents should be easily identified in the accompaniment, however, so that movement can readily be synchronized with them.

It is of the greatest importance that accompanists do not skip a beat or delay or replay notes to correct a mistake in reading. The pulse beats must go

[1] The improvisational devices for the piano with musical examples have been deleted from this edition of *Dance in Elementary Education*. Helpful sections on piano improvisation may be found in *Music for Early Childhood*, Morristown, N.J., Silver Burdett, 1955; Pia Gilbert and Aileene Lockhart, *Music for the Modern Dance*, Dubuque, Iowa, Brown, 1961; Aileene Lockhart and Esther E. Pease, *Modern Dance—Building and Teaching Lessons*, Dubuque, Iowa, Brown, 1973.

on continuously and accurately. Mistakes are less likely when the accompanist is improvising, for it leaves her freer to watch the performance of the class and to keep with them. An accompanist who has had some rhythmic movement experience is the best choice for dance. Such a person feels the rhythm of the music and generally maintains it in spite of an occasional inaccurate note.

Triple measures should be used occasionally for basic locomotor movements rather than always using duple measures. This can be done with younger children without drawing their attention to the fact. In this way ¾ meter becomes familiar to them before they begin to examine its different placing of accents. The best music for skips, slides, and gallops is written in 6/8 meter. The quarter note followed by an eighth note in this timing supports the 2-1 ratio of these movement combinations.

It is not a good idea to use the same walk, run, or skip too often, because children will tend to identify movement with a particular melody rather than with the rhythmic quality of the music. However, it is permissible to change the timing of a familiar piece occasionally so that the children may perform several different locomotor movements to it.

Music for younger children should be simple in arrangement but offer obvious support to the movement it accompanies. Florid arrangements, heavy chords and strongly syncopated rhythms are unsuitable for this age level. Older children, however, enjoy music with *zip, bounce, swing,* as they describe it. College and traditional songs, military marches, and suitable popular music are good choices for locomotor movements and dance steps. Selections which have a feeling of syncopation are desirable if they do not contain highly complex arrangements.

Every dance room should have percussion instruments available. Some will be contributed by the children; others may be purchased at music stores and toy departments. Drums, rattles, wood-blocks, and other instruments made by teacher and children provide excellent and fresh accompaniment for most purposes.[2]

References for Recordings

It is in the choice of records that the musical taste and background of the teacher is immediately evident. If in doubt, it is wise to confer with the music teacher or supervisor as to the suitability of a record.

[2] See footnote 5 in Chapter 16.

Using records for teaching presents special problems:

1. Be sure you understand the record-playing machine you are using and treat it well. Repairs are costly.
2. Be sure you know the speed at which the record was recorded and adjust the machine accordingly.
3. A machine with speed control is highly desirable unless you are sure the tempo of your records is accurate.
4. The placement of the machine is important unless it is one with spring construction. If it is too near the dancers (particularly when a large group is folk dancing), floor vibrations may cause the needle to jump. Dancers lose their place in the music and often cannot continue. A heavy sponge rubber pad placed under the machine will help.
5. Although not too good for the record, a white pencil is useful in marking places on it for starting and stopping. Most long-playing records use bands between pieces; even so, a white mark on the band helps to identify the starting place quickly.
6. To build a more lasting library of recordings, make a tape of the recording while it is new.

Dance Music

Basic Dance Tempos, HYP 501A, Educational Activities Records, P.O. Box 392, Freeport, N.Y. 11520.

Many different pieces to accompany the basic dance steps makes this record useful for teaching them.

DIETRICH, SALLY TOBIN, 134 Sherman Ave., Rockville Center, N.Y. 11570. Three 78 rpm albums, two *Dance and Play* and a third *Rhythmic Play.*

The melodies are fresh and interesting and the music suitable for the indicated movements. Locomotor, nonlocomotor and movement combinations are given, other pieces usable for improvisation, and even short dance studies. It is not necessary to follow the titles, of which "Goblins" and "Curling Smoke" are typical.

GRAY, VERA, *Listen, Move and Dance Records* (four 7″ 45 rpm), Canadian F.D.S. Audio-Visual, 185 Spadina Ave., Toronto 2B, Ontario.

On No. 1 and No. 2 of these valuable teaching aids can be found short excerpts from Saint-Saëns, Poulenc, Bartok, etc., for quick and light, quick and strong, slow and light, slow and strong movements. Each piece is repeated. No. 5 in the series, titled "La Nursery," has six short, useful pieces including Kabalevsky's "A Sad Story" and "A Joke."

HAYDEN, ERMA, *Themes for Children's Rhythms* (one 10″ 78 rpm), Virginia Sanders, 2012 Clifton Ave., Nashville, Tenn. 37203.

The short pieces on this record are all very usable. Good for movement invention of a specific dramatic quality are "Funny," "Angry," and "Fighting." The "Polka" and "Waltz" are excellent for dance-making.

JAMES, PHOEBE, *Creative Rhythm Records for Children,* Box 475, Oak View, Calif. 93022.

Twenty-four 78 rpm records provide music simple in structure but interesting melodically. Usable for younger children are "Animal Rhythms," "Garden Varieties," "Hallowe'en Rhythms," and "Nursery School Rhythms." "Creative Dances" is useful for older children's short dance studies.

KING, BRUCE, and NORDLI, DOUGLAS, *Dance Music for Pre-School Children,* No. 407, S & R Records, 1607 Broadway, New York, N.Y. 10019

The music is of good quality but seems somewhat advanced for preschool children, especially the nursery rhyme variations on side 2. On side 1 the run, skip, slide, polka, and turning pieces would be useful for any age child.

Listen and Move I, II, III, IV, Macdonald & Evans, 8 John St., London, W.C., England.

These short, unusually interesting pieces use percussion instruments, voices, and music of different moods. All are very useful for creative movement exploration and dance-making. They may be ordered through Canadian F.D.S. Audio-Visual, 185 Spadina Ave., Toronto 2B, Ontario.

MILLER, FRIEDA, *Music for Rhythms and Dance,* Frieda Miller Records for Dance, Dept. D, Box 383, Northport, N.Y. 11768.

The music for dance movement of the late Frieda Miller is of exceptionally high quality. The walks, runs, skips, waltzes, polkas have an infectious rhythm that makes moving to them exhilarating for dancers of all ages. Although most of the pieces on this record are long, the phrasing is irregular and parts can be used without doing an injustice to the whole. Music in Parts V and VI is useful as accompaniment for a variety of choreographic problems.

ORTMANS, KAY, *Music for Movement,* No. 1, Kay Ortmans Productions, 2005 Alba Rd., Ben Lomond, Calif. 95005.

Interesting short piano sketches to express ideas and moods. Breezy walk, light running, skipping dance, gently drifting, are typical of side 1; several on side 2 have more definite phrasing. The album cover has hints for children and adults and imaginative ideas for the music's use.

RCA Victor Basic Record Library for Elementary Schools, *The Rhythm Program,* WE 71-76, Vols. I–VI. RCA Records, Educational Dept., 1133 Avenue of the Americas, New York, N.Y. 10036.

There are four 45 rpm records in each of these volumes, three for primary and three for upper grades. The grade placement seems arbitrary, as many of the selections in earlier volumes would be valuable for older children. Especially recommended are Vol. I (locomotor and descriptive music) and Vol. III (lively folk tunes). Vol. IV contains gavottes, gigues, waltzes, and country dances and Delibes's "Passepied," a useful piece for dance-making. Some of the teaching notes are written from the point of view of a music rather than a dance teacher. RCA also issues twelve albums (each with one 12″ LP record) of *Adventures in Music* for elementary schools, from Bach to Webern. There is no duplication of repertoire between this series and the one above. If a school can afford both, rich resources for dance teaching will be available.

WALBERG, B. J., *Dance-a-Long* (two records), FC 7651, Folkways Records and Service Corp., 701 Seventh Ave., New York, N.Y. 10036.

This music is interesting and original; some of it has uneven phrasing and simple but effective syncopation. The "Rhythm Game" could be used for practicing canon, and the "Waltz, Schottische, Mazurka, Polka" is desirable accompaniment for these dance steps. "Circus" and "Out West" are usable with younger children. "Fun and Frolic" and "4/4 Rhythmic Exercises" provide variety in timing, some of it delightfully syncopated, for older children's dance-making.

WHITE, RUTH, Rhythms Productions, Cheviot Corp., Box 34485, Los Angeles, Calif. 90034, *The Rhythms Hour*, CC615; *Adventures in Rhythms*, Vol. I, CC623; *Motivations for Modern Dance*, Vol. II, CC624; *Motifs for Dance Composition*, CC611.

Each album consists of three 7″ 33⅓ rpm records. The first two contain many pieces of value for younger children; the second two are recommended for use by older children. The music is of excellent quality and will have appeal for children of all ages.

WOOD, LUCILLE, ed., *The Small Dancer*, Bowmar, 622 Rodier Dr., Glendale, Calif. 91201.

Each selection is short and most are interesting and supportive of the idea for which it was chosen. The Indian and African dance songs, "Train," "Puppets," "Grasshoppers" are among those recommended.

Music with Narration, Instructions, or Songs

BARLIN, ANNE and PAUL, *Dance-a-Story*, RCA Victor Educational Series LE 101-108.

There are several "Dance-a-Story" albums, each on a different subject—for example, "The Magic Mountain," "At the Beach," "Little Duck," "Noah's Ark." Instructions as to what to dance about with suitable music are on one side and the music alone is on the other side. An imaginative teacher may be able to find less structured ways to use the music. In this freer and more creative version of the old-fashioned story-play, the appeal is to younger children.

BRITTEN, BENJAMIN, *Young Person's Guide to the Orchestra*, Columbia MX 6368 (with Saint-Saëns's *Carnival of the Animals*); London 21007 (with Prokofiev's *Peter and the Wolf*).

Certain variations of this classic record are usable for older children's dance-making.

HAACK, BRUCE, and NELSON, ESTHER, *The Way Out Record for Children,* D 131, and *The Electronic Record for Children,* D 141, Belwin-Mills Publishers, 25 Deshon Dr., Melville, N.Y. 11746.

Of this series the last two of a group of five "Dance, Sing and Listen" records offer particularly good possibilities for exploration and improvisation following the suggestions given. "School for Robots," "Accents," "Rubber-bands," "The Saucer's Apprentice," "Four Seasons," and "Tools" are recommended on D 131; "Dance," "Upside Down," "African Lullaby," "Spiders," and "Clapping with Katy" on D 141.

LOHOEFER, EVELYN, and MCKAYLE, DONALD, *Come and See the Peppermint Tree,* DPT 101, Educational Activities, P.O. Box 392, Freeport, N.Y. 11520.

This record of younger children's imaginative and unusual songs attempts, for the most part successfully, to reproduce the spontaneity, irregular rhythms, and tonality of children's own speech. Of special interest for creative movement are "Follow Me," "My Shoes Went Walking," "Jabbety Jib," "Dance Awhile," "Jump and Spin," "The Moon in the Yard," "The Sandman."

ORFF, CARL, and KEETMAN, GUNILD, *Music for Children (Schulwerk),* Angel Record 3582-B (also available from Magna Music-Baton Inc., 6394 Delmar Blvd., St. Louis, Mo. 63130).

A series of short pieces including delightful and uncommon nursery rhymes and songs, short pieces using drums, triangles, xylophones, sleigh bells, wood-blocks, etc., percussion and speech exercises, and songs and dances. Valuable for children's exploration and composing of dance studies. Music and dance teachers are becoming interested in the Orff method of teaching music, which emphasizes creativity and rhythmic awareness.

PROKOFIEV, SERGE, *Peter and the Wolf,* London 21007 (with Britten's *Young Person's Guide to the Orchestra*); London 6187 (with Saint-Saëns's *Carnival of the Animals*).

Certain themes of this musical story are usable for reproduction in movement.

TANNER, VIRGINIA, *Come Dance with Me,* Hoctor Educational Records, 115 Manhattan Ave., Waldwick, N.J. 07463.

A successful and widely known dance teacher of children sets forth her approaches to creative dance teaching. Fundamentals of movement and rhythm are imaginatively explored.

Records of the Young People's Record Club

Many years ago the Young People's Record Club was formed by well-known musicians and educators. Many of the records were delightful songs for younger children which encouraged different kinds of movement. Later the club was merged with the Children's Record Guild. At present the records (both YPR and CRG) may be obtained from the Franson Corp., 225 Park Ave. So., New York, N.Y. 10003. All are available in 78 rpm and many in 45 rpm, at nominal cost. Because of their popularity and educational value, however, they are now being issued in twelve 331/3 rpm albums each containing two or three related pieces, as well as concert excerpts for listening.

While the majority of the activity records are for younger children, even preschool and kindergarten, some are excellent for older children's problems in dance-making, especially the folk songs sung by artists in their field, such as Charity Bailey and Tom Glazer. There are so many of these records that some are inevitably better than others—musically, in their appeal to children, and in their adaptability to movement interpretation. In this author's experience the following have seemed to be the most useful.

For Younger Children

Building a City	Merry Toy Shop, The
Cap, Spike and Salty Sam	My Playful Scarf
Carrot Seed, The	My Playmate the Wind
Chugging Freight Engine	Out of Doors
Circus Comes to Town, The	Rainy Day
Creepy Crawly Caterpillar	Skittery Skattery
I Am a Circus	Sunday in the Park
Jingle Bells and Winter Fun	Trains and Planes
Let's Play Zoo	Train to the Zoo
Little Fireman, The	What the Lighthouse Sees
Little Indian Drum	When the Sun Shines
Little Puppet, The	Whoa! Little Horses
Lonesome House, The	Who Wants a Ride
Men Who Come to Our House, The	

For Older Children

By Rocket to the Moon

Chisholm Trail (especially title song, "Erie Canal," and "Yankee Doodle")

Look at Michie Banjo (especially title song and "Angelico")

Mozart Country Dances (two records) (excellent for eighteenth-century dance forms)

Slow Jo (a "sound" record)

Timber-r-r (especially title song, "Keep the Logs Movin'," and "Shanty-Boys' Life")

Twelve Days of Christmas, The
We Wish You a Merry Christmas
Working on the Railroad (especially title song, "Paddy," and "The Shiny Silver Rails")

Records of Sounds, Rhythmic Structure, and Certain Ethnic Styles

Adventures in Rhythm, Bowmar 56.7652
Authentic Afro-Rhythms, Educational Activities K6060
Drums of Haiti, Folkways 4403
Fundamentals of Music for Dancers, The (Ruth White), CC609, Rhythms Productions, Cheviot Corp.
Music of the Southwest American Indians, Folkways 4420 (one of a number of recordings of North American Indians)
Play Your Instruments and *Make a Pretty Sound* (Ella Jenkins), Folkways FC 7665
Rhythms of Childhood (Ella Jenkins), Bowmar 56.7653
Rhythms of the World (Langston Hughes), Folkways 7340
Science Fiction Sound Effects Record, Folkways FX6200
Sound Patterns, A Documentary of Various Man-made and Nature Sounds, Folkways FX 1630
Sound, Rhythm, Rhyme, and Mime for Children, Folkways FC 7540
This Is Rhythm (Ella Jenkins), Bowmar 56.7652

Some Distributors of Educational Records

Bowmar Records, Inc., 622 Rodier Dr., Glendale, Calif. 91201
Canadian F.D.S. Audio-Visual, 185 Spadina Ave., Toronto 2B, Ontario
Dancer's Shop, Children's Music Center, 5373 W. Pico Blvd., Los Angeles, Calif. 90019
Educational Activities, Inc., P.O. Box 392, Freeport, N.Y. 11520
Educational Record Sales, 157 Chambers St., New York, N.Y. 10007
Educo Records, P.O. Box 3006, Ventura, Calif. 93003
Folkways Records, 701 Seventh Ave., New York, N.Y., 10036
Franson Corp., 225 Park Ave. So., New York, N.Y. 10003
Macdonald and Evans, Ltd., 8 John St., London W.C., England

RCA Records, Educational Dept., 1133 Avenue of the Americas, New York, N.Y. 10036

Rhythms Productions Records, Cheviot Corp., Box 34485, Los Angeles, Calif. 90034

Note: For specific records of songs see Chapter 18; for others of piano and orchestral music see Chapter 20.

References for Films

The following listing of 16 mm films is in two sections, those for teachers' and those for children's viewing. The films in the latter group should inspire or stimulate movement reactions of various kinds. Content ranges from abstract design to legend to views of nature and her creatures, with other whimsical tours as well.

The films for teachers show mainly teaching methods and materials and children's response. In some, children's dance studies take up a good part of the film, and these will be enjoyed by children as well as their teachers.

For Teachers' Viewing

A Child of Dance (Film Images, a division of Radion Films, 17 W. 60th St., New York, N.Y. 10023), 9 min., color, sound.

Produced by Virginia Tanner. A sensitive and engaging film of young girls' free, lyric dance expression.

A Time to Move (Early Childhood Productions, P.O. Box 352, Chatsworth, Calif. 91311), 30 min., B & W, sound.

Focuses on the meaning of movement for the three- and four-year-old. Each new skill is a composite of simpler ones already attained.

Being Me (University of California Extension Media Center, Berkeley, Calif. 94120), 13 min., B & W, sound.

Shows Hilda Mullin with children's dance classes at Pasadena Art Museum. Emphasizes the inner experience of movement as enhancing self-knowledge.

Children Dance (University of California Extension Media Center, Berkeley, Calif. 94120), 14 min., B & W, sound.

Naima Prevots and Geraldine Dimonstein demonstrate in a classroom environment valuable explorations of movement concepts.

Dance for Joy (Documentary Films, 3217 Trout Gulch Rd., Aptos, Calif. 95003), 15 min., color, sound.

Gertrude Knight, with preschool children, uses music as a catalyst for spontaneous movement reaction.

Dance: The Language of Motion (Idyllwild Arts Foundation, Idyllwild, Calif. 92349).

Valuable in showing the relationships of other arts to dance, and the growth of artistic awareness in the child.

Dancers in School (Pennebaker, Inc., 56 W. 45th St., New York, N.Y. 10036), 40 min., color, sound.

National Endowment for the Arts "Arts Impact" Program shows dance taught by artists, and their effective interplay with children.

Early Expressionists (Contemporary Films, McGraw-Hill, 330 W. 42nd St., New York, N.Y. 10036), 15 min., color, sound.

Rhoda Kellogg shows that movement experiences are crucial to a child's orientation to living and learning.

Free to Move (Brockenhurst Film Studios, Southern Film Productions, Hampshire, England), 30 min., color, sound.

Combines aspects of both movement and dance education excellently, with relationships to the other arts depicted as well.

Haiku (Center for Mass Communications, Columbia University Press, 440 W. 110th St., New York, N.Y. 10025), 28½ min., B & W, sound.

Jane Dudley's dance students use Japanese poetry for creative dance-making in an excellent film.

Learning Through Movement (S-L Film Productions, 5126 Hartwick St., Los Angeles, Calif. 90041), 32 min., B & W, sound.

Anne and Paul Barlin show over a period of time how total involvement in the learning process occurs through creative movement.

Looking for Me (University of California Extension Media Center, Berkeley, Calif. 94720), 29 min., B & W, sound.

Illustrates importance of movement exploration for normal and disturbed children to develop self-awareness.

Movement Speaks (Wayne State University Systems, Distribution and Utilization Center, 5448 Cass Ave., Detroit, Mich. 48202), 16 min., B & W, sound.

Creative movement in an English boys' school shows movement exploration and dance themes with appeal to young boys.

Sound and Movement (Tucson Creative Dance Center, 3131 N. Cherry Ave., Tucson, Ariz.), color, sound.

Barbara Mettler directs movement improvisation to many sorts of unusual sounds.

You Too Can Compose a Dance (S-L Film Productions, 5126 Hartwick St., Los Angeles, Calif. 90041), 20 min., B & W, sound.

Two parts, each 10 min., show movement exploration and discovery, and their structure into a dance study. Useful for teachers and children as well.

A most complete directory of 16 mm dance films, compiled and annotated by Allegra Fuller Snyder and Monica Moseley, can be found in *Dance Magazine,* Vol. XLIII, No. 4, April 1969. Readers are referred to this directory for films of concert ballet and modern dance, and also for European, North American Indian, Far Eastern, Central and South American, African, and Near Eastern ethnic dance films.[2]

For Children's Viewing

Art and Motion (Encyclopaedia Britannica Educational Corp., 425 N. Michigan Ave., Chicago, Ill. 60611), 17 min., color, sound.

Ballade d'Emile (Film Center, Inc., 20 E. Huron St., Chicago, Ill. 60611), 8 min., color, sound.

Between the Tides (A-V Explorations, 505 Delaware Ave., Buffalo, N.Y. 14202), 26 min., color, sound.

Child-Viewing-and-Doing #1 (Learning Through Movement, Anne and Paul Barlin, 192 E. Green St., Claremont, Calif. 91711), 20 min., B & W, sound.

Christmas Cracker (Contemporary Films, McGraw-Hill, 1221 Avenue of the Americas, New York, N.Y. 10020), 9 min., color, sound.

Dance Squared (Contemporary Films, McGraw-Hill, 1221 Avenue of the Americas, New York, N.Y. 10020), 4 min., color, sound.

Ersatz (Contemporary Films, McGraw-Hill, 1221 Avenue of the Americas, New York, N.Y. 10020), 10 min., color, sound.

Fantasy of Feet (Encyclopaedia Britannica Educational Corp., 425 N. Michigan Ave., Chicago, Ill. 60611), 8 min., color, sound.

Hailstones and Halibut Bones, Parts 1 and 2 (Sterling Educational Films, Inc., 241 E. 34th St., New York, N.Y. 10016), 6 min., 8 min., color, sound.

Hoo Ha (Rapaport, 175 W. 72nd St., New York, N.Y. 10023), 5 min., color, sound.

Images from Nature (Indiana University Audio-Visual Center, Bloomington, Ind. 47401), 7 min., color, sound.

Loon's Necklace, The (Encyclopaedia Britannica Educational Corp., 425 N. Michigan Ave., Chicago, Ill. 60611), 10 min., color, sound.

Magic Fiddle, The (Contemporary Films, McGraw-Hill, 1221 Avenue of the Americas, New York, N.Y. 10020), 15 min., color, sound.

Marcel Marceau's Pantomimes (Audio Film Classics, 10 Fiske Pl., Mt. Vernon, N.Y. 10550), 13 min., color, sound.

[2] An August, 1973 Directory of Films on Ballet and Modern Dance by John Mueller may be obtained from Dance Film Archive, Instructional Media Center, University of Rochester, Rochester, N.Y. 14627.

Notes on a Triangle (National Film Board of Canada, Ottawa, Ontario, or 1251 Avenue of the Americas, New York, N.Y. 10020), 5 min., color, sound.

Once Upon a Time There Was a Dot (Contemporary Films, McGraw-Hill, 1221 Avenue of the Americas, New York, N.Y. 10020), 8 min., color, sound.

Paddle to the Sea (National Film Board of Canada, Ottawa, Ontario, or 1251 Avenue of the Americas, New York, N.Y. 10020), 28 min., color, sound.

Purple Turtle, The (Association Films, 347 Madison Ave., New York, N.Y. 10018), 13½ min., color, sound.

Snowy Day (Weston Woods Studio, Weston, Conn. 06880), 6 min., color, sound.

Stone Soup (Weston Woods Studios, Weston, Conn. 06880), 10 min., color, sound.

Toot, Whistle, Plunk and Boom (Bursar's Office, Northern Illinois University, DeKalb, Ill. 60115), 10 min., color, sound.

Selected Readings

The Child in School

ALMY, MILLIE, *Young Children's Thinking: Studies of Some Aspects of Piaget's Theory,* New York, Teachers College, 1966.

ASHTON-WARNER, SYLVIA, *Spearpoint,* New York, Knopf, 1972.

ASHTON-WARNER, SYLVIA, *Teacher,* New York, Simon & Schuster, 1963.

Association for Supervision and Curriculum Development, *Early Childhood Education Today,* 1968 Yearbook, Washington, D.C., National Education Association, 1968.

AXLINE, VIRGINIA M., *Dibs: In Search of Self,* Boston, Houghton Mifflin, 1964.

BLACKIE, JOHN, *Inside the Primary School,* New York, Schocken Books, 1971.

BREARLEY, MOLLY, ed., *The Teaching of Young Children—Some Applications of Piaget's Learning Theory,* New York, Schocken Books, 1970.

BRECKENRIDGE, MARIAN E., and VINCENT, E. LEE, *Child Development,* 5th ed., Philadelphia, Saunders, 1965.

BROWN, GEORGE ISAAC, *Human Teaching for Human Learning—An Introduction to Confluent Education,* New York, Viking, 1972.

DOLL, RONALD C., and FLEMING, ROBERT S., eds., *Children Under Pressure,* Columbus, Ohio, Merrill, 1966.

HOLT, JOHN, *How Children Fail,* New York, Pitman, 1964.

HOLT, JOHN, *How Children Learn,* New York, Pitman, 1967.

JENKINS, GLADYS GARDNER, SCHACTER, HELEN, and BOWER, WILLIAM, *These Are Your Children,* 3rd ed., Glenview, Ill., Scott, Foresman 1966.
KELLEY, EARL C., *Humanizing the Education of Children,* Washington, D.C., National Education Association, Department of Elementary, Kindergarten and Nursery Education, 1969.
ROWEN, BETTY, *The Children We See,* New York, Holt, Rinehart & Winston, 1973.
SUTTON-SMITH, BRIAN, ed., "Leisure Today: Research and Thought About Children's Play," *Journal of Health, Physical Education, and Recreation,* Vol. 43, No. 6, June 1972.
WATSON, GOODWIN, ed., *Changes in School Systems,* Washington, D.C., National Education Association, 1967.

Longer Views for the Teacher

ALLPORT, GORDEN W., *Becoming,* New Haven, Conn., Yale University Press, 1955.
Association for Supervision and Curriculum Development, *Perceiving, Behaving, Becoming,* 1962 Yearbook, Washington, D.C., National Education Association, 1962.
Association for Supervision and Curriculum Development, *To Nurture Humanness,* 1970 Yearbook, Washington, D.C., National Education Association, 1970.
BORTON, TERRY, *Reach, Touch and Teach,* New York, McGraw-Hill, 1970.
BRUNER, JEROME S., "The Act of Discovery," *Harvard Educational Review,* Vol. 31, No. 1, 1961.
BRUNER, JEROME S., *The Process of Education,* Cambridge, Mass., Harvard University Press, 1961.
CRATTY, BRYANT J., *Movement Perception and Thought—The Use of Total Body Movement as a Learning Modality,* Palo Alto, Calif., Peek Publications, 1973.
DEWEY, JOHN, *Art as Experience,* New York, Putnam, 1958.
ERIKSON, ERIK, *Childhood and Society,* New York, Norton, 1964.
FEATHERSTONE, JOSEPH, *Schools Where Children Learn,* New York, Liveright, 1971.
GRANT, BARBARA M., and HENNINGS, DOROTHY GRANT, *The Teacher Moves, An Analysis of Non-Verbal Activity,* New York, Teachers College, 1971.
HERRON, R. E., and SUTTON-SMITH, BRIAN, *Child's Play,* New York, Wiley, 1971.
JERSILD, ARTHUR T., *Child Psychology,* 6th ed., Englewood Cliffs, N.J., Prentice-Hall, 1968.
LEMBO, JOHN M., *Why Teachers Fail,* Columbus, Ohio, Merrill, 1971.
LEONARD, GEORGE B., *Education and Ecstasy,* New York, Delacorte, 1968.
LYON, HAROLD C., *Learning to Feel, Feeling to Learn,* Columbus, Ohio, Merrill, 1971.
MASLOW, ABRAHAM H., *Toward a Psychology of Being,* 2nd ed., New York, Van Nostrand, Reinhold, 1968.
METHENY, ELEANOR, *Movement and Meaning,* New York, McGraw-Hill, 1968.
MURPHY, GARDNER, *Personality: A Biosocial Approach to Origins and Structure,* New York, Basic Books, 1966.
OBERTEUFFER, DELBERT, and ULRICH, CELESTE, *Physical Education,* 4th ed., New York, Harper & Row, 1970.
PIAGET, JEAN, *Science of Education and Psychology of Children,* New York, Orion Press, 1970.
Quest, Monograph II, *The Art and Science of Human Movement,* April 1964, Publication of the National Association for Physical Education of College Women and The National College Physical Education Association for Men. For subscription: Frances Bleick, 1419 9th Ave. So., St. Cloud, Minn. 56301.
RATHS, LOUIS E., *Teaching for Learning,* Columbus, Ohio, Merrill, 1969.
ROGERS, CARL R., *Freedom to Learn,* Columbus, Ohio, Merrill, 1969.

SILBERMAN, CHARLES E., *Crisis in the Classroom,* New York, Random House, 1970.

SKINNER, B. F., *Beyond Freedom and Dignity,* New York, Knopf, 1971.

SMITH, NANCY W., ed., *Focus on Dance IV, Dance as a Discipline,* American Association for Health, Physical Education and Recreation, Washington, D.C., AAHPER Publications, 1967.

WEINSTEIN, GERALD, and FONTIN, MARIO D., *Toward Humanistic Education—A Curriculum of Affect,* New York, Praeger, 1970.

WHITEHEAD, ALFRED NORTH, *The Aims of Education,* New York, Macmillan, 1967.

WITKEN, ROBERT W., *The Intelligence of Feeling,* London, Heinemann, 1974.

The Pursuit of Creativity

ANDERSON, HAROLD H., ed., *Creativity and Its Cultivation,* Addresses Presented at the Interdisciplinary Symposium on Creativity, New York, Harper & Row, 1959.

BRITTAIN, W. LAMBER, and LOWENFELD, VICTOR, *Creative and Mental Growth,* 5th ed., New York, Macmillan, 1970.

GHISELIN, BREWSTER, ed., *The Creative Process,* Berkeley, University of California Press, 1952.

GOWAN, JOHN C., DEMOS, GEORGE D., and TORRANCE, E. PAUL, *Creativity: Its Educational Implications,* New York, Wiley, 1967.

HAWKINS, ALMA, *Creating Through Dance,* Englewood Cliffs, N.J., Prentice-Hall, 1964.

KRIVITSKY, NIK, *The Gift of Heaven,* Tucson, Ariz., Public School District No. 1, 1971.

MEARNS, HUGHES, *Creative Power: The Education of Youth in the Creative Arts,* 2nd ed., New York, Dover, 1958.

METHENY, ELEANOR, ed., *People Make Ideas Happen,* Washington, D.C., AAHPER Publications, 1971.

MOONEY, ROSS, and RAZIK, T. A., eds., *Explorations in Creativity,* New York, Harper & Row, 1967.

STONE, A. H., *The Story of a School,* London, Her Majesty's Stationery Office, 1959.

TORRANCE, E. PAUL, *Creativity* (Series on *What Research Says to the Teacher*), Washington, D.C., National Education Association, 1963.

TORRANCE, E. PAUL, *Encouraging Creativity in the Classroom,* Englewood Cliffs, N.J., Prentice-Hall, 1970.

TORRANCE, E. PAUL, *Rewarding Creative Behavior,* Englewood Cliffs, N.J., Prentice-Hall, 1965.

WILT, MIRIAM, *Creativity in the Elementary School,* New York, Appleton, 1959.

Teachers' Books on Dance

ANDREWS, GLADYS, *Creative Rhythmic Movement for Children,* Englewood Cliffs, N.J., Prentice-Hall, 1954.

BARLIN, ANNE, and BARLIN, PAUL, *The Art of Learning Through Movement,* Los Angeles, Ward Ritchie, 1971.

BOORMAN, JOYCE, *Creative Dance in Grades Four to Six,* Don Mills, Ontario, Longman Canada, 1971.

BOORMAN, JOYCE, *Creative Dance in the First Three Grades,* New York, McKay, 1969.

CANNER, NORMA, . . . *and a time to dance,* Boston, Beacon, 1968.

CARROLL, JEAN, and LOFTHOUSE, PETER, *Creative Dance for Boys,* London, Macdonald & Evans, 1969.

DIMONDSTEIN, GERALDINE, *Children Dance in the Classroom,* New York, Macmillan, 1971.

DIXON, C. MADELEINE, *The Power of Dance,* New York, Day, 1939 (out of print, but available in libraries).

DOLL, EDNA, and NELSON, MARY JARMAN, *Rhythms Today!* Morristown, N.J., Silver Burdett, 1965.

English Ministry of Education, *Moving and Growing, Physical Education in the Primary School,* Part I, London, Her Majesty's Stationery Office, 1952.

FLEMING, GLADYS ANDREWS, ed., *Children's Dance,* Washington, D.C., AAHPER Publications, 1973.

GATES, ALICE A., *A New Look at Movement, A Dancer's View,* Minneapolis, Burgess, 1968.

GRAY, VERA, and PERCIVAL, RACHEL, *Music, Movement and Mime for Children,* New York, Oxford University Press, 1963.

HABERMAN, MARTIN, and MEISEL, TOBY, *Dance—An Art in Academe,* New York, Teachers College, 1970.

HAYES, ELIZABETH R., *Introduction to the Teaching of Dance,* New York, Ronald, 1964.

HUMPHREY, DORIS, *The Art of Making Dances,* New York, Holt, Rinehart & Winston, 1959 (Grave, 1962).

JORDAN, DIANA, *Childhood and Movement,* Oxford, England, Blackwell, 1967.

JOYCE, MARY, *First Steps in Teaching Creative Dance,* Palo Alto, Calif., National Press, 1973.

KING, BRUCE, *Creative Dance, Experiences for Learning,* New York, Bruce King Studio, 1968.

LABAN, RUDOLPH, *Modern Educational Dance,* 2nd ed., rev. by Lisa Ullmann, London, Macdonald & Evans, 1963.

LOFTHOUSE, PETER, *Dance,* London, Heinemann, 1970.

METTLER, BARBARA, *Materials of Dance as a Creative Art Activity,* Tucson, Ariz., Mettler Studios, 1960.

MONSOUR, SALLY, COHEN, CHAMBERS MARILYN, and LINDELL, PATRICIA ECKERT, *Rhythm in Music and Dance for Children,* Belmont, Calif., Wadsworth, 1966.

MURRAY, RUTH L., ed., *Designs for Dance,* Washington, D.C., AAHPER Publications, 1968.

ROWEN, BETTY, *Learning Through Movement,* New York, Teachers College, 1963.

RUSSELL, JOAN, *Creative Dance in the Primary School,* New York, Praeger, 1965.

SAFFRAN, ROSANNA B., *First Book of Creative Rhythms,* New York, Holt, Rinehart & Winston, 1963.

Selected Articles on Dance II, 1958–1967, Washington, D.C., AAHPER Publications, 1968.

SHERBON, ELIZABETH, *On the Count of One,* Palo Alto, Calif., National Press, 1968.

VENABLE, LUCY, and BERK, FRED, *Ten Folk Dances in Labanotation,* New York, Witmark, 1959.

WIENER, JACK and LIDSTONE, JOHN, *Creative Movement for Children,* New York, Van Nostrand Reinhold, 1969.

Dance and Other School Activities

ANDERSON, MARIAN H., ELIOT, MARGARET E., and LABERGE, JEANNE, *Play with a Purpose,* 2nd ed., New York, Harper & Row, 1972.

DAUER, VICTOR, *Dynamic Physical Education for Elementary School Children,* 4th ed., Minneapolis, Burgess, 1971.

Department of Education and Science, *Movement; Physical Education in the Primary Years,* London, Her Majesty's Stationery Office, 1972.

DRIVER, ANN, *Music and Movement,* New York, Oxford University Press, 1958.

FAIT, HOLLIS F., *Physical Education for the Elementary School Child: Experiences in Movement,* 2nd ed., Philadelphia, Saunders, 1971.

GILBERT, PIA, and LOCKHART, AILEENE, *Music for the Modern Dance*, Dubuque, Iowa, Brown, 1961.

GOODRIDGE, JANET, *Creative Drama and Improvised Movement for Children*, Boston, Plays, 1971.

HALSEY, ELIZBETH, and PORTER, LORENA, *Physical Education for Children*, 2nd ed., New York, Holt, Rinehart & Winston, 1963.

HUMPHREY, JAMES H., *Child Learning Through Elementary School Physical Education*, Dubuque, Iowa, Brown, 1965.

HUMPHREYS, LOUISE, and ROSS, JERROLD, *Interpreting Music Through Movement*, Englewood Cliffs, N.J., Prentice-Hall, 1964.

MAYNARD, OLGA, *Children and Dance and Music*, New York, Scribner, 1968.

MCFEE, JUNE KING, *Preparation for Art*, 2nd ed., Belmont, Calif., Wadsworth, 1970.

MONTGOMERY, CHANDLER, *Art for Teachers of Children*, Columbus, Ohio, Merrill, 1968.

NYE, ROBERT EVANS, and NYE, VERNICE TROUSDALE, *Music in the Elementary School (An Activities Approach)*, Englewood Cliffs, N.J., Prentice-Hall, 1970.

OPIE, IONA and PETER, *The Lore and Language of Children*, New York, Oxford University Press, 1959.

PAINTER, HELEN W., *Poetry and Children*, Newark, Del., International Reading Association, 1970.

Preparing the Elementary Specialist, Washington, D.C., AAHPER Publications, 1973.

Promising Practices in Elementary School Physical Education, Washington, D.C., AAHPER Publications, 1969.

SCHURR, EVELYN, *Movement Experiences for Children*, New York, Appleton, 1969.

SHEEHY, EMMA, *Children Discover Music and Dance*, New York, Teachers College, 1968.

SIKS, GERALDINE B., *Creative Dramatics, An Art for Children*, New York, Harper & Row, 1958.

SMITH, JAMES A., *Creative Teaching of the Creative Arts in the Elementary School*, Boston, Allyn & Bacon, 1967.

VANNIER, MARYHELEN, FOSTER, MILDRED, and GALLAHUE, DAVID, *Teaching Physical Education in Elementary Schools*, 5th ed., Philadelphia, Saunders, 1973.

WAY, BRIAN, *Education Today: Development Through Drama*, London, Longman Group, Ltd., 1967.

Music and Rhythm

BAILEY, EUNICE, *Discovering Music with Young Children*, New York, Philosophical Library, 1958.

COLEMAN, SATIS N., *Creative Music in the Home*, rev. ed., New York, Day, 1939 (out of print, but available in libraries).

COPLAND, AARON, *What to Listen For in Music*, rev. ed., New York, New American Library, 1964.

ELLIOT, RAYMOND, *Learning Music*, Columbus, Ohio, Merrill, 1960.

HOOD, MARGUERITE V., and SCHULTZ, E. J., *Learning Music Through Rhythm*, Westport, Conn., Greenwood Press (reprint), 1972.

JACQUES-DALCROZE, EMILE, *Eurhythmics, Art and Education*, Bronx, New York, Blom, 1970.

KATZ, ADELE T., and ROWEN, RUTH HALLE, *Hearing—Gateway to Music*, Evanston, Ill., Summy-Birchard, 1959.

LANDECK, BEATRICE, *Children and Music*, New York, Sloane, 1952.

LIESS, ANDREAS, *Carl Orff, His Life and His Music*, London, Calder & Boyars, 1966.

SHEEHY, EMMA, *There's Music in Children*, 2nd ed., New York, Holt, Rinehart & Winston, 1968.

Movement Education

BARRETT, K. ROSS, *Exploration, A Method for Teaching Movement,* Madison, Wis., University Printing and Typing Service, 1965.

CAMERON, W. MCD., and CAMERON, MARJORIE, *Education in Movement in the Infant School,* Oxford, England, Blackwell, 1969.

CAMERON, W. MCD., and PLEASANCE, PEGGY, *Education in Movement,* Oxford, England, Blackwell, 1963.

COPE, JOHN, *Discovery Methods in Physical Education,* Camden, N.J., Nelson, 1967.

GERHARDT, LYDIA A., *Moving and Knowing,* Englewood Cliffs, N.J., Prentice-Hall, 1973.

GILLIOM, BONNIE CHERP, *Basic Movement Education for Children: Rationale and Teaching Units,* Reading, Mass., Addison-Wesley, 1970.

NORTH, MARION, *Movement Education,* New York, Dutton, 1973.

PORTER, LORENA, *Movement Education for Children,* American Association of Elementary, Kindergarten and Nursery Educators, Washington, D.C., National Education Association, 1969.

STANLEY, SHEILA, *Physical Education: A Movement Orientation,* Toronto, Ontario, McGraw-Hill of Canada, 1969.

SWEENEY, ROBT, ed., *Selected Readings in Movement Education,* Reading, Mass., Addison-Wesley, 1970.

Motor Learning and Analysis of Movement

BROER, MARIAN, *Efficiency of Human Movement,* 3rd ed., Philadelphia, Saunders, 1973.

CRATTY, BRYANT J., *Movement Behavior and Motor Learning,* 2nd ed., Philadelphia, Lea & Febiger, 1967.

DUVELL, ELLEN NEALL, *Kinesiology, The Anatomy of Motion,* Englewood Cliffs, N.J., Prentice-Hall, 1959.

ESPENSCHADE, ANNA S., and ECKERT, HELEN M., *Motor Development,* Columbus, Ohio, Merrill, 1967.

Quest, Monograph VI, *A Symposium on Motor Learning,* May 1966, Publication of the National Association for Physical Education of College Women and The National College Physical Education Association for Men. For subscription: Frances Bleick, 1419 9th Ave. So., St. Cloud, Minn. 56301.

SCOTT, GLADYS M., *Analysis of Human Motion,* 2nd ed., New York, Appleton, 1963.

WELLS, KATHERINE F., *Kinesiology: The Scientific Basis of Human Motion,* 5th ed., Philadelphia, Saunders, 1971.

Dance History and Appreciation

COHEN, SELMA JEAN, ed., *The Modern Dance, Seven Statements of Belief,* Middletown, Conn., Wesleyan University Press, 1966.

H'DOUBLER, MARGARET N., *Dance: A Creative Art Experience,* rev. ed., Madison, University of Wisconsin Press, 1957.

HASKELL, ARNOLD L., *The Wonderful World of Dance* (a book for children), Garden City, N.Y., Doubleday, 1960.

KRAUS, RICHARD, *History of the Dance in Art and Education,* Englewood Cliffs, N.J., Prentice-Hall, 1969.

LANGER, SUZANNE K., *Feeling and Form,* New York, Scribner 1953.

LANGER, SUZANNE K., *Problems of Art,* New York, Scribner 1957.

MARTIN, JOHN, *Introduction to the Dance,* Brooklyn, N.Y., Dance Horizons Press, 1965.

MARTIN, JOHN, *John Martin's Book of the Dance,* Brooklyn, N.Y., Dance Horizons Press, 1963.

MAYNARD, OLGA, *American Modern Dancers, The Pioneers,* Boston, Little, Brown, 1965.

NADEL, HOWARD MYRON, and NADEL, CONSTANCE GWEN, *The Dance Experience, Readings in Dance Appreciation,* New York, Praeger, 1970.

SACHS, CURT, *World History of the Dance,* New York, Norton, 1937.

SORRELL, WALTER, *The Dance Has Many Faces,* New York, Columbia University Press, 1966.

SORRELL, WALTER, *The Dance Through the Ages,* New York, Grosset & Dunlap, 1967.

TERRY, WALTER, *The Dance in America,* New York, Harper & Row, 1956.

VAN TUYL, MARIAN, ed., *Dance, a Projection for the Future,* Impulse Publications, 160 Palo Alto Ave., San Francisco, Calif., 1968.

Periodicals

Childhood Education (monthly), Association for Childhood Education International, 3615 Wisconsin Ave., N.W., Washington, D.C. 20016.

Children Today, An interdisciplinary journal of the professions serving children, Office of Child Development, Children's Bureau, P.O. Box 1182, Washington, D.C. 20013.

Dance Magazine (monthly), 10 Columbus Circle, New York, N.Y., 10019. Devoted primarily to professional dance, dance artists, and dance companies.

Dance Perspectives (quarterly), Dance Perspectives Foundation, 129 E. 9th St., New York, N.Y. 11415. The most scholarly and research-oriented of the present dance periodicals.

Dance Scope (biennially), American Dance Guild, 124–16 84th Rd., Kew Gardens, N.Y. 11415. Contains occasional articles on dance education.

Educational Leadership (monthly), Journal of the Association for Supervision and Curriculum Development, 1201 Sixteenth St., N.W., Washington, D.C. 20036.

Impulse (annually), published 1951–1970 by Impulse Publications, San Francisco, Calif. Available in paperback from Dance Horizons, 1801 E. 26th St., Brooklyn, N.Y. 11229. Issues for 1953 and 1957 are devoted to dance in education and dance for children.

JOHPER (monthly), Journal of the American Association for Health, Physical Education and Recreation, 1201 Sixteenth St., N.W., Washington, D.C. 20036. Occasional articles on dance education.

Keeping Up with Elementary Education (quarterly), Journal of the American Association of Elementary, Kindergarten and Nursery Educators, 1201 Sixteenth St., N.W., Washington, D.C. 20036.

Learning—The Magazine for Creative Teaching (monthly), Education Today Company, 530 University Ave., Palo Alto, Calif. 94301.

Quest (bienially), Publication of the National Association for Physical Education of College Women and The National College Physical Education Association for Men. For subscription: Frances Bleick, 1419 9th Ave. So., St. Cloud, Minn. 56301.

Young Children (monthly), Journal of the National Association for the Education of Young Children, 1834 Connecticut Ave., N.W., Washington, D.C. 20009.

Index